S0-CDO-610

The Sappho History

Anne-Louis Girodet Trioson, engraving, 1827

The Sappho History

Margaret Reynolds

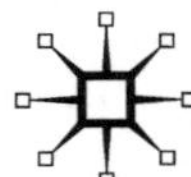

First published 2003 by
PALGRAVE MACMILLAN
Houndmills, Basingstoke, Hampshire RG21 6XS and
175 Fifth Avenue, New York, N.Y. 10010
Companies and representatives throughout the world

PALGRAVE MACMILLAN is the global academic imprint of the Palgrave Macmillan division of St. Martin 's Press, LLC and of Palgrave Macmillan Ltd. Macmillan® is a registered trademark in the United States, United Kingdom and other countries. Palgrave is a registered trademark in the European Union and other countries.

ISBN 0–333–97170–1 hardback

This book is printed on paper suitable for recycling and
made from fully managed and sustained forest sources.

A catalogue record for this book is available from the British Library.

Library of Congress Cataloging-in-Publication Data
Reynolds, Margaret, 1957–
The Sappho history / Margaret Reynolds.
p. cm.
Includes bibliographical references and index.
ISBN 0–333–97170–1
1. European literature—History and criticism. 2. Literature, Modern—History and criticism. 3. Sappho—In literature. I. Title.

PN57.S335 R49 2003
809'.93351—dc21

2002026946

10 9 8 7 6 5 4 3 2 1
12 11 10 09 08 07 06 05 04 03

Printed and bound in Great Britain by
Antony Rowe Ltd, Chippenham and Eastbourne

For Jeanette Winterson with love

Contents

List of Illustrations

Figures

Plates

Acknowledgements

I would like to acknowledge with gratitude the assistance of the staffs of the British Library, the Bodleian Library, the Cambridge University Library, the National Art Library at the Victoria and Albert Museum, the Department of Prints and Drawings at the British Museum, the Warburg Institute, the University of London Library at Senate House, the London Library, the New York Public Library, the Bridgeman Art Library, and the Reunion des Musées Nationales in Paris.

My professional debts are many, but in particular I thank my colleagues and friends in the Department of English and Drama at Queen Mary, University of London and my colleagues and friends and the President and Fellows of Clare Hall, Cambridge – two places where I have spent some very happy years.

So many people have shared this Sapphic project, but the most tolerant (and most irascible) is my girlfriend, who says that she never again wants to hear a word beginning with S and ending with O. All the same, I thank her, with my love.

Thanks to Philippa Brewster and Georgina Capel who are so much more than agents.

Thanks too to Angela Leighton who – as always – has been a dear friend and an inspiring critic; to Gillian Beer who has been creative, supportive and fun; to Lisa Jardine who never fails to fire up; to Jonathan Noakes who made me think again about the poems; to Philip Ogden who is always there with love and learning; and to Isobel Armstrong who gives without reserve both intellectually and emotionally.

Other friends have contributed support and excitement, gems and fragments. They will know what they gave – or perhaps they won't – which doesn't make their gifts any less precious to me. So thank you to Jerry Brotton, Rachel Holmes, Harriet Marland, Marianna Kennedy, Peter Hone, Charles Gledhill, Jim Howett, Dinah Birch, Kate Flint, Oliver Taplin, Beaty Rubens, Edith Hall, Fiona Macintosh, Helen Cooper, Heather Glen, Maud Ellmann, Elisabeth Bronfen, Inga-Stina Ewbank, Kate Challis, Ruth Rendell, Katy Kabitoglou, Jerome McGann, Marion Shaw, Mark Storey, Sophie Tomlinson, Margaret Williamson, Caroline Zilboorg, Sara Davis, Christine Hall, Cath Sharrock, Yopie Prins, Judith Stein, Lisa Corrin, Lesley Howard, Mona Howard, Marina Warner, Frances Spalding, Sally Marmion, Andrew Sanders, Steven Connor, Anne Janowitz, Lynda Nead, Barrie Bullen, Leonee Ormond, Catherine Maxwell, Marilyn Butler, Kelsey Thornton, Tony Davies, Vivien Jones, Markman Ellis, David Fairer, Caroline Michel, Marcella Edwards, Hilary Fairclough, Vicky Licorish, Paul Shearer, Henrietta Llewellyn Davies, Ruth Padel, Jacqueline Rose.

Thanks also to Josie Dixon who has followed the fortunes of this book for some time and is a rigorous and generous publisher, to Emily Rosser, an exemplary editor bringing just the right mix of patience and enthusiasm to the work, and to the anonymous reader of this work whose kind suggestions were of great assistance.

The publishers of my anthology *The Sappho Companion* gave me so much help at a crucial stage of my thinking, and so many of their creative ideas have gone into the shaping of this book that I would also like to thank them here; especially Jenny Uglow, Alison Samuel and Ali Reynolds.

Every time I look at you.
Every time.
Every time I look.
Every time.

EVERY TIME I LOOK AT YOU.

Eyes go dark.
Blood sings in my ears.

Every time.

Tongue grows heavy.
Voice sticks in the throat.

Every time.

Limbs melt with fire.
Gut seizes up.

Every time.

Every time I look at you.

Hands tremble.
I feel that I could die.

Every time.
Every time.

And nothing else is.
All is dark rounding us.

Every time I look at you.

1
Introduction

I

Every time I look at you

Sappho's poems are about desire, and loss, and the memory of desire. The pattern is always the same, and the function of the poem is always to re-light desire – through words. The original desire – as something bodily felt by the subject – may have disappeared. But the shadow of desire – as something re-enacted through the skill of the poet – is communicated to the object: the listener, the beloved, the audience, the reader of the poem. Me. You. Us.

Sappho's speaker may, or may not, have once felt the desire she describes, but through the contrivance of her words, she makes a new feeling, which is authentic. I know it is. Because it is mine. Yours. Ours.

> It seems to me that man is equal to the gods,
> that is, whoever sits opposite you
> and, drawing nearer, savours, as you speak
> the sweetness of your voice
>
> and the thrill of your laugh, which have so stirred the heart
> in my own breast, that whenever I catch
> sight of you, even if for a moment,
> then my voice deserts me
>
> and my tongue is struck silent, a delicate fire
> suddenly races underneath my skin,
>
> my eyes see nothing, my ears whistle like
> the whirling of a top

and sweat pours down me and a trembling creeps over
my whole body, I am greener than grass
at such times, I seem to be no more than
a step away from death

but all can be endured since even a pauper ...

(Sappho, Fragment 31. Translation by Josephine Balmer.)

Fragment 31 – Sappho's most famous poem – comes down to us from antiquity with just that assurance: that the poem has the power to make us feel. 'Are you not amazed', writes Longinus to his first-century audience, 'how at one and the same moment she seeks out soul and body, hearing, tongue, sight, complexion as though they had all left her and were external, and how in contradiction she both freezes and burns, is irrational and sane, is afraid and nearly dead, so that we observe in her not one single emotion but a concourse of emotions? All this of course happens to people in love ...'[1] Sappho's Fragment 31 has been read and re-read many times since Longinus composed his commentary, and scholars dispute the precise situation it is designed to portray. Is this a personal statement? Is it an expression of genuine private feeling? Or an *enkomium* celebrating the good fortune of the lucky bridegroom, and therefore meant for public performance like so many others of Sappho's *epithalamia* (wedding poems)? Has Sappho – official poet – started out rationally, but been seized with sudden desire? Is she guilty? Is she teasing? Is she shocked at her own illicit feeling?[2]

Whatever the circumstances, one thing is clear. This is not the first time that this has happened nor will it be the last. The speaker has been here before. She knows what it feels like; what happens 'every time I look at you', and she knows that she can – and will again – survive it: '... but all can be endured since even a pauper ...'

In the course of this poem Sappho takes her bodily self apart, breaks herself into pieces, dismembers her parts, anatomises herself, and then puts herself back together. And this taking apart replicates the taking apart of her mind, the layering of experiences, past and present, that complicate and enrich her representations of desire, loss, and the memory of desire.

Many-minded

The same premise underlies the only complete extant Sappho poem, Fragment 1, the 'Ode to Aphrodite'.

Immortal Aphrodite, on your patterned throne,
daughter of Zeus, guile-weaver,
I beg you, goddess, don't subjugate my heart
with anguish, with grief

but come here to me now, if ever in the past
you have heard my distant pleas
and listened; leaving your father's golden house
you came to me then

with your chariot yoked; beautiful swift sparrows
brought you around the dark earth
with a whirl of wings, beating fast, from heaven
down through the mid-air

to reach me quickly; then you, my sacred goddess,
your immortal face smiling,
asked me what had gone wrong this time and this time
why was I begging

and what in my demented heart, I wanted most:
'Who shall I persuade this time
to take you back, yet once again, to her love;
who wrongs you Sappho?

For if she runs away, soon she shall run after,
if she shuns gifts, she shall give,
if she does not love you, soon she shall even
against her own will.'

So, come to me now, free me from this aching pain,
fulfil everything that
my heart desires to be fulfilled: you, yes you,
will be my ally.

(Sappho, Fragment 1. Translation by Josephine Balmer.)

Here again Sappho is in love, in thrall to desire. Or rather, she was. Though the speaker tells us that this is happening 'now', that she is at this very moment invoking Aphrodite's aid, the form of the prayer to her goddess means that Sappho is already speaking from the security of a moment after – a moment beyond the actual experience of disabling desire. When Sappho's speaker begins her incantation she is already sufficiently in control, sufficiently past the lived experience, to shape her words into ritual order, to make her poem in performance.

And what does she do in the poem itself? She rehearses a past experience – now realised as an imagined experience – of another time when Aphrodite did come to her, and help her. She memorialises a past which was an invention, and then she repeats it here, in the immediate present of the poem, at the same time as she fantasises a future when that which happened once, will happen yet again. Thus the poem layers time upon time. Past experience, re-imagined, present poetry, and future imagined, are all conjured simultaneously through Sappho's technique. Like the epithet she gives to Aphrodite, 'many-minded, myriad-minded' – 'guile-weaver' in Balmer's translation – Sappho's poetic method is multiple. No experience comes to her speakers – or, therefore to us – singly. Desire, loss, the memory of desire.

The layering of time that stratifies the situations in Sappho's poems is reinforced by the layering of personae. Too often in the past Sappho's fragments have been read as the simple expression of personal feeling. More recently, Margaret Williamson has reminded us that Sappho's poems were written, not only for performance, but for group performance. The singing, she argues, would have been shared between Sappho's girls, the voice passing from one to another.[3]

In fact, if you look closely, that is exactly what happens in the poems anyway. There is always more than one voice. In Fragment 1 Aphrodite speaks. And, in the last line, she will be Sappho's 'ally', her close companion in Sappho's erotic enterprise. More than that, through Sappho's witty invocation, Aphrodite is co-opted also into Sappho's poetic enterprise as her imagined presence and, most importantly, her imagined *voice* shapes the frame of the poem. Even in Fragment 31 the beloved girl gets to speak. It is, remember, the sound of her *voice* that sets the speaker's heart on fire and that consequently makes the moment which makes the speaker speak the poem.

This collective notion of poetry – where many sing, and many consciousnesses are realised – means that Sappho can assert her own identity within the poem. She makes a persona other than herself who can then look at her, recognise her, name her. Even in the few fragments that we have, one of the peculiarities of Sappho's poetry is that she often names herself, brings herself into existence by signing her own name in her compositions. It's in Fragment 1 and it's in Fragment 94.

And many times she told me this

... frankly I wish that I were dead:
she was weeping as she took her leave from me

and many times she told me this:
'Oh what sadness we have suffered,
Sappho, for I'm leaving you against my will.'

So I gave this answer to her:
'Go, be happy but remember
me there, for you know how we have cherished you,

if not, then I would remind you
[of the joy we have known,] of all
the loveliness that we have shared together;

for many wreaths of violets,
of roses and of crocuses
... you wove around yourself by my side

... and many twisted garlands
which you had woven from the blooms
of flowers, you placed around your slender neck

... and you were anointed with
a perfume, scented with blossom,
... although it was fit for a queen

and on a bed, soft and tender
... you satisfied your desire ...'

(Sappho, Fragment 94. Translation by Josephine Balmer.)

As in Fragments 1 and 31, Sappho recalls a moment that is past – the time of her taking leave of the beloved – but that remembrance is itself embellished by the recalling, within that past time, of other better, earlier times. Sappho exhorts her beloved to remember her – 'Go, be happy but remember/ me there' – and she initiates that process of memory that will happen in the future by including a mnemonic for the past – 'I would remind you' – and by making the beloved begin by naming her, for herself, for us: 'what sadness we have suffered,/ Sappho, for I'm leaving you against my will'. The structure of Sappho's time-frames here is reflected also in her repetition of *polla* and *pollois*, 'many'. 'Many times' Sappho's beloved makes her complaint; 'many' were the wreaths, and the garlands; 'many' are the memories of 'satisfied desire'. Nothing comes to us once in this poem. Everything is repeated.

And that repetition includes us. Here. Now. For as Sappho starts to recall what she once said to her beloved – itself a speech recalling what she once did with the beloved – so that scene, those many scenes of desire, are re-enacted, re-created, for us. We too make up the multiplier. We too have desired, have lost, and now recall the memory of desire. Except that, paradoxically, we – hearing this poem, in the moment of attending to Sappho's words – are the ones on whom desire is working, not in the past, but in the present. For to appreciate her meaning, we must imagine her scene. We must put ourselves in her place, on that soft bed, now. Now, recalling desire, now, letting it happen, now, letting love have its way.

Although she is in Sardis

[... Atthis,]
although she is in Sardis,
her thoughts stray here, to us ...

[... for you know that she honoured] you
as if you were a goddess
and, most of all, delighted in your song.

But now she surpasses all the women
of Lydia, like the moon,
rose-fingered, after the sun has set,

shining brighter than all the stars; its light
stretches out over the salt-
filled sea and the fields brimming with flowers:

the beautiful dew falls and the roses
and the delicate chervil
and many-flowered honey-clover bloom.

But wandering here and there, she recalls
gentle Atthis with desire
and her tender heart is heavy with grief ...

(Sappho, Fragment 96. Translation by Josephine Balmer.)

Sappho's audience is built into this poem. She addresses Atthis, who is also a singer – 'most of all, [she] delighted in your song' – and she reiterates Atthis's tune of desire, taking it over, by praising the lost beloved who is in Sardis. It may be that the poem would have gone on to sing that beloved's song too, telling us what she felt, what she said, as she recalled Atthis, her 'tender heart ... heavy with grief'. So Sappho registers many voices or, to put it the other way around, she splits herself – as she splits herself in Fragment 31 – into many selves.

Similarly, she spreads herself out across time, for there is a past, present and future in the poem, as there is in Fragment 94 and Fragments 1 and 31. And she spreads herself across geographical space too, for her view extends up to the sky and across the sea to the city of Sardis where her telescopic eye spies Atthis's distressed girlfriend. Again, it's the same mapping out of the imaginative spaces traversed by desire that also takes place in Fragment 94 and in Fragment 1. So Sappho is everywhere, through time, through space. And she is everyone, more than just her own speaking self.

Which reminds me of Anactoria

Some an army on horseback, some an army on foot
and some say a fleet of ships is the loveliest sight
on this dark earth; but I say it is whatever you desire:

and it is perfectly possible to make this clear
to all; for Helen, the woman who by far surpassed
all others in her beauty, left her husband –
the best of men –

behind and sailed far away to Troy; she did not spare
a single thought for her child nor for her dear parents
but [the goddess of love] led her astray
[to desire ...]

[... which]
reminds me now of Anactoria
although far away,

whose long-desired footstep, whose radiant, sparkling face
I would rather see before me than the chariots
of Lydia or the armour of men
who fight wars on foot ...

(Sappho, Fragment 16. Translation by Josephine Balmer.)

In Fragment 16 Sappho's psychic geography expands to include the public and masculine worlds of history, storytelling and the panoply of war. As in the other fragments she takes over the voice of another woman – in this case Helen – but she is also taking over the voice of another man – Homer. It is tempting to see in her opening picture of the 'lovely sight' of cavalry or infantry or 'a fleet of ships', an allusion to Homer's celebratory lists in *The Iliad*. But Sappho then promptly revises her source by re-telling Homer's story from the woman's point of view, and equating Helen's experience of the imperatives of desire with her own love for Anactoria. So her frame spans hundreds of years of time back to the story of Troy. And it spans space as she conjures the person of the beloved Anactoria who is 'far away' and whose person she values over the contemporary military might of mainland Lydia.

The poem makes clear that it is Sappho's imaginative power that forges these connections, brings all these diverse elements together within the scope of her composition. There may be a surface in this poem which makes it appear to be private in the colloquial intimacy of '[... which]/ reminds me now of Anactoria'. The introduction of a contingent personal concern may masquerade as haphazard free association, but that private story is set within, and indeed above, the public story of warring nations told by Homer. And yet, Sappho's evocation of desire self-consciously appeals to a wide audience – 'and it is perfectly possible to make this clear/ to all; for ...' One argument here is that desire – personal, intimate, peculiar, particular – is in fact more universal, more potent and relevant than any larger civic history.

II

Today I will sing with a clear voice to enchant you all

Sappho of Lesbos lived at the end of the seventh, beginning of the sixth century BC. It was a time when an oral tradition was just giving way to a literate culture. Most of Sappho's poetry would have been improvised and then memorised by her and her audiences. But writing, invented in Egypt, had been known in Greece for some one hundred years before Sappho and though she herself may not have written down her own poetry during her lifetime, some of her work must have been committed to papyrus quite soon after her death, because so much survived that a reputed Nine Books of her works were still in existence by the third century BC.[4] Whether or not they were written down, Sappho's audiences remembered her compositions, relayed them to others, recalled them, kept them in their hearts, treasured them. One of the earliest stories testifying to the distinction of her work is that told by Aelian about Solon of Athens who lived from about 640/635 to 561/560 BC. One night he heard his nephew sing a poem of Sappho's over the wine, and he asked the boy to teach it to him. When a friend asked why he was so eager, Solon replied '… so that I may learn it and die'.[5] In the Fragments extant today Sappho's audience – real and imagined – clearly figures as addressee, as collaborator, and as beloved who will be seduced by her song.

In recent years, translators and critics have made much of this presence – or presences. It is a political move, partly motivated by a wish to rescue Sappho from the more old-fashioned and conventional descriptions of the past which characterised her poetry as personal and private, rather than general and public. The translations by Josephine Balmer that I have quoted here pointedly emphasise the significance of Sappho's audience. Other recent translations – notably those by Mary Barnard, David Constantine, Guy Davenport and Diane Rayor – do the same. Essays on the subject of Sappho's audience include those by Ellen Greene, Judith P. Hallett, John J. Winkler, Charles Segal, André Lardinois and Leslie Kurke.[6]

Of course, the fact is that most of the poems I have discussed here were not known until the beginning of the twentieth century. For readers in the eighteenth century – see Chapter 2 – their notion of the character of Sappho's work relied almost entirely upon two Fragments; Fragment 1 and Fragment 31 – the first complete, the other broken off, but apparently almost complete. Otherwise they had only about fifty other tiny shards, a great number of them only one or two lines long. (I have also cheated a bit in performing this modern Sappho by quoting from an English translation that makes Sappho's fragments effectively into whole poems.) All the same, that key idea of the *audience* figures in Fragments 1 and 31, in the Greek, and in earlier English translations, as it does also in many of the other fragments too. The current revival in Sappho scholarship is partly due to the continuing process of editing and restoring her work that has gone on since the beginning of the twentieth century.[7] But now that there is a fairly substantial text – and Sappho's oeuvre has been considerably enlarged since the mid eighteenth century – there is also a new audience. And that audience cares to know the audience that Sappho knew. Or, at least, cares to imagine it.

Almost all of the scenes that I discuss in this book are the work of the imagination. The stories I tell are about how others have imagined Sappho. We can know so little about Sappho – and even that little is an invention, a reconstruction. I have quoted Balmer's English translations of her poems. Insofar as that assumes the intervention of a voice other than Sappho's, those translations are just that – a 'carrying across', a make believe, a forgery. Even if I were to quote the Greek I would choose to use a scholarly edition, which also can only ever be an intelligent fake. Even if I were to quote exactly from the papyrus remains, or the works of the ancient commentators who cited her, I would still be presenting you with a shadow, or a reflection. We can only ever know Sappho as she is 'carried across' to us by some other. She is always in translation.

But this fact, in itself, reinforces my argument about the importance of Sappho's audience. As I read Sappho's work the premise of the audience in the poem, and the methods Sappho uses to create her poetics of desire, loss, and the memory of desire, give me the model for the form of this book. If we want now to imagine that Sappho had an audience then, it is certain that she has had an audience ever since. Or rather, as then, many audiences.

To begin with, there is that first audience, those who saw and heard Sappho of Lesbos 2600 years ago. In her day, during her life, we might imagine her audience to have consisted of women – and maybe men too – watching her perform at highly charged ceremonial occasions. Her studied attention to the body and the feeling of what happens in the body as expressed in her most powerful work would have been – (so goes my imagined scene) – emphasised and underlined by the presence of her body, and indeed, their bodies. 'This is what happens', sings Sappho. Then she shows it, performs it, with a voice that theatrically fails – 'tongue is broken' – with her wide unseeing eyes – 'eyes go dark' – with the shiver on her skin – 'a subtle fire runs through my limbs'. And then – (so goes my imagined scene) – her listeners would respond by remembering desire, their own experience of desire, lost perhaps, or momentarily present, but being made to happen again in their own bodies by the story set before them in Sappho's words and Sappho's person.

Then there is that second audience, living, say, within a few hundred years of Sappho's death, and close enough in time to have had handed down to them a folk memory which might feel authentic simply because their actual experience and circumstances and ways of thinking may have been that much closer to hers. (Rather as we, now, might remember and imagine the world before the

First World War, or even the world of Wordsworth's lakes.) Solon of Athens was one of these. The Roman poet Horace (65–8 BC) was another, able to recall her poems, and to make up tales about how he might have heard her: 'How narrowly I missed ... seeing ... Sappho complaining to her Aeolian lyre about the girls of her city.'[8]

After that, there are any number of audiences – far too numerous to count, but some of them are in this book. In my collection *The Sappho Companion* I told how Sappho was perceived by different people – individuals and groups – across the years that intervene between her and us. The point is that Sappho is always what we make of her. She may once have performed, but, ever since, others have performed her, as I am performing her now.

This is not a book about the Classical Sappho, and I make no claim to any 'authenticity' either for my readings of her, or for my readings of others' readings of her. Neither is this a book about the history of Greek scholarship or Sappho scholarship. Those stories have been told by Christopher Stray, by Lobel and Page, Richard Jenkyns, Joan DeJean, Margaret Williamson, Page DuBois, Lyn Hatherly Wilson and Jane McIntosh Snyder.[9] Rather, this is a book designed to take snapshots of particular moments in the peculiar history of Sappho's afterlife in cultural transmission and in the cultural imagination. The emphasis, therefore, must always lie with the subject – which is Sappho's latter-day audience. I have made her the eponymous heroine of my tale, but she is only the object. Mary Robinson, Tennyson, the Victorian women poets, Baudelaire, Hilda Doolittle (H.D.) and Virginia Woolf are the true subjects.

One thing I am clear about. It is difficult to write about Sappho. In two of the most important recent books that deal with Sappho's reception, that difficulty seems to me to be implied, for both are unusual works of scholarship, and even awkward at times. Joan DeJean's monumental work on the tradition in French is an original study that has made the way for much of the work that has followed, and I am very glad to acknowledge my own debt to her. But *Fictions of Sappho, 1546–1936* is unwieldy – three massive chapters, which shift scene from, say, eighteenth century political fictions to comparable developments in the twentieth century and then back again in the space of two paragraphs.[10]

For a time, I puzzled over this. But long acquaintance with the way Sappho's reception works has shown me that no history of Sappho can be progressist. There is no straightforward notion of one Sappho here, leading neatly into another and so on through time. Sappho is never handed down in quite that way. Rather, she is handled here in one way. Then that version disappears, goes underground, becomes unfashionable. Other Sapphos take over – contradictions, or opposites, or reactions – but they do not necessarily have a continuous life either. And yet then, centuries on, someone will return to one of the older images and another faked Sappho is overlaid in a criss-cross which makes her history as an icon as chequered as her various legends. Sappho is never black and white. Or else, she is indeed black and white; and – as the riddle goes – *read* all over.

Yopie Prins's inventive and witty book *Victorian Sappho* reveals the same problem except that she has turned it into a strength. She deals, in a way that I do not, with Sappho's Greek – or Sappho's editors' Greek, especially that of H.T. Wharton in his 1885 edition of *Sappho: Memoir, Text and Selected Renderings with a Literal Translation*. She gives an account of the Michael Fields (Katharine Bradley and Edith Cooper) and their aspirations toward Greek, then considers Swinburne, and his complicated and eccentric physical relation to Greek, and finally reads a selection of the Victorian women poets to assess their personal and literary investment in Sappho's story. As a result, her book works its way through a backward chronology which is surprising and odd, but entirely justified by the special nature of her subject in Sappho and her wayward heritage.[11]

My own book does, more or less, work its way through chronologically – from Mary Robinson (1758–1800) to Virginia Woolf (1882–1941). Each chapter is designed to stand on its own, but some themes in my chapters overlap. So, for instance, while Chapter 2 on Robinson has a great deal to say on the question of Sappho's function as a role model for intellectual women, so Chapter 3 on the iconography of Sappho from the 1760s to the late nineteenth century similarly begins with her portrayal as a writing woman. Some of my chapters are about individuals and their very personal interest in Sappho. This is the case with Chapter 4 on Tennyson and those of his juvenile poems that display her influence. In his case the time focus of my reading – or rather *his* reading of Sappho – is also very specific, covering just one intense working period across the summer, autumn and winter of 1830–31.

Other chapters are about groups of people. That on the Victorian women poets, for example, is designed to trace a line of indebtedness that actually is, to some degree, developmental, as the same theme of Sappho's balancing of 'love versus art' is self-consciously re-worked by writers from Letitia Elizabeth Landon (L.E.L.) and Christina Rossetti, to Mary Coleridge, Agnes Mary Frances Robinson and the Michael Fields. Another relatively 'developmental' strand links Chapters 6 and 7, on Baudelaire and Swinburne, because I argue here that much of Swinburne's Sapphic aesthetic (then passed on to George Moore and Thomas Hardy) derives from Baudelaire. The one other 'group' chapter is Chapter 8 on H.D. Richard Aldington and Ezra Pound also figure there because the three of them create quite distinct versions of a Modernist Sappho.

Chapter 3 on Sappho's iconography in pictures and paintings and sculptures is a generic essay. It overlaps with the more literary side of her history, but I have told the whole story of her history as an icon in *The Sappho Companion*, and here I want to be able to deal in detail with these manifestations in popular culture, allowing my readers to create those criss-crossing connections. Or to ignore them, just as they wish.

This method – at once piecemeal and multiple – is one that I learned from Sappho. Or rather from Sappho's poems. Or rather from Sappho's fragments, made into poems by her latter-day audiences.

I have spoken of those audiences, and their importance in my picture of Sappho. But there are other things in the Fragments that seem to me to colour – or shade? – any view of Sappho's history. When Sappho (if she did) broke herself up into her constituent parts in Fragment 31 then she made a template for what she has since become. Parts. In pieces.

When Sappho (if she did) employed her techniques of including the voices or personae of Aphrodite or Atthis or Anactoria or the rest of her girls in her Fragments 1 and 94, in her Fragments 96 and 16, then she initiated the patterns I use here of many consciousnesses singing together, singing separately.

When Sappho (if she did) names her own name in her Fragments 1 and 94 (and in others) then she begins a process of recognition and possession that will be handed down through the centuries as others name her (the Tenth Muse, the Lesbian, the lesbian, Psappho, Saffo, Sapho), and name themselves by naming her (the British Sappho, the German Sappho, the Russian Sappho, the Modern Sappho, the New Sappho).

When Sappho (if she did) invented a psychic geography spread out across past, present and future time, and across wide tracts of her contemporary world, then she made a paradigm for what she would become – spread out for all time and across all Western culture.

When Sappho (if she did) assumed that she spoke her own feelings as a poet to be understood by us as an audience to be the true account of our own feelings, then she set up the pattern of vampiric possession which turns that process back on her. As she once felt and spoke for us, so we have come to feel and speak for her.

When Sappho (if she did) made her performed speaking into a poetic voice that was everywhere and for everyone, then she anticipated her own latter-day extension of self – and loss of self. As I say at the end of my pictures chapter, quoting the late nineteenth century French writer Rachilde, 'Etre Sapho ce serait être tout le monde.'

III

I tell you;
in time to come
someone will remember us

If Sappho lends herself to metaphor, perhaps that is because she is *nothing but* metaphor.

'She was', says the Scholiast quoted by Lucian, 'small and dark and ugly, like the nightingale.'[12] Sappho's life as a legend began soon after her death. She was portrayed, lyre in hand, on a vase dating from the late sixth century BC and appears again on a red-figure *hydria* (water jar) from the mid to late fifth century BC.[13] In both these cases she is shown in the role of a poet, but from quite early on a tussle seems to have developed between those who valued her as a writer – lauding her as the 'Tenth Muse' or as one of the 'garland' of Hellenistic women writers – and those who attempted to put her in her place by telling the stories of how she was a lover of women, how she deserted her girls for Phaon the ferryman who scorned her, and how she leapt from the cliff of Leucadia.[14] The tale of the two Sapphos – one, the poet of Mytilene, the other, the courtesan of Eresus – was invented in ancient times to save Sappho's reputation, but the split becomes an image repeated many times in the later history of Sappho's afterlife.

The legends are certainly not to be relied upon, but they do give us the tropes of the woman and the lyre, the singer 'like the nightingale', the poet of desire who was unhappy in love, the 'masculine' Sappho who was a lover of women. Then there is the leap, the fall, the myth of lyric origin, the idea of the mother, and of the mother of a daughter, and the notion that Sappho's Lesbos may be an ancient poetic home.

Some of these figures are worked through in the imaginations of the audiences I discuss here. In her guise as 'the first' lyric poet – and the 'original' woman poet – Sappho becomes a private 'mother-Muse' for writers such as Tennyson or Baudelaire. Baudelaire's poem 'Lesbos' actually begins 'Mère des jeux latins et des voluptés grecques'. For the women poets, however, the same concept of Sappho's originality leads them alternately to idealise her, and to repudiate the inevitable tragedy of her story. Similarly, the idea of Sappho as an ancient model who took the stage in poetic performance led to the popularity of her image as virtuoso performer worked over in the plays and operas that take her theme.

Then there is the tale of Sappho's leap from the Leucadian cliff. On the one hand it can be construed as a grand gesture of the Sublime as Sappho's poetic voice is merged with sky and sea, and that's how she was portrayed by many Romantic writers including Mary Robinson. Yet, but shortly afterward, and Sappho is incarnated as a suicide who was also a 'fallen' woman – both because of her sexual practices and the mode of her death. Thus 'Sappho' provided a popular pictured image, where the one idea leads into the other in the iconography that I trace through the early years of the nineteenth century. Then, as the nineteenth century wore on and discussions of sexuality became more complex, Sappho's ancient name was denounced and exposed as a dirty word in the works of Swinburne and his followers.

Yet again, for the Modernist poet H.D. – an American who spent most of her life abroad – Sappho's close metaphoric association with the island of Lesbos meant that the ancient poet – and the idea of the island itself – came to symbolise a land of poetic origin, denied, and yet nostalgically desired, a place always out of reach for the exile. To some degree, in his peculiar way, that lost place was similarly the key Sappho image in the imagination of Richard Aldington. While for Ezra Pound Sappho was, first of all, a poet ... a voice, half heard, half guessed, a foreign tongue that would always remain untranslatable.

IV

Tongue is broken

Whether or not any of Sappho's work was written down during her lifetime, none of it survives from that time and such literary remains as we have today are the result of memory, guesswork, and accident. The story of how Sappho's oeuvre was constructed across the 2600 years that intervene between her and us is told in Margaret Williamson's *Sappho's Immortal Daughters* and in my *The Sappho Companion*. For the purposes of this book it is only necessary to know that there are two primary sources for her work.

The first of these two primary sources are the quotations handed down to us by ancient authors. The most important of these are Fragment 1, the so-called 'Ode to Aphrodite' which was quoted in full by Dionysius of Halicarnassus in his 'On Literary Composition' dating from the first century BC, and Fragment 31, 'That man seems to me', which was quoted in part by Longinus in his 'On the Sublime' written in the first century AD.

The second of the primary Sappho sources are the papyrus discoveries that took place at Oxyrhynchus (now called Behnasa) in Egypt as a result of the work of the Egypt Exploration Fund based in Oxford at the end of the nineteenth and beginning of the twentieth centuriesy.

Across the years covered by this book, from the mid-eighteenth century to the early part of the twentieth century, there were many developments in Sappho scholarship, and new editions and translations published during that time helped to create a recognisable Sapphic body of work. In the early part of the period, as Joan DeJean has shown, France was the leader in producing both editions and 'fictions' of Sappho. Then, during the nineteenth century, the major centre for Greek scholarship moved to Germany, while, by the end of that century, Britain had, in effect, taken over. Scholars, and those readers who had Greek, were those most often *au fait* with these events. Tennyson, for instance, was a reasonably accomplished Greek scholar. He knew and used Boissonade's 1825 Paris edition of Sappho. But he also knew enough to know when that work was superseded by Bergk's editions published in Germany in the mid nineteenth century, and he actually went on to purchase a copy of one of these. Similarly, when H.T. Wharton published his important *Sappho: Memoir, Text, Selected Renderings and a Literal Translation* in 1885 Wharton was sufficiently up to date to use Bergk's Greek text. And yet, even as his book went into a second and third edition, he also knew that that work was likely soon to be overtaken by the discoveries then being made in Egypt.[15]

That said, what happened to be going on at any one time in terms of Greek scholarship very rarely affected what was going on in terms of Sappho's story. There are, strictly speaking, only two places in this book where events in Sappho scholarship directly influenced imaginative creations: the first case is where Michael Field's collection *Long Ago* was inspired by Wharton's 1885 *Sappho* volume; and the second is where H.D., Pound and Aldington were influenced by the articles being published in the *Classical Review* about the discoveries in Egypt. Always, it is much more likely that some larger, wider, cultural event or mood leads to a collective interest in Sappho and that, inevitably, focuses on the more accessible aspects of what we choose to call 'Sappho' – that is, the legends or the metaphors. Hence her importance as an intellectual woman at the time when Mary Wollstonecraft and Germaine de Stael were writing. Hence her significance for Baudelaire when lesbianism was topical and fashionable in the Paris of the mid nineteenth century. This is, as I have said, not a book about an authentic Sappho, but about the many different Sapphos who come and go in the popular imagination.

In resisting the hold of these enveloping metaphors you might like to believe that Sappho's poetry could be of more help than her legends. But the poetry presents us with the most extended and persuasive metaphor of all. For Sappho's body of work is in fragments. And once again, there is the figure in the poem, for in Fragment 31 Sappho's 'tongue is broken'.

The romance of Sappho's fragments has been a part of her attraction from the earliest times. One is almost tempted to speculate that it may be the chief reason for her fame. Sappho, as a result, is not a person, not an oeuvre, barely a name. Instead S——o is a space. For joining up the dots. Filling in the blanks. Making something out of nothing.

But making something precious out of nothing.

More golden than gold

If we have very little of Sappho, then that little is all the more to be treasured. In the introduction to her 1796 sonnet sequence *Sappho and Phaon* Mary Robinson wrote:

> In examining the curiosities of antiquity, we look to the perfections, and not the magnitude of those reliques, which have been preserved amidst the wrecks of time: as the smallest gem that bears the fine touches of a master, surpasses the loftiest fabric reared by the labours of false taste, so the precious fragments of the immortal Sappho, will be admired, when the voluminous productions of inferior poets are mouldered into dust.[16]

Tennyson, though better qualified to know what those remains consisted of because he did read Greek, was similarly affected by the lost works and his regret and admiration are expressed in *The Princess* where the lady Professors of Ida's academy deliver lectures on the Classics:

> ...
> With scraps of thunderous Epic lilted out
> By violet-hooded Doctors, elegies
> And quoted odes, and jewels five-words-long
> That on the stretched forefinger of all Time
> Sparkle for ever.[17]

Tennyson was borrowing from his favourite poet of the older generation, Byron, as did the Greek scholar John Addington Symonds in *Studies of the Greek Poets*:

> – these dazzling fragments,
> 'Which still, like sparkles of Greek fire,
> Burn on through time and ne'er expire',
> are the ultimate and finished forms of passionate utterance, diamonds, topazes, and blazing rubies, in which the fire of the soul is crystallized for ever.[18]

By the time we come down to H.D. in the early twentieth century and a dream about a jewel box that belonged to her mother, then Sappho's broken gems, once perfect, still precious and dazzling, have become such a commonplace that the sign substitutes silently for the signified. In Bergk's edition, said John Addington Symonds, 'every vestige that is left of her is shrined'. And holy relics is what the fragments have become, whether in fact – as with the broken *oistrakon*, the shard of terracotta pottery that gives us Fragment 2, excavated by Medea Norsa in the early twentieth century and now housed in a velvet case in the Biblioteca Laurenziana in Florence – or in the imaginations of all her many audiences.

Poring over Sappho's precious relics for clues, scholars and readers find holy writ. Everything is meaningful, even the empty spaces where there may be nothing at all. The history of Sappho scholarship and the rapt attention of her readers – so optimistic, so ecstatic, so wishful and wistful – reminds me of the enthusiasm of the fanatic. Sappho's adherents hoard her every word, enshrine her broken syllables, and garland her fragments in exquisite settings.

Limb-loosening

If the fact of Sappho's fragmented state implies loss, it also confers value. The paradox where dearth equals wealth is one that has obtained in ideas to do with the fragment from the eighteenth century on. But now, in the early years of the twenty-first century, we are familiar with the broken structures of Modernism and the post-Modern, and the fragment has become almost more than the whole. Less, we are told, is more. Today – possibly in opposition to a set of past ideals which we wish to construe as monolithic, imperialist, absolute and intolerant – we applaud multiplicity, variety, difference. Feminist scholarship, ethnic issues, gay politics, popular cultures, have all taught us that diversity is desirable. Angela Carter called her own writings an 'art of bricolage'; Claudine Herrmann described women as 'thieves of language'; the 'unwritten novel' consists of snippets of fiction, diary entries, recipes, pastiche, personal confession and newspaper cuttings; even biography – once trumpeted as the most 'truthful' of genres – now acknowledges its own piecemeal untrustworthiness when it sets an historical account side by side with fictional digressions; and contemporary art of all kinds (and critical views of art) now insist on the participation of the reader or the viewer and leaves space for the insertion of action or reaction.[19]

It may be that this current preoccupation of ours is one reason for Sappho's present popularity: her work is fragmented, her life can only be guessed at through fragments. But the fact is that Sappho's fragmentary state has contributed to her value across the whole period discussed in this book, from the mid eighteenth century on.

To begin with, the language associated with the idea of the fragment allows for a range of wordplay and opens up a whole range of metaphoric discourses. If Sappho – body of work and body, as indeed they both are, the one in fact, the other in legend – is fragmented, then this suggests that they are broken, mutilated, crippled, defective, impaired, maimed, bruised, dismembered, in pieces. Or, in another set of figurative manuscript contexts, they are tattered, torn, shredded, in shards, wispy, stumpy, bitty, scrappy, ragged. Because both Sappho's work and Sappho's person are 'in pieces' it means that it and she are neither whole, nor wholly independent. So it – and she – can be possessed, taken, raped, riddled, rapt, wrapped, ventriloquised, impersonated, forged. On the one hand, she represents a falling short – she is crude, unhewn, unripe, sketchy. On the other hand, she posits an excess, as she is made multiple, decimated, many-sided. Her hand can be forged, her deeds are overwritten, her text is a palimpsest, her imprint is graffiti, her life is an apocrypha and her words are a set of tall stories.

In a larger discourse the paradox of lost and found, of lack and excess, means that Sappho's fragments become a synecdoche, the part that can stand in for the whole. These meaningful remains hint at a larger conception which is grander, more perfect, more sublime that anything fully realised and readily accessible. Our imaginations supply the bigger picture which will always be beyond anything that can actually be achieved. And yet at the same time the implied relationship between the broken-off part and the integrated whole might suggest some conflict between the two, some sense that the whole is authoritarian while the part is resisting, rebellious, oppositional. Then, the inevitability of a dual perspective forced on us, as we switch between a contemplation of the whole that is suggested by the part, sets up a notion of doubleness that pervades discussion of the fragment, whether as a strength through layered meaning, or as a site of conflict and contradiction. Finally, the fragment – whether planned or unplanned, the result of something being unfinished, or interrupted, or broken off – always forces on the reader, the viewer, that necessity of double vision, of actively participating in constructing an imagined entity from the extant ruins or remains.[20]

Though it was not something that I had planned, I realise that many of these larger philosophical positions dictated by notions of the significance of the fragment, underpin many of my conclusions in reading writers reading Sappho. My version of Mary Robinson's reading, for instance, espouses a fragmentary literary method that I see as deliberately provisional because it opposes a range of social imperatives that are construed as destructively authoritarian. The Victorian women poets exploit the multiple possibilities of reflection and reversal, difference measured against similitude. H.D. turns herself into her own active reader, as reading and writing overlap with her dreams and her psychoanalysis.

One thing, however, was certainly planned. And that is the importance of reader-response in this book. I have said that this critical method was dictated by a concern to consider the many audiences of Sappho's poems. But it was also dictated by my continuing awareness that because Sappho always has been, and always will be, in pieces, then her readers' project has always been, and will always be, to reconstruct her. Or to fake her. For that reconstruction can sometimes be true to the reader, but it must always be false to Sappho.

V

I cannot weave my web

Elizabeth Wanning Harries says that, though the concept of the fragment is inextricably bound up with our notions about the ancients, they themselves had no comparable concept of the significance of literary fragments. Rather, the European fashion for the deliberate making of fragments is one that began during the early Renaissance, then fell into decline, only to resurface in the eighteenth century. Since then it has remained more or less permanently in sentimental vogue. Though Harries does not discuss the historical parallels, there is no doubt that the Renaissance fashion for the fragment – her particular example is the *sparsi rime*, 'scattered rhymes' of Petrarch's sonnet sequence – coincided and indeed probably grew out of the concurrent rise in Classical scholarship, which itself was intimately connected to the development of the new printing techniques and the consequent dissemination of Classical texts.[21]

When the printing press was invented in the fifteenth century, one of the results was the promotion of Classical scholarship. Printers needed things to print if they were to exploit and profit from their new technology, and so they scoured the libraries of Europe for manuscripts to convert into print for the markets they wished to create. Scholarship and enterprise go hand in hand at this period, and so it is not surprising that this is also the time when the techniques of comparison and collation – still the staples of textual editing today – were extrapolated from practices in Biblical scholarship to be applied to the ancient texts of the Greek and Latin languages. One of the ancient texts that began to gain a wide audience at this time – because it was made available through the new technologies – was Ovid's *Heroides*, 'Letters of the Heroines', which included Letter XV 'Sappho to Phaon'. Another ancient text suddenly made available to a wider audience was Longinus's first-century treatise *Peri Hypsous*, 'On the Sublime'. The new popularity of that text was to have far-reaching consequences in initiating a whole philosophy of the Sublime whose tenets are with us even today. Some marginal notes from that larger subject are dealt with here in my Chapter 2 on Mary Robinson and Chapter 3 on the pictures of Sappho. But more than that, the new visibility of Longinus contributed to a new bringing into view of Sappho, whose Fragment 31 happens to be one of the texts that he cites.

But it was during the eighteenth century, in particular, that the Fragment became almost more popular than the Whole. Harries rightly points out that the fashion for fragments pre-dates the Romantics with whom it is often now associated. But again – as with the rise of the fragment vogue in the Renaissance – there was a practical and historical reason for the revived interest. Just as the manuscripts of ancient texts were rediscovered (or rather re-presented) in the fifteenth and sixteenth centuries, so antique things were being rediscovered in the eighteenth century.

In June 1738 a 13-year-old girl came to Naples from Dresden. She was Maria Amalia Christina, daughter of Augustus III of Poland (the former Frederick Augustus of Saxony), and she was to marry Charles VII of Bourbon, King of Naples and the two Sicilies. For some time before this date the King had been prevaricating over whether or not to build himself a new seaside villa at the resort of Portici. Maria Amalia decided for him. Her father had just recently acquired three antique statues, bought in Vienna at a public sale, but found at a site along the Naples coast close to Portici. She had the passion of a collector – even at that young age – and she saw her opportunity. 'Build that villa at Portici' she whispered in the ear of her new bridegroom. Accordingly, Charles VII acquired the adjoining plots of land and he appointed Rocque Joaquin de Alcubierre to construct the beach house and excavate the site. From 1738 onwards Alcubierre, and later, Karl Weber, another engineer employed by him, worked on the building-up, but worked even more assiduously on the breaking-down. They discovered small things – marbles, bronzes, scraps of mosaic – and they brought up large things – whole statues, bronzes, walls covered with frescos. But at every stage – through flooding, through heat, through the collapse of their flimsy tunnels, and the deaths of their workers – the villa was delayed and the excavations went on. This story is told in Christopher Charles Parslow's *Re-Discovering Antiquity: Karl Weber and the Excavation of Herculaneum, Pompeii and Stabiae*, but the results for the re-invention of the ancient world and for the re-imagination of Sappho were to be far reaching.[22]

In 1750 Weber came across the so-called Villa dei Papiri. This was evidently the home of a wealthy man – in all probability a scholar – who had collected, during the years of the first century AD, a hoard of pictures and sculptures, bronzes and mosaics. And papyri. As the villa gradually gave up its treasures, one of the most important sites of the finds was described by Camilla Paderni who excavated the remains of an early library. This he described soon after its first discovery in 1752:

> [One room] appears to have been a library, adorned with presses, inlaid with different sorts of wood, disposed in rows; at the top of which were cornices, as in our own times. I was buried in this spot for more than twelve days, to carry off the volumes found there; many of which were so perished, that it was impossible to remove them.[23]

Over the ensuring years many papyrus rolls, or, more correctly, *fragments* of papyrus rolls, were removed from the eponymous Villa dei Papiri and other sites in the archaeological wonderland around the Bay of Naples. Their charred and blackened remains are still to be seen in the galleries of the Museo Nazionale at Naples. They look like nothing at all. It is very hard, even for a scholar, even for a bibliographical scholar, to see what they are. To see what they mean. We look, but we don't understand. Then we look again, and we imagine what we see. Every time I look at you.

But in the eighteenth century there were those who got the message. There were no Sappho fragments found among the scraps of papyri excavated at Pompeii and Herculaneum. But because Sappho's fabled Nine Books of poetry – the total reported to have been held in the library at Alexandria in about the third century BC – were widely thought of as one of the greatest losses of antiquity, people began to make up stories about what might have happened if Sappho *had* been there. The volume most explicitly influenced by this idea was Etienne Lantier's antiquarian novel *Voyages d'Antenor en Grèce et en Asie* (1797) which was translated into English two years later as *The Travels of Antenor in Greece and Asia from a Greek Manuscript found at Herculaneum: Including Some Account of Egypt*. The novel opens with an unnamed narrator playing the Grand

Tourist and visiting the famous sites of the excavations around Naples. There he sees the papyrus finds being exhumed and interpreted:

> They consisted of cylindric rolls, nearly in the form of rolled tobacco. The first folds were so difficult to open, that it was necessary to make use of a machine to draw out, by means of screws, this black and shattered parchment upon linen or unctuous paper. As soon as the decypherer had discovered a word, he wrote it down; guessing at those which were illegible by the sense and connection of the sentence: and though these writings had no points or commas, the learning and intelligence of the persons employed supplied all these defects.

The scholars at work on this collection are fired by imagining that they will find the lost glories of ancient Greek literature and are not interested in a 'very voluminous roll in Greek' noted by the narrator. He persuades the excavators to allow him to carry the manuscript away to Paris. Once deciphered, it turns out to be the autobiography of one Antenor who had lived in the sixth century BC and who had travelled all over the ancient world during his 108 years of life. Antenor had also – as it happened – arrived at Leucadia on the very day when Sappho took the leap. Before she dies, Sappho had confided another manuscript to Antenor which told the whole history of her unhappy *amour*, and we are to suppose that Antenor is actually quoting from this manuscript as he goes on to tell her story.[24]

Lantier's fiction of Sappho is the one that links her story most explicitly with the archeological fantasies brought on by the discoveries at Pompeii. But those events spawned many other quasi-antiquarian novels that were immensely popular throughout Europe during the trend for the Classical revival. You bought the furniture and the vases – the real thing if you could afford it or, like Sir William Hamilton, were in a position to acquire it – and you read the books.

These books included a novel by Alessandro Verri, *Le avventure di Saffo*, which was published in 1780, reprinted many times, and translated into English in 1803 by John Nott. Others were Vincenzo Imperiale's *La faonide: inni et odi de Saffo* (1784), which purported to be a translation from the Greek of a hitherto unknown hymn of praise to Phaon which had been recently discovered written on a papyrus found in a stone box by the 'famous Russian scholar Ossur' while he was visiting the Cape of Leucadia. This work was translated into French by J.B. Grainville in 1796 in his *Hymnes de Sapho, nouvellement découvertes et traduite pour la première fois en français*.

The most important and widely influential work of this kind, however, was Jean-Jacques Barthélemy's *Voyage du jeune Anacharsis en Grèce*. This pseudo-antiquarian novel, larded with footnotes and genuine references to the Classics, was first published in Paris in 1788. It was translated into English in 1794 and many times thereafter, into Italian in 1801, and it was regularly reprinted well into the nineteenth century. In English its title was *Travels of Anacharsis the Younger in Greece during the Middle of the Fourth Century before the Christian Era*. Obviously then the fictional Anacharsis (unlike Antenor) does not actually get to meet Sappho, but in Volume II, chapter 3 (in the 1817 English translation) Anacharsis does visit Lesbos and there he hears the story of Sappho, her works, her life, and her contradictory reputations:

> I was one day repeating these and many similar expressions [of Sappho's] to a citizen of Mytilene, and added: 'The figure of Sappho is seen upon your coins, and you profess the highest veneration for her memory. How is it possible to reconcile the sentiments she has left us in her writings and the honours you publicly decree her with the infamous manners with which she is privately reproached.' He answered me, 'We are not sufficiently acquainted with the particulars to form a competent judgment of her life'. Strictly speaking, no conclusion can be drawn in her favour from the love she professes for virtue, nor from the honours we pay to her talents. When I read some of her works, I dare not acquit her; but she had merit and enemies, and I dare not condemn her.[25]

VI

Little and black, like the nightingale

The antiquarian fictions of the late eighteenth century helped to bring Sappho into focus and this is why my study starts at this period. Barthelemy was one of the chief sources for Mary Robinson's sonnet sequence *Sappho and Phaon* which I discuss in Chapter 2. I would also suggest that the contemporary trend for the Grand Tour and the contemplation of the ruins of the ancient world, combined with (for women artists especially) their particular relation to the lost original of the woman poet in Sappho, led directly to the more up-to-date version of Sappho's story told in Germaine de Stael's influential novel *Corinne* (1807). *Corinne*'s subtitle is *or, Italy* and it was designed, in part, as a travel book, taking the attentive reader on an extended tour of the ancient ruins of Rome and other major sites in Italy. Corinne's own house is set at Tivoli outside Rome, a site well known as the home of the so-called Temple of the Sibyl. It is, moreover, no accident that a crucial scene in Corinne's story is set at Cape Miseno overlooking the Bay of Naples, Vesuvius, and the excavations of Pompeii and Herculaneum.

But many contemporary issues coincide here. There are the excavations, there is the fascination with fragments, there is the pursuit of the Sublime, and there is the new visibility of Sappho who relates to all of these larger interests in the late eighteenth century. So Sappho is always there in the margins of a more conventional history of Romanticism. Poets like Mark Akenside and George

Dyer both composed poems supposed to be by or about her. Robert Southey wrote 'Sappho: A Monodrama' (1793), a poem which places Sappho on the edge of the cliff at the Sublime moment of will that precedes her death. Mary Robinson and Samuel Taylor Coleridge corresponded with each other as 'Sappho' and 'Alcaeus' and addressed poems to each other in these names. More than that, Ruth Vanita has argued that Coleridge's 'Christabel' and even his 'Kubla Khan' owe something to his vision of Sappho. Certainly the Eastern setting and the picture in 'Kubla Khan' of the 'savage place! as holy and enchanted/ As e'er beneath a waning moon was haunted/ By woman wailing for her demon-lover' might well suggest some of Sappho's scenes. And in 'Christabel' there is a direct reference to Sappho's Fragment 105a, on 'the sweet-apple', in lines I, 48–52:

There is not wind enough to twirl
The one red leaf, the last of its clan,
That dances as often as dance it can,
Hanging so light, and hanging so high,
On the topmost twig that looks up at the sky.

There is also a curious personal footnote to Coleridge's more professional uses of Sappho. In 1816 he gave to his daughter Sara a copy of Franz Kleist's German drama based on the story of Sappho with a note that said, 'I have not read this, but am told that it is good.'[26]

Among the younger Romantics, Byron read Sappho in Greek and she appears in both his letters and his poetry, usually in a jokey context and most notably in *Don Juan* (1819) Canto XLII, where she is included in a list of proscribed authors as Byron indulges himself with a pun on 'hymn' that reflects his acquaintance with '*mascula Sappho*':

Ovid's a rake, as half his verses show him,
Anacreon's morals are a still worse sample,
Catullus scarcely had a decent poem,
I don't think Sappho's Ode a good example,
Although Longinus tells us there is no hymn
Where the sublime soars forth on wings more ample.

Percy Bysshe Shelley also studied Greek while he was at school at Eton. The college produced its own textbooks for Greek and Latin studies and in the Eton edition of selected *Poetai Graeci* both Sappho's Fragment 31 and Fragment 1 were included, along with lyrics from Homer, Hesiod, Theocritus and Erinna. Shelley remembered Sappho from these early days, and his 1822 poem 'To Constantia, Singing' is a close revision of Fragment 31. Keats, on the other hand, may not have had access to Greek studies during his schooling, but all the same he does seem to have been familiar with Sappho's two famous poems, and Ruth Vanita makes a good case for his 'Ode to a Nightingale' as a version of Fragment 31.[27]

If the male poets of the Romantic period touched on Sappho, the women poets of the late eighteenth century and early nineteenth century embraced her. For them she figures as a key source and influence, not usually because of her poetry, but for her legends and for her legendary function. One curious aspect of the imaginative apprehension of the fragment, at this time and at others, is its close association with ideas of the feminine. In *The Unfinished Manner* Elizabeth Wanning Harries discusses this question in a chapter on novels such as Richardson's *Clarissa* (1748), Choderlos LaClos's *Les Liaisons dangereuses* (1782) and Frances Sheridan's *Memoirs of Miss Sidney Biddulph: Extracted From Her Own Journal, and Now First Published* (1761). She suggests some of the reasons for this association: that the feminine is understood as contingent while the masculine is absolute, paralleling the relation between the partial Fragment and the autonomous Whole; that the feminine and the fragment are conventionally allied with concepts of Nature, while the masculine and the Whole go with Culture; that the shattered discourse in *écriture feminine* puts it with the fragment, the non-linear and the incomplete. Obviously there is a whole range of philosophical positions within these assumptions and they have been the subject of feminist debate for some years now. But I think that within the early part of the period I explore in this book – from the mid-eighteenth century through the nineteenth century – there is an argument to be made for the feeling that Sappho peculiarly belonged to women and to 'the feminine' for many reasons – because she was a woman, because she composed lyric poetry, and because she was in fragments.

This argument underpins much of my thesis in Chapter 2 on Mary Robinson, and it informs my Chapters 3, on the pictures, and 5, on the Victorian women poets. But related considerations also appear in my Chapter 4 on Tennyson and in Chapter 6 on Baudelaire.

Two historical examples – one to do with a woman artist of the early period, another relating to a woman writer – might help to show how Greek, and the idea of Sappho and the fragment, made this association real for my subjects.

In 1788, on the eve of the Revolution in France, the painter Elisabeth Vigée-LeBrun was reading Abbé Barthélemy's *Voyage du jeune Anacharsis* with its detailed story of Sappho. After one such session (her brother read aloud while she painted), she had the idea of dressing up herself and her friends in 'ancient Greek' draperies. She borrowed some antique vases from an acquaintance, she persuaded another to appear with his lyre guitar, she had her cook produce some authentically 'simple' ancient dishes, she arranged the lighting, and framed her scene with the double doors into her drawing room. So, later that night, when her guests arrived at the appointed hour, they were treated to a scene directly drawn from *Anacharsis*. The event became a scandal – the gossip went about that it had cost millions of francs – and it became an urban folk tale about the extravagances of the rich *beau monde* in a city populated by the dispossessed who were starving and resentful.

But Vigée-LeBrun kept the event as her trademark. When she painted her famous second *Self Portrait with Julie* (1789) she wears those distinctive Grecian robes. She herself called this self-portrait *A la Grecque*.[28] Still later in her career, she was to continue the allusions to the ancient and modern incarnations of her illustrious female 'ancestors'. She painted Emma Hamilton as the Sibyl, and then she painted Madame de Stael as her own fictional character, Corinne. I discuss these paintings in Chapter 3, but the point I am making here is that all of these – completed – pictures are fragments of a larger enterprise which, though contingent and piecemeal, nevertheless aimed at a reconstruction and valuing of female achievement.

My second example is to be found in Mary Shelley's 1826 novel *The Last Man*. The preface tells how the narrator penetrated into the Cave of the Cumaean Sibyl – significantly, a setting near Naples. Finding herself accidentally falling into a still deeper cave, hitherto unknown to the guides, she discovers scattered fragments, scraps of writing in many languages, some known, some unknown, some legible, some not. These – we are to suppose – are the remains of the lost Nine Books of the Sibyl, and the broken record of her prophesies:

> The rest of the furniture of the cavern consisted of piles of leaves, fragments of bark, and a white filmy substance, resembling the inner part of the green hood which shelters the grain of the unripe Indian corn ... At length my friend, who had taken up some of the leaves strewed about, exclaimed, 'This *is* the Sibyl's cave; these are Sibylline leaves.' On examination, we found that all the leaves, bark, and other substances, were traced with written characters.

The narrator then pieces these fragments together in order to tell the story of a coming world and a lost race, which is effectively the novel that follows:

> Doubtless the leaves of the Cumaean Sibyl have suffered distortion and diminution of interest and excellence in my hands. My only excuse for thus transforming them, is that they were unintelligible in their pristine condition ... I hardly know whether this apology is necessary. For the merits of my adaptation and translation must decide how far I have bestowed my time and imperfect powers, in giving form and substance to the frail and attenuated Leaves of the Sibyl.

Sappho and the Sibyl are both included in the reference to the lost Nine Books now in fragments. Mary Shelley's scene here is also a metaphor for entering, penetrating, knowing the mother's body in that secret cave. These are the inscriptions, remains, of the mother's writings that she pieces together, just as she herself had indeed come to know Mary Wollstonecraft only through reading her, both in her private letters and in her published writings. Like her own monster in *Frankenstein* (1818), it is as if Mary Shelley's idea of the feminine is one that is always made of scraps of body parts, and one that is always only coming at an understanding of the narrated world second-hand, at one remove, through other people's books, or other people's writings.[29]

Sappho's fate is much the same. She too becomes a mother over and over in the stories I tell here. But a mother who has to be invented, reconstructed, revised. And yet in those readings my subjects all make a new story which – as with Mary Shelley and Elisabeth Vigée-LeBrun – is, in the end, a story of new powers. This is why this book begins in the mid-eighteenth century. Because Sappho first appears there in many new lights and she begins there in many new fictions.

VII

I loved you once, Atthis, long ago

Or rather, she is used there to begin many new fictions. Again, all my readers' readings may be true to themselves, but they are always false to Sappho. For she is desired by them and, in different ways, possessed by them. Throughout the time of my working on Sappho I have been aware of a distinctly erotic tone that runs through all these readings. It is a strand that goes back a long way.

Towards the end of the sixth century, Paul the Silentiary wrote an epigram that suggests that any access to 'authentic' ancient versions of Sappho's work had already been lost, and that the nostalgic regret about her inaccessibility had already begun:

> Soft Sappho's kisses, soft the embraces of her snowy limbs, but her soul is of unyielding adamant. For her love stops at her lips; the rest belongs to her virginity. And who could endure this? Perhaps one who has borne it will endure the thirst of Tantalus easily.[30]

Tantalising. In the erotics of the fragment – part known, part hidden – in the erotics of the feminine – part veiled, part guessed – Sappho yields, and yet resists us. She is the quintessential poet of desire, and still we never have her.

But that is the paradox. By definition, desire only ever comes to us piecemeal, in fragments. In fantasy – which is the principal engine of desire – I focus upon parts. Your mouth, your beautiful eyes, your hands on my body. Specific, precise, discriminated. Over and over again. Lack, and then excess. My focus is on only one part, one action, one movement or touch, which I then reiterate, return to, rehearse in a cycle which endlessly repeats itself in pieces, deferring consummation, resisting the whole.

'Desire', writes Giuseppe Mazzotta 'knows only shreds and fragments even if plenitude is its ever elusive mirage.'[31] One day I will have all of you. One day I will have enough. But even as I say the words, I know it isn't true. While desire inflames me, there will never be enough, no matter how much I have. When desire is no longer there, everything, will mean – nothing at all.

Sappho has given me much pleasure. As she has pleasured others before. In my imagination she comes to me, she comes for me. I have looked at her with desire. I have imagined that she looks back at me. Every time I look at you.

I am not the only one. I do know that. I am neither first, nor last. In my chapter on the pictures of Sappho I found that one of the peculiarities of this history is the fact that artists so often paint or sculpt her over and over again. Their multiplied images reflect the thwarting of their desire. My own many images, many pictures, of Sappho mirror the failure of my enterprise to own her. In the end, I do know that I have only made another one of the many forgeries that fake her name. I too have gone over that Sapphic pattern, but I have re-made it for my own purposes. Desire, loss, the memory of desire.

One reviewer of my book *The Sappho Companion* wrote:

> Of course, Reynolds's muse – 'difficult, diffuse, many syllabled, many-minded, vigorous and hard' – is as revealing of its author as the fictions that precede it. Her Sappho – butch, proud and prone to silences – is not afraid of leaving gaps unfilled; of beckoning, bitter-sweet and hard to get, from the future.[32]

I first began to think seriously about Sappho as an academic subject when I read Jeanette Winterson's *Art & Lies* in 1994. Her Sappho is fierce and brave, angry about the falsehoods shaped around her life, and angrier still about the forgeries of her work:

> I have a lot of questions, not least, WHAT HAVE YOU DONE WITH MY POEMS? When I turn the pages of my manuscripts my fingers crumble the paper, the paper breaks up in burnt folds, the paper colours my palms yellow. I look like a nicotine junkie. I can no longer read my own writing. It isn't surprising that so many of you have chosen to read between the lines when the lines themselves have become more mutilated than a Saturday night whore.[33]

So in this too my vision is skewed, my picture is distorted. I am willing to confess a personal relation to the many bodies of Sappho that I have since exhumed, celebrated, loved. But now, after many years and many incarnations, it seems to me still that nothing is more true, more honest in its own vision than that one where I first started. In this book you will find many reflections of Sappho. But if you want to find the real Sappho, then you must turn to the fictions that are in *Art & Lies*.

2
Mary Robinson's Attitudes

When Goethe arrived in Naples in March 1787 he was introduced to Sir William Hamilton, His Majesty's British Envoy Extraordinary to the Kingdom of the Two Sicilies. The two men were soon on friendly terms, and Sir William offered Goethe a tour of his secret treasure vault. It was crammed with busts and bronzes, with marble torsos and antique ornaments all lying in a jumble. Goethe spied a long case lying on the floor and could not resist lifting the lid while his host's back was turned. It contained a magnificent pair of ancient bronze candelabra that he was sure he'd seen earlier in the museum of finds from the excavations at Pompeii. He began to wonder if these and other such 'lucky acquisitions' were the reason why Sir William showed his treasures only to his most intimate friends. But the thing that intrigued Goethe most was a box: a chest, standing upright and large enough to hold a human figure, its front taken off, the interior painted black, and the whole set inside a splendid gilt frame.[1]

Sir William had lived in Naples since 1764 and was established as an influential diplomat and a notable connoisseur of antiquities. The neo-Classical revival of the late eighteenth century was at its height and its main venue was set, not in a beleaguered Greece occupied by Turkish forces, but in the great cities of Italy: Florence, Rome, Naples. The spirit of ancient Greece was everywhere felt in those cities; its art could be seen there, in the plundered early statues that thronged the Galleries of the Vatican; and its fragments could be purchased there, in the equally famous shops that sold antiquities imported from archaeological sites in both Greece and Italy. Sir William had made the most of his position. He visited Roman and Etruscan tombs to carry away their grave goods, he purchased wall paintings from the excavations at nearby Pompeii, he had cameos, carved gems, bronzes and he made two comprehensive collections of vases, both Roman and Greek. The small private museum Sir William established at his residence at the Palazzo Sessa became an attractive draw for travellers to Italy – hence Goethe's visit in 1787. But the curious box which Goethe saw in the cellar was not one of Sir William's antiquities. Or not quite. The box was a stage prop for the performance of Lady Hamilton's Attitudes.

The new Campaspe

Emma Hart had come to Naples the previous year to be installed as Sir William's mistress. For some five years before that, from the age of 16, she had been the mistress of Sir William's nephew, Charles Greville. When Greville fell into debt he hit upon the plan of sending Emma on to his elderly uncle:

> at your age a clean and comfortable woman is not superfluous ... She is the only woman I ever slept with without ever having had any of my senses offended, and a cleanlier, sweeter bedfellow does not exist.[2]

All this in exchange for the settling of his bills.

At first, Sir William was reluctant, although he had met Emma in London and admired her. But he had been a widower since 1782, and eventually he was reconciled to the scheme because of her resemblance to the profile of a Greek goddess carved on a cameo. Emma, for her part, set out reluctantly. And when she got to Naples there was the problem of what to do with her. Even as an Envoy's mistress – and most certainly as his wife, which she was to become in 1791 – Emma would be expected to converse, to perform, to entertain. The first Lady Hamilton had been an accomplished musician, but Emma had never been taught an instrument. She could speak no language except her native English. Even that she did not speak very well and, in any case, had nothing to talk about, for she had no education and little inclination to learn. All that Emma had ever done was be. Still, she had done that very nicely, and was much sought after as a model since she had been painted by the likes of George Romney and Joshua Reynolds. Then Sir William hit upon the answer. Emma would do Attitudes to entertain their guests.

Wearing a specially made dress of 'Greek' drapery, with a large Kashmir shawl and a few props – a vase, an axe, a child – Emma performed Attitudes. To begin with she did them inside that black painted chest, and her poses were drawn from Sir William's collection of Pompeiian wall paintings. Later, the box was discarded as too confining, and the sources for her repertoire of Attitudes were extended to include figures from Greek vases, scenes from mythology, or well-known paintings both ancient and modern, and even moods or attributes. Goethe was treated to several performances, and described her swiftly-varying depictions:

> she lets down her hair and, with a few shawls, gives so much variety to her poses, gestures, expressions, etc., that the spectator can hardly believe his

> eyes. He sees what thousands of artists would have liked to express realized before him in movements and surprising transformations – standing, kneeling, sitting, reclining, serious, sad, playful, ecstatic, contrite, alluring, threatening, anxious, one pose follows another without a break. She knows how to arrange the folds of her veil to match each mood, and has a hundred ways of turning it into a head-dress. The old knight idolizes her and is enthusiastic about everything she does.[3]

The Attitudes were a success. The Scottish painter Hugh Douglas Hamilton painted a triple portrait of Emma as the three Muses of song, dance, and epic poetry. Many of Sir William's guests made sketches of the performance, including a German artist, Friedrich Rehberg, who made a number of drawings 'faithfully copied from Nature at Naples'. Twelve of these were engraved and published by Tommaso Piroli in 1794. The twelve images represented in Rehberg and Piroli's publication by no means record all of Lady Hamilton's Attitudes. A tantalising reference in a contemporary account of the performances hints that one of Emma's poses portrayed a woman poet, possibly even Sappho herself. The Comtesse de Boigne – who visited Naples as a young girl in 1792 and was co-opted to perform as an accessory in the Attitudes – gave a list of Emma's props among which she included a lyre: 'Lorsqu'elle consentait à donner une représentation, elle munissait de deux ou trois schalls de cachmire, d'une urne, d'une cassolette, d'une lyre, d'un tambour de basque ...'[4] So famous were they, that Lady Hamilton's Attitudes became an essential component for any fashionable young gentleman completing his Grand Tour. William Artaud dutifully reported his assiduous sightseeing to his father:

> The environs at Naples are truly Classic ground, I have visited Lake Avernus, have been in the Elysian Fields, in the Baths of Nero, and in the Tomb of Virgil ... I have been at Herculaneum and Pompeii, and the Museum at Portici and saw Lady Hamilton's Attitudes ...

Emma became a sight, an art object, an aesthetic experience to rival the Classical antiquities in any connoisseur's collection. 'Elle passait', wrote the painter Elisabeth Vigée-LeBrun, 'de la douleur à la joie, de la joie à l'effroi, avec une telle rapidité que nous etions tous ravis'; 'She passes from sadness to joy, and from joy to terror with such astonishing rapidity that we were all enraptured.' While the Conte della Torre di Rezzonico said that,

> I observed with great delight that just as the Greeks learnt to preserve the beauty of their females' faces even when expressing tears or pain, equally the new Campaspe when adopting an attitude of pain never lost her beauty ... She

> single-handedly created a living gallery of statues and paintings. I have never seen anything more fluid and graceful, more sublime and heroic ...[5]

Everyone was satisfied. Though Goethe judged his fair entertainer 'frankly a dull creature' he saw how she had been transformed in Sir William's eyes: 'After many years of devotion to the arts and the study of nature [he has] found the acme of these delights in the person of an English girl of twenty with a beautiful face and a perfect figure.' In Emma, he said, Sir William saw 'all the antiquities, all the profiles of Sicilian coins, even the Apollo Belvedere'. Horace Walpole said that the device of the Attitudes allowed Sir William to marry his 'Gallery of Statues', and even Emma herself declared that 'Sir William is never so happy as when he is pointing out my beautyies to [his friends].'

Perdita

My story here concerns another set of neo-Classical Attitudes. Whether or not Emma Hamilton included a representation of Sappho in her range of *tableaux vivants*, Emma's fame was admired from afar by another woman artist who called herself 'Sappho'. Though, to be sure, that was only one of her many names.

This was the poet Mary Robinson. Like Emma Hamilton, Mary Robinson was used to assuming a variety of poses. As a poet, she had published under the names of Laura, Daphne, Julia, Louisa, Oberon and Echo. 'Sappho' was just one of her poetic personae, but it was to become her best-known name after she published a sonnet sequence, *Sappho and Phaon, in a Series of Legitimate Sonnets with Thoughts on Poetical Subjects, and Anecdotes of the Grecian Poetess* in 1796.

Mary Robinson was born in 1758, one of the five children of an errant seaman, Captain John Darby. Mary was educated at a school in Bristol and then by Meribah Lorrington in Chelsea who taught her Latin, French and Italian and painting on silk. Unfortunately Lorrington also drank, so that did not last long. But Mary had acquired enough accomplishments to make her education an asset when her impoverished mother – deserted by her husband yet again – tried to set up a school. Through a dancing master, Mary attracted the attention of the actor David Garrick and there was some talk of her going on the stage. Then, at the age of 15, she married Thomas Robinson, an articled clerk who presented himself to Mary and her mother as a man of wealth and family. He was neither; he was a gambler and a libertine, surrounded by rakish friends, who soon saw that 'the pretty child' had financial potential. One of these friends, however, Lord Lyttelton, happened to give Mary a copy of Anna Aikin's poems, which she read 'with rapture'. 'I thought them', she wrote later 'the most beautiful poems I had ever seen, and considered the woman who could invent such poetry as the most to be envied of human creatures.'

After a stint in the King's Bench prison with her debtor husband, and by now, a baby daughter, Mary was persuaded to go back to the plan of the stage to try to earn some money. So, in December 1776, she appeared at Drury Lane as Juliet and a successful career began, though it was to be a short one. Late in 1779 the 17-year-old Prince of Wales (later George IV) saw Mary in *The Winter's Tale*, and, smitten, employed Lord Malden as his ambassador. To begin with she held out:

> I entreated him to recollect that he was young, and led on by the impetuosity of passion; that should I consent to quit my profession and my husband, I should be thrown entirely on his mercy. I strongly pictured the temptations to which beauty would expose him; the many arts that would be practised to undermine me in his affections; the public abuse which calumny and envy would heap upon me; and the misery I should suffer, if, after I had given him every proof of confidence, he should change in his sentiments towards me.

In the end, the Prince offered a bond for £20,000 to be paid when he came of age, and 'Perdita' succumbed to 'Florizel'. In this new role too, Mary Robinson took on many guises. On one occasion the Prince suggested that Mary visit him incognito at his apartments in Buckingham Palace by dressing up in the 'disguise of male attire' – which she was used to doing on stage, for she was well known for her 'very good breeches figure'. Real life cross-dressing was quite another matter, but her later public appearances with the Prince seemed still to include varieties of costumed posturing:

> To-day she was a *paysanne* with her straw hat tied at the back of her head. Yesterday she perhaps had been the dressed belle of Hyde Park, trimmed, powered, patched, painted to the utmost power of rouge and white lead; to-morrow she would be the cravated Amazon of the riding house ...[6]

The Prince, you will be unsurprised to learn, soon lost interest – and that in spite of the wardrobe. After a year, he passed on to another bought-beauty and Mary's bond was still unpaid. She was left with a reputation which made it impossible to return to the stage and a collection of impassioned letters. She offered them back, price £25,000. Eventually, in 1781, King George III paid over to Mary the knockdown sum of £5000 – 'to get my son out of this shameful scrape' – and in 1782 Charles James Fox also persuaded her to hand over the Prince's bond in exchange for an annuity of £500. By this time Mary had been both Lord Malden's and Fox's mistress. After a while she took up with Banastre Tarleton, a veteran of the American War of Independence who was, as it turned out, no more to be relied upon than the Prince or the pauper husband. He left her for the last time in 1798 when he married a young heiress. At that time Mary Robinson was partially paralysed as the result of a miscarriage in 1783, poverty-stricken as the result of Tarleton's gambling, and ... an established author.

Robinson had begun to write for money, and she continued to do so, producing Gothic novels which sold well and had a reliable audience. But that early exposure to Aikin and the illustrious calling of poetry, meant that she saved her best efforts for verse. In 1791, at the suggestion of Edmund Burke, she published a collection of *Poems* and the list of its six hundred subscribers included the Prince of Wales, his brothers the Dukes of York, Clarence and Gloucester, politicians like Fox, George Pitt, Lord North and William Russell, artists like Richard Cosway and Sir Joshua Reynolds, and people from the theatre like Richard Brinsley Sheridan and his wife Elizabeth Linley and the celebrated actress Mrs Jordan. It was followed by *Poems, Modern Manners* in 1793 and *Sappho and Phaon* in 1796.

A series of sketches

Sappho and Phaon consists of forty-four Petrarchan sonnets. After three introductory sonnets – one addressed to Poetry, one to Chastity and one to Love – it traces the story of Sappho's awakening passion for Phaon, her vain attempt to invoke the power of Reason to calm her desire, her efforts to seduce Phaon, his subsequent neglect, her reaction to his departure for Sicily, her following him there, and her final despairing decision to jump off the cliff of Leucadia in order to put an end either to her infatuation or her life. From the first, Mary Robinson conceived the strength of her sonnet sequence as lying in its composite, fragmentary character, where all the diverse pieces would add up to a complete whole:

> It must strike every admirer of poetical compositions, that the modern sonnet, concluding with two lines, winding up the sentiment of the whole, confines the poet's fancy, and frequently occasions an abrupt termination of a beautiful and interesting picture; and that the ancient, or what is generally denominated, the LEGITIMATE SONNET, may be carried on in a series of sketches, composing, in parts, one historical or imaginary subject, and forming in the whole a complete and connected story.[7]

The Attitudes style of Mary Robinson's *Sappho and Phaon* is further underlined by a contents page which gives a careful list of tableaux setting out 'The Subject of Each Sonnet'. So Sonnet IV, for instance, is listed as 'Sappho Discovers Her Passion'; V 'Contemns its Power'; VII 'Invokes Reason'; in VIII 'Her Passion Increases'. XII is 'Previous to her Interview with Phaon'; XIII is 'She Endeavours to Fascinate Him'. In XXX Sappho 'Bids Farewell to Lesbos'; in XXXII she 'Dreams of a Rival'.

'Standing, kneeling, sitting, reclining, serious, sad, playful, ecstatic, contrite, alluring, threatening, anxious' ... Here is Mary Robinson – or Sappho – posing a series of Attitudes, just as Goethe saw Emma Hamilton perform.

The idea of fragmented glimpses that lies behind both Emma Hamilton's Attitudes and Mary Robinson's sonnet sequence is crucial and revealing. Both women were aiming at a personal investment in a culture where they could otherwise have been reduced to a footnote, or displaced to the margins. And yet, paradoxically, they made that effort using a method which was evanescent and liminal. It is almost as though their artistic self-presentation can only be made *through* margins and footnotes. The splitting up of the self into parts practised by both Hamilton and Robinson had a particular resonance given the archaeological and Classical themes of their work. At the same time this fragmentation reflects on their own piecemeal experience of who they were, on their own construction of identity. Remember that both of these women were, quite literally, sold: Emma to Sir William, Mary to the Prince of Wales. They were valuables, goods, luxury items – in Irigaray's terms, 'use-value, exchange value among men'.[8]

But still they knew their own worth. They knew how to use a contemporary interest in the aesthetic to turn themselves into art objects which could be appreciated and valued. The contradictions, especially in Mary Robinson's position, were multiple. On the one hand she was, or had been, a kept woman; on the other, she was a respected writer. On the one hand she was an actress, to be ogled and lampooned; on the other she was a liberal thinker, the friend of Edmund Burke and, later, of Mary Wollstonecraft. On the one hand she was a child of the Enlightenment, committed to the virtues of Reason and Education, and on the other, she was an adherent of the Della Cruscan school of poetry, which was explicitly sentimental.

When Robinson comes to create her portrait of Sappho, she gives the Greek poet a version of her own split personality. Sappho is, on the one hand, 'a lively example of the human mind, enlightened by the most exquisite talents', while on the other, 'yet yielding to the destructive controul of ungovernable passions'. She is, on the one hand, 'a supremely enlightened soul' and on the other she is 'labouring to subdue a fatal enchantment; and vainly opposing the conscious pride of illustrious fame, against the warm susceptibility of a generous bosom'.

Ungovernable passions

Mary Robinson's investment in Sappho's story is personal, but it is also particular to her social context. Commentators on *Sappho and Phaon* have seen that one of its keys is the treatment of feeling, but they have tended to see this trope as one that is purely literary, when, in fact, feeling occupied a troubled terrain in Robinson's own life. The facts of her experience suggest Irigaray's account of the debilitated feminine in 'This Sex Which is Not One': 'The rejection, the exclusion of a female imaginary undoubtedly places the woman in a position where she can experience herself only fragmentarily as waste or as excess in the little structured margins of a dominant ideology.' Irigaray, of course, situates this process within a commercial framework, and from our perspective we see clearly that Mary (and Emma) were turned into commodities. But the things that were bought and sold were not just their bodies, but their feelings, their regard, the 'susceptibilities' of their 'generous bosoms'. So feeling and the condition of femininity begin to elide in Robinson's imagination. She is a woman in the margin of a 'dominant ideology' but it is not the fact of her sex that she experiences as 'waste' or 'excess', but the fact of her feeling. The forty-four feeling Attitudes that we find in *Sappho and Phaon* are Robinson's aesthetic attempt to come to terms with that.

Forty-four varieties of feeling

Robinson's complete range of Attitudes displayed in *Sappho and Phaon* are performed then first of all for herself. Dressed up as Sappho, Robinson distances herself from the scene of sex relations about which she writes in order to analyse and understand her own position. In these secret, broken, coded fragments she attempts to recuperate 'woman's desire'.[9]

Sonnet IV – given in the table of contents as 'Sappho Discovers her Passion' – is the first poem in the sequence supposed to be spoken about her own situation and Robinson has Sappho speak about her body, describing the symptoms of her desire in a version of the Greek poet's Fragment 31:

Why, when I gaze on Phaon's beauteous eyes,
Why does each thought in wild disorder stray?
Why does each fainting faculty decay,
And my chill'd breast in throbbing tumults rise?
Mute, on the ground my Lyre neglected lies,
The Muse forgot, and lost the melting lay;
My down-cast looks, my faultering lips betray,
That stung by hopeless passion, – Sappho dies!

A tug of war then follows between Feeling and Reason. In Sonnet V, Reason 'Contemns [love's] Power'; Sonnet VI 'Describes the Characteristics of Love'; Sonnet VII 'Invokes Reason'; and Sonnet VIII takes up the body theme again, 'Her Passion Increases':

Why, through each aching vein, with lazy pace
Thus steals the languid fountain of my heart,
While, from its source, each wild convulsive start
Tears the scorch'd roses from my burning face?

Her blood, her blush, here rises to visible show on her cheek – and, doubtless, elsewhere – and Sappho hopes, by the end of the sonnet, that Phaon's encouraging response will 'fan the blush of shame'. This bodily picture looks coy enough, but it becomes rather explicitly rude if one remembers the euphemistic strategy, employed by eighteenth and nineteenth century writers, of transferring bodily reactions experienced in the lower, hidden, part of the body, upward to the exposed, public, politer features.

After a couple of sonnets describing Phaon, Sonnet XI 'Rejects the Influence of Reason' and Sonnet XII becomes altogether more steamy. This sonnet is listed as portraying Sappho's position 'Previous to Her Interview with Phaon'. So – to play on that idea – she anticipates him, he is coming ... which he is, in her imagination, if nothing else.

Now, o'er the tessellated pavement strew
   Fresh saffron, steep'd in essence of the rose,
   While down yon agate column gently flows
A glitt'ring streamlet of ambrosial dew!
My Phaon smiles! the rich carnation's hue,
   On his flush'd cheek in conscious lustre glows, ...

The blood which had first risen in the speaker's face is now transposed to Phaon's body, while she displaces a picture of his physical body and its sexual functions into the landscape and the sound-track to her fantasy of a delightful consummation:

   Breathe soft, ye dulcet flutes, among the trees
Where clust'ring boughs with golden citron twine;
   While slow vibrations, dying on the breeze,
Shall soothe his soul with harmony divine!
   Then let my form his yielding fancy seize,
And all his fondest wishes, blend with mine.

The irony is that this scene never happens. Even within the sonnet sequence it is pictured as an imagined scene, a fantasy, it is precisely '*Previous* to Her Interview with Phaon'. For all its seeming transparency and tenderness, Robinson's *Sappho and Phaon* is highly critical of relations between the sexes and is as ironic as anything written from a more overtly political perspective today. Sappho keeps working herself up into a frenzy of desire – forty-four frenzies to be precise – only to find that there is no reciprocal reaction.

It may be that Love, or feeling, is one subject in Mary Robinson's variety of Attitudes in *Sappho and Phaon*, but that could make the sonnet sequence sound trivial, or worse, womanly. It is not love itself that is the subject, but the process of *talking about love*, writing poetry about love.[10] It is the writing, speaking, analysing, and staging of Sappho's experience of love that interests Robinson, and the poses in which she portrays her speaking Sappho are designed to impose a creatively controlled but always questioning shape onto the contingencies of the experience of desire. Phaon is nothing in this sonnet sequence. He is shown to be unworthy of Sappho's love from the start so that we can attach no interest to the possibility of mutual regard or a developing reciprocity between Sappho and Phaon. He never even actually gets to appear in this staging; we only ever see him through Sappho's eyes, in Sappho's imagination. He is simply the necessary object that enables Sappho's discourse of love. He is no more than a stage prop; a vase, an axe, a child, to be used in the enacting of Mary Robinson's Attitudes.

The failure of relations between the sexes is a subject that Robinson returns to many times in her work, but not simply to make a cynical political point. In another Sappho-related poem, 'Lesbia and Her Lover', the layers of artifice and metaphor, as well as the discussion on the function of the art-object and the performance of feeling, make the poem a brilliant example of Robinson's wit and sophisticated thinking.

Lesbia upon her bosom wore
The semblance of her lover;
And oft with kisses she would cover
The senseless idol, and adore
The dear capricious rover.

Lesbia would gaze upon his eyes,
And think they look'd so speaking,
That oft her gentle heart was breaking;
While glancing round with frequent sighs,
She seem's her lover seeking!

One day, says reason, 'Why embrace
'A cold and senseless lover?
'What charms can youthful eyes discover
'In such a varnish'd, painted face?
'Prithee the task give over.'

Cried Lesbia, 'Reason, wherefore blame?
'Must you the cause be told?
'My breathing lover I behold
'With features painted just the same –
'As senseless and as cold!

'Then, reason, 'tis the better way
'The harmless to commend;
'My breathing lover soon would end
'My weary life, to grief a prey –
'This never can offend!'[11]

Lesbia knows a lot about posing. She knows the Attitudes which the conventions of romance and heterosexuality and the sex-market expect her to perform. And if 'reason' – as in commonsense – questions her behaviour in adoring a painted image, then 'Reason' – as in Lesbia's intelligent reckoning of the facts of her experience – explains Lesbia's willingness to promote the make-believe over the real.

In *Sappho and Phaon* Reason is, in the same way, the antagonist set against Feeling.

But this is not the ordinary reason that is the voice of moderation. Robinson's governing principle is the oxymoron of a passionate Reason, an intellectual feeling, an erotic intelligence. Repeatedly invoked in the course of the sonnet sequence, Reason exhorts Sappho to summon up self-control, and to concentrate on those things that are both desirable and attainable – in Sappho's (and Robinson's) case, personal ambition and poetic achievement. Love is only one of the subjects discussed in Robinson's forty-four Attitudes. Others are Mind, Poetry and Fame.

Echo's Song

At the climax of Robinson's sequence is Sonnet XXXIV, listed in the contents as 'Sappho's Prayer to Venus'. This poem occupies a particularly important position in Robinson's series because – like Sonnet IV – it does actually draw on one of Sappho's own poems, the so-called 'Ode to Aphrodite'. Fragment 1 begins by invoking the Goddess and then pleads for her assistance in winning the beloved, begging her to become her ally, her fellow-fighter. Fragment 1 is also interesting because it's one of the places where Sappho actually names herself. Aphrodite responds to her call, and asks, 'Who shall I persuade this time/ to come back to your love?/ who wrongs you Sappho?' Like her model, Robinson's poem begins by calling on the Goddess and goes on to beg for her help in restoring her absent beloved. Also like her model, Robinson puts in her own name, her own signature. This is Robinson's version.

XXXIV

Venus! to thee, the Lesbian Muse shall sing,
  The song, which Myttellenian youths admir'd,
  When Echo, am'rous of the strain inspir'd,
Bade the wild rock with madd'ning plaudits ring!
Attend my pray'r! O! Queen of rapture! Bring
  To these fond arms, he, whom my soul has fir'd;
  From these fond arms remov'd, yet, still desir'd,
Though love, exulting, spreads his varying wing!
  Oh! source of ev'ry joy! of ev'ry care!

Blest Venus! Goddess of the zone divine!
To Phaon's bosom, Phaon's victim bear;
So shall her warmest, tend'rest vows be thine!
For Venus, Sappho shall a wreath prepare,
And Love be crown'd, immortal as the Nine!

Here Robinson presents Sappho invoking Venus (or Aphrodite) as the Greek poet did in her Fragment 1. But she also presents a shadow image of herself invoking Sappho as if *she* were a latter-day goddess of love. The 'Lesbian Muse' is Sappho, but it is also Sappho-as-played-by-Robinson, and the name of the impersonator is encoded in the poem. One of Robinson's literary pseudonyms was 'Echo', and it is Echo-Robinson who 'am'rous of the strain inspir'd,/ Bade the wild rocks with madd'ning plaudits ring!' At the conclusion of the poem this song which tells about love – whether Sappho's own, or Robinson's imitation – will make the 'wreath' of fame both for Sappho herself, and, by implication, for Robinson too. Venus's new crown, as sung by Sappho-Robinson, will be this 'wreath' of poems, the sonnet sequence itself that anatomises and stages Love.

The Sapphic Sublime

Mary Robinson referred to Sappho many times in her work.[12] In a sense we are not even inclined to ask *why* because it seems so inevitable that a woman poet might look to this illustrious ancestor. In addition, given that one of Robinson's subjects was the effect of sensibility, Sappho might seem a natural choice because her legend – at least as told by Ovid and re-told by Alexander Pope – is one that concerns an excess of feeling. But in the late eighteenth century, Sappho flourished in quite another setting and one considerably more dignified and significant.

Sappho's Fragment 31 – as it is in modern editions – survived from antiquity because it was quoted in the first century AD by Longinus in his treatise *On the Sublime*. It was the invention, or rather, the re-discovery of the notion of 'the sublime' in art that made Sappho into a popular icon in the eighteenth century. The earliest English translation of *Peri Hypsous* was published by John Hall in 1652 and a number of others followed, but the eighteenth century obsession with the sublime really began with Nicolas Boileau's popular French translation of Longinus, and Milton's twelve-book edition of *Paradise Lost*, both published in 1674. In England, the immediate results were a Latin edition of Longinus by John Hudson (1710), and an English translation by William Smith (1739), along with numerous articles and essays on language, poetry, rhetoric, aesthetics which addressed the character of the sublime.[13]

Longinus's *On the Sublime* (which may not be by Longinus at all) is an attempt to define and analyse the qualities of great or high writing. From the start Longinus sets up an opposition between writing which may persuade and charm, and writing which astonishes, which ravishes, writing that 'takes the reader out of himself', that 'throws the audience into a transport', and it is this latter kind of writing that he considers 'sublime'. 'Greatness', he says, 'appears suddenly.' Like a thunderbolt it reveals the writer's full power in a flash: 'the sublime ... with the rapid force of lightning has borne down all before it, and shown at one stroke the compacted might of genius'. Longinus cites several ancient writers and works through a number of distinguishing qualities before he gets to section 10 and his Sappho example. There he quotes part of Fragment 31 to show how great writing makes selection of diverse objects and puts them together again to make an instantly convincing whole. Here is Longinus's commentary:

> Let us consider next, whether we cannot find out some other means, to infuse sublimity into our writings. Now, as there are no subjects, which are not attended by some adherent circumstances, an accurate and judicious choice of the most suitable of these circumstances, and an ingenious and skilful connection of them into one body, must necessarily produce the sublime. For what by the judicious choice, and what by the skilful connection, they cannot but very much affect the imagination.
>
> Sappho is an instance of this, who having observed the anxieties and torments inseparable to jealous love, has collected and displayed them all with the most lively exactness. But in what particular has she shown her excellence? In selecting those circumstances, which suit best with her subject, and afterwards connecting them together with so much art.

Here he quotes Fragment 31:

> Are you not amazed, my friend, to find how in the same moment she is at a loss for her soul, her body, her ears, her tongue, her eyes, her colour, all of them as much absent from her, as if they had never belonged to her? And what contrary effects does she feel together? She *glows*, she *chills*, she *raves*, she *reasons*; now she is in *tumults*, and now she is *dying away*. In a word, she seems not to be attacked by one alone, but by a combination of the violent passions ...[14]

'Standing, kneeling, sitting, reclining, serious, sad, playful, ecstatic, contrite, alluring, threatening, anxious'. Here we are again. According to Longinus's description, Sappho's Fragment 31 is a set of Attitudes, swiftly changing and astonishing. Like Vigée-LeBrun or Goethe watching Emma Hamilton, Longinus can hardly believe his eyes, and the transformations of Sappho's varying emotional postures carry him away, strike him in a flash. 'Are you not amazed?' he says to his reader. 'Do you not wonder?'

The key word here is συνοδος the swarm, or concourse of emotions. 'Concourse' or 'intersection' is actually a better translation, because the Greek word – from which we derive 'synod' – can also be used to describe the clash of hostile armies, the meeting of an assembly, or the conjunction of the stars. It is literally, a place where diverging roads come together, a crossroads, or a crossing of paths. And it is the tension implied in holding in mind the idea of individuated manynesses at the same time as blending them into one whole that gives Sappho's poem its power, as it gave Emma Hamilton her effect, or Mary Robinson her politicised method of dealing with the split selves that made up her own experience of herself.

Once Longinus's treatise was translated into English its premises began to underlie many of the discussions that followed. Writers such as John Dennis, Jonathan Richardson, and Joseph Addison (who also wrote some early influential articles on Sappho), Mark Akenside and John Baillie contributed to the dissemination of the idea of the sublime.

According to Samuel Monk, Baillie's *An Essay on the Sublime* (1747) in particular marked the moment 'when speculation withdrew from the search for sublimity in the object and began to be centred in the emotions of the subject'. It's a change in definition that fits with Sappho's analysis of love's physical symptoms in Fragment 31 and it is a bias that was expanded in Edmund Burke's influential book *A Philosophical Enquiry into the Origin of Our Ideas of the Sublime and Beautiful* (1757, revised and expanded edition 1759).

In the preface to the first edition Burke explained that his aim was to distinguish between the attributes that properly belong to the Sublime and to the Beautiful, correcting common abuses of the terms (which he believes even Longinus to be guilty of), by returning to first principles:

> Could this admit of any remedy, I imagined it could only be from a diligent examination of our passions in our own breasts; from a careful survey of the properties of things which we find by experience to influence those passions; and from a sober and attentive investigation of the laws of nature, by which those properties are capable of affecting the body, and thus exciting our passions.

Before he begins to thumb through the attitudes – or Attitudes – that allow for this examination, Burke notes in his 1759 'Introduction on Taste' that taste, 'like all other figurative terms, is not extremely accurate: the thing which we understand by it, is far from a simple and determinate idea in the minds of most men, and is therefore liable to uncertainty and confusion'. Thus, he argues, in order to cultivate taste and discrimination, one must beware of succumbing too readily to pleasure or the experience of feeling, and learn instead discretion and judgement. 'Every trivial cause of pleasure', he says, 'is apt to affect the man of too sanguine a complexion: his appetite is too keen to suffer his Taste to be delicate; and he is in all respects what Ovid says of himself in love, *Molle meum levibus cor est violabile telis,/ Et semper causa est, cur ego semper amem.'* That is, 'Tender is my heart, and easily pierced by the light shaft,/ And there is ever cause why I should always love.'

'One of this character', concludes Burke, 'can never be a refined judge.'[15]

But Burke has made a mistake. Ovid may have written these lines, but he is not speaking of himself. He is speaking of Sappho – *as* Sappho in fact – for the quotation comes from Ovid's *Heroides* (*Letters of the Heroines*) XV, 'Sappho to Phaon'.

So here we have the contradiction. Longinus quotes a real Sappho poem to praise her for her judgement, taste and skill in producing 'great writing', in reaching the sublime. While Burke quotes a made-up story about Sappho to criticise an excess of sensibility, an indiscriminate indulgence of feeling.

The vaunting mind

That Edmund Burke should quote Ovid's Sappho as an example of the too sensible character who 'can never be a fine judge' is particularly important in view of Burke's underlying assumptions about gender stereotypes. His implied opinions in this area, along with his anti-radical views, were part of Mary Wollstonecraft's long-standing quarrel with him. When Burke comes to discriminating the characteristics of 'the beautiful', he puts them under headings like 'Beautiful objects small', or 'Smoothness', or 'Delicacy' and 'Grace'. In a section entitled 'How far the idea of BEAUTY may be applied to the qualities of the MIND', Burke offered the following famous passage:

> Those virtues which cause admiration, and are of the sublimer kind, produce terror rather than love. Such as fortitude, justice, wisdom and the like. Never was any man amiable by force of these qualities. Those which engage our hearts, which impress us with a sense of loveliness, are the softer virtues; easiness of temper, compassion, kindness, and liberality; though certainly those latter are of less immediate and momentous concern to society, and of less dignity.

He does not even mention men and women, or masculine and feminine, but it is easy to see why Wollstonecraft might be offended.[16]

Burke quotes Longinus only once in his *Enquiry*, and it is in a section headed 'Ambition'. This is Longinus, section VII:

> For the mind is naturally elevated by the true sublime, and so sensibly affected with its lively strokes, that it swells in transport and an inward pride, as if what was only heard had been the product of its own invention.

And here is Burke:

> Now whatever either on good or upon bad grounds tends to raise a man in his own opinion, produces a sort of swelling and triumph that is extremely

> grateful to the human mind; and this swelling is never more perceived, nor operates with more force, than when without danger we are conversant with terrible objects, the mind always claiming to itself some part of the dignity and importance of the things which it contemplates. Hence proceeds what Longinus has observed of that glorying and sense of inward greatness, that always fills the reader of such passages in poets and orators as are sublime; it is what every man must have felt in himself upon such occasions.

And, says Mary Robinson, every woman.

When Mary Robinson read Sappho – the real (or as close as she could get to the real) Sappho that is, and not Ovid's or Pope's inventions – then she was reading the sublime. As her mind took 'a proud flight' in response, she imagined that she had invented what she had merely heard. Actually she *did* invent what she heard, or re-invented it, because she took on Sappho's persona and re-wrote her poems in a new form, translating Sappho into forty-four 'Legitimate Sonnets'. And in responding to the Sapphic sublime Mary Robinson was 'transported' or 'ravished', she was 'swelling' beyond the limitations of her condition. 'The essential claim of the sublime', according to Thomas Weiskel, 'is that man can, in feeling and in speech, transcend the human.'[17] Mary Robinson needed to transcend the human which was, in her life, all too confining. More than that, she needed to transcend the feminine, a specific eighteenth century feminine that could be bought and sold, that insisted upon the primacy of feeling, and played fast and loose with a woman's feelings.

The terrible Sublime

Sappho has many claims on the Sublime and she crosses all Burke's boundaries. For although Sappho is a woman, and although her poetry is lyric rather than epic (that is, feeling rather than heroic), Longinus's definitions, as re-worked by the theorists of the eighteenth century, made her into an exemplar of the 'masculine' category of the sublime, rather than the 'feminine' category of the beautiful. For instance, in early eighteenth century writings on the sublime there was considerable emphasis on a move to challenge the authority of tradition and formulaic rhetoric, in favour of the authenticity of individual experience and personal expression. Fragment 31, with its emphasis on the physical experience of desire, and the intimate relation of private feeling, obviously fits in with this move. As the century wore on and theories of the sublime opened out into the promotion of a Romantic sensibility and the moral value of the poet's role, Sappho was easily re-made into a model Romantic poet. Her work (even such little as was available to the eighteenth century) ranged over many topics, was free-thinking and broad in tone, while it retained the character of personal conviction. It was this that linked her writing – and her many legends – with tenets of the sublime, as described, for instance, by Joseph Addison in 1712:

> The mind of man naturally hates everything that looks like a restraint upon it ... On the contrary, a spacious horizon is an image of liberty, where the eye has room to range abroad, to expiate at large on the immensity of its views, and to lose itself amidst the variety of objects that offer themselves to its observation.[18]

Above all, the circumstances of Sappho's legend made her into an icon of the sublime, and one moment in particular seals her claim: the scene of Sappho's leap. Joseph Addison said that the sublime in nature required 'the prospects of an open champaign country, a vast uncultivated desert, of huge heaps of mountains, high rocks and precipices, or a wide expanse of waters, where we are not struck with the novelty or beauty of the sight, but with that rude kind of magnificence which appears in many of these stupendous works of nature'. So this is where the scene is set.

Sappho stands on a high cliff under the open sky. The jagged rocks lie in the abyss beneath, and the expanse of the ocean gapes under feet. She is in despair, she knows herself abandoned and alone. She contemplates the terror of her present situation while her pride and her fierce intellect mean that she keenly understands all that she suffers. Through it all she still holds her nerve enough to discriminate and analyse every shade of her suffering. And when she does leap into space, it is a bold risk, a glorious final fling, a wild flight in a starry sky.

Sappho leaps, but her name survives, and her Sublime legend survives. In the closing sonnets of *Sappho and Phaon* Robinson's Sappho-as-poet-heroine is rescued by Reason and Ambition, even if her Sappho-as-betrayed-lover has to die. In the penultimate sonnet Sappho's 'gaze' is not turned on Phaon, or even inward on herself. Instead she looks on the 'dizzy precipice' and the world recedes as she contemplates the exalted scene of the sublime.

XLIII

While from the dizzy precipice I gaze,
  The world receding from my pensive eyes,
  High o'er my head the tyrant eagle flies,
Cloth'ed in the sinking sun's transcendent blaze!
The meek-ey'd moon, 'midst clouds of amber plays
  As o'er the purpling plains of light she hies,
  Till the last stream of living lustre dies,
And the cool concave owns her temper'd rays!
  So shall this glowing, palpitating soul,
Welcome returning Reason's placid beam,
  While o'er my breast the waves Lethean roll,
To calm rebellious Fancy's fev'rish dream;
  Then shall my Lyre disdain love's dread control,
And loftier passions, prompt the loftier theme!

The poem is replete with masculinised emblems – the 'tyrant eagle' over her *head*, 'the sinking sun's transcendent blaze', 'this glowing, palpitating soul', 'rebellious Fancy' – and these signal Sappho's masterly achievement at the moment of the leap. Reason, elided here with the 'meek-ey'd' and 'concave' moon, is construed as feminine, but it is that 'cooling', tempering and ordering of her ambition that will allow Sappho to look forward into a glorious future and the extension of her poetic ambitions beyond the grave: 'Then shall my Lyre disdain love's dread control,/ And loftier passions, prompt the loftier theme!' In the last poem of the sequence, 'Sonnet XLIV. Conclusive', the subjects are figurative and allegorical (Fancy, Time, Fate), but the imagery focuses on flight, on wings, on the stars and heavens, and ends with an address to 'Sky-born VIRTUE': 'Yet shall thou more than mortal raptures claim,/ The brightest planet of th'ETERNAL SPHERE!'

In another poem – 'To a False Friend, In Imitation of Sappho' – Robinson is even more explicit in suggesting that Sappho's assurance of immortality is the direct result of her transcendent 'flight' in the leap. She will haunt the lover who has betrayed her because she will overreach her human condition. Her words will be repeated by the sea and the sky, and her name will endure, along with her claim to the Sublime.

> In vain you fly me! on the madd'ning main
> SAPPHO shall haunt thee 'mid the whirlwind's roar;
> SAPPHO shall o'er the mountains chaunt her strain,
> And Echo bear it to thy distant shore!
> No scene upon the world's wide span shall be
> A scene of rest, ungrateful man, to thee!
>
> When the wind howls along the forest drear,
> Or faintly whispers on the curling sea,
> My voice upon the dying gale to hear
> Thou shalt awake – and call, in vain, on me!
> And when the morning beam illumes the sky,
> My faded form shall meet thy sleepless eye!
>
> False Lover! no, upon the tow'ring steep,
> Where Fame her temple rears, defying Time,
> SAPPHO shall mark unaw'd the bounding deep,
> And while thy name to blank Oblivion fades,
> SAPPHO shall smiling seek th'Elysian shades.[19]

The unperishable lustre of MENTAL PRE-EMINENCE

At the end of one of her prefaces to *Sappho and Phaon* Mary Robinson addressed her audience:

> I cannot conclude these opinions without paying tribute to the talents of my illustrious countrywomen; who, unpatronized by courts, and unprotected by the powerful, persevere in the paths of literature, and ennoble themselves by the unperishable lustre of MENTAL PRE-EMINENCE.

In *Sappho and Phaon* Mary Robinson is indeed, as Jerome McGann says, 'a woman speaking to women'. And those women who receive her confidences are her own kind, other intellectual woman, perhaps other women poets:

> Among the many Grecian writers, Sappho was the unrivalled poetess of her time: the envy she excited, the public honours she received, and the fatal passion which terminated her existence will, I trust, create that sympathy in the mind of the susceptible reader, which may render the following poetical trifles not wholly uninteresting.

I have said that Phaon is nothing in this sonnet sequence. So it is. But he and Sappho are not the only characters in the series. There are also Sappho's girls, and they are there all the time. Even in the steamiest scenes of Sappho's imagination her girls are present. In Sonnet IV she says, 'Come, tuneful maids, ye pupils of my care/ Come, with your dulcet numbers soothe my breast'. In Sonnet VIII she says, 'Go, tuneful maids, go bid my Phaon prove/ That passion mocks the empty boast of fame;/ Tell him no joys are sweet, but joys of love'. And even in Sonnet XII, the fantasised consummation with Phaon, there they are again: 'Breathe soft, ye dulcet flutes among the trees'.

And in Sonnet XXXII Mary Robinson performs a telling sleight of hand. Under the many layers of her guise as Sappho she succeeds in writing a love poem by a woman to a woman. It is another re-writing of Sappho's Fragment 31 where Sappho expresses her jealousy of the man who is 'blessed as the gods' because he is enjoying the favours of the girl she herself desires. In Robinson's version the scene is posed under the title of Sappho 'Dreams of a Rival'. That is, of course, a girl who rivals her for the attentions of Phaon. But look what happens in the poem: the address is actually to the girl, the 'Sicilian maid', and with the pretence of imaging Phaon's pleasure in the girl's charms, Robinson succeeds in smuggling in an expression of woman-to-woman desire:

XXXII

BLEST as the Gods! Sicilian Maid is he,
  The youth whose soul thy yielding graces charm;
  Who bound, O! thraldom sweet! by beauty's arm,
In idle dalliance fondly sports with thee!

Blest as the Gods! that iv'ry throne to see,
  Throbbing with transports, tender, timid, warm!
  While round thy fragrant lips light zephyrs swarm,
As op'ning buds attract the wand'ring Bee![20]

Women, or the claims of women, fire Robinson's imagination. That is why she wrote about Sappho. That is why she admired Emma Hamilton's fame, that is why she made friends with Mary Wollstonecraft, and that is why she wrote *A Letter to the Women of England on the Injustice of Mental Subordination*.

Their proper sphere

Mary Robinson's pamphlet was first published in 1799 under the title of *Thoughts on the Condition of Women*. It was reissued later the same year with its new title, but still under the pseudonym of 'Anne Frances Randall' – yet another name, yet another pose. It begins:

> Custom, from the earliest periods of antiquity, has endeavoured to place the female mind in the subordinate ranks of intellectual sociability. WOMAN has ever been considered as a lovely and fascinating creation, but her claims to mental equality have not only been questioned, by envious and interested sceptics; but by a barbarous policy in the other sex, considerably depressed, for want of liberal and classical education.[21]

The *Letter* goes on to cite a range of eminent females, from Sappho herself and other examples in antiquity, to Robinson's immediate predecessors like Anne Dacier or Lady Mary Wortley Montagu, and her own contemporaries such as Lady Harriet Ackland and Mary Wollstonecraft. Robinson also makes practical suggestions as to how to improve the status of women, and these range from a woman's right to duel to defend her reputation, to a call for female representatives in parliament. Above all it is ambition and fame that motivate Robinson, and that she believes will motivate her sex.

Her own first experience of fame and intellectual approbation came, she said, with the applause Garrick heaped upon her: 'I then experienced, for the first time in my life, a gratification which language could not utter. A new sensation seemed to awake in my bosom; I felt that emulation which the soul delights to encourage, where the attainment of fame will be pleasing to the esteemed object.'[22] Her most fulsome compliments in the *Letter*, however, are reserved for scenes where women display 'fortitude' and achieve the 'heroic' and the 'sublime'. Interestingly, the examples that she gives, while they do speak of mental power and decision, often include a clear admiration for *physical* strength. She admires the 'Welsh girls' carrying basket-loads of heavy fruits at Covent Garden market; she tells of an incident that took place among a family she knew where the daughter, improperly importuned by her lover, promptly presented him with a pistol, drew out one for herself, and shot him; she describes from first-hand knowledge all the privations that Lady Harriet Ackland had to undergo while accompanying her soldier husband in Canada and though 'far advanced in a state in which the tender cares, always due to the sex, become indispensably necessary'. In speaking of the Queen of France, but lately executed, she describes a scene reminiscent of her own version of the sublime moment of Sappho's leap:

> If there are political sceptics, who affect to place the genuine strength of soul to a bold but desperate temerity, rather than to a sublime effort of heroism, let them contemplate the last moments of Marie Antoinette ... Behold her hurled from the most towering altitude of power and vanity; insulted, mocked, derided, stigmatized, yet *unappalled* even at the instant when she was compelled to endure an ignominious death!

Even while she argues against the practice of 'mental subordination' Robinson's examples betray the same concerns as those that figure in her *Sappho and Phaon*. She is still addressing the body, and the freedoms (or restrictions) of the female body. The first requirement, Robinson argues, is that the strengths, talents and powers of her countrywomen (among them Emma Hamilton) be recognised. After that, she says, 'Let WOMAN once assert her proper sphere, unshackled by prejudice, and unsophisticated by vanity; and pride, (the noblest species of pride,) will establish her claims to the participation of power, both mentally and corporeally.' She concludes: 'Should this Letter be the means of influencing the minds of those to whom it is addressed, so far as to benefit the rising generation, my end and aim will be accomplished.'

What actually happened was that Mary Robinson got forgotten.[23] In the aftermath of the French Revolution, and with the rise of Napoleon, a new era in sexual politics was ushered in. The sight of women on the barricades, the terrors of men who feared powerful women and their claims, meant that reaction set in. In 1798 Erasmus Darwin was already writing that, 'The female character should possess the mild and retiring virtues rather than the bold and dazzling ones; great eminence in almost anything is sometimes injurious to a young lady ... great apparent strength of character, however excellent, is liable to alarm both her own and the other sex.'[24] Robinson knew what she was up against. 'I remember hearing a man of education,' she wrote in the *Letter*, 'an orator, a legislator, and a superficial admirer of the persecuted sex, declare, that "the greatest plague which society could meet with, was a *literary woman*!"' So the work of literary and politically active women like Robinson, like Madame de Stael, like Wollstonecraft, came to nothing. Wollstonecraft died, Robinson died, de Stael was exiled.

At the beginning of her *Letter* Robinson had referred to the 'genius' of Mary Wollstonecraft to explain that though she was 'avowedly of the same school', her contribution was no servile imitation of the *Vindication.* In her view many women needed to stand up for their rights and their claims; many attempts to imagine new powers would be needed; many Attitudes of power needed to be assumed. 'For it requires', she said, 'a *legion of Wollstonecrafts* to undermine the poisons of prejudice and malevolence.'

'Her soul is free/ She is where'er she wills to be'

Mary Robinson died at her daughter's cottage at Englefield Green near Windsor in 1800. But relatively late in her life her powers were recognised by someone who is not now, and never has been forgotten: Samuel Taylor Coleridge. The two poets corresponded and exchanged complimentary poems, Coleridge said 'had she but been married to a noble Being, what a noble Being she herself would have been', and to another friend he wrote: 'She is a woman of undoubted Genius … She overloads everything; but I never knew a human Being with so *full* a mind – bad, good, & indifferent, I grant you, but full, & overflowing.'[25]

After Coleridge recited 'Kubla Khan' to Robinson (or he may have sent her a manuscript copy) she replied with a poem, 'To the Poet Coleridge', where she enacts a hearing (or reading) of his poem to emphasise her commitment as a competent reader, capable of appreciating this display of his '*Minstrelsy*, SUBLIMELY WILD'.[26]

Robinson signed the poem 'SAPPHO'.

In September 1800 she wrote him another poem addressed 'To the Infant Son of S.T.Coleridge Esq.', and shortly before her death Coleridge replied with 'A Stranger Minstrel'. In this poem Coleridge envisaged himself on the heights of Mount Skiddaw in the Lake District, wishing that Mary Robinson were with him to appreciate the magnificence and terror of the scene. He imagines that the mountain, 'ancient Skiddaw, stern and proud', speaks to him about her, scornfully dismissing her capacity to understand this Sublime scene and putting her back in her woman's place: 'she dwells belike in scenes more fair/ And scorns a mount so bleak and bare'. But then the mountain relents, and admits that he too 'ancient Skiddaw, stern and proud' does know her poetry because it has reached even his mountainous wilderness:

'Nay, but thou dost not know her might,
'The pinions of her soul, how strong!
'But many a stranger in my height
'Hath sung to me her magic song,
   'Sending forth his ecstasy
   'In her divinest melody,
'And hence I know her soul is free,

'She is, where'er she wills to be,
'Unfetter'd by mortality.

...

'I too, methinks, might merit
'The presence of her spirit!
'To me too might belong
'The honour of her song and witching melody!
'Which most resembles me.
'Soft, various and sublime,
'Exempt from wrongs of time!'[27]

In his poem 'Alcaeus to Sappho' (1800) Coleridge pays Robinson a similar compliment. As 'Alcaeus', he sets up 'the beautiful' in the person of a girl who loves him and who looks at him with tenderness and admiration:

How sweet, when crimson colours dart
Across a breast of snow,
To see that you are in the heart
That beats and throbs below.

All Heaven is in a maiden's blush,
In which the soul doth speak,
That it was you who sent the flush
Into the maiden's cheek.

But still 'Alcaeus' writes that, while others may think this the most exquisite sight in the world, he knows that 'Sappho's' sublime intellectual powers make *hers* 'The fairest face on earth':

And, can a lip more richly glow,
Or be more fair than this?
The world will surely answer, No!
I, Sappho, answer, Yes!

Then grant one smile, tho' it should mean
A thing of doubtful birth;
That I may say these eyes have seen
The fairest face on earth![28]

When Mary Robinson's daughter published a three-volume edition of her *Poetical Works* in 1806 she prefaced the collection with twenty-two 'Tributary Poems' from eminent writers, friends and admirers. 'Laura! when from thy beauteous eyes', begins the first poem. But then comes, 'When SAPPHO, from the lofty steep', and, 'Transcendent SAPPHO', and then, 'Think not thy numbers SAPPHO's woes declare', and, 'As LESBOS' SAPPHO boasted first in fame!' and, 'What voice attun'd to the soft Lesbian lute/ Breathes in this rugged clime such accents clear?/ What British SAPPHO warbles thro' the year,/ When ev'ry grove in Greece is lorn and mute?'[29]

Mary Robinson was a woman on the margin. In many ways 'Mary Robinson' was only a footnote to the life of the woman who was ... Juliet, Perdita, the mistress of the Prince of Wales, the lover of General Tarleton, the politician who called herself Anne Frances Randall, the poet who called herself Laura and Oberon, Echo, Louisa, Julia, Daphne and Sappho. Her lived identity was provisional, haphazard, improvisatory, conditional and circumstantial.[30]

And yet. And yet, in her work Mary Robinson aimed at a transcendent unified character, just as the Romantic poets who were her contemporaries aimed at transcendence, at a wholeness and a Sublime vision that was beyond the contingencies of the human condition. As Sappho, in the name of Sappho, Robinson attempted that Sublime. But Robinson was an actress; she performed all the different aspects of her own life, just as Emma Hamilton performed her Attitudes. The difference is, perhaps, that Robinson was always in control of her assumed poses, and whatever her ambition, she knew that she could only ever be Robinson-performing-Sappho, or – as she became in those 'Tributary Poems' – Robinson-performing-many-Sapphos.

And if she did forge a signature – or many signatures – if she did claim many names, perhaps that, in itself performed an identity which was Sublime. An identity that took her 'out of herself', that allowed her 'proud mind' to make that glorious leap into space beyond the confines of all that contained the woman called 'Mary Robinson'.

Emma Hamilton had a signature too: her Attitudes. And they were – in exactly the same way – performed, forged, multiple. She couldn't give them up. They were who she was. They were who she had become; who she wanted to be.

Quite early on, you will remember, Emma Hamilton found that she could not go on performing her Attitudes in the special framed box that Sir William had had made for her. It was too confining. She burst out of its bounds. As the years went by Emma grew fat, and yet still she went on performing her Attitudes. There were those who thought she had become a joke. Gillray, the famous cartoonist, produced a new engraved version of Emma's Attitudes, modelled on Piroli's set of engravings and bringing them up to date.[31] It was advertised as 'considerably enlarged' and dedicated to 'all admirers of the grand and the sublime'. I used to think that this moment in the story was elegiac. But when I showed Gillray's picture of the older Emma dancing the tarantella to the poet Liz Lochhead she told me I was wrong. It was lyric, it was even heroic, she said.

It was 'wild', she was still doing it, she was still herself, or she was still the many *herselves* she had invented.

And then I knew that Liz Lochhead was right. And I remembered that Vigée-LeBrun had indeed been 'ravished', taken out of herself, by the sight of Emma's performance, and that the Conte della Torre di Rezzonico had seen in Emma Hamilton's Attitudes exactly the same thing that was in Mary Robinson's Attitudes played out in *Sappho and Phaon*. That is, both the Beautiful and the Sublime: 'I have never seen', he said, 'anything more fluid and graceful, more sublime and heroic'.

1. Portrait of a young girl, called 'ritratto di Saffo', Pompeii *c.* 1st century AD.

2. Portrait of Josephine Budaevskaya by Mlle Rivière, 1806.

3. Angelica Kauffmann, *Sappho Inspired by Love*, 1775.

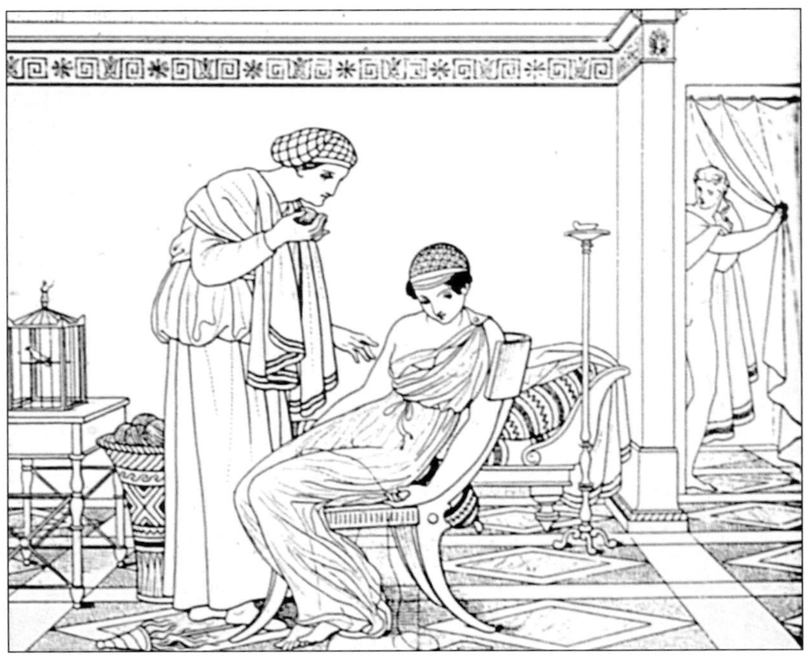

4. Anne-Louis Girodet Trioson, *Sapho dédaigne les occupations de son sexe*, 1827.

5. Elisabeth Vigée-LeBrun, *Self-Portrait with Julie*, called *A la Grecque*, 1789.

6. Hugh Douglas Hamilton, *Portrait of Emma, Lady Hamilton, as the Muses Terpsichore, Polyhymnia and Calliope*, *c.* 1789–90.

7. Elisabeth Vigée-LeBrun, *Portrait of Madame de Stael en Corinne*, 1807.

8. Richard Westall, *Portrait of the Artist's Wife as Sappho*, before 1802.

9. Jacques Louis David, *Sappho and Phaon*, 1809.

10. Baron Gros, *Sapho*, 1801.

11. Charles Gleyre, *Le Coucher de Sapho*, 1868.

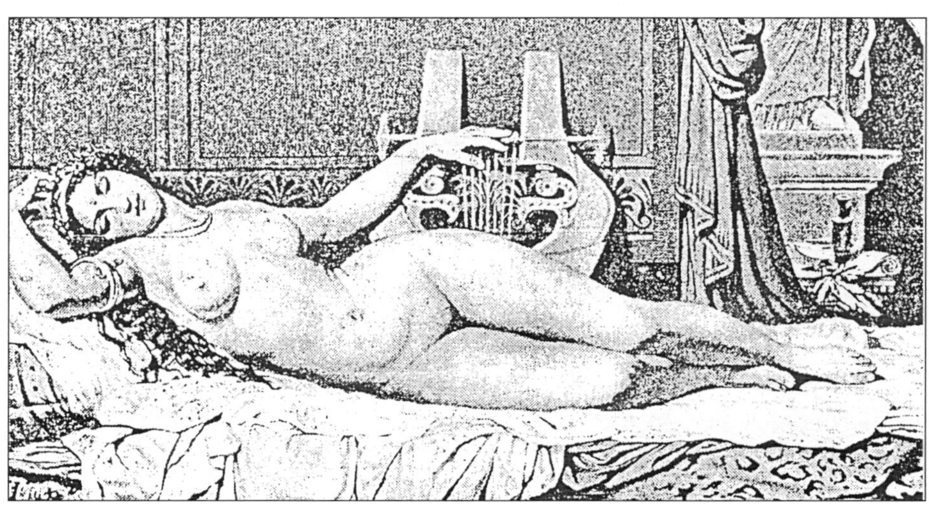

12. Felix Joseph Barrias, *Sapho d'Ereze*, 1847.

13. Charles Auguste Mengin, *Sappho*, 1877.

14. Albert Moore, *Beads* or *The Fan*, 1880.

15. Frederick Dudley Walenn (fl. 1894–1930), *Famous Women of Antiquity*. Sappho is fifth from the left.

3
Picturing Sappho

Sappho is nobody. She has no body. We know, or think we know that she existed, but if we try to reach out to her there is nothing there. Her text is insubstantial, her body of work is all second hand, because other writers have consumed her, digested her remains. The rest is dust. The closest we can come to Sappho is a tiny scrap of papyrus, nearly one thousand years old, found on a rubbish heap at Oxyrhynchus, or a triangular bit of broken pottery with some words scratched on it. Both of these are preserved like precious holy relics: the scrap of papyrus is hidden away from the light and only brought out at intervals; the broken shard is kept in a velvet case. Yet even these are substitute bodies, changelings even, for the lines in soot ink were written belatedly by someone in the first century and the potsherd was scratched by some other hand in the third century BC.

In the legends too, Sappho has no body. When she threw herself from the Rock of Leucadia her body was broken in pieces and carried away by the sea. But the stories say that she began in the same way, for when Orpheus failed to save Eurydice he wandered the world until a group of maenads, tormented by his mournful song, tore him into pieces and tossed his severed head, still singing, into the Hebrus so that it floated with his lyre out into the Aegean and on to the island of Lesbos. Thus it was that Sappho became the lady with the lyre … though, as we shall see, she is sometimes more lyre than lady.

In spite of her having no body, many people remember pictures of Sappho. They do not always remember what they saw and they did not always see what they remembered, but the image of her body remains material with them, for these many people – many women to be precise – recall pictures of Sappho for many different reasons. Felicia Hemans said her poem 'The Last Song of Sappho' was 'suggested by a sketch, the design of the younger Westmacott. There is a desolate grace about the whole figure, which seems penetrated with the feeling of utter abandonment'; Caroline Norton's poem 'The Picture of Sappho' began by invoking her popularity as an artistic subject, 'Thou! whose impassion'd face/ The Painter loves to trace,/ Theme of the Sculptor's art and Poet's story'. In George Eliot's *The Mill on the Floss* Maggie told Philip Wakem that she did not want to be a new Corinne because 'the Muses were uncomfortable goddesses ... obliged always to carry rolls and musical instruments about with them'. And in June 1927 Virginia Woolf watched her lover Vita Sackville-West fall asleep on a train and she wrote 'She looked like Sappho by Leighton, asleep.'[1]

In the memories of all these writers Sappho does become, in Judith Butler's phrase, a body that matters. Sappho's image can never be 'real'; it is made up in one time by some interested party for one set of reasons, and then it is viewed in another time and cited, subverted, questioned, or praised by another interested party and for another set of reasons. All of these writers could be referring to the same picture. They are not, but each one of them would recognise the genre, could easily guess at its content, because the material representation of 'Sappho' stays more or less within the same repertoire of postures, or displays the same attributes. And yet, even across this hundred-year span of quotations, different matter is pressed out of Sappho's many bodies depending on the bias of the viewer. Hemans sees the melancholic genius (which is herself); Norton sees the abused woman (which is herself); Eliot's Maggie sees an absurd icon (because she wants to substitute a realist heroine made through prose, not poetry); while Woolf sees erotic possibility in repose.

One reason why memories of Sappho's pictures persist is because there are so many. Her legends have generated a huge number of images over the last 250 years, and one of the stranger things about Sappho as a subject is that so many artists return to her again and again. Angelica Kauffmann painted at least four pictures, Jean Honore Fragonard two or three, Richard Westall painted three, Théodore Chasseriau two, James Pradier made two statues, Gustave Moreau seems to have painted about twelve Sappho versions, as well as designing costumes for a production of Gounod's opera, and Henry Tresham and Anne-Louis Girodet Trioson both engraved whole suites of images. Once, it seems, is never enough with Sappho. Her imaginary body is a property to be enjoyed by these artists – in the sense that it must give them some pleasure to choose to portray her – and yet it is also a property to be 'enjoyed' as in used, owned, manipulated, and policed.

My terms are borrowed from definitions of Lacan's concept of feminine *jouissance*, and that perhaps is a clue to Sappho's persistence. Feminine *jouissance* is judged insolent and self-absorbed because it defies the law. Our originary experience of it is prior to the entry into the symbolic, known in the unmediated mother–child unity when her body was yours, your body was hers, and there was no separation. But then the law, the word, the facts of conscious life in the world, intervene and that union is lost or compromised. All that remains is the secondary, fantasised experience of *jouissance* that replicates that past through desire; that moment when, once again, her body is yours, yours hers. But the law and the word forbid this undifferentiated experience, and it becomes an excess of enjoyment, transgressive and outlawed, likely only to be offered by a defamed woman, a *femme fatale* whether she is Isolde or Carmen, Rita Hayworth or Elizabeth Taylor, or ... Sappho.[2]

In tracing the key trends in visual representations of Sappho the images that will be discussed in this chapter fall under five particular headings: Sappho figures as the original woman artist and a politicised icon for her successors; as a lover of women; as a highly sexualised woman swooning with desire; as a suicide; and as a vamp, or a *femme fatale*. And in every case, the viewer's attention is drawn to her body. Whatever she is, Sappho is figured as a transgressive who resists, or goes against the norm. Sometimes in Sappho pictures the image portrayed is that of proud rebel. Sometimes the message in the image is one that condemns the subject, labels her as a pervert, or punishes her with dissolution. There is always a tussle between the attraction to Sappho-as-subject, and her perceived status as an outlawed breaker of taboos.

The picture of Sappho

This portrait of Sappho's picture begins in the 1760s. Before that date there had certainly been many pictures of Sappho, generally celebrating her role as a poet and often figuring her as the only woman in a Pantheon of men. Such representations included images on Greek vases dating from the sixth century BC on, heads on ancient coins from Mytilene, illuminations in medieval manuscripts of Ovid's *Heroides* or Boccaccio's *De Claris Mulieribus*, and grand scenes portrayed in public rooms such as Raphael's *Parnassus* in the Vatican, Giovanni da Giovanni's *The Destruction of Mount Parnassus* in the Pitti Palace, and Corneille Michel II's ceiling painting *Sapho chantant et jouant de la lyre* for the Salon des Nobles de la Reine at Versailles. But from the 1760s until about the 1820s ladies with lyres were everywhere. There were illustrated editions of Sappho and Anacreon, there were antiquarian novels which included pictures of Sappho, there were prints by Bartolozzi and Cipriani, there were paintings by famous artists like Fragonard, Angelica Kauffmann, George Romney and Jacques Louis David, statues by sculptors who were well known, like Canova, and by others long-forgotten, like Chinard and Dannecker. Sappho appeared regularly at the Paris Salon and at the Royal Academy, she was to be found in suites of engravings by Henry Tresham and Anne-Louis Girodet, she figured in private sketchbooks, on vases and cameos produced by Messrs Wedgwood and Bentley, on ormolu clocks, on transfer printed china, and in schemes for interior decoration.[3]

There was one specific reason for Sappho's popularity in the second half of the eighteenth century. Just at this time her 'authentic' face seemed to appear out of the past. In 1759 excavators at Pompeii unearthed a painted tondo of a portrait bust of a young woman (along with a companion tondo of a man). It shows a girl, curly-haired and wearing a distinctive netted head-dress, holding a writing tablet in one hand and a stylus in the other, which she places thoughtfully to her lips as if in search of inspiration (see Plate 1). The picture is now in the Museo Nazionale in Naples, and if you want to see it you must ask for 'il ritratto di Saffo'.[4] It cannot be a real portrait. It almost certainly was not meant to represent Sappho when it was painted in the first century AD and the identification was repudiated in the early twentieth century. But 'Sappho' is what it was called in 1759, and the image is still widely sold today as 'Portrait of a Girl (Sappho?)'. The link between this image and the idea of Sappho seems as obvious now to any marketing director in Naples or postcard seller at the Louvre because we inherit that version of who and what Sappho is. And in the eighteenth century this intellectual was what many people wanted her to be.

'Sweet mother, I cannot weave my web': I

Many people; but I should say 'many women'. What is significant about this early cluster of Sappho images is how many of these pictures were produced by women, either directly as artist-maker, or indirectly, as sitter or commissioner. These include Angelica Kauffmann's (at least) four pictures of Sappho, a drawing by Maria Cosway, a painting by Nanine Vallain, a portrait by Mlle Rivière, Elisabeth Vigée-LeBrun's celebrated portrait of Madame de Stael, at least one (possibly more) painting by her pupil Marie Guillaume Benoist, and a wall painting by the English artist Marianne Birch Lamartine.[5] Mario Praz long ago noted the prevailing fashion in this period for 'lady with the lyre' pictures. 'Let a woman', he wrote, 'have even the slightest talent as a poetess or singer, and behold, she has the right to a portrait in the garb of a Muse, with a red mantle, a laurel crown and an elegant lyre.'[6] But for these practitioners this was considerably more than just play-acting.

Sappho as a writer – or the concomitant position of Sappho as performer – was the posture these women preferred. At this time Sappho sits up straight and she performs, for she either plays her lyre or she writes. Vigée-LeBrun's portrait of Madame de Stael shows her in the act of improvising poetry. We are the implied audience, as we are to the performance given on the lyre-guitar by Josephine Budaevskaya in Mlle Rivière's picture (see Plate 2). In the same way we witness Sappho at work in Maria Cosway's drawing where she has carved Phaon's name on a tree, or in Fragonard's painting where she writes 'inspired by love'. In some cases Sappho even gets to write her own poetry: two of Kauffmann's paintings show her composing Fragment 1, the 'Ode to Aphrodite' (see Plate 3), and in one (engraved in 1778 by John Boydell, see Figure 1) the strong diagonal of Sappho's rhetorical writing gesture points at the text in her lap and her hand holding the pen. In one of Bartolozzi's stipple engravings, published in London in 1793, Sappho is shown bending over her lyre while the caption is a version of Fragment 102:

> Cease gentle mother, cease your sharp Reproof
> My hands no more can ply the curious Woof,
> While on my Mind the Flames of Cupid prey,
> And lovely Phaon steals my heart away.[7]

At first glance it looks like this might be one of Sappho's negative images, because it sets up a scene where she is unable to act. But in its eighteenth century context Sappho's Romantic sensibility leads directly to an identity as a writer. In her portrait of Budaevskaya (Plate 2) Mlle Rivière has had her subject put aside her woolwork to take up her lyre in a most becoming attitude; and in one

Figure 1 Engraving of Angelica Kauffmann's *Sappho Inspired by Love*, by John Boydell. Published 1778

of Anne-Louis Girodet's engravings entitled *Sapho dédaigne les occupations de son sexe* (see Plate 4) his heroine ignores the (archeologically correct) ancient Greek wool-basket.[8] It seems to me that these pictures of performing women offer a riposte to Rousseau's strictures on the 'nature' of girls which – according to him – makes them prefer the needle to the pen because of necessity (an innate love of finery means that they want to adorn themselves), and vanity (they are distressed by the unbecoming posture required by the act of writing). These new Sapphos refuse to follow their mothers: they will make poetry, rather than weave. Or rather, they choose to follow their Classical mothers, Penelope or Philomela, and what they weave will be not a garment, but a story. And if – as Freud has suggested, somewhat in the manner of Rousseau – a woman weaves to cover her shame, then we shall see the consequences of choosing the pen over the needle in later pictures of Sappho.[9]

Images of women in Classical drapery writing, reading, performing, playing the lyre, were immensely popular during the Romantic period. There is no doubt that Sappho became so visible because she was, especially for the women artists who invoked her, a model, and a promise. But what does it mean to call on Sappho's name? to perform Sappho? to make your body her body, or to make hers yours?

Living Muses

In Angelica Kauffmann's 1775 painting it is not just Sappho that appears, for she is 'inspired by Love' (Plate 3). The Cupid image shadowing Sappho was common, and it re-works other familiar icons, whether a Classical Venus and Cupid, or a Christian Madonna and Child. But here, in spite of the terms of representation, this child – normally the product of the body – is the product of mind, or spirit. This Cupid is not a separate persona, but rather a reflection of Sappho's sensibility, and out of that split self this woman produces a text – the poem in her lap – which names her, gives her a signature. Similarly the emphasis on the naked left breast at the centre of the composition and framed within the pyramidal structure by the fillet of her dress and the jewelled armband, implies the subject's feeling heart rather than her nurturing bosom.[10]

It is too easy to dismiss this appeal to the mother-and-child icon as reactionary, as one designed to placate Kauffmann's contemporary opponents of women's education and achievement by dressing up Sappho as a Madonna. The womb in eighteenth century medical discourse is the seat of the emotions in woman, and her peculiar susceptibility to feeling was supposed to lie in her unknowable organic recesses. When this painting was engraved by John Boydell in 1778 he added a volcano (Figure 1). It may be Vesuvius and refer to Naples and the excavations there, but it is also emblematic of a woman's body with its strange productive spaces. Hence the child of Sappho's mind and heart – the poem she is in the act of writing – is borne in her lap. I would argue here for a parallel with Vigée-LeBrun's two 'Self-Portraits with Julie' (especially the second in her trademark Greek costume) (see Plate 5). Often condemned in the past as a merely pretty picture that pandered to conventional modes of femininity, recent critics have suggested that, on the contrary, Vigée-LeBrun presents herself here as both a mother and an artist: she may have produced the child, but she has also produced the picture of the child, and so made this double picture of herself as creative producer.[11]

The device of the split self is one that Angelica Kauffmann often uses, and in paintings such as *The Artist in the Character of Design Listening to the Inspiration of Poetry* (1782) or *Self-Portrait Hesitating Between the Arts of Painting and Music* (1794) it suggests – in the manner of Emma Hamilton's Attitudes or Mary Robinson's sonnet sequence – many possibilities in process. In this way Kauffmann evades the monolithic representation inevitably invoked by the static form of painting, to create a kinetic self-presentation where who she is, and what she might be, is always moving on. She is not unique in exploiting this method, but it is one that is distinctively associated with the representation of the creative woman in this period. Hugh Douglas Hamilton's triple portrait of Emma, Lady Hamilton as three Muses refers to the transformations of her Attitudes, but it also suggests her mutability and versatility (see Plate 6). Another example of a similarly kinetic treatment of the theme of the artistic woman is Richard Samuel's *The Nine Living Muses of Great Britain* (1779) which purports to show nine artists – actors, painters (including Kauffmann), writers and musicians – but which effectively portrays 'woman' and her range of aspirations.[12]

Sappho becomes a fashionable subject during the Romantic period because her multiplicity in having many stories, inhabiting many bodies, mimics a developing strand in women's (self) representation. Simply by the device of alluding to Sappho – or indeed the Muse, or the Sibyl or any other ancient model – that multiplicity is brought into view.

When Elisabeth Vigée-LeBrun painted her *Portrait of Emma Hamilton as a Sibyl* (1792) showing a writing block in her lap, just like Kauffmann's earlier *Sappho*, this was not meant to be an accurate portrayal of the more-or-less uneducated Emma. This was – as Vigée-LeBrun constantly called it – 'my Sibyl'. It is a conflation of the many bodies it implies: that is, the flesh of the sitter and her potentialities; the image of the Sibyl and her achievements; and the hand of the artist who has executed this work of art by consulting her own perspicacious vision. Vigée-LeBrun repeated this enterprise in her important portrait of *Madame de Stael en Corinne* (1807) (see Plate 7). You may think that there is only one woman in this text, but there are several: Madame de Stael and her fictional heroine Corinne, plus Sappho, the Muse, and the Sibyl, as well as Vigée-LeBrun's previous Sibyl painting (which is mimicked in this later picture in the dress and pose of the subject and in the compositional shape), and, perhaps above all, the artist, Vigée-LeBrun herself, whose capacity for a kaleidoscopic vision has produced this multi-faceted image.[13]

Portrait of —— as Sappho

At the end of the eighteenth century and early in the nineteenth century there were many women who had their portrait painted specifically 'as Sappho' – and many more who alluded to her simply by holding a lyre. An early picture by Vigée-LeBrun posed Laure de Bonneuil as Sappho (1773); François Gérard painted Madame de la Pleigne in this guise; in about the 1830s Juliette Récamier was portrayed 'en Sapho' by A.E. Fragonard; Chinard's bust of Sappho was modelled on the mistress of his patron; Canova's statue of Alexandrine Bleschamps, Princess of Camino (*c.* 1808–12) began as an image of 'Sappho' (though it was later sold as 'Terpsichore').[14] The trouble with this eliding of identities is that the urge to recuperate and claim a positive image out of the past means that either – or both – figures end up with no name. The very self that is striving to establish its identity by analogy, can get absorbed into the masquerade and disappear altogether. 'Sappho' in all these 'Portrait of —— as Sappho' pictures is, strictly speaking, absent. But once her name and her attributes are summoned up, these real women may no longer inhabit her. Instead, she inhabits them; she becomes present as a revenant, a ghost haunting the living beings who bring her back to life, as a vampire inhabits or usurps the body, draining it of individual identity. In this way the woman who wished – by calling herself Sappho – to make herself more visible, has paradoxically disappeared, made away with her own body, and let Sappho take on her flesh, her dress, her name.

One of the strangest pictures in this genre is by the British artist Richard Westall. It is dated sometime before 1802 and it is titled *Portrait of the Artist's Wife as Sappho* (see Plate 8).[15] You will see only one Sappho attribute – the laurel crown – but otherwise it would be impossible to know who she was, if it were not for the title. There are clues; the uplifted eyes, the stormy sky, the jewelled armbands as in Kauffmann's portrait, the Greek-style tunic – see through, so that you can just about glimpse her breast. But to recognise all these references one would have to be pretty well-versed in the manners and modes of ladies with lyres to guess that she is one, even though she has not got one.

For me, the really troubling thing about this picture is that I do not know who it is. Yes, it is Sappho. Yes, it is the Artist's Wife. But who is she? Where has she gone? What did she do? What was her name? What were her credentials for dressing up as Sappho? I have no idea. Once upon a time, that this was a picture of Sappho was immediately obvious to the viewer, and, once upon that time, the viewer might have known who this sitter was. Now she has disappeared. Her portrait remains – the print by Sartain is still fairly common – but she has vanished because the real woman has been absorbed into, consumed by, Sappho. It is a risky business, collaborating with Sappho. You attempt to incorporate her attributes by memorialising her, by pinning her name to your breast, and all you end up doing is turning your own authentic signature into Sappho writing your name.

Sappho exposed

It is a risky business, collaborating with Sappho. It is not only your name that is at stake, but your good name.

I have said that the close identification with Sappho, or with any of the ancient Classical models of intellectual women, was perceived as a means of positive self-promotion for the ambitious woman of the Romantic period. This strategy was reflected in the close political, social and cultural allegiances that were built up between these women; between, for instance, Madame de Stael and Vigée-LeBrun, between de Stael and Juliette Récamier, between Mary Robinson and Mary Wollstonecraft. Female friendship was a relatively new theme in the eighteenth century, and one promoted by both Wollstonecraft and de Stael, the two best-known intellectual women of the period. De Stael wrote 'What the Greeks understood by friendship existed between men ... only because their customs prevented them from imagining that one can meet in a woman, a being equal in spirit ... a companion for life.'[16] It was this prevailing fashion for the bonds of female friendship that led to the celebrity of Marie Antoinette's intimacy with the Duchesse de Polignac or the Princesse de Lamballe; to the widespread admiration for Lady Eleanor Butler and her companion Sarah Ponsonby known collectively as the Ladies of Llangollen; and to curiosity and interest in the lives of the devoted spinsters Miss Marianne Woods and Miss Jane Pirie.

But now I have named names that speak more than they dare. For Miss Woods and Miss Pirie took a certain Dame Helen Cumming Gordon to court in 1811 on the grounds that in removing her granddaughter from their school in Edinburgh, she had destroyed their reputation. (It was this case that gave Lilian Hellmann the plot for her 1934 play *The Children's Hour*.) Miss Woods and Miss Pirie won their case because the House of Lords ruled that they couldn't have done what they were supposed to have done. 'No such case was ever known in Scotland, nor in Britain', the House decreed, but that did not stop the gossip. Nor did Wordsworth's visit to the Ladies of Llangollen stop the stories about them. And in France? In the days leading up to the Revolution an anonymous scandal sheet entitled *La Vie privée* included a crude engraving of Marie Antoinette *in flagrante* with one of her ladies in waiting, and her circle was nicknamed the 'Tribades of the Trianon'.[17]

Later Madame de Stael complained: 'Ever since the Revolution, men have deemed it morally useful to value women at the most absurd mediocrity.'[18] And one of the ways of ensuring that the ambitious woman was policed, restricted and downgraded, was by invoking the very name that they had once called on, the name that had been adopted as a badge of pride: Sappho.

Across the same period when Sappho was becoming so visible in European culture, she was also putting in a number of appearances in pornographic literature. In a vulgar satire on one Lady Frances Brudenell, the anonymous author of *The Toast* could explain at length what went on between Lady Frances (or Myra) and her friend Lady Allen (or Ali) and, for his authority, he turned to Classical sources:

> What if *Sappho* was so naught? [ie. naughty]
> I'll deny, that thou has taught
> How to pair the Female Doves,
> How to practise *Lesbian* Loves:
> But when little AL is spread
> In her Grove, or on thy Bed,
> I will swear, 'tis Nature's Call,
> 'Tis exalted Friendship all.

Then there was *The Sappho-an* which was widely read – by men – in London coffee houses. Published in 1740, its subtitle was *An Heroic Poem of Three Cantos, in the Ovidian Stile, describing the Pleasures Which the Fair Sex Enjoy with Each Other, according to the Modern and most Polite Taste; Found Among'st the Papers of a Lady of Quality, a great promoter of Jaconitism.* And in around the 1770s or 1780s the pseudonymous *A Sapphick Epistle from Jack Cavendish to the Honourable and most Beautiful Mrs D—* was addressed to the sculptor Anne Seymour Damer, Horace Walpole's heir, an independent woman, well known for her love of women.[19]

None of these dubious publications were illustrated, but one published in the 1790s was. This was *La Nouvelle Sapho, ou histoire de la secte anandryne*, the tenth volume of *L'espion anglais; ou correspondance secrète entre Milord All'Eye et Milord All'Ear.* This may have been written by Matthieu François Pidansat de Mairobert, who was a friend of the police chief in Paris and a member of a Salon especially famous for its salacious gossip. *L'espion anglais* purported to be stories about contemporary London life, and it had a wide circulation in London as well as Paris. But the *La Nouvelle Sapho* volume was a satire directed at a group of independent women who gathered in Paris around the actress Judith Raucourt, and whose secret sect was supposed to meet at the house of Madame Furiel to indulge in lesbian practices. *La Nouvelle Sapho* gave a thoroughgoing account of the meetings of the Anandrynes, and offered pictures to match (see Figure 2).[20]

Yet, these pornographic publications were not the only place where erotic representations of Sappho appeared. The Danish artist Nicolai Abildgaard painted a picture *Sappho and the Lesbian Maid* (*c.* 1806–09) toward the end of his life. It shows two women in a glade, the one lying virtually naked with her head on

Figure 2 Illustration to *La Nouvelle Sapho* (Paris, 1789)

Figure 3 Anne-Louis Girodet Trioson, *Songe de Sapho*, 1827

Sappho's bosom as she reaches up to embrace the poet who leans down, also half clothed. Abildgaard's sketchbooks include at least three studies for this painting, as well as numerous other sketches, more or less erotic in tone, of Sappho with other women.[21] Though there were no more full-blown canvases dedicated to the subject of Sappho as a lover of women, there were hints in later pictorial representations, especially in Anne-Louis Girodet Trioson's 1827 suite of engravings (see Figure 3) where three illustrations in particular – plate 3, *J'ai dormi délicient, en songe, dans les bras de la charmante Cytherée*, plate 4, *Sapho fait les apprets de sa noce* and plate 14, *Sapho implore les secours de Venus* – suggest the pleasures which dare not speak their nineteenth century name.[22]

'Sweet mother, I cannot weave my web': II

But the predominant fictions of Sappho in the Romantic period made her heterosexual. They told, with varying details, the story of her love for Phaon, ending, as it does in Ovid's *Heroides*, in Sappho's debilitation, despair and eventual suicide. Before they arrived at that end, however, these stories frequently dealt in detail with the *amours* of Sappho and Phaon, and this was a theme that went into many of Sappho's pictures.

One striking version survives in Jacques Louis David's *Sappho and Phaon* (1809) (see Plate 9). Here again Sappho becomes incapable of 'weaving her web' – writing her poetry, playing her lyre – as Cupid takes it out of her hands and she swoons into Phaon's arms while he caresses – significantly – her mouth, and silences her. The presence of the bed, of the matching pair of exposed breasts –

male and female – of Phaon's central upright spear particularly, but also of his bow echoing Cupid's bow and quiverful of arrows, make it quite clear what is going to happen next, so that we hardly need the signal of the lascivious billing doves on the windowsill. Every one of Sappho's usual list of attributes is here: the lyre, the scroll, the laurel crown, possibly even the volcano in the background, though this looks like a smilingly benign, definitely dormant volcano here. For this Sappho is not feeling herself. She has lost her lyre. She has lost her upright posture. The laurel crown is going to come off at any moment, and the bed in the background beckons. Even the 'other self' Cupid in this picture belongs not to Sappho, but to Phaon, whose stance he mirrors and whose accomplice he is. Phaon dominates here, and Sappho is just another prize.[23]

During the early years of the nineteenth century, following on from the cult of Sappho as a woman's icon, there developed a reactionary response that made Phaon into a male god. This trend actually began with Henry Tresham's series of aquatints from 1784 where a well-endowed Phaon manages to star in several of Tresham's twelve illustrations to Verri's *Le avventure di Saffo* (see Figure 4).

Figure 4 Henry Tresham, *Le avventure di Saffo* (Rome, 1784)

Interestingly, though Tresham seems to have had no allegiances, other than a love of the gracious male form which he shared with the bisexual Fuseli and others in his circle at Rome, Joan DeJean makes a case for Verri's novel – and then Tresham's series – as 'proto-Napoleonic' fictions of Sappho. She points out that when Verri's novel was reissued in 1797 it was dedicated to Napoleon's sister, Caroline Murat, the wife of his Neapolitan general Joseph Murat.[24] DeJean deals with other Sapphic fictions where their authors were linked, in one way or another, to Napoleon, but she does not deal with the group that most explicitly worked this transfer of power from Sappho to handsome Phaon: the painters from the Napoleonic camp.

Jacques Louis David was a painter who identified with Napoleon Bonaparte, and whose work helped to identify the Emperor Napoleon I. He was the official artist who depicted the moment during Napoleon's coronation when he impatiently placed the crown on his own head. As we have seen, he also painted *Sappho and Phaon*, with its prominent homage to the male body. Anne-Louis Girodet Trioson, a pupil of David's, was another who, on the one hand, produced celebratory Napoleonic scenes including *L'Empereur recevant les clefs de la ville de Vienne* (1810), and who, on the other, painted at least one Sappho picture *Paysage avec Sapho, en train d'écrire sur des tablettes* (1793). And in 1827 when Girodet made a suite of engravings to accompany his own translation of Sappho, five of the sixteen plates depicted luscious naked male bodies, centre stage (see Frontispiece, this volume). Of the many other painters who either held official appointments, or painted propaganda pictures for Napoleon – artists such as Ingres, Vien, Ducis, Vafflard, Baron Gros, Gerard and Meynier, as well as Girodet and David – several also painted pictures of Sappho. Pictures where, for the most part, Sappho is represented in a vulnerable or debilitated position.

Pierre Vafflard's picture, for instance, was *Sapho retirée de l'eau par les soins d'un étranger* (1819); Louis Ducis's was *Sappho Recalled to Life by the Charm of Music* (1811), a scene that was based on events in Lantier's novel *Voyage d'Antenor* where she is tended by a male doctor. François Gerard produced a melancholy portrait of 'Sapho' which was engraved by J. Reverdin, but his most important contribution to the Sappho genre was his *Corinne at Cape Miseno* (1821) where Corinne, Sappho's modern alter ego, has lost her power.[25] The volcano (Vesuvius) is still there in the background, but Corinne sits on a broken column. The lyre has fallen from her hand, and her performance here – or rather her existence, her improvised body – is on display for the benefit of the man in the picture, her lover Lord Nelvil, who takes up a large part of the image and who is the hero, the calm controlling centre of the image. He, the viewer within, gazes on Corinne in the stress of artistic and emotional *sturm und drang*. His is the viewpoint of the artist that orders the scene, and we are encouraged to identify with him, to look coolly on her breakdown, just as he does.

It is no accident that Gerard should here give us a picture of Sappho-Corinne silenced and, in effect, defeated; for Madame de Stael, Corinne's creator and Sappho's successor, was Napoleon's enemy. He saw her Salon of outspoken women as a dangerous nest of insurgents, and he forced her into exile in Switzerland where she continued to complain about Napoleon's restriction of democratic debate, and his state control of both art and public opinion. Napoleon's anxieties about strong women were shared by many of his contemporaries, and the seeds of the problem went back at least as far as the French Revolution, when a perceived breakdown in sex differentiation was blamed for the break-up of social structures. More generally, as Nancy Armstrong has suggested, the end of the eighteenth century saw the development of an oppositional system of sex and gender, where the desirable definition of masculinity was increasingly dependent upon the concomitant construction of its feminine other.[26] So this is where Sappho comes to be inhabited by yet another body. Once she was upright, active, centre frame. In Gerard's *Corinne at Cape Miseno* she is pushed to the margin, she is chaotic, awash with feeling. Her artistic ambition is cut down like the column upon which she sits, just as the phallic power she had once usurped is cut off, while her mind is dispersed, fragmented. Corinne here is in the position of the defeated enemy, weak and dependent on the hero's will, like the broken bodies that are trodden underfoot in Gerard's *Le General Rapp présente à Napoleon les drapeaux pris à l'ennemi après la bataille d'Austerlitz, le 2e Décembre 1805* (1810), or in Baron Gros's key picture of triumph *Napoleon visitant le champ de la bataille d'Eylau le 9 Février 1807* (1808).[27]

As it happens, this moment in the story of Corinne is not only the last time that we see her in performance, but it immediately precedes the unfolding of a family history which makes a separation between Corinne and Lord Nelvil inevitable. By choosing to portray this particular point in Corinne's story Gerard dramatises the pivotal scene when power passes, as it does in David's *Sappho and Phaon*, from the woman to the man. From this moment on, Corinne's future contains only loss; first her lyre is laid aside, and then her life.

But it was another of Napoleon's official painters who produced the work that epitomised this declining trajectory. Baron Gros's painting of 1801 was considered a masterpiece at the time, and it still figures in art history as a landmark in the Romantic style. It was a picture of Sappho. A picture of Sappho as suicide (see Plate 10).

Portrait of the artist as suicide

Sappho's leap, though part of her legends from ancient times, does not become a subject for pictorial representation until the eighteenth century. In the 1760s a French translation of Ovid's *Heroides* included an engraving of *The Leucadian Leap*; in the 1770s another French translation, this time of Anacreon, Sapho, Bion and Moschus, had another illustration of the leap. In 1782 the printmakers

Bartolozzi and Cipriani published an engraving in London entitled *Sappho Throwing Herself from the Rock*, and about this time Richard Westall made his picture of Sappho's leap as she falls toward the little crowd huddled on the beach below. Westmacott produced a sketch of Sappho's fall – the one recalled by Felicia Hemans – and Henry Tresham included the leap in his suite of engravings. In Germany Jacob Carsten made a sketch of Sappho's death; in England Sir William Beechey made another of her frenzy as she approached the precipice.[28] All over Europe innumerable Sapphos jumped off numberless cliffs, and by the 1790s Sappho Leaping from the Rock of Leucadia became a popular subject for large-scale paintings exhibited at the Paris Salon and the London Royal Academy.

The first important painting was Jean-Joseph Taillasson's *Sappho Throwing Herself from the Rock of Leucata* (1791), but it was followed ten years later by Baron Gros's famous 'Sapho' of 1801 and many others. Most of these paintings are lost, though enough titles have been recorded to give some idea of the tip of this Leucadian Rock iceberg. There were statues called *The Despair of Sappho* or *Sappho Falling into the Abyss*; there were paintings such as *Sappho Despairs of Phaon's Love* or *Sappho on the Rock of Leucadia* or *The Last Moments of Sappho*, as well as slightly more cheerful versions such as *Sappho Rescued from the Water* by Nereids or *Recalled to Life by the Charms of Music*. So ubiquitous had this image become, that by 1832 an anonymous reviewer in the *Edinburgh Review* (ostensibly discussing an array of new editions), could write that there were four headings to any consideration of Sappho, each of them '... almost equally important in the history of a woman and an authoress – her love, her leap, her looks, and her lyrics'. In that order. Ten years later in 1842 Honoré Daumier could include a less than flattering image of Sappho about to leap – actually being pushed – in his *Histoire ancienne*, and be pretty certain that his readers would get the joke (see Figure 5).[29]

Why? One can point to the popularity of Classical themes at this period, or the fashionable character of Romantic melancholy, the suicidal despairs of a Chatterton or a Werther, or to trends in the treatment of the Sublime, or the Gothic. But none of this goes to explain the predominance of this one artistic theme, endlessly repeated up until about the 1850s by any number of artists, including Chasseriau, Burthe, Pradier and Clesinger, but still continued by some obsessives, notably Moreau, LeRoux and Ary Renan, until the 1880s and 1890s.[30] Other images of Sappho do appear during the nineteenth century, and I shall come to those, but across the whole period, this one, of the moment of Sappho's suicide, remains consistently attractive.

To begin with, there can be no doubt that some kind of punishment is at work here. The intellectual woman may aspire to the condition of artist, but she is still woman, and the conflict between her mind and her body, between her culture and her nature, or between her art and her love will ... destroy her. It is a common enough pattern, and it is certainly one that does dominate the

Figure 5 Honoré Daumier, *La Mort de Sapho* from *Histoire ancienne* (1842)

Sappho versions in the writings of, say, the women poets of the first half of the nineteenth century. However – setting aside what I have said about the antipathy of the Napoleonic regime – there is obviously no overall conspiracy at work in these pictures. The subject drew painters for a set of contemporary cultural reasons which it is possible to decode in our retrospective view.

Of all these many paintings, that by Baron Gros is still the most famous, the best known (Plate 10). In art history it is cited as an example of the Sublime, and attention is particularly drawn to the portrayal of a Romantic extravagance of emotion (*sturm und drang*) in the handling of ... the moonlight. Now I concede that the moonlight is good. But I do find it amazing that, as far as the academy is concerned, we are supposed to look at this picture and think about the moonlight. And I'd argue that this suggests just how powerful the ideology encoded here is, and how far we have inherited the assumptions about woman, about feeling, and about nature and art, that underlie this image.

This is a picture of woman in an extreme state of mind. A state represented by the flux and reflective movement in the air and water, all illumined by that famously evanescent moonlight. And yet that state of *mind* is expressed in Sappho's *body*. She turns her face and body so far upward, so far in the opposite direction to the imminent downward fall, that she almost seems to be bending backward. She teeters on the balls of her feet, one last fold of drapery is wrapped around a rock, her last connection with earth, as she hurtles toward the moment of transition that will annihilate her body and make her all spirit. In contrast to her fluctuating shape and to her liminal position expressed by the diagonal line of her body, is the altar in the background which stands four-square and solid, the flame burning steadily, in spite of the wind suggested by the hurrying clouds. And at the foot of the altar is an overturned vase, pouring out a libation that parallels Sappho's self-sacrifice on some altar of order and law.

Here, you will notice, Sappho does not play her lyre. Instead, she clutches it to her bosom – as she does also in Chasseriau's 1849 watercolour. Far from being an instrument to display her powers, the lyre is now a badge, an identity tag that tells us – and Sappho herself – who she is. Or rather, who she *was*. At this moment of dissolution the presence of the lyre says 'Sappho', while she says nothing at all, and all her lyrics fade into the silence that follows her death. Yet in one sense this is precisely the scene that must follow on from the previous scene of performance.

In all those earlier Sappho pictures of real women – of Angelica Kauffmann, Josephine Budaevskaya, Richard Westall's wife, and, above all, in Vigée-LeBrun's portrait of Madame de Stael, those women were performing themselves as they performed Sappho. And whether or not they did it in real life – whether they actually did write, or paint, or sing – they insisted on the significance of the idea of performance by having their picture painted in that act. Thus they made their contemporaries *look* at them, and they achieved that by exerting the kind of violence that Edward Said suggests marks every act of performance in art and makes it an 'extreme occasion'. Quoting Richard Poirier he says that performance partakes of 'brutality and even savagery' because

> Performance is an exercise of power, a very anxious one. Curious because it is at first so furiously self-consultive so even narcissistic, and later so eager for publicity, love and even historical dimensions. Out of an accumulation of secretive acts emerges at last a form that presumes to compete with reality itself for control of the mind exposed to it.[31]

In their day-to-day moments of living as an artist Angelica Kauffmann or Vigée-LeBrun, Madame de Stael or Mary Robinson improvised themselves, made themselves happen in process, just as Emma Hamilton performed her Attitudes and so became what she presented. But these performances were fleeting. So, craving that 'publicity', and especially craving an 'historical dimension', these women recorded their performance in life, through writing, through painting, and by inhabiting the body of the woman model to whom they aspired: Sappho, the original woman artist.

Yet their own methods could so readily be turned against them. The force of will contained in this effort at individual performance implies a thoughtful attention to self. An attention which can easily be interpreted as excessive or abnormal, and to the detriment of both body and, especially, mind. The volcano that John Boydell added to his engraving of Angelica Kauffmann's painting of Sappho might be emblematised as the hidden caverns of the woman's body, the labyrinths that are always liable to fluctuation and movement, subject to mysterious secretions and unpredictable eruptions. When Madame de Stael and Kauffmann and all the others inhabited Sappho's body, they did so to foreground their art, and to display the achievements of their minds. When these later painters of Sappho's suicide portrayed Sappho's body, they indexed the dissolution of her art, and the breakdown of her mind.

In Gros, in Tresham, and in Chasseriau Sappho has become an hysteric. Her range of Attitudes in these pictures often resemble those described and categorised in the second half of the nineteenth century by Jean-Martin Charcot during his work at the Salpetriere hospital in Paris. In the 1860s he collected photographs of his patients to demonstrate the stages of an hysteric fit in what he called the various 'Attitudes passionelles' (see Figure 6). A comparison of these Sappho pictures and Charcot's – supposedly clinical, but actually staged – photographs makes the connection clear. The parallel is particularly striking when one sets Henry Tresham's plate 17 of his series of aquatints *Le avventure di Saffo* (see Figure 7) beside Charcot's photographs which portray the characteristic spasm he called 'arc de cercle', or opisthotonus, where peculiar muscular contractions – according to Charcot – mark the second major phase of an hysterical attack. As Janet Bezier says, the pose bears 'a marked resemblance to the attitude of a body in the throes of passion'.[32] Sappho's female successors inhabited her body to express their minds. In these pictures her mind is broken down as she succumbs to sex, to the body, and to nature.

And, once broken, she disappears. I was sceptical about the function of the moonlight in Baron Gros's picture. But I left out one reading that does indeed make the moonlight the most significant feature in the work. In many of these Sappho-as-suicide paintings she gets absorbed into the landscape. The moonlight takes over in Gros. The vivid blue sky takes over in Chasseriau's 1840 watercolour. In his 1849 painting it is the solid brown and red rocks that predominate. In all of Gustave Moreau's many Sappho paintings it is the sheer chasms and the startling skies that draw the eye, so that it is often hard to make out where the body of Sappho lies in among the vivid colours and organic riot of nature that engulfs her. In Anne-Louis Girodet Trioson's suite of engravings, plate 16 (the last in the series) shows Sappho's body undulating with the wave (see Figure 8). Nearly eighty years later and the same conceit was used by Ary Renan in his painting *Sapho* where she drifts, rootlike, among the flora of the seashore. In another of Girodet's Sappho oeuvres, his painting *Paysage avec Sapho*, she appears

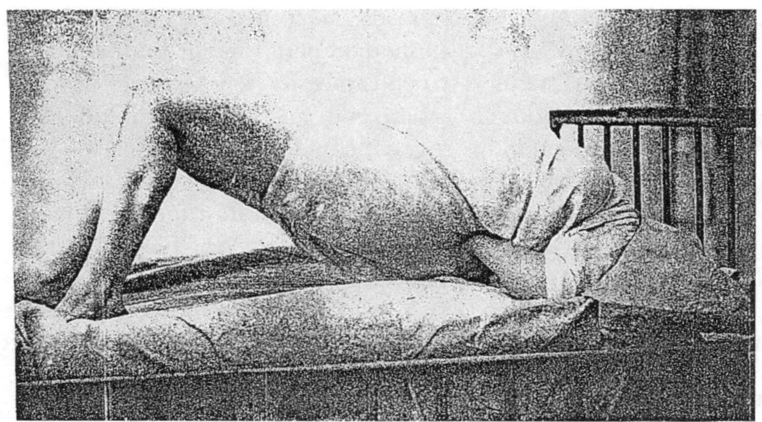

Figure 6 'Arc de cercle', photograph of a patient by Jean-Martin Charcot, Salpetriere hospital, Paris

Figure 7 Henry Tresham, *Le avventure di Saffo* (Rome, 1784)

as a tiny figure dwarfed by a much larger landscape. The premise is the same in a sketch by Jacob Carsten (1792–98) and in a lithograph by Corot (1871). In an 1860s painting by Heinrich Dreber his massive work is all landscape, sea, sky, rocks, greenery. Only if you had the title before you, spelling out 'Sappho', would you start to look for the broken column, the discarded lyre, the half-hidden figure of a woman who turns away from the viewer, and heads toward the sea which, we are to assume, will shortly absorb her.

Figure 8 Anne-Louis Girodet Trioson, engraving, 1827

My favourite picture in this genre of Sappho-absorbed-into-nature pictures is a little watercolour by Edward Lear. It is called *Sappho's Leap*, but she is not there at all. It is just a picture of rocks, sea and sky.[33] As with Richard Westall's *Portrait of the Artist's Wife as Sappho* we can read nothing into the picture without a title, without the insistence of the name of 'Sappho', without the guidance of the word.

The dead letter ...

It is the imposition of the word, of logos, law and culture on world, chaos and nature that makes the predominance of these Sappho-as-suicide pictures so intriguing. Feminist scholars have argued that the whole concept of 'nature' has a history, and is not a given. The figuring of 'nature' as a blank page, an empty space which is always already 'dead', needing to be brought to life by the interpretation of the viewer, is a specifically modern trope emerging probably at the time of increased technological domination. That is, from the middle to the end of the eighteenth century.

When the women thinkers and artists invoked the name of Sappho in the pictures they painted or instigated, they brought to life an inanimate thing; they turned an idea into their mother-artist, and they made her into themselves, invoking a renewed feminine *jouissance* where the identities of mother and child were merged. When the later artists painted Sappho-merged-into-nature and on the point of suicide, they literally and figuratively made her die again, decomposed her like organic matter, while their controlling view of the story, the symbolic order or culture, word and law, was given predominance. In the rules governing the hierarchy of painting in the French Academy, portraiture ranked lower than history-painting. A portrait painter was merely a copyist, a slave to nature which itself was a blank. The artists who depicted their sitters 'as Sappho' were attempting to complicate and elevate their portraits. But the canvases that took 'Sappho-as-suicide' as their theme so much more obviously claimed the higher rank of history-painting, because they exploited the imaginary to tell a story. But their story, their imposed word, condemned to death not only Sappho, but any female aspirations beyond their 'nature'.[34]

... and the competent reader

Sappho poised on the edge of a cliff, between sea and sky, between earth and heaven, is a liminal image. She is at a point of transition, or many transitions: between life and death, between culture and nature, between past, present and future. She crosses or criss-crosses many thresholds, but she also functions as a door through which the viewer may pass into another space, or as a ship which might carry him there. Sappho's pose on the cliff resembles a version of the heterotopia that Foucault describes as most fully represented by the idea of the ship, which is a place, and no place: '... a floating piece of space, a place without a place, that exists by itself, that is closed in on itself and at the same time is given over to the infinity of the sea'.

As Sappho stands on this edge her image fills up with meaning – but only if you have the 'word' of the story. You have to know something of what has gone before, you have to know that the leap comes immediately after, otherwise the scene is an emotive blank – full of meaning, but inexplicable. We are invited to contemplate this self-contained moment, but at the same time the references multiply outward like the 'infinity' of the surrounding sea. The ideal viewer for whom these Sappho-as-suicide pictures are created is not expected to be passive. He must interpret, must work at reading the picture, and he must feel.

The whole genre of 'Sappho-as-suicide' pictures is an affective one, inspired by, perhaps even made possible by, the influence of the contemporary theories of the sublime with which Sappho at this period was so closely linked. I have explained in the previous chapter how Sappho's relation to the eighteenth century sublime was confirmed by the new significance of Longinus's treatise which quoted, and popularised, Sappho's Fragment 31. All of the early theorists of the sublime emphasised the role of feeling and reaction in discriminating its functions. Here is Joseph Addison in one of his 1712 *Spectator* essays on 'The Pleasures of the Imagination':

> When we look on hideous objects, we are not a little pleased to think that we are in no danger of them. We consider them at the same time as dreadful and harmless; so that the more frightful appearance they make, the greater is the pleasure we receive from the sense of our own safety.

And here is Edmund Burke on the same subject in his 1757 *A Philosophical Enquiry into the Origin of our Ideas of the Sublime and the Beautiful*:

> In all cases, if the pain and terror are so modified as not to be actually noxious; if the pain is not carried to violence, and the terror is not conversant about the present destruction of the person, as these emotions clear the parts, whether fine or gross, of a dangerous and troublesome encumbrance, they are capable of producing delight; not pleasure, but a sort of delightful horror, a sort of tranquillity tinged with terror; which as it belongs to self-preservation is one of the strongest of all the passions. Its object is the sublime.[35]

You thought – I thought – that these Sappho-as-suicide pictures were about Sappho's body. They are. But they are also about the body of the viewer: the viewer who is terrified by this image of a woman *in extremis*, suffering in mind, on the point of suffering in body, and on the verge of dissolution and decomposition, and who – because he, by contrast, is safe and at one remove from this experience of the sublime – can derive pleasure from the contemplation of her threatened position. Thus we are pleasured by the picture of Sappho's body. She abandons herself (in every sense), and we have her (in every sense).

This suggests yet another different reason for the popularity of the Sappho-suicide theme. The period of the late eighteenth and early nineteenth centuries was one that celebrated the rake, often making him into a hero, and even a hero of the risk in the sublime, in works like Richardson's *Clarissa*, Choderlos LaClos's *Les Liaisons dangereuses* or Mozart's *Don Giovanni*. Susan Griffin argues in her book *Pornography and Silence* that while we all live in terror of death, imperfection and decay, men in a dominant cultural position able to produce and propagate images – in command, therefore, as the history painter is in command of the story – came to associate woman with nature, with the body, and the organic inevitability of vulnerability. Therefore, they took their revenge on the feminine by producing images that destroyed women, silenced them, took them apart, as a totem of their own control.[36] So that is what happens to Sappho ... to all these many suicidal Sapphos, 1003 and many more, in a list that can compete with Leporello's catalogue of Don Giovannni's conquests 'in Spain alone', as told in Mozart's opera.

Which takes me back to one of the quotations I began with – Felicia Hemans on the sketch of Sappho by the younger Westmacott: 'There is a desolate grace about the whole figure, which seems penetrated with the feeling of utter abandonment.' By the early part of the nineteenth century this is exactly what has happened to Sappho. She has been penetrated, abandoned. She has leapt over and over again from the Rock of Leucadia and the story spreads that she is a fallen woman.

Sappho for sale

By about the middle of the nineteenth century there was a brisk trade in pictures with titles like 'Lost', or 'Found'. The contemporary fallen woman – prostitute, *demi-mondaine*, *grisette*, streetwalker, courtesan – call her what you will, became a popular subject in literature and in art in both Britain and France. But the most popular scene of all in her story, was the scene of her death, whether it took place in the Seine or the Thames, and that scene was called 'Found Drowned'. This was a time when reformers and police chiefs were extremely exercised about the prevalence of prostitution in cities, and Lynda Nead says that the number of pictures on this theme was taken as evidence for the extent of the problem. In fact, as she argues, the pictures are numerous not because they represented a social fact, but because they sold well. And for two reasons: there was an element of social policing in the genre – here was a warning to women who might break out of conventional familial structures – but there was also an element of sentimental prurience that guaranteed those pictures' value in the marketplace. In Paris, a gruesome fascination with the Morgue made it the object of many tourists' pilgrimages, and nothing was considered more moving than the fate of the young woman drowned in the Seine, preferably with a babe in arms.

Elisabeth Bronfen has described the commercial success of a plaster cast of a girl's face, widely sold during the 1850s, and known as 'L'Inconnue de la Seine'. It is not in any way a particularly interesting piece in itself. But it becomes morbidly attractive once invested with the imagined story of degradation and despair that lived behind it in the imagination of thousands of purchasers. That same story lies behind many English pictures too, including plate VIII of George Cruikshank's 1836 series of engravings, *The Drunkard's Children*. Here the girl gone wrong throws herself from the parapet of a bridge, her body bent backwards in that attitude of abandonment and on the downward trajectory that symbolises the character of her double 'fall'.[37]

As another who was well known for having thrown herself into the water, Sappho came to be metaphorically associated with the idea of the fallen woman. In France this trend was confirmed by various pseudo-scholarly publications that proposed or disputed her role as courtesan. At the same time, a contemporary fashion for lesbianism, in literature and in life, meant that Arsene Houssaye could begin a gossipy account of the *amours* of George Sand with the much quoted statement: 'At this time Sapho was resuscitated in Paris, not knowing if she loved Phaon or Erinna.'[38]

The consequences for images of Sappho were specific and peculiar. In 1848 the sculptor James Pradier produced a statuette in silvered bronze and gilt called *Sappho* (see Figure 9). They showed her standing, leaning on a column which bears a scroll in Greek, and – in one version – a libation jug beside her with two

Figure 9 James Pradier, *Sappho*, 1848

billing doves and a tortoiseshell lyre by her side. Her drapery is carefully rendered, as is her elaborate necklace and her earrings, and, though fully clothed, her contemplative pose and downcast head suggest an erotic mood. Janis Bergman-Carton points this out, quoting Gautier's reaction to the piece, and comparing the statuette itself with the sensationalised engraving of it published in *l'Illustration* (see Figure 10).

Figure 10 Engraving after James Pradier's *Sappho*, published in *l'Illustration* 11 (1848)

If this Sappho was portrayed as a courtesan, she was also literally 'for sale'. In a new commercial endeavour Pradier produced a number of luxurious copies of his statuette in silver, and he licensed the Maison Susse with the right to sell small-scale reproductions. He did something similar with his next 'Sappho'. This was a monumental marble, executed in 1852 and showing a gloomy, seated Sappho. Even before that date Pradier seems to have made a small version and licensed it for reproduction, so that the image became widely known in both France and England where it was reproduced in Parian by Minton.

There is some dispute over who acted as the model for this second version: according to some it was the great tragic actress Rachel, according to others it was Louise Colet, the author, and mistress of Gustave Flaubert (among others). Whoever was the model, the implications for this association with Sappho are the same. Both Rachel and Louise Colet were intellectual women, therefore sexually suspect, and 'no better than they should be'. In the popular mind the life of the independent and artistic woman was inextricably mixed with the slur of sexual availability.[39]

In Sappho's case this became literally true as she was bought and sold throughout Europe. Besides Pradier's two images there were at least two other Parian versions of 'Sappho' sold in England by Worcester and Copeland. You could also buy a small multicoloured marble showing Sappho on a liverish green bench, lyre to one side and a scroll on her knee. By far the most intriguing of these domestic Sapphos was a Parian model by Copeland, issued in 1851 for the Great Exhibition, and again in 1869. It was based on a full-sized marble statue by William Theed. But where Theed's original showed Sappho naked from the waist up, the miniaturised Copeland model acquired a substantial necklace and a little top to cover her breasts and shoulders.[40]

When the French novelist Alphonse Daudet published *Sappho: Parisian Manners: A Realistic Tale* in 1884 he drew on these facts about Sappho's image in the marketplace (though his source was said to be one of Clesinger's statues of 'Sappho'). Daudet's heroine is a prostitute who has acquired the nickname of 'Sapho' because she had modelled for a famous statue created by a sculptor who was one of her lovers, and because she had been the inspiration for a poem, 'The Book of Love', composed by another. When her new lover, a young provincial called Jean Gaussin, discovers her story, he is disgusted at the thought of how her body in miniature can be pawed by many a lecher admiring the adornments of his own mantelpiece. Daudet's novel was adapted for the stage and widely performed in France and England. It was also turned into a popular opera by Jules Massenet, premiered in 1897.[41]

So, by the close of the nineteenth century, Sappho's name had thoroughly declined. And if I tell you that the real name of Daudet's contemporary incarnation was 'Fanny Legrand' then you can see how far she had fallen.

The whole lyre

In the scene in Daudet's novel where the sculptor Caoudal explains to Jean Gaussin how Fanny acquired her nickname, he reminisces about her youth:

> Such arms, shoulders still a trifle thin – but that suited the ardent Sappho. And as a woman, a mistress! What rapture to be drawn from that fleshly form, what sparks from that flint; a key-board where never a note was wanting. The whole gamut! As La Gournerie used to say.

La Gournerie, the fictional poet, here stands in for the real life Alphonse de Lamartine (1790–1869), who had written 'L'Elégie antique' (1816) in imitation of Sappho's Fragment 31, and who made a declaration about the nature of passion that was to become a catchphrase: 'L'amour, c'est la lyre à sept cordes, et j'ai joué de toutes' ... 'Love is a lyre with seven strings, and I have played them all'.

He wasn't the only one. In siren pictures painted in England and France during the mid-nineteenth century the lyre became a suggestive cliché. The implications for Sappho were irresistible. Charles Gleyre's 1868 painting *Le Coucher de Sapho* (see Plate 11) places her rounded lyre intriguingly alongside her equally rotund bottom. And Felix Joseph Barrias's *Sapho d'Ereze* (1847) is even more explicit (see Plate 12).[42] 'Fanny Legrand' indeed.

From this time on the lyre means only one thing. In the paintings of Gleyre and Barrias the sexual allusion is clear. In later paintings the same reference is included, but the positioning of the lyre hints at female vice, whether shared or solitary. In pictures which show Sappho with another woman – like Simeon Solomon's *Sappho and Erinna in the Garden of Mytilene* (1864) – it lies teasingly put aside, while she concentrates on the girl. In pictures where Sappho is on her own – like Charles Mengin's melancholy *Sappho* of 1877 (Plate 13) – she holds her lyre unobtrusively down by her side, but it is still the signal of her solitary occupation. The same autoerotic trend is in numerous pictures by Frederic Leighton, William Reynolds Stephens, Albert Moore and many others. One painting by Moore of two sleeping girls in Greek-style costume is sometimes called *Beads* and sometimes called *The Fan* (see Plate 14).[43] Either way we can guess what it means, and what these girls, together or separately, have been up to. Like the lyre, these hints suggest so much more than they say. They function as wordless clues leading back to the (improper) pleasures of feminine *jouissance*. But the knowing reader, equipped with the story, can interpret and read them, and diagnose their transgression.

In the 1860s Algernon Charles Swinburne wrote a letter to Dante Gabriel Rossetti about some of Christina Rossetti's poems for children. He compared Christina's poetry to that of Sappho, and made a joke about how the ancient poetess would not have written poems for children, because she was so adverse to the process by which they were created. Then he added that, on second thoughts, Sappho 'might have sung and played to children with the same mouth and the same hand which made music on the Lesbian lyre and on another feminine organ not necessary to specify ...' Once upon a time the lyre had been an instrument enabling women's artistic performance, then it had become a badge, a name tag saying 'Sappho'. Now it was reduced to a body part, spelling woman, speaking sex – as in one particularly explicit Sappho image designed by Félicien Rops as a frontispiece for a late nineteenth century edition of Stéphane Mallarmé's *Poésies*.[44]

Sappho's haunted body

But that is not the whole picture. At no stage is there only one current image, for Sappho is always many. At the turn of the nineteenth century she was recuperated through a combination of factors: a rise in the scholarly status of the Classics; the publication of Bergk's Sappho edition in Germany and Wharton's in England; and then the publicity surrounding the Egyptian excavations of the late nineteenth and early twentieth centuries. While these things were going on, the New Woman was also reclaiming Sappho, making her into a heroine much like the one she had been a hundred years earlier for artists like Mary Robinson, Angelica Kauffmann, Germaine de Stael or Elisabeth Vigée-LeBrun. So a painter like Hector LeRoux in France could portray Sappho upright again, playing her lyre and standing in front of her 'school' (see Figure 11). Similarly Alma Tadema's 1881 *Sappho* effectively placed her in her schoolroom as she sits surrounded by some of her girls on a marble rank of benches engraved with the names of her pupils and listening to a performance by Alcaeus (see Figure 12). (The picture became famous so rapidly that it was soon used as the basis for a *Punch* cartoon on 'Sap-pho-tography' – see Figure 13.) Sappho came in for the same celebrity as her image, and the English artist Frederick Walenn could include her in a pantheon of 'Famous Women in Antiquity' (see Plate 15). And in 1895 it was a selection of pictures of Sappho that opened an exhibition of engraved portraits 'Women Writers from Sappho to George Eliot' at The Grolier Club in New York.[45]

Through the twentieth century Sappho's image has similarly undergone many makeovers, but, especially recently, the style favoured by artists is one which is allusive rather than representational. Sarah Baylis's illustration for Josephine Balmer's 1984 translation attempts a portrait, but the fact that the face is half in dark shadow suggests how unknowable Sappho is. In two senses this image resembles some of the ways in which Sappho was used in the past. The emphasis on the landscape – it takes up half the frame – is one. The other is the fact that photographs of the artist suggest that this is a self-portrait of Baylis herself, though here Sappho is a rebellious punk daughter, rather than a consoling mother. One particularly interesting feature of Baylis's picture is Sappho's adornment – the coral, the crab earring, the shells – all fragments, found objects, rather like Sappho's own Fragments, which are excavated from the earth, or buried in other texts. And this idea of the glittery, highly coloured, jewelled, but piecemeal character of the Fragments is one that Gillian Ayres took up in her 1985 picture *Sappho's Fragments*. Similarly Rose Frain's artist's book *Sappho Fragments* (1989) focuses on the idea of Sappho as lost text or as palimpsest. It consists of twenty leaves of handmade paper, some bearing words, slivers of text, while others are blank, marked only with faultlines, fine silver thread, or faint traces of paint, feathers, muslin, tatters of silk, or human hair. In Frain, as

Figure 11 Hector LeRoux, detail from *Sappho's School*, *c*. 1860s

in Ayres and Baylis, it is the effect of the poetry, rather than the person, that takes precedence. And you will notice that there is no lyre here at all.[46]

Sappho may have no body, be nobody, but her picture survives. Whatever is done to her image, she haunts us still. She is a ghost which can be laid (in one sense) and which can never be laid (in the other sense). And Sappho pleasures us, however fleetingly, however illicitly, and even where punitive injunctions cut in, addressed to the women who are her successors.

In the tensions that lie between Sappho as a figure of originary feminine *jouissance*, and Sappho as an icon of transgression who must be contained, there lies an explanation for so many of the scenes that are re-enacted in these pictures. Here is one possible reason for the mother-and-child icon that glimmers

Figure 12 Laurence Alma Tadema, *Sappho*, 1881. Walters Art Gallery, Baltimore

Figure 13 Caricature of Alma Tadema's *Sappho*, published in *Punch*, 14 May 1881

behind Angelica Kauffmann's Sappho and Cupid pictures. The idea of Sappho as a figure for feminine *jouissance* also offers an explanation for the blurring of the boundaries of identity that go on in the 'Picture of —— as Sappho' trend. It helps with reading those multiple pictures – by Kauffmann, Vigée-LeBrun others – where one woman is portrayed, but split into multiple selves. It works too with the mirroring reflections of woman-with-woman in the lesbian images that feature in the Sappho story. But it also helps to explain why Sappho's seductions work for men too: they also had mothers, and the originary experience of *jouissance*, and they quite probably know desire, and, therefore, its fantasised return.

That extinguishing of all boundaries that goes with *jouissance* might help also to explain the dissolution of the self in the Sappho-as-suicide images. For then, at the moment of death, she becomes one with nature and the world at large, returning to the absence of consciousness that existed prior to the entry into the symbolic. There is no doubt that these suicide pictures must be read as negative statements, but they are also, paradoxically, true to the concepts of Sappho as mother, and as other-self, that had immediately preceded them in the works of the women artists like Kauffman and Vigée-LeBrun. The technical characteristics that appear in the range of Sappho paintings point the same way. The chiaroscuro in pictures, say, by Gros or Taillaisson, or the figure-merging-into-landscape such as that in Hreber's painting, suggest the same impulse of engulfment. Even the bright images of Chasseriau or Burthe, imply an ecstatic surrender in the predominance of that vibrant colour. Sappho is being obscured here, or absorbed or overcome, but she always was shady, liminal, multiple, even in the more celebratory pictures from the earlier period. Indeed that was her strength, later turned into a failing.

And I think it is no accident that Sappho – in most of these pictures – is represented alone. Whether she is posed as artist, suicide, sex object, or melancholic, the point is that the viewer is invited to place himself or herself alongside. Sappho's experience elides with our experience. We feel with, in, or through her, and thus are permitted a glimpse of the *jouissance* that moves beyond the law, even when the apparent facts of the story told about Sappho seem to maim or confine her.

Interestingly, it is a scenario that brings us back to the circumstances of Sappho's poetry. Just as her actual works – in terms of the written letter – have disappeared, so the *idolon*, the concept of her work, survives. Not the signifier, but the signified. Sappho is the ultimate picture of ecstatic engulfment. She descends into the abyss. She blends with the sky. She is swallowed up by the infinity of the sea. She can be condemned or punished in this way, but she still returns in yet another guise. There may be few poems, but there are many Sapphos and no one story can contain her. If 'woman', is beyond the word, and more than the story, then so with Sappho, who is everyone and no-one, everywhere and nowhere. 'Etre Sapho', said the late nineteenth century French writer Rachilde, 'Etre Sapho ce serait être tout le monde!' ... 'To be Sappho is to be everyone' or, 'to be all the world'.[47]

4
Fragments of an Elegy

In January 1831 a young man sat down to write a poem. He was not quite 20, and he had been studying at Trinity College Cambridge for just over two years. He was good-looking and clever, and he was the centre of a circle of admiring friends. He was a competent Classical scholar, having taken Latin and Greek while at Eton. He was a serious reader, as well as an aspiring poet, and his particular passions were the works of Dante, and Shakespeare – especially the Sonnets – and the fragments of Sappho.

The title of his poem was 'To the Loved One', a conscious reference to Sappho, because one of her only two more-or-less-complete poems was regularly known in the nineteenth century as 'A l'Aimée' in French, 'To a Beloved Girl' or 'To a Maiden' in English. It is Fragment 31 in all modern scholarly editions of Sappho. The Loeb Classical Library edition gives the following prose translation:

> He seems as fortunate as the gods to me, the man who sits opposite you and listens nearby to your sweet voice and lovely laughter. Truly that sets my heart trembling in my breast. For when I look at you for a moment then it is no longer possible for me to speak; my tongue has snapped, at once a subtle fire has stolen beneath my flesh. I see nothing with my eyes, my ears hum, sweat pours from me, a trembling seizes me all over, I am greener than grass, and it seems to me that I am little short of dying. But all can be endured, since ... even a poor man ....

Here is a recent poetry translation by Josephine Balmer:

> It seems to me that man is equal to the gods,
> that is, whoever sits opposite you
> and, drawing nearer, savours, as you speak
> the sweetness of your voice

> and the thrill of your laugh, which have so stirred the heart
> in my own breast, that whenever I catch
> sight of you, even if for a moment,
> then my voice deserts me
>
> and my tongue is struck silent, a delicate fire
> suddenly races underneath my skin,
> my eyes see nothing, my ears whistle like
> the whirling of a top
>
> and sweat pours down me and a trembling creeps over
> my whole body, I am greener than grass,
> at such times, I seem to be no more than
> a step away from death
>
> but all can be endured since even a pauper ...[1]

Although this poem survives in a fragmentary state, it survives at all only because it was quoted by Longinus in his treatise *On the Sublime* written in the first century AD. Longinus cites the poem for its accuracy in rendering the symptoms of 'love's madness', and the persuasive physicality of Sappho's description of desire – the eyes dark, the voice stuck in the throat, the fire in the gut – have become the standard repertoire of love's effects recited throughout Western culture, from the high to the low. Barthes puts the poem into *A Lover's Discourse*:

> ... for when I glance at you even for an instant, I can no longer utter a word: my tongue thickens to a lump, and beneath my skin breaks out a subtle fire: my eyes are blind, my ears filled with humming, and sweat streams down my body, I am seized by a sudden shuddering; I turn greener than grass and in a moment more I feel I shall die ...[2]

In Barthes, this poem figures under the heading of 'Love's Languor: subtle state of amorous desire, experienced in its dearth, outside of any will-to-possess', with which I do not agree, for it seems to me that this does replicate the bodily effect of an active female desire in the presence of the desired. So I offer another recent version that puts the urgency back into the poem, this time by the Canadian poet Marilyn Hacker:

> Didn't Sappho say her guts clutched up like this?
> Before a face suddenly numinous
> her eyes watered, knees melted. Did she lactate
> again, milk brought down by a girl's kiss ...[3]

Sappho's poem has been copied and re-worked many times, by Ovid, by Catullus, by John Donne and Philip Sidney, by Smollett, Shelley and many others. In the early nineteenth century two of the best-known versions were a French translation by Nicolas Boileau and an English translation by Ambrose Phillips published in 1711:

> Blessed as the immortal gods is he,
> The youth who fondly sits by thee,
> And hears and sees thee all the while
> Softly speak and sweetly smile.
>
> 'Twas this deprived my soul of rest,
> And raised such tumults in my breast;
> For while I gazed, in transport tost,
> My breath was gone, my voice was lost:
>
> My bosom glowed; the subtle flame
> Ran quick through all my vital frame;
> O'er my dim eyes a darkness hung;
> My ears with hollow murmurs rung.
>
> In dewy damps my limbs were chilled;
> My blood with gentle horror thrilled;
> My feeble pulse forgot to play;
> I fainted, sank, and died away.[4]

From Longinus on, Fragment 31 has been re-read and re-interpreted, especially recently, so it is worth running through some of the key questions which these versions and readings set up.

The first thing to say is that between Sappho and Marilyn Hacker this poem often has not been about a woman desiring a woman. In the Greek it certainly is a woman who speaks because *chlorotera*, 'I am greener', has a feminine ending.[5] But from Catullus on, Sappho's Fragment 31 has been imitated by male poets and revised to make the speaker of the poem male. This erasure of the feminine signature turns the poem into the conventional love triangle where two men compete for the attentions of one woman. This, in turn, makes the way back to a male homoerotic reading of the poem where the two men are more interested in each other, and the girl addressed disappears out of the picture. Thus all the feminine in the poem can be rubbed out so that there is no woman in this text.

On the other hand, if you keep the feminine signature, many modern critics – convinced by the model of heterosexual desire that has become a commonplace across the centuries that intervene between us and Sappho – end up with readings that privilege heterosexuality and stigmatise homosexuality.

Thus Fragment 31 becomes a 'surprise poem': that is, we are lulled into thinking the speaker is a man, until deviant Sappho springs her shock-horror statement with 'I (feminine) am greener'. Or, it becomes a homosexual guilt poem: that is, Sappho suddenly realises the perversion of her desire for the girl half way through, and so that's why she feels like dying at the end.[6]

Other recent readings have tried to place the poem in a more self-consciously literary context: there is actually no man present at all, he is simply an imagined future bridegroom, who, on the model of an elaborate Homeric compliment, has deserved his good fortune in finding such a bride. Or, putting Sappho at the end of the great period of oral poetry, critics have suggested that she looks forward here to a new literate tradition by performing in this poem her own 'death-by-writing' – which, of course, is simultaneously reversed by the expectation of her future 'life-by-reading'. Most recently, Margaret Williamson has argued that many of Sappho's poems work in a context of shared singing, where all her girls participate and pass the song from one to another.[7] This is particularly helpful because it reminds me that, although this is a poem about *looking*, the girl in Sappho's poem does actually get to speak, and it is that speaking, and the effects of that speaking, that are given priority:

> He seems as fortunate as the gods to me
> the man who sits opposite you
> and listens nearby to your sweet voice …
> truly that sets my heart trembling in my breast …

Desire, and its bodily effects, woman to woman, or man to woman; fraught with possibilities both homosexual and heterosexual; a love triangle however constituted; a poem about looking, about memory, about the self, about subject and object; a poem about fragmentation and death, about performing poetry and about the survival of writing. All of these things are in Sappho's Fragment 31.

'To the Loved One'

The young man who set out to write 'To the Loved One' in 1831 did not have the benefit of these readings. But he did have Sappho. His poem is addressed to a beloved, apparently now absent, who is still present to his imagination, and whose words he can still recall, as he explains in his first stanza:

> My heart is happy now, beloved,
> Albeit thy form is far away;
> A joy that will not be removed
> Broods on me like a summer's day.

Whatever evil fate may do,
It cannot change what has been thine;
It cannot cast those words anew,
The gentle words I think divine.

It's conventional enough in its Romantic sensibility and its Victorian acquiescence to fate, but at the very centre of the poem are three stanzas which suggest a close reading of Sappho's Fragment 31 and which justify the borrowing in the title.

Sometimes I dream thee leaning o'er
The harp I used to love so well;
Again I tremble and adore
The soul of its delicious swell;
Again the very air is dim
With eddies of harmonious might,
And all my brain and senses swim
In a keen madness of delight.

Sometimes thy pensive form is seen
On the dear seat beside the fire;
There plainest thou with Madeline
Or Isabella's lone desire.
He knows thee not, who does not know
The tender flashing of thine eye
At some melodious tale of woe,
And the sweet smile and sweeter sigh.

How oft in silent moonlight air,
When the wide earth is full of rest,
And all things outward seem more fair
For the inward spirit less opprest,
I look for thee, I think thee near,
Thy tones are thilling through my soul,
Thy dark eyes close to mine appear,
And I am blest beyond control!

As in the Sappho original, this section of the poem begins with the poet-speaker looking at and – crucially – *listening to*, the beloved, and what happens to him as a result is straight out of Sappho. The speaker 'trembles'; his sight fails, 'the air is dim'; his brain and senses 'swim', picking up on the ideas of melting and wetness in Sappho's *idros*.[8] And what doesn't come from Sappho, comes from the sources that have accrued around her: his 'keen madness of delight' suggests

Longinus's commentary; his ending up 'blest beyond control' is out of Ambrose Phillips's translation, 'Blest as the immortal gods is he ...'

In the middle stanza of this section the speaker imagines his beloved singing, performing poetry. The harp in his first stanza is interchangeable with the lyre – Sappho's instrument – and is a metaphor for the performance, or even simply the writing, of poetry in the early nineteenth century. In this case the actual subject matter of the beloved's song is named – 'There plainest thou with Madeline/ Or Isabella's lone desire'. It could be Keats, of course, 'The Eve of St Agnes' or 'Isabella and the Pot of Basil'. But this is also a very Sappho-like subject, the complaints – of love presumably – the expression of desire in woman, and interestingly here, more than one woman.

In the second part of this second stanza, very late in his Sappho-revision, we meet a version of the man in Sappho's poem. Here his role is much reduced, for this 'he' is imagined *without* the knowledge of the beloved which is the exclusive property of the speaker; 'He knows thee not, who does not know/ The tender flashing of thine eye/ At some melodious tale of woe,/ And the sweet smile and sweeter sigh.'

What is particularly telling here is that the beloved's 'flashing eye', 'sweet smile and sweeter sigh' etc. are all prompted by something specific – that is, the beloved's own performance of the miseries of Madeline and Isabella, poetically rendered. This beloved certainly is not 'seen and not heard', nor is the beloved simply a lovely object of desire. Rather, this beloved sings for a purely personal pleasure, is moved by that song of 'some melodious tale of woe' and the privileged viewer is only he, the speaker, who has witnessed this performance.

When this poem was composed in January 1831 the writer was unofficially engaged to a girl whom he had known since December 1829. His family did not approve of the connection, but he had written her a number of poems since that first meeting, often addressing her by name – she was called Emily – and punning on the derivation of her name from the Latin verb 'to love', *amare*:

> Consent to be 'Beloved'; I ask no more
> Than to fulfil for thee thy warning name,
> And in a perfect loving live and die.

Even keeping his Sappho reference, he could have used the pun again in this title. But he didn't. His title is ungendered, 'To the Loved One'.

Who then does he address? Who is it that he admires performing poetry? The writer of 'To the Loved One' was Arthur Hallam.[9] And the writer of 'Madeline' and 'Isabel', both published in 1830 in *Poems, Chiefly Lyrical*, was Alfred Tennyson.

Those far-renownèd brides of ancient song
Peopled the hollow dark, like burning stars ...

Alfred Tennyson, 'A Dream of Fair Women' (1832)

Tennyson did not need Arthur Hallam to introduce him to Sappho. Tennyson was taught Greek and Latin by his father, and during his years at Louth Grammar School he first came across a textbook which gave him phrases and words that stayed with him all his life. This book was a selection of extracts from the classics in two parts, the *Analecta Minora* and *Analecta Maiora*, edited by Andrew Dalzel, and revised by George Dunbar. When Tennyson returned from Louth in 1820 to be taught at home, his father bought a copy of Dalzel's *Analecta Minora sive Collectanea Graeca Majore ad usum academica juventutis accommodata cum notis philogis* (Cadell, London, 1820–21) which is still in the Tennyson collection at Lincoln. It clearly became Tennyson's book, because he has written his name in it twice and 'Trin.Coll. Cambridge' on the flyleaf of Volume I.[10]

Dalzel prints Sappho's Fragment 1, the so-called 'Ode to Aphrodite', and Fragment 31, 'To a Beloved Woman'. Both poems are closely and copiously annotated in Tennyson's hand with explanations of phrases, and variant readings drawn from Dalzel's notes and, presumably, Tennyson's own or his tutor-father's interpretations. Many of the notes in schoolboy Greek are an attempt to render Sappho's Aeolic dialect into Attic Greek. The annotations are in Greek, in Latin, and in English, and on one page Tennyson has written out in full Catullus's version of Fragment 31, 'Ille mi par esse Deo videtur'. There is no way of telling when Tennyson wrote these notes; it may have been as early as 1821, soon after the book was purchased, or it may have been as late as 1829 or 1830 when he took the book with him to Cambridge. Certain it is, however, that Tennyson read these two poems and knew them thoroughly.

The other edition of Sappho's Fragments that Tennyson knew in these early days was Jean-François Boissonade's 1825 *Lyrici Graeci*. Again, Tennyson has written his name on the flyleaf and annotated the book in pencil (now much faded). Boissonade's edition prints seventy-seven fragments attributed to Sappho beginning with the 'Ode to Aphrodite' and 'To a Beloved Girl'. This book, like the Dalzel, was obviously a major influence in the literary lives of the young Tennysons. Sixty-five years after its publication Frederick Tennyson recalled Boissonade's edition when he published his own version of Sappho in *The Isles of Greece: Sappho and Alcaeus* which, he explained,

> is not so much one poem, as a collection of poems, which have been mostly founded on the solitary fragments to be seen in a weird little volume, which came into my possession, I know not how, bearing the title of 'Lyrici Graeci' or Greek Lyricists; one of a series of duodecimos published in Paris in 1825.[11]

That Alfred Tennyson also kept up his early interest in Classical scholarship is borne out by the presence of another book in his library, Theodor Bergk's 1843 Greek and Latin edition of *Poetae Lyrici Graeci*.[12] In 1846 Edward Fitzgerald referred to three Sappho fragments in a letter, and Tennyson wrote back: 'Lovely lines, but I knew them before, the first ages ago, and the two last two years ago in Scheidwin's or Scheidewin's greek fragments – a book Frank Lushington had and which I have ever since intended to get – I fancy those two last lines have only been lately recovered ...'[13]

Quite apart from these stray remains of evidence concerning editions bought and fragments quoted, Tennyson's poetry is saturated with references that suggest his special debt to Sappho. This has always been acknowledged, but in a general way, where she jostles for position with Theocritus and Ovid, Alcaeus and Horace, and many other Classical lyric poets.[14] In fact, Sappho's influence was early, particular and enduring, but the period when his borrowings were most overt is very specific.

Our thought gave answer each to each, so true –
Opposed mirrors each reflecting each –
That though I knew not in what time or place
Methought that I had often met with you,
And either lived in either's heart and speech

Alfred Tennyson, 'To ... [As when with downcast eyes]' (1832)

Here follows a familiar story. Alfred Tennyson went up to Trinity College Cambridge in November 1827. Arthur Hallam arrived a year later, and they met in April 1829. Their liking was immediate and their friendship intense. It survived their competition for the Chancellor's Gold Medal for Poetry, for which they both entered, but which Tennyson won. Hallam recognised the superior power, but he did not give up his own poetic ambition. They wrote sonnets to each other, they even collaborated on at least one poem.[15] Hallam read Tennyson's manuscripts, advising and correcting. Tennyson reciprocated. Hallam dug out his notebooks, and he had some of them printed up in a trial edition. The idea was to publish a book together, just like Wordsworth and Coleridge. Brothers under the skin, together in one volume. Their relationship seemed still more firmly cemented when Hallam met Tennyson's sister Emily in December 1829 and decided that he was in love.

But then something happened. Arthur's father, the historian Henry Hallam, of a much grander and wealthier family than the ramshackle Tennysons, seems to have frowned on this increasing intimacy. The exact reason why is not clear, nor, without spelling it out, was there much that Hallam senior could do. But he could suppress the outward shows of the relation, and he did. He declared that he would not recognise an engagement to Emily and decreed that Hallam and she should not meet for one year. They obeyed. Further, he requested that Arthur should give up the idea of a collaborative publication with Alfred. Which he did. Arthur conceded, and put his little trial edition away.[16]

No matter. There were other things, other pleasures. Some things Henry Hallam could not forbid or prevent. Arthur wrote to Emily, and he set himself to promoting his friend's work, duly published as *Poems, Chiefly Lyrical* (the Wordsworth and Coleridge reference stayed in the title) in June 1830. And even this heavy-handed father could not stop the two men going off together for three happy summer months on a walking tour through France and down to the Pyrenees during the long vacation of 1830. Back at Cambridge in the autumn and winter, they read together, and squabbled over what Alfred should and should not publish. 'Boylike', Tennyson later said, Arthur admired everything that Alfred wrote. Arthur tried to rescue even Alfred's most juvenile pieces, so that Alfred called him 'point-blank mad'.[17] Injudiciously admiring he might have been, but this was the private face of their intimacy. Arthur's public role, the one he so clearly began to map out for himself at this time, was as the poet's champion and guide. The earliest official result of this calling was Hallam's well-known review essay on Tennyson, published in the *Englishman's Magazine* in August 1831.

But among the earliest personal evidence of Hallam's role as Tennyson's critic is a letter to one of their friends. Writing to William Bodham Donne in February 1831, Hallam copied out Tennyson's draft for the poem which became 'Mariana in the South': 'I expect you to be properly grateful to me for sending you by these presents another poem, of which to say that I love it would be only saying that it is his.' Tennyson was clearly Hallam's property. The subject and scene, he explains, were conceived while they were together the previous summer in the South of France, and he goes on to explain the poem's originality as well as to relate it to its poetic predecessors. These ancestors, he says, are Greek:

> It is observable in the mighty models of art, left for the worship of ages by the Greeks, & those too rare specimens of Roman production which breathe a Greek spirit, that their way of imaging a mood of the human heart in a group of circumstances, each of which reciprocally affects & is affected by the unity of that mood, resembles much Alfred's manner of delineation ... I believe you will find instances in all the Greek poems of the highest order, at present I can only call into distinct recollection the divine passage about the sacrifice of Iphigenia in Lucretius, the desolation of Ariadne in Catullus, and the fragments of Sappho, in which I see much congeniality to Alfred's peculiar power ...[18]

That Hallam and Tennyson should share a passion for Greek is not surprising. Hallam gave Tennyson an 1825 edition of the *Epigrams and Greek Anthology*, and Alfred wrote in this copy '*A. Tennyson hanc anthologiam mihi d. amicissiumus Arth. Hallam*'.[19] That they should both care about Sappho in particular is also not surprising. Tennyson had read her and alluded to her work in his earliest writings. Hallam had impressed at least one of his acquaintances, probably a tutor, with his interest in the 'short poems and fragments of Sappho'.[20] But that Hallam should compare Tennyson's poetry to Sappho's fragments just at this particular time – early in 1831 – is telling.

In January 1831 Hallam wrote a version of Sappho's Fragment 31 in his poem 'To the Loved One'. In February of the same year he linked Tennyson's 'Mariana in the South' with Sappho. And at some point during late 1830 to early 1832 – I would suggest at around this very time, the beginning of 1831 – Tennyson himself wrote no less than three poems that were versions of Sappho's Fragment 31.

'Eleänore'

The first of these was 'Eleänore' which Tennyson published in his *Poems* (1832). You will see that we do not actually get to the close Sappho reading until the last section, stanza VIII, but like Sappho's Fragment 31, this poem is about a girl who is looked at by the poet-speaker. Beginning with the line 'Thy dark eyes opened not/ Nor first revealed themselves to English air ...', the poem emphasises the idea of the gaze, eyes looking and being looked at, even while it goes on to make the fairytale setting which is the story of Eleänore's fancied babyhood. Eleänore is a kind of Sappho: she is not English, but foreign, exotic, and she lives in an imaginary garden landscape which is a fantasised ancient Greece, 'some delicious land/ Of lavish lights, ... And shadowed coves on a sunny shore ...'[21] And she begins as a baby, and alone, which both hint at Sappho's place in Tennyson's imagination that makes her belong to that far-off time of the world's infancy and implies her position as the original woman-poet, exemplary and unique.

No one comes close to Eleänore: 'Who may minister to thee?' in stanza III. But in stanza IV the poem's project is revealed, and that is to take 'Eleänore' out of that obscurity and to 'express' her in 'full-sailed verse'. The enterprise is not, however, the usual lover's difficulty of enumerating his mistress's attractions. Eleänore herself is, in effect, a poet. Tennyson's verse has to do justice to her 'full-flowing harmony', to her 'luxuriant symmetry', to her capacity to fuse 'Thought and motion' modulating 'To an unheard melody,/ Which lives about thee, and a sweep/ Of richest pauses, evermore/ Drawn from each other, mellow-deep ...'

The juxtaposition here of an ' unheard melody' with 'a sweep of richest pauses' effectively suggests the status of Sappho's work which does indeed exist only as fragments, much of it 'unheard' because the rest is lost in the 'pauses', the silences of mutilated texts, lost manuscripts, broken potsherds.[22] Stanza IV ends with the question 'Who may express thee, Eleänore?' Express, in the sense of conjure up, speak out, distil the essence of, Sapphic poetry.

Then comes the answer. Tennyson volunteers: 'I stand before thee, Eleänore'. So he gazes at her, 'I muse, as in a trance', much as Sappho's poet-speaker in Fragment 31 gazes at her beloved girl. But in Tennyson's scenario the gaze is mutual, she looks back at him, and it is this reciprocity which promotes the magic space where poetry happens:

I muse, as in a trance, whene'er
    The languors of thy love-deep eyes
Float on to me.

But in this mutual gazing the poet-speaker sees Eleänore's thoughts unfolded too, thoughts which are intimidating, which might suggest his own belatedness, his failure to live up to his poetic model: 'Gazing, I seem to see/ Thought folded over thought ... grow so full and deep/ In thy large eyes, that, overpowered quite,/ I cannot veil, or droop my sight,/ But am as nothing in its light ...'

In stanza VIII, which is the part that most explicitly re-works Sappho's Fragment 31, all the sensations described here are direct borrowings: the humming ears, the broken tongue, the change of colour, even the awkward wetness is transposed into a respectably poetic image:

But when I see thee roam, with tresses unconfined,
While the amorous, odorous wind
    Breathes low between the sunset and the moon;
        Or, in a shadowy saloon,
On silken cushions half reclined;
            I watch thy grace; and in its place
        My heart a charmèd slumber keeps,
            While I muse upon thy face;
        And a languid fire creeps
            Through my veins to all my frame,
    Dissolvingly and slowly: soon
            From thy rose-red lips MY name
    Floweth; and then, as in a swoon,
        With dinning sound my ears are rife,
            My tremulous tongue faltereth,
        I lose my colour, I lose my breath,
        I drink the cup of a costly death,
Brimmed with delirious draughts of warmest life.
        I die with my delight, before
            I hear what I would hear from thee;
            Yet tell my name again to me,
    I *would* be dying evermore,
    So dying ever, Eleänore.

On second thoughts, given the erotic context and the nineteenth century euphemism in 'to die', perhaps it is not such a respectable image after all.

Whatever is going on here, there is one innovation that owes nothing to Sappho. The speaker in Tennyson's poem looks at the beloved girl and, as in Sappho, hears her speak. But in Tennyson we learn what she says, and what she says, the specific utterance that inflames him into desire, is the saying of his name: '... soon/ From thy rose-red lips MY name/ Floweth; and then, as in a swoon ...' and then, further down, '... Yet tell my name again to me,/ I *would* be dying evermore,/ So dying ever, Eleänore.'

Imagined not once, but twice, Tennyson's speaker fantasises a continual naming and 'dying' which, paradoxically will make him – or his poetry – live. Having set up the mutuality of the gaze between the poet-speaker and the girl-object, and having construed her as a 'natural' lyric poet in the Sappho mould, Tennyson's poem seals the reciprocity of their relation in this detail. Just as he speaks her name (several times) in the course of the poem, so she speaks his name. If Tennyson's 'Eleänore' is brought into existence by the process of his writing a poem about her, so similarly, 'Eleänore' brings him into existence, into 'warmest life' by the process of naming him.

'Fatima'

The exact same detail goes into Tennyson's next version of Sappho's Fragment 31, 'Fatima'. When it was first published in 1832 this poem had no title, but only an epigraph, the first line of Sappho's Fragment 31. Again, it is a poem about a girl, set in a garden topos, with an oriental flavour and a strong erotic context.[23] In this case, as in his 'Mariana' poems, Tennyson speaks with the voice of the woman who waits, rehearsing in anxious enchantment, the desired arrival. There are, in fact, at least three Sappho allusions in this poem, but it is Fragment 31 that appears in the third and in the last stanza:[24]

> Last night, when some one spoke his name,
> From my swift blood that went and came
> A thousand little shafts of flame
> Were shivered in my narrow frame.
>   O Love, O fire! ...

and,

> My whole soul waiting silently,
> All naked in a sultry sky,
> Droops blinded with his shining eye:
> I *will* possess him or will die.
>   I will grow round him in his place,
>   Grow, live, die looking on his face,
>   Die, dying clasped in his embrace.

The physical symptoms of desire in the blood are here, as is Sappho's 'fire', though in this case Tennyson extends the metaphor of love's 'fire' to make the cliché of 'burning' desire, unrelieved in the lover's absence, into a full-scale drought of sun and heat. And the 'gaze' frame from Sappho's poem, so thoroughly exploited in 'Eleänore' also appears in 'Fatima'. The speaker wishes finally to 'Grow, live, die looking on his face', but curiously, even in the lover's absence, she still seems to be being looked at. The sun itself looks on her, exposes her, and threatens her own capacity to see, to return the gaze: 'My whole soul .../ All naked in a sultry sky,/ Droops blinded with his shining eye ...' Not just the look of the lover, but the very fact of her own desire, is what puts Fatima on show, makes her an object of unrelenting scrutiny.

And then there is that Tennysonian detail of the name: 'Last night, when some one spoke his name ...' As in 'Eleänore' it's the utterance of 'his name' that brings on the Sapphic fit of fire in the blood. But in 'Fatima' it is not the lover who speaks her name, nor she who speaks his. There are no longer only two present here. A shadowy third is introduced, a 'some one' who 'spoke his name'. Some one who may figure like the third in Sappho's poem, the man who 'seems as fortunate as the gods' because he has the attention of the beloved who is desired by the speaker. A some one who may have an interest in uttering 'his name'. A some one whose interest may be the same as Fatima's, and focussed on the same beloved. The possibilities in Sappho's poem triangulate desire.

'Love and Friendship'

Tennyson's third version of Sappho's Fragment 31 was never published in his lifetime. It was called 'Love and Friendship: An Indian Tale', and part of it (the only fragment now existing, though this draft may be all there ever was), was copied out into his Commonplace Book by Tennyson's Cambridge friend J.M. Heath.

O Friend, dear Friend, I cannot speak of her,
I cannot think a moment of her face,
I cannot name her name thus passingly,
But my blood leaps and dances in my veins
Like a fire-fountain: 'tis a lava stream
Thrown on with fierce convulsions of the heart,
Which in its passage through me still shoots off
Small sparks and shafts of fire which tingle through me.
I am a wreath of flame lit on a hill
And the winds blow me fiercer: but for thee,
My sense, my tongue, mine eyes, my breath, my life,
Long since the fiery forethought of the wish
Had blotted out the wish and laid me here
Stiff in the creeping surf.[25]

The subtitle points again to the oriental frame that Tennyson regularly associated with Sappho, and the title 'Love and Friendship' helps to explain the threesome which appears here. In 'Eleänore' the male poet addressed the female beloved; in 'Fatima' the male poet speaks for the woman who desires her male lover, and a third 'someone' hovers in background. In 'Love and Friendship' the (presumably) male speaker bemoans his love for a woman, but addresses a (presumably) male friend who saves him from the 'death' that desire initiates.

The premise of Sappho's Fragment 31 lies immediately behind this fragment of Tennyson's. He should be writing a poem about the beloved girl, conjuring her presence, and listing the symptoms of desire brought on by that presence. He does actually get around to doing all that, but the set of negatives that open the poem suggest that he won't do it, that he might not follow his model here: '... I cannot speak of her,/ I cannot think a moment of her face,/ I cannot name her name thus passingly,/ But my blood leaps and dances in my veins ...' and so on, according to Sappho's pattern.

Note that naming the name of the beloved happens here too, as it does in 'Eleänore' and 'Fatima'. This time it is, however, different once again. The lover speaks the name of the beloved and it is his own utterance that leads to desire.

Yet there is a distraction in this poem. Apparently the speaker has named his beloved girl, immediately before the poem starts: 'I cannot name her name thus passingly.' But the occasion for the poem itself is not the girl, but the presence of the 'Friend' to whom the poem is addressed. Like Sappho's Fragment 31, this poem begins with the third, the man apparently outside the relation between the speaker and the beloved girl. But here that third assumes primacy. He only appears twice: in the opening line, 'O Friend, dear Friend', and in line 10, '... but for thee ...', but he (presumably he) is still the pivot of the poem. If the speaker cannot name the girl, he can 'name' his 'Friend'. If the speaker is brought, as in Sappho's original, to disintegration, loss of sense, self-fragmentation and to the verge of death by the effects of desire, still that 'Friend' will rescue him:

> ... but for thee,
> My sense, my tongue, mine eyes, my breath, my life,
> Long since the fiery forethought of the wish
> Had blotted out the wish and laid me here
> Stiff in the creeping surf.

Love and friendship. But where does one end and the other begin?

O darling room, my heart's delight,
Dear room, the apple of my sight,
With thy two couches soft and white,
There is no room so exquisite,
No little room so warm and bright,
Wherein to read, wherein to write.

Alfred Tennyson, 'O Darling Room' (1832)

Sappho is Tennyson's mother-poet. She had always been there – 'Lovely lines – but I knew them before ... ages ago ...' – and she gave Tennyson oral and aural satisfaction, being one of his first teachers in the pleasure of delicious sound. Her body (of work) broken though it was, nurtured him. In his earliest poetry he lives, as it were, in the happy symbiosis of the mother–child dyad; he takes her themes, her images, her vocabulary, her sounds, and can recognise no differentiation between his own writing self and this poetic Other. Then, as he comes to define an individual identity, he looks in the mirror which is held up by this other poet, and sees difference. Tennyson is himself, not Sappho. And he finds this out by re-writing, three times over, Sappho's famous poem about looking.

Freud privileges the sense of sight, of seeing, in his account of the maturing subject, and in *Sexuality in the Field of Vision* Jacqueline Rose points out the places in Freud where visual representation is linked to the child's journey into adult sexual life, where very often the child is looking at little scenarios about himself and his relation to his parents to learn sexual difference, or sex. 'Each time', she says, 'the stress falls on a problem of seeing. The sexuality lies less in the content of what is seen than in the subjectivity of the viewer, in the relationship between what is looked at and the developing sexual knowledge of the child. The relationship between viewer and scene is always one of fracture, partial identification, pleasure and distrust.'[26]

In many ways this exactly characterises the fluctuating subjectivity of the poet in his three revisions of Fragment 31. Tennyson identifies with Sappho, yet breaks away from her, he is pleasured by her, and yet he distrusts and denies her. Sappho is the focus of erotic attraction, and her poem is the site. What the poet sees is not a mirror, but a misrecognition, for this eroticism is really about himself. In writing about Tennyson's early work Matthew Rowlinson rightly calls many of the 1830 and 1832 poems 'autoerotic'.[27] The poet is constantly turned on by his own words, by his own performance, and he brings himself off in 'Eleänore' and in 'Fatima' with the repetition, rhythm and intense concentration that ends in 'dying'.

But this is not what happens in 'Love and Friendship'. Here the 'fracture' begins as Tennyson separates himself from the haunting scene of Fragment 31. In 'Love and Friendship' he is saved from the 'dying' which must end any copy of Sappho's poem, by his 'Friend'. The 'dying' is still there of course, the death that might have happened, that would have laid him out 'Stiff in the creeping surf'. But this death is not his. It is, in fact, Sappho's own death pictured here, as she lies in the sea, in the 'creeping surf', having taken her life, as she did, according to the legend, when she leapt from the cliff of Leucadia.

Except that, on this occasion, she didn't jump. She was pushed. The fact is that Tennyson doesn't need her any more. At least, not in quite the same way. Tennyson knew Sappho's body (of work). He, quite literally, wrote all over it. Then he broke up her body (of work) and put it back together again. He made his own image by re-vising, re-seeing Sappho. He made himself into Tennyson by seeing that he was Other, that he was not-Sappho. But it was his erotic knowledge of her body (of work) that brought him to this stage. Peter Brooks calls this 'dynamic of curiosity' which is centred in the intellectual apprehension of sexuality 'epistemophilia', and he defines it as the 'explicit or implicit postulation that the body – another's or one's own – holds the key not only to pleasure but as well to knowledge and power'.[28] Sappho, or rather her formulation in Fragment 31, is the very origin and essential expression of desire in the body; she is body, and Tennyson makes himself into a poet by covering that body, by replicating it, by distilling it, by pressing the life out of it: 'Who may *express* thee, Eleänore?'

In effect, Tennyson uses Fragment 31 as a reflection for learning his own identity. And that is why Tennyson's distinctive mark appears in all three of his inscriptions on Sappho's work. Just as he once wrote notes on the texts of her poems, so now he writes his name into her poem. The 'naming' of my/his/her name in each of his revisions of Fragment 31 changes Sappho's poem into Tennyson's poem, writes his signature at the bottom of the page.

In each of his three revisions of Fragment 31 Tennyson experiments with the positioning of Subject and Object. At first, in 'Eleänore' Tennyson is the Subject and Sappho-Eleänore the Object, though they are locked into mutual recognition. Then Tennyson turns himself into Sappho-Fatima and so makes both himself and her into the Subject.[29] Finally, in 'Love and Friendship' Tennyson makes himself again the Subject, while Sappho dwindles into a distant Object, threatened always with displacement by a new Object of desire in the 'Friend'. Working through these positions Tennyson comes to a theoretical perspective on his poetic world. One where there is co-adaption between subject and object, where there is, in Lacan's punning coinage, 'co-naissance', knowledge (*connaissance*), coinciding with the birth (*naissance*) of the self.[30] And in Tennyson's case his 'co-naissance' contains another pun. For this 'birth' into knowledge and identity was shared – with Arthur Hallam.

Tennyson wrote three versions of Sappho's Fragment 31. Hallam wrote one, and Hallam's poem is preoccupied with the same poetic enterprise that motivates Tennyson's. That is, to bring Tennyson into existence as a poet. His coming to power is a coming to poetry, and Hallam is his handmaiden, even if in 'To the Loved One' Hallam makes Tennyson play the girl.

Of course, the literal-minded may object that Hallam's poem is supposed to be addressed to Emily Tennyson. But the fact of the matter is that in this poem too, there is a naming of names – 'There plainest thou with Madeline/ Or Isabella's lone desire' – and that naming obliquely, or explicitly, might name the author of those two poems ... which could be Keats ... or, Tennyson. Anyway, given that Hallam's poem is about a reciter of poetry enjoying their own performance – 'He knows thee not who does not know/ The tender flashing of thine eye/ At some melodious tale of woe ...' – and remembering that throughout his life Tennyson had a terrible addiction to reading aloud from his own poetry at every opportunity, sometimes going on into the small hours, whether his audience was willing or not ... and one suspects that Hallam's portrait here was taken from life.

Hallam forgave Tennyson his self-obsession. He was obsessed too, and by the same thing: Tennyson.[31]

> **There are three things which fill my heart with sighs,**
> **And steep my soul in laughter (when I view**
> **Fair maiden-forms moving like melodies)**
> **Dimples, roselips, and eyes of any hue.**
>
> **Alfred Tennyson, 'Sonnet', 'There are three things' (1831)**

'For Freud', as Kristeva says, 'binds the state of loving to narcissism.'[32] As the ego comes into being it paradoxically makes itself into an Other, and exploits others to make that self. Effectively pulling its selves together with Lacan's 'imaginary' the ego subsists in a world of mirrors, of doubles, of reflected selves where their purpose is at once to differentiate and to endorse; to be separate, and to be the same, in a measuring of subject against object which blurs the boundaries between each. Thus a confirmation of identity strangely courts the dissolution of the self which is made and unmade in the presence of the desired (because defining) other. Or others.

Sappho's Fragment 31 is enacted on, or at, this stage. She makes herself an 'ideal ego', bringing herself into being in the course of the poem. She faces the threat of self-fragmentation and pulls her-selves together ('... but all can be endured ...'), and she does this in a specular world where she looks at the Others, the girl and the man, who reflect the self that she also looks at. She desires the girl, she desires the state of the man. Love beckons, and she sees her own face in the pool.

When Tennyson and Hallam revised Sappho's Fragment 31 they also became Narcissus. Together and separately. Sappho is their mirror-pool, but so is (are) each other. And so is (are) Emily Tennyson, Eleänore, Fatima, the nameless woman in 'Love and Friendship' and her rival the 'Friend'. Cohorts of desired objects are pressed into service to make the scenes that will make the poet.

And it doesn't stop there. I have always thought it strange that so little critical attention has been given to the huge number of girl-poems written by Tennyson in his early years and published, for the most part, in the collections of 1830 and 1832. 'Girlie' poems is what they have become, simpering illustrations for a soft-porn collection parading their vital statistics. Modern critics are embarrassed by this display, either lamely suggesting that the poet's contemporaries 'found these chaste celebrations of the mystery of womanhood more erotic than we do', or bravely going for a feminist point: 'they were what people (men?) wanted to believe about maidens'.[33]

Tennyson does have a lot of girls: Claribel, Lilian, and Isabel, Mariana, Madeline, Juliet, and Adeline, Oriana, Amy, Anacaona, Marion, Lisette and the Lady of Shalott, Mariana, Eleänore, Fatima, and Oenone, Rosalind, Margaret, Kate, Semele, and My Mab, Rosa, Dora and Lady Clara Vere de Vere, not to mention assorted Gardener's Daughters, Miller's Daughters, and Beggar Maids. Like a Don Juan of letters, his list is long and all encompassing.

For that is what Tennyson is, or that is the persona Tennyson adopts in these early volumes, one sanctioned, in fact, by two of his closest poetic models: by Byron, who lived it and wrote the poem, and by Sappho, who may have lived it and who wrote the poems. That is, poems to lots of different girls. And, like Don Juan, what Tennyson is doing here is using these girls to make himself. Don Juan is a Romantic hero who is a Narcissus, using women as mirrors to reflect himself to twice his size.[34] Tennyson is a Romantic poet who is also a Narcissus, using women as mirrors to reflect himself into poetry. Tennyson said that none of these girls existed, they were all invented – 'All these ladies were evolved like the camel, from my own consciousness' – and we should believe him.[35]

Tennyson seems to have learned his imaginary (and Imaginary) philandering with Hallam, perhaps from Hallam. Tennyson's line-up of named beauties start their parade in 1830 and 1832, but Hallam had been writing similar poems on his own account much earlier.[36]

Hallam liked the girlie poems. This predilection has always been a trial to those who want to make Hallam into the ideal Tennyson critic. In his 1831 review of Tennyson's *Poems* (1830) Hallam praises this 'singular' – an odd choice of word here given their plenitude – 'and very beautiful class of poems'. Like a lascivious customer in a brothel, he cannot choose between these lovelies: 'We must hasten to make our election; so, passing by the "airy, fairy Lilian" ... We shall fix on a lovely, albeit somewhat mysterious lady, who has fairly taken our "heart from out of our breast" ... Adeline ...'[37]

There is, however, no mystery as to why Hallam liked the girlie poems. It's because Tennyson wrote them for him. He performed these women – as he performed Sappho – and, as Hallam's 'To the Loved One' makes clear, Hallam himself was the audience. The women are irrelevant: the true subject of these poems is Tennyson-performing-poet. And their true object is Hallam, the voyeur, who looks on their bringing into being, who is the one they are formed to pleasure. These women are indeed nothing but text, they are 'pure representation' and, as Teresa de Lauretis says, the 'absence of woman' here tells 'the story of male desire'.[38]

Some while after Tennyson and Hallam returned from the South of France in 1830 Tennyson wrote a curious sonnet about 'three things'. Three things which turn out to be the same thing after all, and that thing is not the subject of the poem.

> There are three things which fill my heart with sighs,
> And steep my soul in laughter (when I view
> Fair maiden-forms moving like melodies)
> Dimples, roselips, and eyes of any hue.
> There are three things beneath the blessèd skies
> For which I live, black eyes and brown and blue:
> I hold them all most dear, but oh! black eyes,
> I live and die, and only die for you.
> Of late such eyes looked at me – while I mused,
> At sunset, underneath a shadowy plane,
> In old Bayona nigh the southern sea –
> From an half-open lattice looked at *me*.
> I saw no more – only those eyes – confused
> And dazzled to the heart with glorious pain.[39]

The 'three things' are girls, or rather, parts of girls, taken at random from any old girls; either 'Dimples, roselips, and eyes of any hue', or 'black eyes and brown and blue'. It matters not which, just as it matters not to whom these abstracted body parts belong. The woman is, as ever, absent. She simply puts on the costume of the feminine worn by any one of Tennyson's interchangeable lovelies. But though they may be 'airy, fairy' like his Lilian, Tennyson can still translate these lists of anonymous limbs into poetry, for it is out of these fragmented bits that he makes his 'Fair maiden-forms moving like melodies'. 'There Are Three Things ...' is a joke poem, but Tennyson's consciousness of his technique is striking. This sonnet may be a tease, but the joke is a smutty one which wipes out the woman in order to address another man.[40] For it was Arthur Hallam who was Tennyson's companion in 'old Bayona', the city of Bayonne in the Pyrenees, in the summer of 1830. And so it could be that it is Hallam's penetrating gaze that he recalls; 'Of late such eyes looked at me ... looked at *me*./ I saw no more – only those eyes – confused/ And dazzled to the heart with glorious pain.'

The triangle formed here, Tennyson/Hallam/various women, mimicks the triangulation of desire that appears in Sappho's Fragment 31. It may be that that is one reason why Fragment 31 retains its literary pre-eminence, enacting as it does, a psychic geometry which has become familiar throughout Western cultural representation. Sappho may have been an early analyst of the triangle, she may also have had two women and one man in hers, but ever since, from Shakespeare's sonnets to *Jules et Jim*, the pattern, like that here of (irrelevant) woman/Tennyson/Hallam, is always, in Eve Kosofsky Sedgwick's phrase, 'between men'.[41] And it is always the third – sometimes rival, sometimes ally, sometimes beloved, very often unseen – it is always the third who is the point of the triangle.[42]

I cannot love thee as I ought,
For love reflects the thing beloved;
My words are only words, and moved
Upon the topmost froth of thought.

Alfred Tennyson, *In Memoriam*, LII, 1–4 (1850)

'Ode to Memory' was one of Tennyson's own favourite early poems. The idea of memory he invoked there is both a personal one, derived from childhood, and a more generalised memory of a cultural, particularly a poetic, inheritance. The Classical context, the feminine personification, the garden setting, and the bridal occasion in this poem, all suggest a Sapphic background. More than that, the epithet that Tennyson gives to his Memory-Muse here is 'many-minded', which is a borrowing from Sappho's invocation to Aphrodite in her Fragment 1:

We may hold converse with all forms
Of the many-sided mind,
And those whom passion hath not blinded,
Subtle-thoughted, myriad-minded.

Quite soon after he met Arthur Hallam, Tennyson added 'To ——' to the title and inserted a three-line stanza that indicates how Hallam had taken Sappho's place as the 'myriad-minded' Muse of Tennyson's imagination:

My friend, with you to live alone,
Were how much better than to own
A crown, a sceptre, and a throne![43]

In the event, it was not to be Hallam's living, but his dying, that provided Tennyson's inspiration. In September 1833, while away in Vienna, Arthur Hallam suffered a brain haemorrhage. During their four years of friendship Hallam and

Tennyson had shared Sappho as their Muse-Mother: they were two, she the absent third. From 1833 to the end of his life it was Hallam's own absence that became the wellspring of Tennyson's poetry. With his idea, with his memory measured against his loss, Tennyson played the *fort-da* game that patterned *In Memoriam* and all his strong lyrics.

But Hallam's role as Tennyson's Muse is not an uncomplicated one and, as the nineteenth century wore on and attitudes to sexuality hardened – indeed, as sexuality was invented – Hallam's role as Tennyson's Muse became positively fraught. Sappho became positively taboo.

When Tennyson and Hallam were young men in the 1830s, lyric poetry flourished in a feminine context which was not necessarily effeminate. Sensibility, inherited from the previous generation of Romantic poets and endorsed by the literary dominance of the women poets, was the keynote. It was that sensibility that Hallam found, and praised, in his account of Tennyson's poetic strengths in his August 1831 review, and Sappho, as the first lyric poet, was a respectable source and model.[44]

The adopting of a female voice, as Tennyson does in 'Fatima' and other early poems, was by no means awkward, nor was a swapping of gender – as he does in cross-dressing the 'young spirit' of the poet in 'Ode to Memory' – embarrassing. More than that, even same-sex desire carried no opprobrium in these innocent poetic imaginations. Hallam and Tennyson read Sappho in Greek. They knew what was there, but it was her poetry that mattered. And between themselves? Did they know what was there? How much did they do in that Pyrenean summer that produced all their Sappho poems – 'Mariana in the South', 'Eleänore', 'Fatima', 'Love and Friendship', 'To the Loved One' – and which lingered in Tennyson's memory, significant in time and place?[45]

Much more than we can know. And much less than we can imagine.

What is certain is that Sappho, Sappho as a named or referenced source of lyric passion, disappears altogether from Tennyson's work after the death of Hallam. She is, it is true, mentioned in *The Princess* (1847), but there she is scaled down to a heroine for girls, cited as an example of feminine achievement in Lady Psyche's lecture (Section II, lines 147–8), and she has to compete with that other model of the woman poet, Corinna, who appears embroidered on the Princess's picnic-tent (III, 329–35). Sappho also appeared in the unobjectionable guise of poetic technician when Tennyson composed a Sapphic stanza for R.C. Jebb's *Greek Literature* (1877). And finally, she is mentioned as 'the poet' of the evening star in 'Locksley Hall Sixty Years After' (1886) in a re-worked phrase from an 1830 poem 'Elegiacs' where she had been, more recognisably, 'the ancient poetess'. This change of sex and status is not necessarily a compliment.

Across the years of the nineteenth century the 'separate spheres' of masculine and feminine became more widely diverse, while anything that crossed that divide became more certainly perverse. Tennyson had risked a charge of effeminacy from the beginning, and with *In Memoriam* his risk was publicly noticed.[46] Yet there was worse to come: inversion. Towards the end of the century, just when new thinking on and naming of homosexuality was being attempted in liberal circles, social and legal sanctions clamped down. John Addington Symonds's anxious but brave account of 'Greek love', *A Problem in Greek Ethics*, was privately printed in 1883 and two years later – just when Tennyson was writing 'Locksley Hall Sixty Years After' – the Labouchère Amendment to the Criminal Law Amendment Act of 1885 made all male homosexual acts, whether consenting, whether in public or private, illegal.[47]

'Historically', Barthes says, 'the discourse of absence is carried on by the Woman ...'

> Woman is faithful (she waits), man is fickle (he sails away, he cruises). It is Woman who gives shape to absence, elaborates its fiction, for she has time to do so; she weaves and she sings ... It follows that in any man who utters the other's absence something feminine is declared: this man who waits and who suffers from his waiting is miraculously feminised. A man is not feminised because he is inverted but because he is in love.[48]

But this particular man who waited and suffered for his waiting, while happy enough to be feminised – he had done it to himself time and again – did not wish to be thought inverted, nor did he identify with those who '... Affected An Effeminate Manner'. This was partly a resistance to naming where doing was, in certain circumstances, entirely acceptable; where it was, perhaps, even inevitable as one evolved from boyish 'wild oats' to the mature 'grain by which a man may live'. It was partly a resistance to a pattern that Foucault sees in the late nineteenth century study of psychology which had increasingly led to the presumption that literature, and poetry especially, was a skewed 'confession' producing 'true discourses concerning sex'.[49] And it was partly a reaction to a change in attitudes and fashions which had taken Tennyson's Muse-Mother, Sappho, his origin and source of lyric, and turned her into a disreputable Lesbian. She had become all too risky to be quoted. Gautier had done his work, Baudelaire had taken her, and Swinburne too. Louys would soon have her. Tennyson dared not speak her name. She became 'the poet'.[50]

And yet, in a sense, that designation was the true one. For Tennyson, Sappho was the original poet: she gave him the instrument of lyric verse; she was one of the mirrors that reflected him into poetry; she was the third in the geometry of the triangle that shaped him. Her images, her tone, her vocabulary, her subjects, her style, are glimpsed in the lyrics of *The Princess*, and in the gardens of *Maud*, she is one of the maidens with whom the poet dwells when he meets the veiled figure of the beloved in *In Memoriam*, CIII. And in that poem – at one stage entitled 'Fragments of an Elegy' – Tennyson considers how Sappho's textual fate, broken into pieces, torn into strips, could so easily be his own:

What hope is here for modern rhyme
  To him who turns a musing eye
  On songs, and deeds, and lives, that lie
Foreshortened in the tract of time?

These mortal lullabies of pain
  May bind a book, may line a box,
  May serve to curl a maiden's locks;
Or when a thousand moons shall wane

A man upon a stall may find,
  And, passing, turn the page that tells
  A grief, then changed to something else,
Sung by a long-forgotten mind.[51]

The substance of Sappho was what mattered to Tennyson, the text, the body of work, fragmented though it was, riddled though it was, possessed though it could be. But Tennyson lived long, and when the Egyptian papyrus discoveries of the 1880s and 1890s seemed to promise a resurrected Sappho, Tennyson knew of it. In 1892 the elderly poet told Mrs Montagu Butler that 'the discovery for which he had always hoped the most was of some further writings of Sappho'.[52]

Alfred Tennyson died in October 1892. He was 83. His wife – another Emily Tennyson – was with him, and his son. As he died, Tennyson cried out 'Hallam, Hallam'. His son thought he called to him.[53] Another triangle; but it was not Hallam Tennyson who made the third.

It was more than sixty years since Arthur Hallam and Alfred Tennyson had set out for France and Spain; more than sixty years since they had read Sappho together, since they re-made her in their versions of Fragment 31. Sappho's late reappearance in Tennyson's life may have revived those memories of his own distant making as a poet. It must have seemed far away.

Remembering his early childhood, Tennyson had said that 'The words "far, far away" had always a strange charm for me.' In old age he returned to those words. 'I loved thee once, Atthis, long ago', sang Sappho. This was Tennyson's version. And there was a verse in the manuscript of 'Far-far-away' that Tennyson never published. It read:

Ghost, can you see us, hear us, do we seem
Far, far away, a truth and yet a dream,
Far-far-away?[54]

5
The Woman Poet Sings Sappho's Last Song

The action stops. The music slows, fades, dwindles away. Into the silence a woman's voice is lifted and the music follows her. She is Tosca, an opera singer, a performer, and she sings, 'Vissi d'arte, vissi d'amore' – 'I lived for art, I lived for love'. Alone in her distress, nothing exists except her pain and her song. But she is not quite alone. Someone watches her. On stage she may have an audience of one, but off stage she has an audience of thousands. For behind Tosca the Diva stands Sappho the poet. And so the audience knows that this is a Last Song. Soon there will be no Tosca, no Sappho. Their bodies will be flung into space and dashed to pieces on the rocks. There will be no remains. Except the song.

I lived for art, I lived for love

Puccini's opera *Tosca* was premiered in 1900, but it is set in 1800, and it looks back to a time which saw the beginnings of a Sappho myth that exerted lasting influence on the popular idea of what the woman poet was, and how she conceived of herself. One group who worked and re-worked the image of Sappho were the women poets of the nineteenth century.

At the beginning of that period the dominant idea of Sappho shared by her followers such as Mary Robinson and Madame de Stael, was as the female embodiment of the Romantic hero: passionate, enthusiastic, intellectual, artistic, lonely and doomed. Best known as a poet, a free thinker and a suicide, this Sappho was heterosexual.[1] She had to be, because the essential burden of her song was a gloomy analysis of what it meant to be a Romantic hero trapped in a woman's body, and all too conscious therefore of the dictates of contemporary constructed sexual difference. At a time when women were becoming increasingly radical in their demands for political and social freedoms at the expense of domestic claims, this fated nineteenth century Sappho sang a song where art and love were mutually exclusive. What is very peculiar is how closely women poets identified themselves and their subjects with this fiction of Sappho. The slippage between the real historical situations of the nineteenth century and the made-up stories of Lesbos in the sixth century BC is everywhere apparent. But the assumption continually made by Sappho's latter-day successors is that the condition of the poet is always the same, whatever her time and place. Of course this parallels the Victorian conviction that the condition of femininity is always the same. But the results for the women poets were ambivalent. To be identified as a 'modern Sappho' was both an inspiring blessing and an inhibiting curse.[2]

In spite of the fact that there had been a recent 'British Sappho' in the person of the poet Mary Robinson – the subject of my second chapter in this book – for many of the Victorian woman poets it was not their own countrywoman, but Madame de Stael in France who most effectively appropriated Sappho's image and re-made it in hers. Her novel *Corinne, or Italy* (1807) was the most popular and enduring of her many versions of the Sappho myth, but of her other works *Delphine* (1802) and *Sapho: drame en cinq actes* (1821), as well as the folk-song from her juvenilia 'Romance to the tune: We loved each other since childhood', all draw on the Sappho plot. Corinna was the other well-known Greek poetess of antiquity, and de Stael's heroine blends into the Sapphic model to produce the nineteenth century archetype of the woman poet. The influence of this model was immense, and Byron related how he took de Stael to task over her bad example to impressionable young women:

> I continued saying, how dangerous it was to inculcate the belief that genius, talent, acquirements, and accomplishments, such as Corinne was represented to possess, could not preserve a woman from being a victim to an unrequited passion, and that reason, absence, and female pride were unavailing.
>
> I told her that 'Corinne' would be considered, if not cited, as an excuse for violent *passions* by all young ladies with imaginations *exalté*, and that she had much to answer for.[3]

And so she did. For de Stael's Corinne-Sappho, glorious in her intellectual achievements but, as a consequence, thwarted in love and condemned to melancholy self-destruction, soon became the marker for the destiny of the woman poet. Most obviously this was exactly what happened when Bentley published an English translation of *Corinne* in 1833 where the prose text was translated by Isabel Hill, but the verses and songs of Corinne were specially commissioned in English 'metrical versions' from Letitia Elizabeth Landon. It was a clever move on the part of the publisher, for did he not have here, in living flesh, the very person of the fictional poetess? L.E.L. was one of the first of the nineteenth century women poets to write the despairs of Corinne and Sappho into her verse. Her long verse-story *The Improvisatrice* (1824) re-worked de Stael's *Corinne*, and there the first inset poem is 'Sappho's Song'. In the public mind (and in her own) the trajectory of L.E.L.'s life – a glittering career, a failed love affair, a (probable) suicide – made her seem to act out the inevitable pattern inherited from Sappho.

For other women poets the identification was not so disastrous. But it was potent. Elizabeth Barrett Browning, for instance – and perhaps with L.E.L.'s example in mind – seems to have tried to avoid the comparison. True, she once described herself as '"little & black" like Sappho',[4] but in general – and somewhat surprisingly, given her training as a Greek scholar – she mentions Sappho only occasionally and seems always conscious of her threatening legacy rather than her empowering example. When Sara Coleridge met Barrett Browning in 1851 she wrote of the younger poet:

> She is little, hard-featured, with long ringlets, a pale face, and plaintive voice, something very impressive in her dark eyes and brow ... She has more poetic genius than any other woman ever shewed before, except Sappho ...[5]

Except Sappho. Always Sappho. For she is the pinnacle of female poetic achievement to which her belated rivals can only aspire. The curious thing is that for much of the Victorian age, very little of Sappho's transcendent reputation was based on her poetry. To begin with, there wasn't much of it. For the most part only Fragment 1, the so-called 'Ode to Aphrodite' and Fragment 31, 'That man seems to me', along with a few other fragments were known. There were Greek editions available, published in France and, later, in Germany, as there were also a number of English translations published in the eighteenth century and on into the early nineteenth century.[6] But for the most part – unlike the men such as Shelley or Tennyson – the women poets did not read Greek, so it was the legends that they knew. The legends, and the apparent tone of Sappho's poetry. For what little there was – in the current translations by Ambrose Phillips, John Addison, Francis Fawkes or E. Burnaby Greene – seemed to accord exactly with the nineteenth century's idea of what women should write and indeed with the nineteenth century's idea of what poetry itself should be.

Because Sappho's remains were about love and feeling, because they were intense and (albeit the result of an accident of history) short, they seemed to epitomise the form of women's lyric poetry. Thus we can trace a progression from Mary Ann Stodart's argument that Sappho's work is the Ur-text of women's poetry, through to Swinburne's later assertion that Sappho's is the finest of all poetry. In her *Female Writers: Thoughts on Their Proper Sphere and on Their Powers of Usefulness* Stodart writes:

> We have but few remains of the earliest and best Greek poetesses: or her who earned the high title of the Lesbian muse; but those remains 'more golden than gold', are all breathings from the dearest affections of the heart.

Swinburne follows her lead:

> Judging even from the mutilated fragments fallen within our reach from the broken altar of her sacrifice of song, I for one have always agreed with all Grecian tradition in thinking Sappho to be beyond all question and comparison *the very greatest poet that ever lived.*[7]

Sappho is the essence of poet. Of course this says more about Swinburne and contemporary attitudes to poetry – and to women – than it can about her. But then this is part of the problem with Sappho and all the fictions of Sappho. For most of the nineteenth century the main body of daughter-texts by women poets descend not from the authentic writings of the real Sappho, but from the imposter phantoms that throng into the spaces between the fragments of her text and her story. From the few scraps of 'Testimonia' in the Classical sources that gave (true or false) stories of Sappho there are a number of specific tropes that attracted her nineteenth century successors. All of these cluster around the (true or false) moment when Sappho makes herself into the picture of living art as she improvises her farewell song to art and love, before leaping off the Leucadian rock into the sea. This moment encompasses ideas which appear again and again in Victorian women's poetry: the woman poet as art object; her artless, improvising performance; the leap into space which expresses her abandon; the nothingness and absence which follow her self-immolation; and the farewell song, the text which represents her only remains.

The picture of Sappho

As I have explained in Chapter 3, Sappho was a popular subject for painters and sculptors of the Romantic period and, perhaps not surprisingly, the poems on Sappho written by women early in the nineteenth century focus not on any imagined 'real' woman, but on her invented portrait. When Felicia Hemans published her poem 'The Last Song of Sappho' she introduced it with a reference to a sketch by 'the younger Westmacott' and so made it clear that the voice in her poem is that of the deserted, soon-to-be-dead Sappho.[8] L.E.L.'s poem 'Sappho's Song' follows the same pattern, except that it is slightly more complicated in that the picture that accompanies the poem has been – we are to suppose – painted by the Improvisatrice herself. The popular association of painting and poetry, in part promoted by the illustrated annuals of the time, dictates the opening scenes of *The Improvisatrice* where the poet-painter heroine describes her early canvases which themselves sketch out the story of her own fate told in the poem. The first of her pictures shows Petrarch, separated from Laura. Her second picture, however, blends the poet-subject and the muse-object:

> My next was of a minstrel too,
> Who proved what woman's hand might do,
> When, true to the heart pulse, it woke
> The harp. Her head was bending down,
> As if in weariness, and near,
> But unworn, was a laurel crown.
> She was not beautiful, if bloom
> And smiles form beauty; for, like death,
> Her brow was ghastly; and her lip
> Was parched, as if fever were its breath.
> There was a shade upon her dark,
> Large, floating eyes, as if each spark
> Of minstrel ecstasy was fled,
> Yet leaving them no tears to shed;
> Fixed in their hopelessness of care,
> And reckless in their great despair.
> She sat beneath a cypress tree ...
>
> I deemed, that of lyre, life and love
> She was a long, last farewell taking; –
> That, from her pale parched lips,
> Her latest, wildest song was breaking.

And then follows 'Sappho's Song' enacted by the Improvisatrice, enacted by L.E.L., so that the pictures here multiply and reflect on each other:

> SAPPHO'S SONG,
> Farewell, my lute! – and would that I
> Had never waked thy burning chords!
> Poison has been upon thy sigh,
> And fever has breathed in thy words.
>
> Yet wherefore, wherefore should I blame
> Thy power, thy spell, my gentlest lute?
> I should have been the wretch I am,
> Had every chord of thine been mute.
>
> It was my evil star above,
> Not my sweet lute, that wrought me wrong;
> It was not song that taught me love,
> But it was love that taught me song.

If song be past, and hope undone,
And pulse, and head, and heart, are flame;
It is thy work, thou faithless one!
But, no! – I will not name thy name!

Sun-god! lute, wreath are vowed to thee!
Long be their light upon my grave –
My glorious grave – yon deep blue sea:
I shall sleep calm beneath its wave![9]

Caroline Norton's poem 'The Picture of Sappho' might well have been, like Hemans's, based on Westmacott's sketch or indeed on any one of the many other famous pictorial Sapphos produced in the early years of the nineteenth century in a tradition with which she seems to be familiar. But in this case, Norton writes herself into the poem as the viewer of that picture, and she questions its likeness to 'life':

I

Thou! Whose impassion'd face
The Painter loves to trace,
Theme of the Sculptor's art and Poet's story –
How many a wand'ring thought
Thy loveliness hath brought,
Warming the heart with its imagined glory!

II

Yet, was it History's truth,
That tale of wasted youth,
Of endless grief, and Love forsaken pining?
What wert thou, thou whose woe
The old traditions show
With Fame's cold light around thee vainly shining?

And the American poet Elizabeth J. Eames took up a similar position in her poem 'On the Picture of a Departed Poetess' which begins: 'This still, clear radiant face! doth it resemble/ In each fair faultless lineament thine own?'[10]

These poets know about representation and construction. The painter, the sculptor and the poet make and re-make the image of the woman. The woman poet herself then reproduces that image for her own purposes, but she questions its historical veracity and its likeness to life. The slide from fact to fiction and back again to measuring against fact, suggests the ways in which these writers recognised the temptations of the motherless poet. When you only have one ancestor, and that ancestor is part speculation and part myth, the anxiety which results makes the axis for many a Sappho poem.

Christina Rossetti, who so often takes up and refines the subjects of her contemporaries, wrote two poems specifically about Sappho, as well as many where Sappho is not named, but where similar themes are re-worked. 'A Study (A Soul)' suggests the posed image of the woman as art object – ' She stands as pale as Parian statues stand' – and her longer poem '"Reflection"' implies through its ambiguous title, a sophisticated version of the later woman poet who looks and questions and puzzles over the image of her own self who is at the same time her ancestor. This other woman who gazes 'through her chamber window' belongs to the speaker, is part of the speaker – 'my soul's dear soul' – and yet she 'never answers' the speaker to whom she presents a mystery: 'Who can guess or read the spirit/ Shrined within her eyes?' In the end, the speaker allows her vision to die into an art object though it still provokes her curiosity.

I will give her stately burial,
Tho', when she lies dead:
For dear memory of the past time,
Of her royal head,
Of the much I strove and said.

I will give her stately burial,
Willow branches bent:
Have her carved in alabaster,
As she dreamed and leant
While I wondered what she meant.[11]

Most convincing readings of this poem place it within a courtly love tradition, making the speaker male.[12] Certainly Rossetti's speaker here, like any male voyeur, kills the woman-object of her gaze into art, and it is right to situate this poem in the long pattern of gaze narratives which runs from Chaucer's *Book of the Duchess* to Adrienne Rich's ironic reverie on the theme:

When to her lute Corinna sings
neither words nor music are her own;
only the long hair dipping
over her cheek, only the song
of silk against her knees
and these
adjusted in reflections of an eye.[13]

But there is nothing in Rossetti's poem to suggest that the sex of the speaker is definitely male, and the frequency with which Victorian women wrote poems about pictures of *other women poets* makes it possible to read '"Reflection"' as a poem addressed to that entrancing but troubling icon. That the 'gazing' is done twice over, by both the speaker who looks at the woman, and the woman herself who looks elsewhere, also implies an identification between the speaker-subject and the woman-object. The poem begins: 'Gazing through her chamber window/ Sits my soul's dear soul ...' So this suggests a self who gazes through the window which is the eye of the soul. And the reiteration never lets up; the next three lines all start with the word 'Looking', and the third stanza repeats 'Gazing gazing still'.

Then there's the title. '"Reflection"' is in inverted commas which hints in typographical terms at the repetitions we should perceive: the double of one woman reflecting on another; the double of the mirror image; the double of the self who analyses the self; the double sets of quotation marks so that we cannot know who speaks the poem. If the one-word title is a typical Rossetti pun, then the punctuation is a pun too. That the title of the poem was 'Day-Dreams' in the first draft manuscript and in the 1896 and 1904 editions reinforces the suggestion that this is a poem about poetic ambition and the models available to the woman poet.[14]

Abandoned women

These images of the looked-at woman poet include questions about and criticisms of assumptions of sexual difference.[15] Rossetti's mysterious image may be a cool puzzle to the viewer, but the more usual Sappho picture is set at the moment of her most intense distress, at the moment when she is indeed 'abandoned'. Here she is exposed, her dress slips to reveal her breast, she is ecstatic, vulnerable, about to leap into space and 'die'. The viewer can do what he likes with her. That's what she is there for. Scarpia certainly thinks so; Phaon does too, and Lord Nelvil in *Corinne*. As Lawrence Lipking puts it, 'The woman forgets herself, the man's attention is pricked.'[16]

But the Victorian women poets are often sophisticated critics of the 'male gaze', partly because they do it so well themselves. When they picture the image of Sappho they too succumb to the lure of the gaze and admit the excitement offered by the image. But they are excited as much as anything because this is a titillating picture of themselves. It is the picture of their own image that they desire and get, with all the paradoxes and difficulties that result. This self-conscious looking at the self looking at Sappho who is, and is not, a self-portrait, overlaps into how the woman poet, quite literally, presented herself, dressed herself. Either she could acquiesce in the masquerade – like Caroline Norton, L.E.L. and Eliza Cook who all at times adopted the fashion for hair bound up in ribbons à la Sappho. Or she could resist the idealised picture of the poetess –

like Christina Rossetti who put herself down as a 'fat poetess' looking distinctly 'incongruous especially when seated by [t]he grave of buried hope'.[17]

The trouble is that in the process of being made into a picture at the point of suicide, this Sappho is twice dead. She is admired at the threshold of self-extinction because she will shortly die, and then she is frozen into the necessity of that imminent death as an art-object.

This is the story traced in Landon's 'A History of the Lyre'. The speaker first sees the poet Eulalie among the ruins of a lost civilisation:

> We stood beside a cypress, whose green spire
> Rose like a funeral column o'er the dead.
> Near was a fallen palace – stain'd and gray
> The marble show'd amid the tender leaves
> Of ivy but just shooting; yet there stood
> Pillars unbroken, two or three vast halls,
> Entire enough to cast a deep black shade;
> And a few statues, beautiful but cold, –
> White shadows, pale and motionless, that seem
> To mock the change in which they had no part, –
> Fit images of the dead.

At the end of the poem Eulalie dies, as prophesised by this first vision, but not before she has commissioned the statue which will be her monument:

> ... and in the midst
> A large old cypress stood, beneath whose shade
> There was a sculptured form; the feet were placed
> Upon a finely-carved rose wreath; the arms
> Were raised to Heaven, as if to clasp the stars
> EULALIA leant beside; 'twas hard to say
> Which was the actual marble ...[18]

As the poem ends even L.E.L., in the persona of her speaker, seems to perceive the problematic situation for the woman poet who is indistinguishable from the object which she has made of herself. 'Peace to the weary and the beating heart,/ That fed upon itself!', are the last lines of the poem. It may be that Elizabeth Barrett Browning had Eulalie's fate in mind when she re-cast it in *Aurora Leigh*. In Book II she exposes the sexualised assumptions of difference which the beautiful image of the performing woman poet so dangerously courts:

> I drew a wreath
> Drenched, blinding me with dew, across my brow,

And fastening it behind so, turned and faced
.. My public! – cousin Romney – with a mouth
Twice graver than his eyes.
                                        I stood there fixed, –
My arms up, like the caryatid, sole
Of some abolished temple, helplessly
Persistant in a gesture which derides
A former purpose.[19]

Barrett Browning clearly saw that the Sappho/Corinne/Eulalie poems written by her forerunners had had a 'purpose', but that its paradoxes made it an 'abolished temple'. Like the haunting images which accrue around the picture of Aurora's mother painted after she was dead (*Aurora Leigh*, Book I, lines 128–63) – as Sappho's image too must always portray a corpse – Barrett Browning argues that while such mementoes of the dead can always provide fruitful metaphors for the imagination, they can never represent the living woman.

Last songs

Many of the earliest Sappho poems of the period make a point of reproducing the poet's performance. Hemans's poem 'The Last Song of Sappho', Landon's 'Sappho's Song' and Rossetti's 'Sappho' all aim to give the (supposed) actual words in the mouth of the ancient poet in the process of utterance. The authenticity of this expression of woman's experience is partly guaranteed by the improvised, immediate and urgent sense of the poem happening now, in process.

It is a problematic strategy. Certainly it gives Sappho a voice and makes her speak out, as if alive again. In Hemans's related poem 'Corinne at the Capitol' she makes a parade of the performance happening – as it were – before our very eyes by using the present tense throughout and by repeating 'now': 'Now thou tread'st the ascending road'; 'Thou hast gained the summit now'; 'Now afar it rolls – it dies –/ And thy voice is heard to rise'; 'All the spirit of thy sky/ Now hath lit thy large dark eye'; 'Now thy living wreath is won'. As if to further emphasise the living presence of Corinne in performance, Hemans contrasts her heroine with the dead things of the past around her:

While from tombs of heroes borne,
From the dust of empire shorn,
Flowers upon thy graceful head ...

Hemans celebrates the demise of the old rule and projects the vitality of the new. That Hemans ends this poem with a brief moral on the virtues of hearth and home is really irrelevant because it comes altogether too late in the wake of this glittering vision. In another Sappho-related poem, 'To a Wandering

Singer', she also conjures up the immediacy of the poet's performance, but this time makes herself the audience who listens to and interprets the poet's song, reading therein her recorded distress: 'I know it by thy song.'[20]

If the project to re-animate Sappho by singing her song for her is a positive one of recuperation, it is also an awkward one, always threatening to dwindle into ventriloquism. This danger is one which Rossetti's two Sappho poems acknowledge. Her 'Sappho' is, in part, one of the 'last songs' posed on the clifftop, but, as Leighton has explained, it also prophesies and enacts a performance set beyond death, on the other side of the grave.[21] Using a technique which is trademark Rossetti, repetition evokes the blankness of death in life, and a series of negatives mark out the imagined afterlife where the dead speaker is still capable of speech.

Even more explicitly, Rossetti's 1848 poem 'What Sappho would have said had her leap cured instead of killing her' acknowledges its task, however teasingly, of putting words into a dead woman's mouth. And of what does this cured Sappho sing? A song of rest certainly, for she is grateful for the pause, having been suffering, singing and leaping for some 2500 years.

> I would have quiet too in truth,
> And here will sojourn for a while.
> Lo; I have wandered many a mile,
> Till I am footsore in my youth.
> I will lie down; and quite forget
> The doubts and fears that haunt me yet.

And yet this Sappho, who is supposed to be dead, still will not lie down. This ghost who haunts all her followers is herself haunted by the burning memory of what she has been. Being 'cured' is nothing if it means that Sappho – the sign, the ultimate icon of suffering in love – is empty and has rubbed out the essence of her selfhood:

> Ah, would that it could reach my heart,
> And fill the void that is so dry
> And aches and aches; – but what am I
> To shrink from my self-purchased part?
> It is in vain; is all in vain;
> I must go forth and bear my pain.

Calling upon 'Love', this 'cured' Sappho asks to be herself once more: 'Oh come again, thou pain divine,/ Fill me and make me wholly thine.'

Rossetti recognises here that this art-object Sappho, the puppet speaker, can only be animated by the co-operative imagination of another. There is no real

Sappho, there are hardly any poems, there are only a few fragments of evidence. But there are still the performances when she comes alive again under pressure of the pose, the leap, the loss.

But the great days of the *improvisatrice* were gone by the middle of the nineteenth century, and Sappho had passed into another related form where she could continue her performance – opera. The women poets seem to have recognised the succession and endorsed the displacement. Barrett Browning's Aurora Leigh, for instance, is not a performer on the Sappho model. She improvises a poem-in-process certainly, but it is a private written document offered for the edification of the reader and the poet-narrator herself. It is an internal drama composed by an author who 'will write no plays' (Book V, line 267) but who will 'take for worthier stage the soul itself' (Book V, line 340). More than this, Aurora consciously refuses to perform 'woman', to become a collectable art-object for Lord Eglinton, who wants her primarily as an adornment for his home, and directs him instead to the actress, the dancer, or the opera singer (Book V, lines 898–909). George Eliot picks up the same thread with *Armgart*. Her work is a verse-drama, but her heroine is an opera singer whom we never see perform. Instead, her off-stage triumph is related by her teacher who – like the man who proposes to her – wants to possess her, to add her to his collection. We are back with the idea of the spectacle, and neither of these women poets likes the view.[22]

Posing the fall

Elizabeth Barrett Browning had seen the problem in her 1844 poem 'A Vision of Poets'. Sappho is the only woman poet to appear there and the vision of her is not unequivocally glorious:

> And Sappho, with that gloriole
>
> Of ebon hair on calméd brows
> O poet-woman! None foregoes
> The leap, attaining the repose.[23]

The 'repose' here is both the serenity which allows the woman poet to write, the confidence which allows her to perform, as well as the 're-pose', the pose of that performance which is endlessly repeated by the other women who are Sappho's successors. No sooner does Barrett Browning think of Sappho than she thinks of all the other women poets who follow her – including herself. And the price for this re-posing is the leap, and the fall. The leap of feeling that throws itself at life and self-expression; the leap of daring and risk that challenges conventions of containment; the leap of desperation and despair that wipes out the self thrust into empty space.

From Lucifer to *Rebel without a Cause*, from Jane Austen's *Persuasion* to François Trauffaut's *Jules et Jim*, the fall, the leap, the plunge, suggests a set of metaphors to do with pride, display, self-promotion, rebellion, punishment and dissolution. In the nineteenth century, 'fallen woman' meant something quite different from fallen angel. As I have explained in Chapter 3 on the pictures of Sappho, 'Found Drowned' had become such a recognisable cliché in the London and Paris of mid-century that G.F. Watts's 1848 painting of that name needed no further gloss to encourage the audience to speculate on the manner of this woman's life and the explanation for her suicidal jump. How could the women poets not look at Sappho's leap and remember all of this? How could they not recall that their nearest bold ancestor, Mary Wollstonecraft herself, had once emulated Sappho – as well as all those anonymous women who leapt into the Thames?

Barrett Browning knew very well that Sappho's leap meant much more than a pedant's quibble over fact or fiction. Even scholarly writers of the time inadvertently betray their own censorious attitudes to Sappho and her kind. In his monumental textbook *A Critical History of the Language and Literature of Ancient Greece* (1850) William Mure devotes several pages to the story of Sappho's plunge and to the phenomenon of the 'Lover's Leap' in general, and decides in favour of the tale on the grounds that 'a female of her temperament and habits' and suffering from an unrequited passion, would be highly likely to throw herself off a cliff. He goes on to list the historic reasons for the practice, whether voluntary or not. They are: punishment, sacrifice and remedy.

The first two are obvious, and fit with Victorian meanings given to the Leap. The third, he explains, works by way of a transition from passion to reason. 'The revulsion of feeling and temperament consequent on the plunge, the terror, and the excitement of the whole ceremony, would be such as to banish the dominant passion from the breast, and to give place to the sway of reason or other counteracting influences.'[24] Assuming of course that the leaper survived.

Mure's language here, albeit coded, makes it clear that the spectacle of Sappho's leap is itself a substitute for the scene which she is denied and which Victorian sensibility would not allow to be depicted: the scene of erotic consummation. He wasn't the only Victorian to see it this way. Writing about 'the girls who leap into space' Catherine Clément quotes a passage from Søren Kierkegaard's *Diary of a Seducer*:

> For a girl infinity is as natural as the idea that all love must be happy. Everywhere a girl turns she finds infinity surrounding her, and she is able to jump into it; her leaping is feminine and not masculine ... her jump is a gliding flight. And when she reaches the other side she finds that, instead of being exhausted by the effort, she is more beautiful than ever, even more full of soul. She throws a kiss to those of us who remained behind. Young, newborn, like a flower growing from mountain roots, she sways over the abyss until we are almost dizzy.[25]

Here is Sappho again, posing, performing, leaping, being watched. But Clément is impatient with Kierkegaard's pretty story and wants to call things by their names. '[She] does everything he wants. She jumps; she jumps again, keeps jumping until the final leap. Oh you do veil it with modest names. She fucks. And your hero ditches her.'[26] Leaping into space is one thing. Ending in a ditch is quite another. But is that not where the abandoned woman, the fallen woman must end? Either in a ditch, or drowned, which is what happens to Sappho. And what might happen to the many daughter-heroines portrayed by the Victorian women poets. L.E.L.'s Sappho says 'it was love that taught me song' hinting that sexual experience and textual expression go together, both parts of the erotic display which exposes the body and recognises desire. There is no separation here between the process of writing/singing/performing, and the imperatives of self-expression written through the body.[27] Once read like this, Hemans's moral at the end of 'Corinne at the Capitol' is curiously prohibitive in its sexual implications. Her conclusion 'Happier, happier far than thou/ ... She that makes the humblest hearth/ Lovely but to *one* on earth' (my emphasis) suggestively condemns the woman poet who exposes herself, not to one, but to many. Perhaps this also explains Barrett Browning's decision later in the century to make her poet-heroine resolutely blameless and virgin even though she allows Aurora to champion the cause of the fallen woman by taking up with Marian Erle.

But Sappho's leap is not just a fall. It is also brave. When Sappho leaps, she flies, she risks herself and she escapes the cage. Again, the image of the bird, caged or free, runs as a metaphor for female containment or release from Mary Wollstonecraft's *Vindication of the Rights of Woman* to Angela Carter's *Nights at the Circus*. This is what Sappho does with her performance, this is what the *improvisatrice* does, along with the woman poet and the diva. In Clément's words, 'with her own death she will make singing's most symbolic gesture. Floria Tosca hurls herself from the top of the ramparts ... "Look look how I can fly".'[28] Feminist theory has proposed the connections between flying and writing, between sexual and textual expression, but the Victorian women poets anticipated the image. Hemans, for instance, puts this 'flight' into 'A Parting Song' where the speaker is a Corinne figure and one 'For whom 'tis well to be fled and gone –/ As of a bird from a chain unbound'. And in her 'The Last Song of Sappho' she actually has her Sappho looking at the seabirds wheeling round the cliff and following their example:

> I, with this winged nature fraught,
> These visions wildly free,
> This boundless love, this fiery thought –
> *Alone* I come – oh! give me peace dark Sea!

And after the fall, after the leap, what is left? Nothing. Silence. Empty space, and the song fading into silence. Hemans's Sappho will have 'peace', and so shall we. L.E.L.'s Sappho will 'sleep calm', Rossetti's will be 'unconscious' and 'forgetful of forgetfulness'.

But then there wasn't much there in the first place. By definition, a 'last song of Sappho' is only about itself and only lasts for the length of the performance. Once she is gone, it's all over. That is why Lawrence Lipking calls the song of the woman poet derived from Sappho via Ovid's *Heroides* an 'anti-epic': 'No action ensues. No plot ever reaches an end. Instead one love-letter follows another, and each is full of tears.' This is why Catherine Clément describes Tatiana in Tchaikovsky's version of Pushkin's *Eugene Onegin* as a 'woman poet'. Because she writes a letter-poem which is about nothing, nothing except herself and her focussed but inchoate desire. When the voice stops, the body disappears. When she stops singing, when she makes the leap, whether shameful or glorious, Sappho kills herself.[29]

Elisabeth Bronfen argues that the act of suicide by a woman can be read as a 'communicative act', a performance, a self-authored text where the woman takes control of her story which is otherwise denied her in her particular cultural or familial position. Clarissa, composing herself in death, is a case in point. Bronfen further suggests that 'the representation of a woman killing herself in order to produce an autobiographical text can serve as a trope for the relation of the writing process to death in general', and that the 'choice of death emerges as a feminine strategy with which writing with the body is a way of getting rid of the oppression connected with the feminine body'.

In the case of Victorian women's Sappho poems the argument is persuasive. Their Sappho dies, but writes in the process. She only writes in fact – composes a 'last song' – *because* she dies. Hence the attraction of the subject for women writers at a period when their own authority as writers, their own permission to write, could not be taken for granted. By writing Sappho's autobiographical lament they are permitted to write, even if they kill her (and themselves) every time. They also reassure themselves about their own literary survival. As the woman poet died, but is remembered in her song, so they too will own remains in the poem.

Bronfen quotes Michael Ryan's suggestion that death offers 'the possibility of an absolute alterity', a 'passage into otherness' which has a literary analogy where the writing process promotes this 'otherness' or alterity by splitting the self into subject-writer and object-text.[30] When death is suicide there is another stage still: for this passage to otherness ambivalently makes the writer simultaneously subject and object like her text. The suicide is poised between 'self-construction and self-destruction'. In annihilating the body in order to make the story of that body, the self is the subject-writer who creates an object-text, and at the same time makes a subject-text where that self can speak out of the object-self who has been reduced to the thing looked at by the text.

When a woman poet writes an autobiographical poem for another woman poet the sense of 'otherness' in writing is further complicated. Paradoxically, while the woman poet doubles herself by imagining a second woman poet, she also diminishes herself by splitting her consciousness which has to be shared with that other. Furthermore, if the suicide triumphs by constructing a new self out of self-destruction, the woman poet who retrieves and rehearses that other simultaneously celebrates the successful self-creation of the first and original woman poet while she yet destroys her own self. She hurls herself into space, makes herself into a void to be filled up with Sappho's translated fragments, denies her own subjectivity and speaks words which belong to another. It is not Sappho who is the puppet now, but the daughter-descendant made in her image who ventriloquises the song that Sappho throws her. There is an anxiety of self-destruction in many of these 'last songs'. Each time the woman poet takes Sappho as a subject she courts self-annihilation, and not just in the time of the poem-in-process, but for all time. When the woman poet writes Sappho's text it may be that she is being written off. The shadow of this particular precursor looms large and threatening, and yet these women poets risk self-destruction by re-affirming her even though they know her resurrection means their own dissolution. This is what worried Mary Robinson when she set out to impersonate Sappho in 1796. 'The merit of her compositions', she wrote, 'must have been indisputable, to have left all contemporary female writers in obscurity.'[31] Every time a woman writes 'Sappho's Last Song' she skirts suicide, literally deconstructing herself in allowing herself to be absorbed into the mother-poet who is original and singular.

Yet in Victorian society this will-to-disappear may be as much a strategy of self-protection as self-mutilation. Putting the self on display results in subjection, possession and objectification as art-object. Willing the self to expression in performance results in sexual exploitation and silence. When a Victorian woman poet wills herself to death by covering her 'real' self with a borrowed mask she may well be choosing that textual suicide as a way, in Bronfen's words, 'of getting rid of the oppression connected with the feminine body'. It is hardly surprising that the one early nineteenth century poet who really did commit suicide – Letitia Landon in 1838 – is also the one who most consistently invoked and impersonated (and was impersonated by) the ideal of Sappho. In life, L.E.L. was punished by society for her display. John Forster broke off his engagement to her on the grounds of some sexual impropriety, she married an entirely unsuitable man, the governor of a slave-trading post on the Gold Coast of Africa, and she left England for good. In literature, she sang songs for others not herself – for Eulalie, for the Improvisatrice and for Corinne. And when both life and writing were over, her contemporaries wrote songs for her, just as they wrote them for Sappho.

Monuments, memorials and remains

The 'last songs' of the Victorian women poets are funerary monuments, they are suicide notes attached to the corpse of the poet, they are souvenirs and mourning mementoes. But they are also love songs. Like Barthes's love letters these songs are empty except for the one message, 'I am thinking of you.' And that reiterated message is only necessary at all because this thinking is 'blank'.

The lover is in danger of forgetting the beloved. She does forget her. And then she recalls and remembers her. As Barthes says, 'I do not think *you*; I simply make you recur (to the very degree that I forget you).'[32] The recalled songs of Sappho and Corinne are often farewells that include an injunction to remember, or to forget. Ostensibly they may be addressed reproachfully to the lover who has injured her. But in fact the audience they address is the audience who is writing the poems – the other women poets who inherit Sappho. Hemans's 'A Parting Song' begins with an epigraph from de Stael's *Corinne* which is taken up in the refrain of the song: 'When will ye think of me, my friends?' Apart from her named Sappho poems, L.E.L. wrote two short farewell poems, 'Song' ('Farewell! and never think of me/ In lighted hall or lady's bower'), and 'The Farewell'. Each of these poems literally remembers the woman poet, puts her real presence back on stage, whether it is a constructed character or the writer herself.

That these 'farewell, remember me' songs imply an interested audience is not surprising. They had one. For these women poets were writing for and to each other. This became especially apparent when L.E.L. assumed Sappho's role of poet-suicide. Elizabeth Barrett wrote a 'memory song' for L.E.L. when she took the words from the mouth of the poet – 'Do you think of me, as I think of you?' – and turned them into a voiced poem in her 'L.E.L.'s Last Question'. Then Christina Rossetti took one line from Barrett Browning's poem about L.E.L. – 'One thirsty for a little love' – and remade it into a new line – 'Whose heart was breaking for a little love' – and that became the epigraph and occasion for Rossetti's own poem called 'L.E.L.'[33]

These memory love-letter poems throw a powerful sidelight on all Rossetti's many farewell poems. Her well-known 'Song' ('When I am dead my dearest') takes on quite another significance if it is put into the pattern of the woman poet singing Sappho's 'last song', for it becomes about that very tradition.

When I am dead, my dearest,
Sing no sad songs for me;
Plant thou no roses at my head,
Nor shady cypress tree:
Be the green grass above me

With showers and dewdrops wet;
And if thou wilt, remember,
And if thou wilt, forget.

I shall not see the shadows,
I shall not feel the rain;
I shall not hear the nightingale
Sing on, as if in pain:
And dreaming through the twilight
That doth not rise nor set,
Haply I may remember,
And haply may forget.[34]

With a typical swerve Rossetti utters the injunction not to sing even as she contradicts it and does begin to sing a new 'sad song'. Here is the woman poet singing yet another of Sappho's 'last songs'. The cypress tree is borrowed from Eulalie's stage set, the dissolved self made into a blank ('I shall not see the shadows') is the empty space where Sappho disappears. The song which the woman poet sings is the familiar one where Sappho is associated with the nightingale who sings 'as if in pain'. And the alternate and haphazard remembering and forgetting is done by both the audience of woman poets to whom she addresses herself, and by the woman poet herself who may, or may not, write poems which remember Sappho or any other woman poet.

Whatever else happened within the tradition of Sappho poems in the nineteenth century it is clear that Sappho – sometimes threatening, sometimes empowering – represented a powerful Muse figure for the Victorian women poets, a Muse figure that was perennially interesting because she was so much about their own selves and their own projects. Even when a poet seems to resist all the persuasions of the glorious-Sappho myth, she can't help hoping for a new beginning.

Armgart, for instance, loses out altogether. Punished for her ambition, cured of her pride, she loses her voice and can no longer sing. But what does she do at the end of George Eliot's verse drama? She retires into obscurity to teach girls – presumably girls – to sing. Like Sappho, she becomes a guide and teacher and gathers disciples around her. It is a humble end to a brilliant career. And yet it is not quite the end. Others will follow.

Sappho resurrected

Nor is it the end of Sappho's Victorian story. For most of the nineteenth century in Britain and in France, though there were a number of editions and translations to be had, it was the *myths* of Sappho that had most influence. But in Germany scholars were at work producing new editions and commentaries on the recorded works of Sappho. Of these contributions the works of Volger (1810), Welcker (1816) and Neue (1827) were all, for different reasons, critically significant. But it was the painstaking work of Theodor Bergk in his *Anthologia Lyrica* (1854) and his *Poetae Lyrici Graeci* (1882) that provided an accurate (as far as possible) and (for the time) up-to-date edition of the poems and fragments.[35] Bergk's work encouraged the English scholar Henry Thornton Wharton to prepare an English translation of Sappho and this appeared as *Sappho: Memoir, Text, Selected Renderings with a Literal Translation* in 1885. This edition, which took Bergk's Greek as its text for the poems, was highly influential: it dismissed the web of myths around Phaon and the Leucadian leap; it made claims for Sappho's importance as the first lyric poet; it established a standard for English translations; it quietly reproduced Bergk's feminine pronouns; and it persuasively argued for the resilience of her poetic model throughout English literature. And there was more to come. By the time Wharton published a second edition only two years later in 1887 his text had already changed and Sappho had started to reappear.[36]

During the 1880s and 1890s new archaeological interest in Egyptian antiquities, combined with a newly 'scientific' approach to excavation, meant that Sappho's body of work began to be reconstituted. Many of the very earliest records of Sappho's poems had been written on papyrus, a form of paper made from reeds. But a piece of paper has many uses and if the words were not valued, then the object that bore them was. Tombs and rubbish heaps were excavated and scraps of papyrus discovered, scraps with words written on them. And among them, Sappho's words, or at least versions thereof.[37]

The women poets of the nineteenth century had not been entirely excluded from Greek scholarship in spite of lack of opportunity and in spite of George Eliot's Dorothea being given to understand by Casaubon that Greek accents were beyond a woman's understanding (*Middlemarch*, Book I, chapter 7). Elizabeth Barrett Browning managed, and so did George Eliot herself. And by the end of the century the younger generation, agitating for education and independent lives, regularly nurtured Classical ambitions. Among these young New Women none were more directly affected by the resurgent Sappho than Katharine Bradley and Edith Cooper, 'Michael Field' to their public, 'the Fields' to their friends.[38]

Directly out of Wharton's book Michael Field made a new Sappho in their own *Long Ago* (1889). Like all their predecessors – L.E.L., Hemans, Barrett Browning, Rossetti – they also make the book and their revision of the 'last song' out of their own experience as poets, as women, and as lovers. But their changed circumstances, and changes in the circumstances of the time, meant that this same set of experiences were radically altered. For a start, they wrote in collaboration, so that there was none of the lonely Romantic hero mode that marks the early nineteenth century idea of Sappho and the woman poet. Then they wrote – by deliberate choice – not as women who performed to be slavered over by the male spectator, but as a man and an equal, under the pseudonym of Michael Field.[39] And finally, though they wrote as lovers, just like L.E.L. and her kind, they certainly didn't have the same problems of heterosexual assumption because they wrote as lesbian lovers, subject and object both, and both together.

In *Long Ago* Bradley and Cooper take first lines or tiny fragments of Sappho's Greek text – following Bergk and Wharton – and then extrapolate their own poem out of that. In effect, they improvise.

> Δεῦρο δηῦτε Μοῖσαι, χρύσιον λίποισαι.
>
> Hither now, Muses! Leaving golden seats,
> Hither! Forsake the fresh, inspiring wells,
> Flee the high mountain lands, the cool retreats
> Where in the temperate air your influence dwells,
> Leave your sweet haunts of summer sound and rest,
> Hither, O maiden choir, and make me blest.

This is the first poem in Field's *Long Ago* although, strictly it functions rather as an epigraph or invocation as it comes after the preface and before the poem numbered '1'. Like all the verses, it starts with a Greek quotation which may, or may not, then be translated in the first line of Field's version. In this case it is, for Wharton's literal translation of the Greek fragment is 'Hither now, muses, leaving golden …'

The ellipses are suggestive. Into this space the Fields insert their poem, making a continuum between the ancient Greek and the nineteenth century English where the one slides easily into the other and the original Sappho is revised by a disciple who mimics her scenes and her phrases. In this case the vocabulary and the tone is borrowed from the two pieces of the Sappho poem now known as Fragment 2, and which Wharton included as poems 4 and 5 in his edition. This poem has only been available in a complete(ish) form since 1937 when Medea Norsa published her transcription from a third century BC potsherd excavated in Egypt. In the nineteenth century only the second and fourth stanzas were known, the text being derived from quotations found in Hermogenes and Athenaeus.[40] All the same, then and since, scholars have recognised that this invocation – which is addressed to Aphrodite in the original – provides the essentials of the Sapphic scene. The natural landscape in Fragment 2 is relished in a frank and uninhibited way by Sappho's speaker. There is, as Richard Jenkyns says, nothing 'bookish' here.[41]

Cooper and Bradley return to this landscape in many of the poems in *Long Ago*. Not for them any dramatic posing on the clifftop. Here instead is a feminised place of springs and woods and hidden places, obscurely libidinous and seductive.

XLIII

'Αμφὶ δὲ [ὕδωρ] ψῦρον κελάδει δι' ὔσδων
μαλίνων, αἰθυσσομένων δέ φύλλων
κῶμα καταρρεῖ.

Cool water gurgles through
The apple-boughs, and sleep
Falls from the flickering leaves,
Where hoary shadows keep
Secluded from man's view
A little cave that cleaves
The rock with fissure deep.[42]

In tone and style, in its choice of location and its address to women, in the very fact that this is the first time any actual *Greek* appears in a woman's poem (as opposed to the numerous epigraphs in French borrowed from de Stael), Michael Field's *Long Ago* consciously attempts an authentic 'last song' of Sappho; one that is true to her atmosphere and themes even while it is still a pastiche. The book even re-works the old 'picture of Sappho' problem by offering as illustration, not the abandoned *déshabillé* of the art-object, but two historical artefacts. An 'archaic head of Sappho … taken from a nearly contemporary vase, inscribed with her name' is reproduced on the cover of *Long Ago*, and the frontispiece is 'from a figure of Sappho, seated and reading, on a vase in the museum at Athens'.[43] The very presentation of the book itself conspires to make this Sappho 'real', for it is printed in red (for the Greek) and black (for the English) on thick handmade paper and bound with vellum.

In reconstructing their 'authoritative' Sappho, the Fields were assisted by Greek scholars, historians and other learned men. The Fields cite Wharton and Bergk and 'Mr Murray at the British Museum', but they were also friendly with John Addington Symonds who recommended his own *Studies of the Greek Poets* (1873) to Edith Cooper.[44] And Cooper was not the only attractive young poet befriended by Symonds. When Agnes Mary Robinson (later Darmesteter, later Duclaux) published her first volume *A Handful of Honeysuckle* in 1878 Symonds wrote to congratulate her and soon began a correspondence in which all things Greek, including Sappho, were discussed.[45]

Agnes Mary Robinson did not then, like Michael Field, go on to re-produce Sappho, but her poetry shows clear signs that she knew the work through her own studies in Greek, and that she was influenced by the tone, the brevity, and the nuances in the extant works of Sappho. The subtle influence runs throughout her work. For instance, in the poem 'Love Without Wings (Eight Songs)' we are given a series of short lyrics which work on the Sapphic themes of art, love, desire and the memory of desire which read like a meditation on a selection of Sappho's fragments:

I.

I thought: no more the worst endures!
   I die, I end the strife, –
You swiftly took my hands in yours
   And drew me back to life!

II.

We sat when shadows darken,
   And let the shadows be:
Each was a soul to hearken,
   Devoid of eyes to see.

You came at dusk to find me;
   I knew you well enough …
O lights that dazzle and blind me –
   It is no friend, but Love!

III.

How is it possible
   You should forget me,
Leave me for ever
   And never regret me!

I was the soul of you,
   Past love or loathing,
Lost in the whole of you …
   Now, am I nothing?

IV.

The fallen oak still keeps its yellow leaves
   But all its growth is o'er!
So, at your name, my heart still beats and grieves
   Although I love no more.

V.

And so I shall meet you
   Again, my dear;
How shall I greet you?
   What shall I hear?

I, you forgot!
   (But who shall say
You loved me not
   – Yesterday?) …[46]

Another late Victorian woman poet clearly influenced by the scholarly reconstituting of Sappho's text rather than the myths of Sappho's life is Mary Coleridge. Like the Fields and like Robinson, she had a Classical education, this time with William Cory, one time Classics master at Eton whose *Ionica* (1891) was suggestively homoerotic. Coleridge not only writes poems with Sapphic themes – 'Marriage', for instance, which celebrates Hymen while it deplores the loss of maiden freedoms, or 'Gifts', or 'Broken Friendship' – but she also writes memorialising poems of desire, loss, and the memory of desire which are set out in an imitation of the Sapphic metre:

CCXXIV

Only a little shall we speak of thee,
  And not the thoughts we think:
There, where thou art – and art not – words would be
  As stones that sink.

We shall not see each other for thy face,
  Nor know the silly things we talk upon.
Only the heart says, 'She was in this place,
  And she is gone.'[47]

The Sappho re-created by these women poets of the late nineteenth century is one whose work is important, rather than her image. Nowhere is this more apparent than in the radical change of genre and style that takes place over the hundred years that span the space between the work of Mary Robinson and Michael Field. When Robinson wrote her *Sappho and Phaon* in 1796 she used the stylised form of the sonnet sequence, and she went to great lengths to claim poetic authority for her work by making it clear on her title page: 'Sappho and Phaon, in a series of Legitimate Sonnets ...' Robinson was anxious about Sappho as a poetic model partly because she was so acutely aware of her own marginalised status, partly because all the work she knew by Sappho was in fragments, pieces, scraps. While this (co-incidental) incompletion guaranteed Romantic authenticity – '[the works of Sappho] possessed none of the artificial decorations of a feigned passion; they were the genuine effusions of a supremely enlightened soul' – it also risked a descent into chaos. So Robinson tidied up her Sappho and made her story in 'Legitimate' or Petrarchan sonnets in an effort to establish poetic stature and artistic control for her own work.[48]

Through the nineteenth century the women poets who wrote on Sappho had to negotiate this problem. How to convey authenticity at the same time as maintaining control? For much of the period the 'last song' was the answer. Here was the fragment-cum-suicide-note-cum-self-erected-monument which was innocently 'true' – because it happened at a moment of extreme provocation – and at once artistically contrived – because it was the last testament of a self-conscious poet. This combination was what Laman Blanchard recognised when he published L.E.L.'s uncollected epigraphs and manuscript pieces under the title of *The Life and Literary Remains of L.E.L.* in 1841. Authentic, sacred, and venerated like holy relics, L.E.L.'s 'literary remains' modelled on those of her predecessors – including Sappho – endorse her womanly *naïveté* and yet imply the artfulness of her last words.

At the end of the century fragmentation seemed no longer problematic. On the contrary, it was encouraging, illuminating, liberating. Perhaps this was because Sappho herself was no longer static, but resurgent and alive again with new discovery, and so these late Victorian women poets embraced Sappho's literary remains for the freedoms she offered in her lost phrases, her ellipses, and empty spaces. Instead of being posed and still, instead of the formulaic model of the 'last song', writers like Michael Field, Agnes Mary Robinson and Mary Coleridge experimented with a kinetic verse which is suggestive and subtle, hinting at more than is said and leaving space for guessing. May Probyn's teasing 'Rondelets' and 'Triolets' belong to this development, as does the delicate erotic charge in the poetry of Charlotte Mew. In all this these poets anticipate the Modernists and show a way to later writers such as Ezra Pound and H.D. whose constructive use of Sappho's silences followed on from these earliest experiments.[49]

The new emphasis on the work of Sappho did not, however, mean that an idealised image of the woman poet disappeared altogether from their verse. Sappho's image does appear, but here is no fixed icon rigidly posed at the moment of self-display and self-destruction. Instead we are given a vision of a working poet whose song is full of nuance and possibility. Michael Field's 'Fifty Quatrains' recalls the loss of Sappho's oeuvre but it celebrates the power of 'The Woman' whose song is one about women which gives 'marvellous rich pleasure' to all her hearers:

> 'Twas fifty quatrains: and from unknown strands
> The Woman came who sang them on the floor.
> I saw her, I was leaning by the door,
> – Saw her strange raiment and her lovely hands;
> And saw … but that I think she sang—the bands
> Of low-voiced women on a happy shore:
> Incomparable was the haze, and bore
> The many blossoms of soft orchard lands.
> 'Twas fifty quatrains, for I caught the measure;
> And all the royal house was full of kings,
> Who listened and beheld her and were dumb;
> Nor dared to seize the marvellous rich pleasure,
> Too fearful even to ask in whisperings,
> The ramparts being closed, whence she had come.

And in Mary Coleridge's 'A Day-dream' – which itself may refer back to Christina Rossetti's poem called '"Reflection"' – the speaker is transported to a land, ancient Greece or present day Egypt, where 'all lay clear/ Betwixt the sunshine and the shining sand':

> … Three tombs of Kings, each with his corners three,
> Shut out three spaces of the golden sky,
> Clear, flat, and bright, they hid no mystery,
> But painted mummies, of a scarlet dye,
> That lay embalmed there many a long term,
> Safe from unkindly damp and creeping worm.

The reference to Egypt and the preservation of mummies suggests an identity for the 'ancient crone' and for the 'maiden' that the speaker finds in this landscape, for both of them are versions of Sappho:

> Deep set beneath a sibyl's wrinkled brow,
> The ancient woman's eyes were full of song.
> They held the voice of Time; and even now
> I mind me how the burden rolled along;
> For I forgot the music of the birds,
> And music's self, and music knit to words.
>
> Then did I turn me to the maiden's eyes,
> And they were as the sea, brimming and deep.
> Within in them lay the secret of the skies,
> The rhythmical tranquillity of sleep.
> They were more quiet than a windless calm
> Among the isles of spices and of balm.
>
> Now music is an echo in mine ear,
> And common stillness but the lack of noise;
> For the true music I shall never hear,
> Nor the true silence, mother of all joys.
> They dwell apart on that enchanted ground
> Where not a shadow falls and not a sound.[50]

Coleridge's doubled Sappho is a suggestive strategy. To some extent it echoes and repeats the techniques used by all the Victorian women's Sappho poems when the ancient Sappho is impersonated by the younger living poet. But the old version of Sappho's Last Song was often a trap, where the younger poet could only rehearse the destructive cycle of posing and singing, leaping and falling silent. In these late Sappho poems, however, something quite different begins to happen, and the youthful poet re-writes Sappho's legacy.

The pleasure of similitude

In the preface to *Long Ago* Michael Field explains the character of their project:

> When, more than a year ago, I wrote to a literary friend of my attempt to express in English verse the passionate pleasure Dr. Wharton's book had brought to me, he replied: 'That is a delightfully audacious thought – the extension of Sappho's fragments into lyrics. I can scarcely conceive anything more audacious'.
>
> In simple truth all worship that is not idolatry must be audacious; for it involves the blissful apprehension of an ideal; it means in the very phrase of Sappho –
>
> Ἔγων δ' ἐμαύτα
> τοῦτο σύνοιδα
>
> ['And this I feel in myself.']
>
> Devoutly as the fiery-bosomed Greek turned in her anguish to Aphrodite, praying her to accomplish her heart's desires, I have turned to the one woman who has dared to speak unfalteringly of the fearful mastery of love, and again and again the dumb prayer has risen from my heart –
>
> σὺ δ' αὔτα
> σύμμαχος ἔσσο
>
> ['... be thyself my ally.'][51]

In one sense Field's 'audacious' new project is very similar to the old ones of Hemans, L.E.L. or Rossetti. From the start it is clear that this is yet another of the self-reflexive poems about the tradition of the woman poet who sings Sappho's song. Poem I (as opposed to the first poem in the collection which I discuss above) begins with a fragment which Wharton translates as 'But charming [maidens] plaited garlands', and which he glosses with the explanation that this fragment was quoted by the Scholiast on Aristophanes' *Thesmophoriazusae* 401 'to show that plaiting wreaths was a sign of being in love'.[52]

I.

Αὔταρ ὀραῖαι στεφανηπλόκευν.

They plaited garlands in their time;
They knew the joy of youth's sweet prime,
  Quick breath and rapture;

Theirs was the violet-weaving bliss,
And theirs the white, wreathed brow to kiss,
  Kiss, and recapture.

They plaited garlands, even these;
They learnt Love's golden mysteries
  Of young Apollo;
The lyre unloosed their souls; they lay
Under the trembling leaves at play,
  Bright dreams to follow.

They plaited garlands – heavenly twine!
They crowned the cup, they drank the wine
  Of youth's deep pleasure.
Now, lingering for the lyreless god –
Oh yet, once in their time, they trod
  A choric measure.[53]

As the Greek grammar makes plain, this 'they' is feminine. They are the women poets, Sappho's disciples and Field's own ancestors who 'unloosed their souls' in the song to the lyre and who 'once in their time' performed the song of Sappho. But they are also poets, and the 'garlands' which they plait refer to the laurel crown worn by the poet, the crown once presented to Corinne on the Capitol, the crown which Aurora Leigh tried out on herself.

So much for the old tradition of the woman poet re-enacting her inevitable destiny. But at the end of *Long Ago* Sappho's story is given a curious new twist in this late version. The very last poem in the volume is a form of epilogue where, certainly, Sappho leaps off the cliff yet again. But the last *numbered* poem is a hymn to Eros which imagines the continuation of Sappho's enterprise and a peculiarly appropriate punishment for Phaon's failure to return Sappho's love. Either he will find that no one remembers him anymore now that Sappho's song no longer applauds and praises him, or ...

Or will Damophyla, the lovely-haired,
    My music learn,
Singing how Sappho of thy love despaired,
    Till thou dost burn,
      While I,
Eros! am quenched within my urn?[54]

Damophyla is Sappho's successor and she, like those later successors among the Victorian women poets, sings a song which is for and about Sappho and which is still designed to make the listener 'burn'. The passing on of Sappho's song to her younger inheritor suggests also the concept of collaboration between women poets which is, so crucially, Michael Field's unique contribution to the poetic tradition of 'last songs'. This is what is boasted in the preface to *Long Ago*, and in this these two writers truly are 'audacious'. Field collaborates with Sappho, as Sappho collaborated with Aphrodite, as she collaborated with her own companions, as she collaborated (in Field's fiction) with Damophyla, as the Victorian women poets collaborated with each other, singing songs for and to each other. In the particular case of Michael Field, of course, this partnership is more than literary, for the Fields were both lovers and poets together, and when the pseudonymous writer of the preface says that he turned 'to the one woman who has dared to speak unfalteringly of the fearful mastery of love' we can guess that Cooper and Bradley are speaking of and to each other, as much as of and to the ancient poet.[55]

One reason why Michael Field succeeded in breaking out of the Victorian pattern of destructive repetitions of the Sappho myth may be because the shared project of collaborative living and loving and writing meant that Bradley and Cooper could revise the old dualities of Sappho and her descendants in the light of their own happy experience. That they lived and wrote at a time when a 'real' text for Sappho was being slowly rediscovered, and at a time when their own authentic 'Greek' sexuality was being slowly named and recognised, meant that they could make, not yet another reprise of Sappho's last song, but a new kind of Sapphic song which was actually a duet. A duet, a collaboration, a singing in unison, which gave new freedoms and permissions.

They weren't the only poets to make this leap from solo to duet. Agnes Mary Robinson does a similar thing in her poem 'Love Without Wings'. In eight short songs she tells a story which appears to be a narrative addressed to and about a lover whom she remembers and, in effect, resurrects. The sex of this 'other' is not revealed but, as in Rossetti's '"Reflection"', it is clearly a version of the self:

I was the soul of you,
   Past love or loathing,
Lost in the whole of you ...
   Now, am I nothing?

The relation between the two is one which revolves around poetry and song:

VII.

I know you love me not ... I do not love you
   Only at dead of night
I smile a little, softly dreaming of you
   Until the dawn is bright.

I love you not: you love me not; I know it!
  But when the day is long
I haunt you like the magic of a poet,
  And charm you like a song.

And at the end of the poem it is the singing together, the duet created by the poet and the poem, which is recalled and which survives to be celebrated:

VIII.

O Death of things that are, Eternity
  Of things that seem!
Of all the happy past remains to me,
  To-day, a dream!

Long blessed days of love and wakening thought,
  All, all are dead;
Nothing endures we did, nothing we wrought,
  Nothing we said.

But once I dreamed I sat and sang with you
  On Ida's hill.
There, in the echoes of my life, we two
  Are singing still.[56]

For all of Agnes Mary Robinson's self-referential terms, it is Michael Field who most consistently and powerfully evoked the idea of a shared song, and Bradley and Cooper's enterprise was to offer a convincing model for the Modernist Sapphic writings of Renée Vivien, Natalie Barney, Gertrude Stein, H.D. and Sylvia Townshend Warner.[57] This two-singing-together happens throughout the many voices of *Long Ago*. It is written into the very title which echoes the Sappho fragment quoted on the title page: 'I loved thee once, Atthis, long ago.' It also refers to Christina Rossetti's poem entitled 'Echo', which itself refers back to Sappho:

Come back to me in dreams, that I may give
  Pulse for pulse, breath for breath:
  Speak low, lean low,
As long ago, my love, how long ago.

And it refers too to Field's own poem 'An Invitation' where reading – and reading Greek in particular – and writing, together combine with a Sappho citation to frame a world of erotic suggestion:

Come and sing, my room is south;
Come with thy sun-governed mouth,
Thou will never suffer drouth,
  Long as dwelling
In my chamber of the south ...

... Books I have of long ago
And today; I shall not know
Some, unless thou read them, so
  Their excelling
Music needs thy voice's flow ...

... And for Greek! Too sluggishly
Thou dost toil; but Sappho, see!
And the dear Anthology
  For thy spelling.
Come, it shall be well with thee.

There are duets and dualities also in Michael Field's poem 'A Girl', where the first speaker leaves the page 'half-writ' so that the object of the poem may become its subject by completing the work. They are there too in Field's 'A Palimpsest' where the same method is evoked so that the double text – old writing under new writing – reflects their dual authorship.[58]

And here is one final Field 'double' poem. In 'Old Ivories' published in their *Wild Honey from Various Thyme* (1908) Field composes a poem about two images of woman which work together to provide a seductive 'pleasure of similitude' that implies both sexual and textual sameness. One element of the double is still the static art-object, the cameo or 'old ivory' of the title. But the other is living, for the real presence of a woman beloved is described by a speaker who creates the poem out of this dual vision. A poem which itself is doubled – because it is written by 'Michael Field' – and which therefore is actually the product of two women who look at each other and love, and who look at each other and write.

Old Ivories

A window full of ancient things, and while,
Lured by their solemn tints, I crossed the street,
A face was there that in its tranquil style,
Almost obscure, at once remote and sweet,
Moved me by pleasure of similitude –
For, flanked by golden ivories, that face,
Her face, looked forth in even and subdued
Deep power, while all the shining, all the grace

Came from the passing of Time over her,
Sorrow with Time; there was no age, no spring;
On those smooth brows no promise was astir,
No hope outlived: herself a perfect thing,
She stood by that time-burnished reliquary
Simple as Aphrodite by the sea.[59]

This is quite a new 'last song' for Sappho. It does still include the picture or art-object element which suggests that Sappho is a narcissistic reflection of the woman poet herself. There may, after all, be no other young woman here for the poet to see. When the speaker arrives at the shop window we are told that 'a face was there', and this could be her own face, a reflection much like Rossetti's '"Reflection"' on Sappho's song of art and love. But the sense of newness in the old 'at once remote and sweet', and the persuasion that this image of a woman, whether reflected or genuinely doubled, is a clean sheet, a blank page, a space not yet written upon – 'On those smooth brows no promise was astir,/ No hope outlived ...' – makes the poem look like a revision and a promise.

During the nineteenth century, Sappho and Sapphism plunged to a variety of disreputable dooms, but for the women poets she retained her pre-eminence. So that even at the time when a popular version of the lonely suffering Sappho like Puccini's *Tosca* goes on singing her familiar aria – 'Vissi d'arte, vissi d'amore' – before falling into silence, among the women poets and writers at the turn of the century a new song of 'art and love' was heard. Not a 'last song' but one endlessly re-written, and not an introspective solo, but a duet where Sappho is, not a rival, but a partner.

6
Poisonous Honey

ART AND LETTERS – A former functionary of the Empire told me a curious anecdote concerning *Mademoiselle de Maupin*. In 1871 this functionary was dining at Chislehurst. The conversation turned on literature ...

The functionary: 'Your Majesty is aware that poets enjoy the supernatural gift of a kind of second sight, which allows them to depict, with all sincerity, feelings which they have never had and to lend the appearance of truth to imaginary facts: ... will give you an example. When Théophile Gautier, whom I knew very well in his youth, wrote *Mademoiselle de Maupin*, he was barely twenty-five, and led a perfectly regular life with his family ... and never saw or did a hundredth part of all that he relates in his famous novel.'

'What!' interrupted the Empress, 'it is not possible. There are in this book things so risky, things which one could not invent ——'

The Emperor, who had been a silent listener to the conversation, raised his head, and in his nasal tones said gently to the Empress: 'So you have read *Mademoiselle de Maupin*? You did not tell me that!'

At this unexpected interruption, the Empress held down her eyes, while the Emperor laughed behind his big moustache.[1]

The Empress is silenced. She has exposed herself and will speak no more of 'risky' things. Things which she believes – knows? – are true, '... things which one could not invent ...', but things which cannot be named, except, of course, in code. And in naming the name of *Mademoiselle de Maupin* the Empress has already said too much.

The holy writ beauty

Théophile Gautier's 1835 novel was one of the Sapphic fictions growing out of a Sapphic fashion which flourished in Paris in the 1830s and 1840s. It was one of the first of the 'Fatal Books' which traced the fall into Decadence from the middle of the century to the Victorian *fin de siècle* and with which Sappho descended. If Tennyson's treatment of Sappho was private, personal and obscure, then Baudelaire's and Swinburne's handling of her, though similarly coded, was public, graphic, perverse and excoriating. Gautier's novel was Sapphic only in a generalised sense, but Baudelaire and Swinburne specifically invoke the name Sappho, and the three works, Gautier's *Mademoiselle de Maupin* (1835), Baudelaire's *Les Fleurs du mal* (1857) and Swinburne's *Poems and Ballads, First series* (1866) are linked by public acknowledgement of friendship, debt and influence.

Charles Baudelaire admired Gautier and his works, and dedicated the 1857 edition of *Les Fleurs du mal* to him:

> Au poète impeccable au parfait magicien ès lettres françaises a mon très cher et très vénéré maitre et ami Théophile Gautier avec les sentiments de la plus profonde humilité je dédie ces fleurs maladives, C.B.[2]
>
> To the impeccable poet and perfect magician of French letters, to my dear, venerated master and friend, Théophile Gautier, I dedicate these sickly flowers with my profound respects, C.B.

On Baudelaire's death in 1867 Gautier wrote a brief but influential 'Life' and assessment of his works. In England, Algernon Charles Swinburne produced a study of *Les Fleurs du mal*, wrote a poem 'In Memory of Charles Baudelaire' called 'Ave Atque Vale' (1878), and contributed ten poems, 'two in English, two in French, one in Latin, and five "Epigrams" in Greek after the Anthologic pattern', to a book of memorial verses on Gautier's death *Le Tombeau de Théophile Gautier* (1874).[3]

One of Swinburne's Gautier poems was 'Sonnet (with a copy of Mademoiselle de Maupin)':

> This is the golden book of spirit and sense,
>   The holy writ of beauty; he that wrought
>   Made it with dreams and faultless words and thought
> That seeks and finds and loses in the dense
> Dim air of life that beauty's excellence
>   Wherewith love makes one hour of life distraught
>   And all hours after follow and find not aught.
> Here is that height of all love's eminence
> Where man may breathe but for a breathing-space
>   And feel his soul burn as an altar-fire
>   To the unknown God of unachieved desire,
> And from the middle mystery of the place
>   Watch lights that break, hear sounds as of a quire,
> But see not twice unveiled the veiled God's face.[4]

Supplanting the Bible with Gautier's new 'holy writ', Swinburne's poem gestures both backward and forward to other 'fatal books'. Walter Pater's 'Conclusion' to *Studies in the History of the Renaissance* (1873) is recalled – '... And feel his soul burn as an altar-fire ...'/ 'To burn always with this hard gemlike flame ...' And Lord Henry Wotton's decisive present of a book 'bound in yellow paper' in Oscar Wilde's *The Picture of Dorian Gray* (1891) suggests an allusion to Swinburne's image of Gautier's 'golden book of spirit and sense'.[5] Swinburne's focus is Gautier's apotheosis of beauty. 'Art for art's sake' was not an aphorism devised by Gautier, but certainly it was one which he endorsed, and that is the distinctive theme which Swinburne praises in *Mademoiselle de Maupin*. This is the effort which '... seeks and finds and loses in the dense/ Dim air of life, that beauty's excellence/ Wherewith love makes one hour of life distraught/ And all hours after follow and find not aught'.

Mademoiselle de Maupin tells the story of d'Albert, unpublished poet and aesthete, who is in search of ideal beauty. To his friend Silvio he relates how, in default of anything better, he takes Rosette, a pretty young widow, as his mistress. He tells how a young man, Théodore, recently arrived at Rosette's idyllic country estate, has attracted his attention. The narrator then intervenes to describe a scene between Théodore and his young page Isnabel, alone in their apartment, which contrives to suggest that all is not as it seems here. A conversation between Théodore and Rosette reveals that Rosette is in love with Théodore who, for some mysterious reason, has previously rejected her and fled from her chateau. Out riding the next day Rosette has to come to the assistance of the page Isnabel, and in loosening 'his' clothing sees

> ... something which to a man would have been one of the most agreeable surprises in the world, but which did not seem to afford her much pleasure ... She saw a very white throat, still unformed, but giving the most admirable promise, and already very beautiful, and a round, polished, ivory bosom, delightful to see, more delightful to kiss.

The tale returns to d'Albert's narrative in a letter to Silvio which confesses, and deplores, his own growing interest in Théodore. D'Albert admits to the 'mad, culpable and odious passion' which has possessed him: 'At last through all the veils enveloping it I discovered the frightful truth. Silvio I am in love. Oh no; I shall never be able to tell you. I am in love with a man!'[6]

But then d'Albert begins to suspect that, after all, Théodore is a woman. Sure enough, in the following chapter 10 we find Madeleine de Maupin taking over the narrative as she writes to her friend Graciosa to explain how she came to disguise herself as 'Théodore de Serannes'. While d'Albert's narrative goes on to explain how he attempts to uncover Théodore's secret by persuading him to play the part of Rosalind in *As You Like It*, Madeleine's tale relates her past experiences with Rosette. Having made friends with Rosette's brother Alcibiades, she had stayed at Rosette's chateau, strenuously resisting, though seduced by, Rosette's attempts to woo her. Then came the night when Alcibiades found Rosette half naked in 'Théodore's' bedroom, and challenged Madeleine/Théodore to a duel. Madeleine wounded Alcibiades and had then run away and settled at an inn in the company of a group of boisterous young men with whom she learned to drink, to flirt and to fight. In this way she acquired a tremendous reputation as a womaniser and a formidable opponent. At this time she met and befriended Ninon, a girl of 15:

> One would have said that she had golden hair powdered with silver; her eyebrows were of a tint so soft and melting that they were hardly visible; her eyes, of a pale blue, had the most velvety look and the most silky lashes imaginable; her mouth, too small to put the tip of your finger into it, added still more to the childish and exquisite character of her beauty.[7]

Madeleine decided to rescue Ninon from her scheming mother and stole her away (without ever revealing the secret of her own sex). Giving Ninon the name of Isnabel, Madeleine dressed her in a 'very rich and very elegant page's costume'. She accepted her caresses, and shared her bed, allowing the child to believe 'most seriously' that she was 'Théodore's' mistress. It was in this way that the two disguised girls had come again to Rosette's chateau where d'Albert pursued his ambiguous courting.[8]

Madeleine confesses to Graciosa that her situation is now awkward. Though not in love with d'Albert, and still inclined toward Rosette, she is 'possessed with the most violent desires. I languish and I die of voluptuousness, for the dress I wear, while engaging me in all sorts of adventures with women, protects me only too perfectly against the enterprises of men.' Madeleine decides to reveal herself to d'Albert, dresses in her Rosalind costume, and goes to bed with him.

> You alone have divined my sex, and if I have made conquests they have been over women; very superfluous conquests they have been, and more than once most embarrassing. In a word, I have always preserved my virginity, and that is why I am sad, now that I feel that I may not be able to give to-morrow that which I have today.[9]

But that is not quite the end. After leaving d'Albert 'Rosalind' goes straight to Rosette:

> What she said there and what she did I have never been able to find out ... I have not found anything either in the papers of Graciosa or in those belonging to d'Albert and Silvio relating to the visit. Only a maid of Rosette apprised

> me of a singular circumstance. It was that her mistress had not slept that night with her lover; but the bed was disturbed and had been used, and bore the impression of two bodies; and moreover, she showed me two pearls, perfectly resembling those which Théodore wore in his hair when acting in the part of Rosalind. I leave this remark to the sagacity of the reader and leave him to draw what inferences he will. As to myself, I have made above a thousand conjectures, all most unreasonable, each and all so absurd that I truly dare not write them even in the most virtuously periphrastic style.[10]

Like the Empress Eugenie, Gautier keeps silent on the subject of 'risky things'. One thing, however, he does make clear. The events of this twice acted consummation – the subtitle of the novel is 'A Double Love' – happen once and once only. On the next morning Théodore saddles his horse and rides away with Isnabel. A brief letter to d'Albert explains:

> You had an inclination for me, you loved me, I was your ideal; very well. I accorded to you at once what you desired ... Now that I have satisfied you it pleases me to go away. What is there so monstrous in that? You have had me entirely and without reserve all one night. What would you have more? Another night, and then another. You would even want the days ... I have at least the satisfaction of thinking that you will remember me rather than another. Your unsatisfied desire opens still its wings to fly to me. I shall be always something desirable to you, where your fancy loves to return ...[11]

The artistic perfection of this once – or twice – realised and possessed ideal of beauty is what Swinburne's poem admires in Gautier's novel. This thing, book, art-object, 'The holy writ of beauty' is made out of momentary possession and subsequent loss:

> ... he that wrought
> Made it with dreams and faultless words and thought
> That seeks and finds and loses in the dense
> Dim air of life that beauty's excellence
> Wherewith love makes one hour of life distraught
> And all hours after follow and find not aught.

The book-as-art-object allows the reader a brief interlude with 'the unknown God of unachieved desire', but that is all, because he will 'see not twice unveiled the veiled God's face'.

Aspiration toward an ideal beauty and the brevity of the moment of recognition is one of the themes in *Mademoiselle de Maupin* reiterated in the aesthetic inheritance which passes through Baudelaire and Swinburne to Pater and Wilde as well as to the works of their later disciples such as George Moore and Arthur Symons. Connected to this theme are a related group of ideas and images which similarly appear in *Mademoiselle de Maupin* and her descendent works, and which are often identified with late Victorian 'decadence'. These include the image of the art-object, significant and possibly pernicious; the risks which single-minded commitment to one idea may take of courting the monstrous or the perverted; the concomitant fear or courting of the possibilities of breakdown and degeneration; and the appeal to a pre-Christian or 'pagan' memory where more modern moralities may not check the search for the ideal in either life or art.

Throughout *Mademoiselle de Maupin* no one ever creates a work of art, but they are constantly aspiring to be one. Madeleine, lifting water to Rosette's lips in her two hands considers how 'we made a pretty group, and would that a sculptor had been present to make a sketch'. And in a curious passage which seems to anticipate Oscar Wilde's *The Picture of Dorian Gray* d'Albert wishes that he was himself beautiful in person and describes how he envies the beautiful faces to be seen in old galleries, fantasising that they might, 'leave their frames and come to rest upon my shoulders' ... 'Jealousy writhes deep down in my soul in knots more twisted than a viper, and I have the greatest difficulty in preventing myself from rushing at the canvas and tearing it to bits.'

But, for the most part it is the women, or woman, who represents ideal beauty and, at least in d'Albert's view, their function is as object:

> I look upon woman according to the ancient manner as a beautiful slave destined for our pleasures. Christianity has not rehabilitated her in my eyes. She is to me always something unlike and inferior to myself, something to be adored and enjoyed, a plaything more intelligent than if it were of ivory or gold ... I have been told, on that account that I thought ill of women; on the contrary, I consider that I think very well of them ...
>
> They are pleasure machines, pictures which need no frame, statues which come if they are called when the fancy takes their master to look at them from close quarters. A women has over a statue this incomparable advantage: she turns of her own accord in the desired direction, instead of, as in the case of the statue, having to be turned and placed by oneself at the right angle; that is fatiguing. You can see that with such ideas I am out of place in this century and world, for a man cannot subsist like that outside time and space ...[12]

If d'Albert's provoking sexism is wittily punished through the independently-minded Madeleine, then his amoral devotion to beauty is taken to its limits by the plan of Gautier's narrative. D'Albert seeks first of all for 'satisfaction of the eye', for 'the perfection of form and purity of line', and 'they are accepted wherever they are met'. No nineteenth century moral, social or cultural conditions are invoked. Only the aesthetic is under consideration, and that means that he can be led down unsanctioned paths.

At the end of chapter 9 d'Albert concludes that 'Even if I were to find out with certainty that Théodore is not a woman, alas, I do not know whether I should not love him still.' But in contemplating the possibility of such a love he describes the risk that he takes of reaching for 'the impossible or monstrous'. He portrays Théodore as the unnatural embodiment of his dream of beauty: 'I have discovered the body of my phantom ... I have shaken hands with my chimera.' His blood, he says, has been poisoned, his foot is 'suspended over the abyss'. And Théodore, while still beautiful, seems the model for Hermaphrodite, and his white hand a cruel deception: 'Ah! without a doubt Satan's claw is covered by such a skin; some jesting demon is playing with me; it is sorcery. This thing is too monstrously impossible.'[13]

D'Albert tries to persuade himself that his love is 'abominable', that it is a 'horrible passion' and that his search for beauty has led only to deformity and to decadence. Quite literally he fears a 'germ of corruption' which has led to 'gangrene' eating up 'all that was pure and holy'; he finds that all the 'threads connecting me with other persons and objects have been broken' and he is 'terrified at the rapidity of this decomposition' which is the result of his loss of moral fibre: '... if it continues I shall have to be salted, or else I shall inevitably rot, and the worms will attack me when I have lost my soul, for that comprises the only difference between a body and a corpse'. And if d'Albert degenerates as a result of his love for a man, Madeleine degenerates and decays into death because she cross-dresses and so also breaks all the 'threads' which connect her to her life:

> There, with my dresses and skirts, I had left my claim to womanhood; into the room where I dressed were crowded twenty years of my life which no longer counted nor concerned me. Upon the door might have been written 'Here lies Madeleine de Maupin' ... The drawer which contained my now useless dresses appeared to me like the shroud of my white illusions; I was a man, or at least I appeared to be; the young girl was dead.[14]

Yet, as d'Albert himself had recognised, it is only the conventions, the 'threads' of a particular place and time in history which make either Madeleine's cross-dressing (and cross-living) or d'Albert's own perverse passion into formulas for degeneration. D'Albert calls himself 'a real pagan' on account of his obsessive love of beauty. He can, he says 'perfectly understand the mad enthusiasm of the Greeks for beauty'. He is 'a man of Homeric times' and the ancients' love of beauty is, 'the explanation of those strange aberrations of ancient love'. Before he begins to experience these 'strange aberrations' in his own person, d'Albert ponders the modern cleaning-up of Classical writers:

> Those strange loves, of which the elegies of the ancient poets are full, which surprise us so much, and which we cannot conceive, are therefore likely and possible. In our translations we substitute the names of women for those already there. Juventius ends as Juventia, while Alexis becomes Ianthe. Handsome boys become good-looking girls, and in this way we reconstruct the monstrous seraglio of Catullus, Tibullus, Martial and Virgil. It is a bold task, which shows how little we understand the ancient genius.[15]

His argument goes this way; the Greeks loved beauty and form, and made perfect statues where male and female were equally the repository of beauty, and the hermaphrodite, containing at once both male and female, was therefore 'one of the most ardently caressed chimerae of ancient idolatry' and is still, 'one of the most pleasant creations of pagan genius'. With the arrival of Christianity, however, 'Woman has become the symbol of moral and physical beauty; from that day man has really declined.' Yet in Théodore/Madeleine d'Albert has effectively found both Apollo and Aphrodite, though he decides that she has to be a woman even if he is going to be true to his Hellenic ideal:

> we are not now in transformation times, Adonis and Hermaphrodite are dead, and it is no longer by a man that beauty shall be realised; for since the gods and heroes are no more you alone conserve in your body of marble, as in a Greek temple, the precious gift of form ...[16]

Gautier's *Mademoiselle de Maupin*, with its Hellenic background, its religion of beauty, its play with sexuality wilfully skewed, and its flavour of corruption and decay is a book which became an iconic art-object in itself, influencing other texts. Its relation to the specifically homoerotic texts of the late nineteenth century which deal with love between men is pretty clear, and its traces are in the self-consciously jewelled prose of Pater or the sumptuous settings in Wilde's fiction. But it is notable that, in fact, no homosexual activity *between men* ever actually takes place in *Mademoiselle de Maupin*. It is contemplated, certainly. But, in the end of course, Théodore is a girl, and all's right with the heterosexual world. On the other hand what does actually take place – though it is unnamed – is sex between women, and we are repeatedly teased – in various different combinations (Rosette/Madeleine, Graciosa/Madeleine, Rosette/Ninon, Madeleine/Ninon) – with the possibilities for sexual relations between women.

Of course there can be no doubt that most of these scenes are provided for the pleasure of the voyeur, and that the reader is consciously made into a voyeur is made clear by the provocative ending which refuses to tell what happened between Madeleine and Rosette. This absence of explicit naming, and the rapid breaking off of other encounters between women, makes them ghostly, evanescent. In Terry Castle's phrase, these lesbians are indeed 'apparitional' and, as she has pointed out, there are a number of places in the text of *Mademoiselle de Maupin* where the women seem, either to themselves or to others, to be no more than phantoms.[17]

But the idea of the lesbian haunted the fiction, the drama and the paintings produced in France in the 1830s and 1840s, and Sappho herself became its most persistent revenant passing into the English tradition in the latter half of the century.[18]

Risky things

One of the most fugitive sightings, and yet the one which was to prove the most influential, was the volume of poems announced as forthcoming by Charles Baudelaire in October 1845 and entitled *Les Lesbiennes*. It was announced again in 1846 and 1847 but it never appeared. In the event the one hundred or so poems which Baudelaire had been working on since the early 1840s were published under the new title of *Les Fleurs du mal* in June 1857. Baudelaire himself described his original title as a *titre pétard*, a 'firecracker', but his contribution was only one of a number of Sapphic – though not necessarily sapphic – fictions produced in Paris during this period. Arsène Houssaye, a poet in Baudelaire's circle, wrote in 1845 that 'At this time Sappho was resuscitated in Paris, not knowing if she loved Phaon or Erinna.'[19]

Baudelaire's poem 'Lesbos' was published in Julian Lemer's anthology *Les Poètes de l'amour* in July 1850; the first act of Arsène Houssaye's *Sappho: drame antique en trois actes* was published in *l'Artiste* in the issue for 15 October 1850; Philoxene Boyer's *Sapho: Drame en une acte* was staged on 13 November 1850; and Baudelaire was often asked during this period to recite his sapphic poem 'Delphine et Hippolyte' in public.[20] Gautier himself, the most effective populariser of the image of the woman-loving-woman, might have also competed for Sappho as his notes for a planned article make clear. He too however, like Houssaye and Boyer, made his Sappho chaste and heterosexual, 'mascula' only because of her intellect, her artistic calling, her social alienation and her political engagement.[21] Baudelaire was the first to make Sappho lesbian, to people her Lesbos with women, and to dispense with the heterosexually corrective figure of Phaon.

There is, however, indeed a man present in Baudelaire's version of Sappho, and that man is Baudelaire himself. In the poetry of Baudelaire's close follower in English, Algernon Charles Swinburne, Sappho also appears as a lesbian and her landscape is womanly. But in neither case does this restoration make Sappho whole again. Quite the contrary; Baudelaire and Swinburne break up Sappho, dissect her, fragment her and insert themselves into her spaces.

Limb-loosening

Charles Baudelaire's *Les Fleurs du mal* finally appeared in June 1857. It included three lesbian poems which may have been the remains of an abortive longer work implied by the earlier, discarded, title of *Les Lesbiennes*. These three poems were 'Lesbos' and two poems which came under the joint heading of 'Femmes Damnées', the first called 'Delphine et Hippolyte' and the second called 'Femmes Damnées'. When the Public Prosecutor committed Baudelaire, his publisher and his printer for trial all copies of the book were ordered for confiscation. As a result of the trial six pieces were removed from the book on the grounds that they were 'offensive to public morals and accepted standards'. Among these six pieces were 'Lesbos' and 'Delphine et Hippolyte'.[22]

IV. – LESBOS

Mère des jeux latins et des voluptés grecques,
Lesbos, où les baisers, languissants ou joyeux,
Chauds comme les soleils, frais comme les pastèques,
Font l'ornement des nuits et des jours glorieux,
Mère des jeux latins et des voluptés grecques,

Lesbos, où les baisers sont comme les cascades
Qui se jettent sans peur dans les gouffres sans fonds
Et courent, sanglotant et gloussant par saccades,
Orageux et secrets, fourmillants et profonds;
Lesbos, où les baisers sont comme les cascades!

Lesbos, où les Phrynés l'une l'autre s'attirent,
Où jamais un soupir ne resta sans écho,
A l'égal de Paphos les étoiles t'admirent,
Et Vénus à bon droit peut jalouser Sapho!
Lesbos, où les Phrynés l'une l'autre s'attirent,

Lesbos, terre des nuits chaudes et langoureuses,
Qui font qu'à leurs miroirs, stérile volupté!
Les filles aux yeux creux, de leur corps amoureuses,
Caressent les fruits mûrs de leur nubilité;
Lesbos, terre des nuits chaudes et langoureuses,

Laisse du vieux Platon se froncer l'œil austère;
Tu tires ton pardon de l'excès des baisers,
Reine du doux empire, aimable et noble terre,
Et des raffinements toujours inépuisés.
Laisse du vieux Platon se froncer l'oeil austère.

Tu tires ton pardon de l'éternel martyre,
Infligé sans relâche aux coeurs ambitieux,
Qu'attire loin de nous le radieux sourire
Entrevu vaguement au bord des autres cieux!
Tu tires ton pardon de l'éternel martyre!

Qui des Dieux osera, Lesbos, être ton juge
Et condamner ton front pâli dans les travaux,
Si ses balances d'or n'ont pesé le déluge
De larmes qu'à la mer ont versé tes ruisseaux?
Qui des Dieux osera, Lesbos, être ton juge?

Que nous veulent les lois du juste et de l'injuste?
Vierges au coeur sublime, honneur de l'Archipel,
Votre religion comme une autre est auguste,
Et l'amour se rira de l'Enfer et du Ciel!
Que nous veulent les lois du juste et de l'injuste?

Car Lesbos entre tous m'a choisi sur la terre,
Pour chanter le secret de ses vierges en fleurs,
Et je fus dès l'enfance admis au noir mystère
Des rires effrénés mêlés aux sombres pleurs;
Car Lesbos entre tous m'a choisi sur la terre.

Et depuis lors je veille au sommet de Leucate,
Comme une sentinelle à l'oeil perçant et sûr,
Qui guette nuit et jour brick, tartane ou frégate,
Dont les formes au loin frissonnent dans l'azur;
Et depuis lors je veille au sommet de Leucate,

Pour savoir si la mer est indulgente et bonne,
Et parmi les sanglots dont le roc retentit
Un soir ramènera vers Lesbos, qui pardonne,
Le cadavre adoré de Sapho, qui partit
Pour savoir si la mer est indulgente et bonne!

De la mâle Sapho, l'amante et le poète,
Plus belle que Vénus par ses mornes pâleurs!
– L'œil d'azur est vaincu par l'oeil noir que tachète
Le cercle ténébreux tracé par les douleurs
De la mâle Sapho, l'amante et le poète!

– Plus belle que Vénus se dressant sur le monde
Et versant les trésors de sa sérénité
Et le rayonnement de sa jeunesse blonde
Sur le vieil Océan de sa fille enchanté;
Plus belle que Vénus se dressant sur le monde!

– De Sapho qui mourut le jour de son blasphème,
Quand, insultant le rite et le culte inventé,
Elle fit son beau corps la pâture suprême
D'un brutal dont l'orgueil punit l'impiété
De celle qui mourut le jour de son blasphème.

Et c'est depuis ce temps que Lesbos se lamente,
Et, malgré les honneurs que lui rend l'univers,
S'enivre chaque nuit du cri de la tourmente
Que poussent vers les deux ses rivages déserts.
Et c'est depuis ce temps que Lesbos se lamente![23]

Baudelaire's 'Lesbos' conflates woman, place and practice. The opening four stanzas which chant the name of Lesbos, realise her as an independent world where other laws obtain, which is both the island and the body of woman. She is addressed by the poet as mother, 'Mère des jeux latins et des voluptés grecques', in an invocation of Greek and Roman practices which is reminiscent of the nostalgia for antiquity expressed by d'Albert in *Mademoiselle de Maupin*. An erotic and closely focussed attention to the body is spelt out in the opening stanzas with its obsessive listing of kisses and caresses which 'adorn' ('Font l'ornement') the nights and days of Lesbos. And this landscape is that of the specifically female body as these kisses, 'like waterfalls' ... 'plunge without fear into the fathomless crevices' ('Qui se jettent sans peur dans les gouffres sans fonds').

The voyeurism of this lewd examination is confessed in stanza 3 with a reference to Phryné who, by definition of her story, must always appear naked. According to the legend Phryné was a celebrated courtesan of Athens who was accused of impiety. Brought before her judges and seeing that the case was going against her, Phryné unveiled herself. Entranced by the speaking beauty of her nakedness, her judges declared that such a form affirmed her innocence and she was acquitted. Phryné was a popular subject with the painters of the nineteenth century and the moment portrayed is always that which shows her unveiling.[24] Yet in Baudelaire's 'Lesbos' this Phryné is not one but several. And here it is not male judges who look at her, but other girls:

Lesbos, où les Phrynés l'une l'autre s'attrirent,
Où jamais un soupir ne resta sans écho ....

The self-sufficient femaleness of this scene on Lesbos is continued with the introduction of Venus who, it would seem, is also looking at another woman, Sappho: 'A l'égal de Paphos les étoiles t'admirent,/ Et Vénus à bon droit peut jalouser Sapho!' Stanzas 5 to 8 however introduce other lookers-on: 'vieux Platon', the Gods who 'judge', and the 'laws of the just and the unjust', whose gaze is similarly desiring but more critical. They enter the poem to be dismissed by the poet as irrelevant to the quasi-religious dedication of Lesbos. Yet their very presence permits a perverse satisfaction which is the pleasure of the executioner and the cool precision of the torturer. For what goes on now, in spite of (because of?), the condemning eyes of these judges are 'an excess of kisses' ('l'excès des baisers'), 'refinement always inexhaustible' ('Raffinements toujours inépuisés'), an 'eternal martyrdom/ Inflicted without release' ('l'éternel martyre,/ Infligé sans relâche aux coeurs ambitieux') and a labouring of physical pain, 'your face pale with effort' ('ton front pâli dans les travaux').

The stresses of Lesbos may be sexual, the condemnation of the observing outsiders may be legal, but Baudelaire's typical method of blurring subject and object, sensation and contemplation, means that the examining view directed at Lesbos, Baudelaire's and ours included, is also sexual – and pornographic.

At stanza 9 the poet-speaker introduces himself. With a pun on the title of the volume, *Les Fleurs du mal*, the speaker explains that he has been chosen above all others on earth 'to sing the secrets of her virgins in flowers' ('Pour chanter le secret de ses vierges en fleurs'). Not only does he now, in effect, take over Sappho's own special role as the singer of Lesbos, he actually takes her very place on the cliff of Leucata. Unlike Sappho, however, he is not there with the intention of taking his own life. Far from it. This latter-day usurper of Sappho survives and sings and acts as an infallible look-out, ('à l'oeil perçant et sûr'), whose task is to scan the horizon for signs that the sea might return the body of Sappho ('Le cadavre adoré de Sapho'). Sappho then, is dead, and another sings in her place. Another, it would seem, who has both vanquished her and become her, translated across language, time and gender:

> De la mâle Sapho, l'amante et le poète,
> Plus belle que Vénus par ses mornes pâleurs!
> – L'oeil d'azur est vaincu par l'oeil noir que tachète
> Le cercle ténébreux tracé par les douleurs
> De la mâle Sapho, l'amante et la poète!

Joan DeJean, following Walter Benjamin, sees Baudelaire's strategy here as one which makes his 'poet-double' heir to Sappho and which initiates a new literary strand which makes the lesbian, Sappho in particular, into 'the heroine of modernism'. As she says, Sappho's part in Baudelaire's 'Lesbos' associates her with Orpheus as her body floats in the sea and her songs are sung by others.[25] But in effect it is Baudelaire's poem which has done this to her. Like Orpheus, her body – 'Le cadavre adoré de Sapho' – has been torn apart, fragmented, to make a poem for her successor.

In the penultimate stanza of 'Lesbos' we learn how and why Sappho died. There is no Phaon in this story, nor is there any of the conflict between art and love, celebrated and mourned by the women poets of the early nineteenth century. Baudelaire's explanation of her death is original and unique. His Sappho dies on the day of her 'blasphemy' when she insulted 'the rite and the cult which she had invented', when she 'made her beautiful body the supreme conquest (fodder) for a brutal man whose pride punished her impiety' ('Elle fit son beau corps la pâture suprême/ D'un brutal dont l'orgueil punit l'impiété'). Her consequent death seems to be a direct result of this event, for there is no suicide mentioned. But ever since that day Lesbos 'laments', and is 'intoxicated every night with the cry of torment' ('Et c'est depuis ce temps que Lesbos se lamente/ ... / S'enivre chaque nuit du cri de la tourmente ...').

What is strange and telling about this version of Sappho's death is that this is exactly what the poet has done to her in his poem. She has been made into 'fodder' ('pâture') for him. She is his muse certainly, but she is also his victim; his observing eye has reduced her to a sum of isolated parts, broken her, with the expertise of the torturer and discarded her 'adored cadaver' in order that he may take her place, sing her song, and have a subject for that song. 'Lesbos' in this poem represents woman, place, practice, but it also represents the original site of lyric poetry, and as such, Baudelaire regards it with a piercing ('perçant') and with an envious eye. Sappho dies when she gave herself to a 'brute' and thereafter her heir, 'from childhood admitted to the black mystery' ('je fus des l'enfance admis au noir mystère'), becomes the voice of Lesbos which sings this poem; 'Et c'est depuis ce temps que Lesbos se lamente'.

'Femmes Damnées'

In the second of the two 'Femmes Damnées' poems, curiously the only one of the three lesbian poems which was not banned in 1857, Baudelaire sets up a similar world, landscape and practice, and again makes himself the Singer of Lesbos. There is no direct reference in this poem either to Sappho or to Lesbos, but there is that distinctive setting of sand and sea, groves and purling streams which suggests the parts of the woman's body.

CXI – FEMMES DAMNEES

Comme un bétail pensif sur le sable couchées,
Elles tournent leurs yeux vers l'horizon des mers,
Et leurs pieds se cherchant et leurs mains rapprochées
Ont de douces langueurs et des frissons amers.

Les unes, coeurs épris des longues confidences,
Dans le fond des bosquets où jasent les ruisseaux,
Vont épelant l'amour des craintives enfances
Et creusent le bois vert des jeunes arbrisseaux;

D'autres, comme des soeurs, marchent lentes et graves
A travers les rochers pleins d'apparitions,
Où saint Antoine a vu surgir comme des laves
Les seins nus et pourprés de ses tentations;
Il en est, aux lueurs des résines croulantes,

Qui dans le creux muet des vieux antres païens
T'appellent au secours de leurs fièvres hurlantes,
O Bacchus, endormeur des remords anciens!

Et d'autres, dont la gorge aime les scapulaires,
Qui, recélant un fouet sous leurs longs vêtements,
Mêlent, dans le bois sombre et les nuits solitaires,
L'écume du plaisir aux larmes des tourments.

O vierges, ô démons, ô monstres, ô martyres,
De la réalité grands esprits contempteurs,
Chercheuses d'infini, dévotes et satyres,
Tantôt pleines de cris, tantôt pleines de pleurs,

Vous que dans votre enfer mon âme a poursuivies,
Pauvres soeurs, je vous aime autant que je vous plains,
Pour vos mornes douleurs, vos soifs inassouvies,
Et les urnes d'amour dont vos grands coeurs sont pleins![26]

Here are women, separate, independent, consecrated, who reach out to one another, touching feet and hands; who whisper 'in the depths of groves where streams flow' ('Dans le fond les bosquets où jasent les ruisseaux'), who 'carve the green wood of young saplings' ('Et creusent le bois vert des jeunes arbrisseaux'), and who walk among the haunted rocks where Saint Anthony saw 'The breasts naked and purple of his temptations' ('Les seins nus et pourprés de ses tentations'). As in 'Lesbos' the reader is presented with a voyeuristic dissection of the body of woman which is both sacramental and perverse. The women are named both as 'sisters' and as 'virgins', and with the consequent punning implications of a religious order, they wear scapularies and hide whips ('un fouet') under their trailing robes or vestments ('longs vêtements'). Their experience is of 'bitter thrills' ('frissons amers'), 'shrieking fevers' ('fièvre hurlantes'), of the 'sweat of pleasure in the tears of torments' ('L'écume du plaisir aux larmes des tourments'). They are addressed as virgins, demons, monsters, martyrs, and in their role as 'seekers of the infinite' ('Chercheuses d'infini'), they are 'devotees and satyrs' ('dévotes et satyres').

The same scheme of torture and pleasure is sketched out, and the landscape of Lesbos, along with the body of woman is displayed, examined, put to the question, through the conniving scrutiny of the poet and reader. In the final stanza, the poet's pursuit ('mon âme a poursuivies') of his quarry, as well as his function, in admiring and singing their 'mournful pains' ('vos mornes douleurs') is made clear. As in 'Lesbos' where the poet-speaker strings out the broken body of Sappho to make her into an instrument for his song, so here Baudelaire plays upon the fragmented bodies of his 'Damned Women' to make his poem.

'Delphine et Hippolyte'

'Delphine et Hippolyte', the third of Baudelaire's lesbian poems in *Les Fleurs du mal*, and the second, along with 'Lesbos', to be condemned and removed from the censored editions, also places Baudelaire in the position of voyeur who makes his song out of that illicit seeing. The image of the gaze is reinforced here by repeated reference to the 'curtain' which is lifted, or the 'veil' which is raised. In the first stanza Hippolyte reclines 'dreaming of the powerful caresses/ Which raised the curtain of her young innocence' ('Hippolyte rêvait aux caresses puissantes/ Qui levaient le rideau de sa jeune candeur').

Delphine, whom we must cast in the role of seducer, promises that she can offer still more delights in this line by 'lifting the veils' of 'more obscure pleasures' ('Des plaisirs plus obscurs je lèverai les voiles'). Hippolyte hopes that 'our closed curtains will separate us from the world ('Que nos rideaux fermés nous séparent du monde'), but her wish is already in vain, for Baudelaire's own rude peepshow has exposed what is otherwise hidden, and his readers are implicated as judges of this unveiling, just as they were made into the appraisers who looked at Phryné.

DELPHINE ET HIPPOLYTE

A la pâle clarté des lampes languissantes,
Sur de profonds coussins tout imprégnés d'odeur
Hippolyte rêvait aux caresses puissantes
Qui levaient le rideau de sa jeune candeur.

Elle cherchait, d'un oeil troublé par la tempête,
De sa naïveté le ciel déjà lointain,
Ainsi qu'un voyageur qui retourne la tête
Vers les horizons bleus dépassés le matin.

De ses yeux amortis les paresseuses larmes,
L'air brisé, la stupeur, la morne volupté,
Ses bras vaincus, jetés comme de vaines armes,
Tout servait, tout parait sa fragile beauté.

Étendue à ses pieds, calme et pleine de joie,
Delphine la couvait avec des yeux ardents,
Comme un animal fort qui surveille une proie,
Après l'avoir d'abord marquée avec les dents.

Beauté forte à genoux devant la beauté frêle,
Superbe, elle humait voluptueusement
Le vin de son triomphe, et s'allongeait vers elle,
Comme pour recueillir un doux remerciement.

Elle cherchait dans l'oeil de sa pâle victime
Le cantique muet que chante le plaisir,
Et cette gratitude infinie et sublime
Qui sort de la paupière ainsi qu'un long soupir.

– « Hippolyte, cher coeur, que dis-tu de ces choses?
Comprends-tu maintenant qu'il ne faut pas offrir
L'holocauste sacré de tes premières roses
Aux souffles violents qui pourraient les flétrir?

Mes baisers sont légers comme ces éphémères
Qui caressent le soir les grands lacs transparents,
Et ceux de ton amant creuseront leurs ornières
Comme des chariots ou des socs déchirants;

Ils passeront sur toi comme un lourd attelage
De chevaux et de boeufs aux sabots sans pitié ...
Hippolyte, ô ma soeur! tourne donc ton visage,
Toi, mon âme et mon coeur, mon tout et ma moitié,

Tourne vers moi tes yeux pleins d'azur et d'étoiles!
Pour un de ces regards charmants, baume divin,
Des plaisirs plus obscurs je lèverai les voiles,
Et je t'endormirai dans un rêve sans fin! »

Mais Hippolyte alors, levant sa jeune tête:
– « Je ne suis point ingrate et ne me repens pas,
Ma Delphine, je souffre et je suis inquiète,
Comme après un nocturne et terrible repas.

Je sens fondre sur moi de lourdes épouvantes
Et de noirs bataillons de fantômes épars,
Qui veulent me conduire en des routes mouvantes
Qu'un horizon sanglant ferme de toutes parts.

Avons-nous donc commis une action étrange?
Explique, si tu peux, mon trouble et mon effroi:
Je frissonne de peur quand tu me dis: « Mon ange! »
Et cependant je sens ma bouche aller vers toi.

Ne me regarde pas ainsi, toi, ma pensée!
Toi que j'aime à jamais, ma soeur d'élection,
Quand même tu serais une embûche dressée
Et le commencement de ma perdition! »

Delphine secouant sa crinière tragique,
Et comme trépignant sur le trépied de fer,
L'oeil fatal, répondit d'une voix despotique:
– « Qui donc devant l'amour ose parler d'enfer?

Maudit soit à jamais le rêveur inutile
Qui voulut le premier, dans sa stupidité,
S'éprenant d'un problème insoluble et stérile,
Aux choses de l'amour mêler l'honnêteté!

Celui qui veut unir dans un accord mystique
L'ombre avec la chaleur, la nuit avec le jour,
Ne chauffera jamais son corps paralytique
A ce rouge soleil que l'on nomme l'amour!

Va, si tu veux, chercher un fiancé stupide;
Cours offrir un coeur vierge à ses cruels baisers;
Et, pleine de remords et d'horreur, et livide,
Tu me rapporteras tes seins stigmatisés ...

On ne peut ici-bas contenter qu'un seul maître! »
Mais l'enfant, épanchant une immense douleur,
Cria soudain: — « Je sens s'élargir dans mon être
Un abîme béant; cet abîme est mon coeur!

Brûlant comme un volcan, profond comme le vide!
Rien ne rassasiera ce monstre gémissant
Et ne rafraîchira la soif de l'Euménide
Qui, la torche à la main, le brûle jusqu'au sang.

Que nos rideaux fermés nous séparent du monde,
Et que la lassitude amène le repos!
Je veux m'anéantir dans ta gorge profonde,
Et trouver sur ton sein la fraîcheur des tombeaux! »

– Descendez, descendez, lamentables victimes,
Descendez le chemin de l'enfer éternel!
Plongez au plus profond du gouffre, où tous les crimes,
Flagellés par un vent qui ne vient pas du ciel,

Bouillonnent pêle-mêle avec un bruit d'orage.
Ombres folles, courez au but de vos désirs;
Jamais vous ne pourrez assouvir votre rage,
Et votre châtiment naîtra de vos plaisirs.

Jamais un rayon frais n'éclaira vos cavernes;
Par les fentes des murs des miasmes fiévreux
Filtrent en s'enflammant ainsi que des lanternes
Et pénètrent vos corps de leurs parfums affreux.

L'âpre stérilité de votre jouissance
Altère votre soif et roidit votre peau,
Et le vent furibond de la concupiscence
Fait claquer votre chair ainsi qu'un vieux drapeau.

Loin des peuples vivants, errantes, condamnées,
A travers les déserts courez comme les loups;
Faites votre destin, âmes désordonnées,
Et fuyez l'infini que vous portez en vous![27]

The first version of this poem ended at stanza 21 with Hippolyte's speech where she accepts Delphine's love, this 'action étrange', and desires to 'annihilate myself in the depths of your bosom' – literally 'in your deep gorge' – 'and to find on your breast the coldness of the tomb' ('Je veux m'anéantir dans ta gorge profonde/ Et trouver sur ton sein la fraîcher des tombeaux'). Conscious that he was somewhat at risk here, Baudelaire added the explicitly condemning last five stanzas just before the original publication. But his first version, like 'Lesbos' and the other 'Femmes Damnées' poem, neither condemns nor praises.

He resorts here, as in 'Lesbos', to a remote antiquity, suggesting in the names of his characters an earlier world of fantasised feminine power and autonomy. Hippolyte is named for Hippolyta, warrior queen of the Amazons, and though she is portrayed as 'fragile' and 'frail', she also retains some gestured memory of her legendary glory in stanza 3 where her 'arms are defeated, thrown down like useless weapons' ('Ses bras vaincus, jetés comme de vaines armes'). Delphine is named for the Sibyl or the priestess of the oracle at Delphi, and she too is an inheritor of a race-memory, shaking her mane of hair and trembling as if seated on the tripod of the Pythian oracle:

Delphine secouant sa crinière tragique,
Et comme trépignant sur le trépied de fer,
L'oeil fatal, répondit d'une voix despotique:
– « Qui donc devant l'amour ose parler d'enfer? »

Delphine's argument, like that set out in 'Lesbos' and in 'Femmes Damnées' is that this is a separate world, consecrated and remote, and not governed by commonplace moralities. Anyone who attempts to 'mix the things of love with honesty', to reconcile the shadow with fervid heat ('L'ombre avec la chaleur' – literally suggesting 'on heat'), the night with the day, is bound to fail, and such a one will, says Delphine, 'Never warm their paralytic flesh/ At that red sun which we call Love' ('Ne chaffera jamais son corps paralytique/ A ce rouge soleil que l'on nomme l'amour!').

But the terms of Delphine's love, as in Baudelaire's two other lesbian poems, are perverse and cruel. In an image reminiscent of the way in which Baudelaire himself exploits the body of Sappho, Delphine is pleasured by her own performance on the body of Hippolyte. As Baudelaire strings up Sappho's body to make his song, so Delphine scans her lover's flesh for 'the silent hymn which sings of pleasure' ('Le cantique muet que chante le plaisir'), and there is no doubt here but that this is the song of the sexualised body which can be played upon and made to perform in response.

Delphine's voracious and unforgiving sexual demands are derived from Baudelaire's near ancestor in de Sade, for she surveys 'her prey' which, like an animal, she has marked with her teeth:

> Delphine la couvait avec des yeux ardents,
> Comme un animal fort que surveille une proie,
> Après l'avoir d'abord marquée avec les dents.

But Delphine's attentions – she argues – are kind in comparison with those of heterosexual desire, which always destroy. Her kisses are light as air, while others will carve Hippolyte in furrows ('Et ceux de ton amant creuseront leurs ornières/ Comme des chariots ou des socs déchirents'). As in 'Lesbos', strange lesbian loves are unreachable and bizaare, tortured even, but they are not destructive and mutilating as are the loves of the brute ('un brutal') who makes Sappho's body into fodder ('un pâture'), or the boorish lover who will trample Hippolyte: 'Ils passeront sur toi comme un lourd attelage/ Des chevaux et de boeufs aux sabots sans pitié ...'

One immediate reaction to the suggestive seduction of Baudelaire's poem was the well-known painting by Gustave Courbet, generally called *Sleep* (1866). It was produced as part of the Second Empire fashion for lesbianism, but Courbet specifically acknowledged Baudelaire's 'Delphine et Hippolyte' as a source and said that he saw his painting as an illustration of the poem. Commissioned, like the infamous *L'Origine du monde*, for the wealthy collector Khalil Bey, *Le Sommeil* shows two women, one dark, one blonde, naked and abandoned in each other's arms, their limbs intertwined and their clothes thrown hastily aside. The voluptuous and quasi-oriental setting is emphasised by flowers, rich brocades, and a coloured glass decanter and goblet. Tellingly, a tortoiseshell comb and two pearl earrings are discarded unremarked in the rumpled sheets. Courbet too, it would seems, had read the 'risky things' in *Mademoiselle de Maupin*.

Curiously 'Delphine and Hippolyte' was a decadent, a 'fallen', poem even before the Decadence was invented. The poem refers repeatedly to the 'abyss', the depths of female sexuality which is endured, invited, explored by its protagonists. And with the last five condemning stanzas which Baudelaire's own self-censorship added, the connection becomes complete. 'Descendez', he says, 'Descend', 'Go down':

> – Descendez, descendez, lamentables victimes,
> Descendez le chemin de l'enfer éternel!
> Plongez au plus profond du gouffre, où tous les crimes,
> Flagellés par un vent qui ne vient pas du ciel,
>
> Bouillonnent pêle-mêle avec un bruit d'orage ...

Probing the abyss of the Lesbian's body, Baudelaire sends her down, makes her decline, turns her into a fallen woman, a Decadent, and takes Sappho down with her.

'Sapho'

In 'Lesbos' and in both the 'Femmes Damnées' poems Baudelaire casts himself as looker on and appears either as judge and commentator or as poet-inheritor of Sappho's role. On one occasion, however, Baudelaire may have had Sappho speak for herself. Or rather, he may have ventriloquised her, for the pattern of degradation which he uses there is the same as in his lesbian poems from *Les Fleurs du mal*.

An early poem, published in 1845 in a book which was the result of a collaboration with three other poets (so that the poem may not have been composed by Baudelaire) is called 'Sapho' and here it is Sapho who speaks:

> Pour aimer les bergers, faut-il être bergère?
> Pour avoir respiré la perfide atmosphère
> De tes tristes cités, corruptrice Lesbos,
> Faut-il donc renoncer aux faveurs d'Antéros?
> Et suis-je désormais une conquête indigne
> De ce jeune berger, doux et blanc comme un cygne?[28]

If this is by Baudelaire then it does in many ways anticipate the uses to which he put Sappho in *Les Fleurs du mal*. Here, as in 'Lesbos', she is submitting to a (possible) 'brute' in the person of the shepherd who, in any case, is certainly portrayed as not her social equal: 'To love shepherds, must a girl become a shepherdess?' And in that process he, or rather her desire for him, has reduced her to 'an undignified conquest'. Here, as also in 'Lesbos' and as in 'Femmes Damnées' there is a collision between the corrupt world of Lesbos with its 'sad cities' and the other, equally desired, favours of Anteros. As Anteros was the son of Venus and Mars and the god of mutual (heterosexual) love, the implication must be also that this is an opposition set up between lesbian and heterosexual practice. Baudelaire's Sappho seems to wish to transcend or cross between all categories of class and sexual practice. Or, Baudelaire wishes to use Sappho to cross between all categories. She, like her 'sisters' in 'Femmes Damnées' is a 'chercheuse d'infini', a seeker of infinity, who gives herself to be broken in pieces in that pursuit.

Le cadavre adoré de Sapho

Baudelaire's sadism is well known. His is a poetry, as Kristeva argues, which is founded wholly on metaphor. A metaphor which paradoxically 'destroys bodies', rends them apart, in order to spread that body out over the largest space – to make them emblematic of the infinite. For Kristeva, the two distinctive characteristics of Baudelaire's poetry – a sadistic and destructive passion, and an elated veneration of a supreme ideal – are not necessarily mutually exclusive. In considering Baudelaire's exploitation of Sappho, Kristeva's analysis is helpful. She dismisses the simplistic notions of Baudelaire's vengefulness directed at a loving but tyrannical mother, or versions which split his experience of sex (with Jeanne Duval) from ideal love (with Marie Daubrun or Sabatier), and instead focusses on the metaphor contained in his setting 'carrion' (the woman's body) against 'paradise' (the desired infinite). This is what she says:

> ... the 'carrion' refers to a limitless, nonsensed body, harrowed by a crisis that one might call deeply narcissistic. Indeed if one grants that in literature as in dreams that of which 'I' dream or 'I' speak is what 'I' am, then Baudelaire's abjections are just as many blurrings between subject and other – corruptions of an identity that is acknowledged as impossible.[29]

In Baudelaire's three, or perhaps four, lesbian poems woman's body is indeed 'carrion'. Quite literally so in 'Lesbos', where the poet-speaker looks out over the sea on the watch for the 'adored cadaver' of Sappho. But his Sappho is both woman and poet, and her 'body' means both her imagined (and broken) flesh, and her actual (and fragmented) body of work. It is her 'corpus' which interests Baudelaire, and the 'nonsensed' version which he makes of Sappho – which is in fact what it is, because he hardly refers to the extant works, borrows little from the legends, and anachronistically muddles in reference to Roman gods and Christian symbolism – is 'harrowed by a crisis' which is Baudelaire's own. That is, the crisis of the poet who is both anxious about belatedness and desirous of a state of negative capability.

Baudelaire's own identity as a poet is at stake here – remember that *Les Fleurs du mal* was his first volume, though he had been working for many years – and yet, awkwardly, his own special character as a poet was one which was always divesting of self, entering into the consciousness of another, shedding personal concerns, and taking on the 'impersonality' which was to be so much admired by his successor T.S. Eliot. In fact, it may be that Baudelaire's decision not to go ahead with the title (the volume?) of *Les Lesbiennes* is directly connected to the 'narcissistic crisis' which is written into his lesbian poems. For how could a man, writing in the nineteenth century, hope to cross the infinite spaces across gender, or across time, in order to write the poetry of *Les Lesbiennes*? And yet of course he did make that attempt, at least insofar as one can judge from the 'remains' of that endeavour.

In one sense, however, Baudelaire's invention of the 'carrion' Sappho is not nonsensed, for it did have an authentic tradition derived from Sappho's own work, and it went on to have a notable function in literary history as an image of Decadence.

Sappho herself was the first to break her body into pieces, even if she said that it was love, sexual desire, *eros* that was doing it to her. Her Fragment 130 uses an image of dismemberment, 'limb-loosening' that was a commonplace in Greek poetry when she first used it, and which has become a familiar, even clichéd image since. In the Loeb translation by D.A. Campbell it appears as 'Once again limb-loosening Love makes me tremble, the bitter-sweet, irresistable creature'; in Mary Barnard's translation it goes, 'With his venom/ Irresistable, and bittersweet/ that loosener/ of limbs, Love/ reptile-like/ Strikes me down'; in Josephine Balmer's it is 'Love makes me tremble yet again/ sapping all the strength from my limbs;/ bittersweet, undefeated creature –/ against you there is no defence'; Diane Rayor's translation is 'Once again that loosener of limbs, Love/ bittersweet and inescapable, crawling thing,/ seizes me'.[30]

The three key constituents of Sappho's erotic experience represented in this fragment are the character of desire as a 'creature', bestial, 'crawling' and overpowering, whose actions are physically violent and consistently overpowering; the weakness of the 'victim' whose limbs are 'loosened', and who is powerless to resist, and yet whose experience is paradoxically and simultaneously both 'sweet' and 'bitter'; and that strand, which John Winkler has called the 'double consciousness' in Sappho, means that her texts seem to operate effectively on two levels, for she evokes here both the predatory and singularly focussed intent of lust, alongside the helplessness of desire, fire in the belly, weak at the knees.[31]

'Eros' may break up Sappho's body, but literary self-consciousness is also a 'splitting' device. In Fragment 130 Sappho's doubled feeling/recording self is suggested in 'yet again', or 'once again' in translation, which makes it clear that Sappho's poem incorporates a memory of desire, deriving from another place and time, which can be measured against the present being described.

In Sappho's famous Fragment 31, 'He seems as fortunate as the gods to me ...', the experience of desire is also presented as a scene of self-fragmentation when the amorous speaker dissects her body to produce a list of parts, at the same time splitting herself into body-acted-upon and mind-recording-that-feeling:

> my tongue has snapped, at once a subtle fire has stolen beneath my flesh, I see nothing with my eyes, my ears hum, sweat pours from me, a trembling seizes me all over, I am greener than grass, and it seems to me that I am little short of dying ...

Sappho's list is compared by Lyn Hatherly Wilson to the catalogues of Homer which also list pains in variously discriminated body parts but which, typically, are evoked in describing an embattled warrior rather than a lovesick woman.[32]

Sappho's associative description of desire and bodily debilitation has become such a familiar image in Western culture that all our readings can only be re-readings, and it is hard now to recognise the shock and the danger which is in an alliance between pain and desire unless it is construed as a perversion.

In many ways Baudelaire is an inheritor of the poetic self-consciousness in the construction of lyric which passes down from Sappho; in others he is a latecomer whose jaded appetites require the inventiveness and variety of the roué. Here is Baudelaire writing to his mother in 1853 and making himself into a poet-hero who, like Sappho, is in tatters, only the sum of his parts:

> I am used to physical suffering to a certain degree. I am adept at making do with two shirts under torn trousers and a jacket which lets in the wind, and I am so experienced in using straw or even paper to plug up the holes in my shoes that moral suffering is almost the only kind I perceive as suffering. However, I must admit that I have reached the point where I don't make any sudden movements or walk a lot because I fear that I might tear my clothes even more.[33]

Baudelaire was a dandy, conscious of his public surface, as Gautier was in his red waistcoat, or as d'Albert is in *Mademoiselle de Maupin*. And yet also, in Walter Benjamin's coining, he was a 'ragpicker' who creates himself out of parts: 'Because he did not have any convictions, he assumed ever new forms himself. Flâneur, apaché, dandy, ragpicker were so many roles to him. For the modern hero is no hero; he acts heroes.'[34]

But what then occurs if, in order to act the hero, the poet not only disintegrates and reassembles himself, but also unpicks and re-members the body of woman? In her essay on Baudelaire Kristeva confronts 'the problem of the dandy'. She acknowledges its reliance on 'mere appearance', the purely artificial, the singlemindedly aesthetic. This is, in effect, a version of the 'art for art's sake' formula which Baudelaire found in Gautier even if he did not adopt its positions until after the publication of *Les Fleurs du mal*.[35] But Kristeva takes the idea of the dandy on to argue that the adoption of this pose, this 'seeming', is also 'an attempt to slip from feigned virility to an equally feigned femininity, only thus finally neutralized'. She goes on:

> In this domain of transference where identities are carried away by their inappropriateness, pretending to be a woman (those flowing locks, pink gloves, colored nails as well as hair) is not really a transition to homosexuality. What is lacking is the erotic obsession with the sado-masochistic quest of an object of the same sex. The dandy decked out as a woman is in fact rebelling against whatever (in others or in himself) tends to believe that the feminine, the maternal, is essential. Nothing is essential outside the seeming, the sign, the text, which have consumed affects – such is the dandy's facade; and that stifled cry in its elegant and ecclesiastical rigidity, is one aspect of his struggle against maternal feminine abjection (the 'carrion'), from which he ceaselessly separates himself. The femininity the dandy allows himself is a symbolic creativity – poetry itself – that recognizes that its cause is external, even if he appropriates it to himself and uses it.[36]

Setting aside Kristeva's curious assumptions about the character of homosexuality, there are elements in this argument which are especially relevant when the poet under discussion is one who uses a woman, Sappho, for and through his poetry, and when that woman is the first, the 'mother', of lyric poets. In *Mademoiselle de Maupin* Théophile Gautier, Baudelaire's close associate and friend, and the dedicatee of *Les Fleurs du mal*, had shown, long before the work of Joan Rivière or Simone de Beauvoir, that femininity (and masculinity) are 'masquerades'.[37] Taking this a stage further, Baudelaire exploits the 'feigned femininity' of the dandy who is concerned with surface, in order to recoup the function of creativity – in this case, writing poetry – which, according to 'essentialist' accounts is an exclusively female property. Kristeva does not refer to Baudelaire's Sappho poems or to *Les Lesbiennes*, but the fact of his invocation and exploitation of Sappho, as both woman and poet, reinforces her point.

It is odd, however, that Kristeva denies that this 'pretending to be a woman' has to do with homosexuality. If she is thinking of Baudelaire's own life then, of course, I must agree. The proclivities of the work need have nothing to do with the biography and vice versa. But the fact is that Baudelaire's writing which 'pretends to be a woman', in 'Lesbos' and the two 'Femmes Damnées' poems, most certainly does include a transition to homosexuality, albeit female homosexuality.

More than that, while I have my own doubts about the legitimacy of Kristeva's generalisation in her aside on how homosexuality is constituted ('... the erotic obsession with the sadomasochistic quest of an object of the same sex ...'), it is certainly true that in Baudelaire's verse erotic experience between those of the same sex is portrayed as obsessive, dedicated and driven, and it is also true to say that the mood of those poems is suggestively lurid, mixing pleasure and pain, 'douces langueurs et des frissons amers'.

Yet if Baudelaire's depiction of *Les Lesbiennes* is set within a frame of sado-masochism, so is his own attitude to them. His (poetic) pleasure is being invoked by their (poetic) pain, and what are we to make of his two frequently quoted observations, that the 'sole, supreme voluptuous pleasure in love lies in the certainty one has of doing evil', and that 'There is in the act of love a great resemblance with torture or a surgical operation'?[38]

Baudelaire's remarks are set in a heterosexual context, and of course sado-masochistic practice and fantasy does colour many sexual situations. In Angela Carter's meditations on de Sade she makes the same point about sex and torture. In both cases the lover, or the victim, become their parts, individuated, manipulated parts, broken down to a fragmented body which is worked upon in discrete sections to bring about pleasure or pain. What the comparison does not allow for is mutuality, reciprocity. One party has to be in charge, while the other suffers, one party acts, the other is acted upon. One party, as in Carter's witty scene from her short story 'The Bloody Chamber', has to be fully clothed, while the other is naked.[39] So Baudelaire is still a dandy; he is still dressed, although in tatters, while his Sappho is exposed, and he tears her to pieces.

L'Origine du monde

The taking apart of woman in this way, her reduction to parts, was not a new phenomenon in the poetry of the mid nineteenth century, nor was Baudelaire its only exponent. Sappho, whom Baudelaire broke up to make his own poetic self, was a particularly apt subject for the process because her body was, according to legend, broken on the rocks and her work was, in fact, fragmented and torn. But Baudelaire's Sappho is not so much a genuinely Hellenic creation as a woman of the nineteenth century.

The form of love poetry which particularises the charms of the beloved's body had been refined in the Renaissance by the poets who praised 'the body emblazoned'.[40] Baudelaire too was a practitioner of these 'blasons anatomiques', especially in such poems as 'Le Beau Navire' (which begins 'Je veus te raconter, ô molle enchanteresse!/ Les diverse beautés qui parent ta jeunesse'), 'Le Serpent que Danse' and 'Les Bijoux'. That it is the practice of the male artist, whether painter or poet to view, to examine, the displayed body of his subject-beloved in pieces, dissecting and anatomising her parts, has become a familiar theme in modern criticism. The dangerous dismemberment which thus takes place, the reduction of woman to a collection of truncated limbs and fetishised body sites has further been made the focus for politicised agitation especially over the representation of the female body whether in so-called high art, or in the perhaps more insidious – because more widespread – conventions of popular culture found in, say, advertising.[41] But from the late eighteenth century to the end of the nineteenth century, the anatomisation of the female body was a distinctive and obsessive theme.

Elisabeth Bronfen and Elaine Showalter point to the popularity of wax anatomical models displayed in cities and towns across Europe throughout the nineteenth century. Their original purpose was to allow for the detailed study of the workings of the body, its internal organs and constituent parts, without the gruesome necessity of working with an actual dead body in decay and putrefaction. According to Sander Gilman the techniques used in producing these wax models were adapted from those employed in making effigies for church rituals. From that, he extrapolates a connection between the increasing secularisation of society – which took place from the eighteenth century on – and the parallel privileging of the 'rational' sense of sight. Thus scientific investigation and an objective unveiling of the body's mysteries promoted an interest in the study of anatomy which was supposed to be austere, analytical and exploratory. In fact, many of these wax models were of the female body – they were nicknamed the 'wax' or 'anatomical Venuses' – and paintings of the highly popular genre subject of the 'scene of post-mortem' invariably included a fully dressed male doctor examining the naked body of a woman.[42]

The prurience in these paraded inspections is made clear by Elaine Showalter's account of a 'scandalous' painting by Gustave Courbet which was commissioned in 1866 by the Turkish collector Khalil Bey. It was called *L'Origine du monde*, and it depicted a woman's cunt while the rest of its owner disappears out of the frame:

> In the dressing room of this foreign personage one sees a small picture hidden under a green veil. When one draws aside the veil one remains stupified to perceive a woman, life-size, seen from the front, moved and convulsed, remarkably executed, reproduced *con amore*, as the Italians say, providing the last word in realism. But, by some inconceivable forgetfulness the artist, who copied his model from nature, had neglected to represent the feet, the legs, the thighs, the stomach, the hips, the chest, the hands, the arms and the shoulders, the neck, and the head.[43]

That this contemporary spectator, writing in 1889, felt driven to describe this picture by listing all the missing limbs as separate parts, rather than representing it as a failure to portray the model's whole person, let alone an individual with character and spirit, name and independent existence, suggests how familiarly automatic the dissection of woman had become in the late nineteenth century.

That this insistence on the part for the neglect of the whole suggests a metonymic anxiety about the character of female sexuality in late nineteenth century culture has been argued by Dijkstra, Showalter, Bronfen, Dowling, Stott, and others.[44] In the early case of Baudelaire, however, the representation of the parts of the body chopped into pieces and made into an auto-icon, suggests not just an anxiety about sexuality, but the obsessions of the fetishist, who is also a poet, and for whom poetic 'maternal space' is figured by Sappho. Just as the worrying cunt in Courbet's picture represents 'the origin of the world', so Sappho, for the poet-arrived-late-in-time represents the beginnings of poetry.

According to Freud's account of fetishism, the subject denies what he imagines to be the castration of the mother by investing some other loved thing with the power of the mother's lost phallus. Thus he (usually he) both explains the apparent emptiness and absence at the centre of the mother (the cunt which is nothingness, a not-phallus) and yet simultaneously renews a relationship with creative 'maternal space' by keeping by him the symbol of his fantasy of the mother's power (the previous moment, which is always false, when he believed that she possessed a penis).[45]

In Baudelaire's 'Lesbos' the first word of the poem is 'mother' ('Mère des jeux latins et des voluptés grecques') and the first reference, to the Romans and Greeks, gestures back to early Western civilisation, to 'the beginning of the world'. Lesbos is both the land and the mysterious body of the mother, and Sappho herself is reduced to an inanimate object, a fetish, which is absent or lost. Sappho's 'adored cadaver' ('Le cadavre adoré de Sapho') is what the poet looks out for. He has his sight which is 'piercing and sure' ('l'oeil perçant et sûr'), which is, in effect, potent, like the phallus with which it is conceptually associated. And he waits, looks out to discover if 'the sea' or rather 'the mother' – given the sounding pun which works in the French – will be 'indulgent and good' ('Pour savoir si la mer est indulgente et bonne') and will restore the absent, cut-off, body of Sappho. According to this reading Sappho has become a thing, a fetishistic object which can be made into 'food' for another, absorbed therefore, into another ('Elle fit son beau corps la pâture suprême'). And that thing, which represents her notional castration, can be taken over by another – in this case the poet who seeks the fetish-part – who will thereby annexe her space and acquire her potency. This is indeed the 'feigned femininity' of the poet-dandy who makes woman into 'pâture' (in Baudelaire), or 'carrion' (in Kristeva's account of Baudelaire) in order to counteract whatever it is in himself which 'tends to believe that the feminine, the maternal, is essential'.

Théophile Gautier said that Baudelaire was not remotely interested in a 'natural' woman, but only ever in femininity 'feigned': 'It is not he who would write virtuous tirades against painting, rouging and the crinoline. All that removed a man, and especially a woman, from the natural state found favour in his eyes.' Gautier links this, first of all, to 'the individual taste of the poet for artificiality', but he then expands this apparently personal predilection to include the more general tastes of the age: 'He takes pleasure in this kind of composite beauty, and now and then a little artificiality that elaborates advanced and unsound civilisations.' Then, over the page, still in speaking of woman-*au-naturel* versus carmined-and-bejewelled, he declares that: 'These tastes explain themselves and ought to be understandable in a poet of the decadence ...'[46]

Gautier saw Baudelaire, as he saw himself, as a late-arrived sophisticate ('advanced and unsound civilisations') whose jaded tastes were for the contrived, the rarified and the bizaare. He construed himself and his friend as real-life versions of his own d'Albert, bored with the 'natural' and requiring ever more piquant experience. Like Gautier's version of Baudelaire, d'Albert finds no pleasure in a 'natural' woman because when he examines her parts, he finds several of them wanting:

> Rosette is not bad. She might even pass as beautiful, but she is far from realising my dream. She is a statue, several bits of which are very clearly developed. The others are not so striking; some parts are modelled with much skill and charm, while others are done in a more careless and loose fashion. To the ordinary observer the statue appears quite finished and complete in its beauty; but a more careful scrutiny soon discovers spots where the work is not concise enough ...[47]

Judged in terms of the art-object ('She is a statue ...') and the artificial ideal, Rosette inevitably fails to survive the examination of critical scrutiny, '... she is far from realising my dream'. If the trend in Baudelaire's lesbian poems, and in 'Lesbos' in particular is toward a denial that 'the feminine ... is essential' then similarly in Gautier's *Mademoiselle de Maupin* it is a 'feigned femininity', a contrived and artificial representation, which will most please. It is Théodore, a man (apparently), who most nearly resembles d'Albert's ideal 'dream', and who indeed realises it completely when 'he' dresses up as Rosalind. And remember, that it is in that costume – that is, as-man-dressed-as-woman – that he goes to d'Albert.

So too in Baudelaire's 'Lesbos' the male poet dresses up in drag to become 'the male Sappho, lover and poet/ More beautiful than Venus ...' Kristeva's 'feigned femininity' is, after all, just such an account of artificial self-creation, constructed by the man in drag '(those flowing locks, pink gloves, colored nails as well as hair)'. But this transvestism, enacted by Baudelaire's poems where he masquerades as Sappho, far from suggesting any identification or sympathy with real femininity, does away with the feminine altogether.[48]

7
Sappho's Fatal Book

'Ave Atque Vale'

In England, Baudelaire's most ardent admirer was Algernon Charles Swinburne, and his own relation to the French poet whom he called the 'sweet strange elder singer' created a pattern that mimicked the connection between Baudelaire and Sappho. In his valedictory poem 'Ave Atque Vale, In Memory of Charles Baudelaire' written after Baudelaire's death and published in 1878, he quotes an epigraph from *Les Fleurs du mal* and memorialises the departed body of the poet as part of a landscape and seascape which is pure Baudelairian-Sapphic:

I

Shall I strew on thee rose or rue or laurel,
　　Brother, on this that was the veil of thee?
　　Or quiet sea-flower moulded by the sea,
Or simplest growth of meadow-sweet or sorrel,
　　Such as the summer-sleepy dryads weave,
　　Waked up by snow-soft sudden rains at eve?
Or wilt thou rather, as on earth before,
　　Half-faded fiery blossoms, pale with heat
　　And full of bitter summer, but more sweet
To thee than gleanings of a northern shore
　　Trod by no tropic feet?

II

For always thee the fervid languid glories
　　Allured of heavier suns in mightier skies;
　　Thine ears knew all the wandering watery sighs
Where the sea sobs round Lesbian promontories,

> The barren kiss of piteous wave to wave
> That knows not where is the Leucadian grave
> Which hides too deep the supreme head of song.
> Ah, salt and sterile as her kisses were,
> The wild sea winds her and the green gulfs bear
> Hither and thither, and vex and work her wrong,
> Blind gods that cannot spare.[1]

Vying with his two heroes, Gautier and Baudelaire, in the artifice of art, Swinburne's limping and elaborate metrics for this poem are replicated in the complicated acknowledgement of literary debt and reference. As with Baudelaire's treatment of Sappho's body, the French poet's body seems similarly to have become a free-floating relic or fetish, just out of the reach of the desiring follower. Swinburne clearly knows the text of Baudelaire's 'Lesbos' well, and recalls the exact terms of Baudelaire's imaginary seascape. Swinburne's 'wandering watery sighs/ Where the sea sobs' includes a literary memory of the last stanza in 'Lesbos', and his 'barren kiss of wave to wave' refers to the mirror and the sterility images which are expressed in the presentation of same-sex love in Baudelaire's 'Lesbos' and in both of the 'Femmes Damnées' poems. But Swinburne's peculiar, and distinctively skewed suggestion of sexuality, means that he hears and acts on, extends, all the refined hints in the earlier poems, and something titillatingly prurient seems to seep through his description of Baudelaire's expertise in 'Lesbian promontories'.

Part of this comes out of Swinburne's own hothouse imagination, but part also comes out of a delicate and discerning receptiveness to the possibilities of an artificial language which can play and pun. For instance, in the phrase 'the wild sea winds her', the word is both 'winds' – as in blown about by the winds – and 'winds' – as in wraps around like a shroud. Or, for example, in 'the green gulfs bear/ Hither and thither, and vex and work her wrong', the image is both as in 'tease and torture her body in a wicked manner', and alternatively as in 'use mercilessly and exploit all the imagined variations of her own unsanctioned behaviour'.

Swinburne is one of those poets who points constantly to the fact that poetry is a nothingness; that it is only air and wind, breath and singing, and that it fades in the instant of utterance. So Baudelaire, the dead poet, no longer singing, is lost and yet pursued by Swinburne's poetry itself, which thus attempts to resurrect the body of Baudelaire's work:

> Thou art far too far for wings of words to follow,
> Far too far off for thought or any prayer.
> What ails us with thee, who art wind and air?
> What ails us gazing where all seen is hollow?

Yet with some fancy, yet with some desire,
Dreams pursue death as winds a flying fire,
Our dreams pursue our dead and do not find.
Still, and more swift than they, the thin flame flies,
The low light fails us in elusive skies,
Still the foiled earnest ear is deaf, and blind
Are still the eluded eyes.

Not thee, O never thee, in all time's changes,
Not thee, but this the sound of thy sad soul,
The shadow of thy swift spirit, this shut scroll
I lay my hand on, and not death estranges
My spirit from communion of thy song –
These memories and these melodies that throng
Veiled porches of a Muse funereal –
These I salute, these touch, these clasp and fold
As though a hand were in my hand to hold,
Or through mine ears a mourning musical
Of many mourners rolled.

Those critics interested in poetry who condemn Swinburne's work tend to focus on its insubstantiality, its lack of fact and body, its airy nothingness, all sound without substance. Browning and Tennyson were among these.[2] But, conversely, critics interested in moral statements condemn Swinburne's poetry for its materiality, its focus on the body – in the term made famous by Robert Buchanan – on its 'fleshliness'. Buchanan's primary target for attack in his 1871 article 'The Fleshly School of Poetry' was Dante Gabriel Rossetti, but he also argued that Rossetti had learnt from Swinburne's example:

> Mr Swinburne was wilder, more outrageous, more blasphemous, and his subjects were more atrocious in themselves; yet the hysterical tone slew the animalism, the furiousness of either lowered the sensation; and the first feeling of disgust in such themes as 'Laus Veneris' or 'Anactoria', faded away, with comic amazement. It was only a little mad boy letting off squibs, not a great strong man, who might be really dangerous to society. 'I *will* be naughty!' screamed the little boy; but, after all, what did it matter? It is quite different, however, when a grown man with self-control and easy audacity of actual experience, comes forward to chronicle his amorous sensations ...[3]

There is a split here. Buchanan sees the bodilyness of Swinburne's poetry, its 'animalism', its 'fury', just as he sees the physicality in the poet which produces the 'hysteria' and fact of 'sensation', and just as he sees – or rather feels – the physical fact of his own reaction as reader, the 'feeling of disgust', and the 'comic amazement'.

And yet, Buchanan ultimately lets Swinburne get away with it, because these are only 'squibs and naughtiness'. Crucially, because the stories of the erotic body in Swinburne's poetry are not – so Buchanan says – based on 'actual experience'. The propensity which is in Swinburne' s verse to play, to pun, to disperse solid representation into word-games and poetry's airy nothingness may be one reason why Buchanan does not see how genuinely 'fleshly' Swinburne is.

But there are also two other reasons. And both are invisible to Buchanan because he seems to have a very limited idea of exactly what erotic experience may consist of. For Swinburne personally – insofar as one can say or know anything about another's experience – it would appear that beating, flagellation, 'sporting an arse', was the key erotic experience that informed his poetry. Beating, being beaten, and beating time mean that this body experience translates into poetry and its strict beating rhythm. Yopie Prins has ingeniously argued the case precisely for the materiality of Swinburne's verse by showing how Swinburne's childhood experience of – and continuing interest in – the whip, coloured both his early lessons, his apprehension of Greek metre, and his later exploitation of the varieties of poetic metre along with the varieties of perversely beaten bodies displayed in his poetry. Certainly Swinburne was an expert in this area and made himself a connoisseur of the literature of flagellation, so that it cannot be surprising that he took this excitement and urgency into the terms, the practices and the methods of his poetry.[4]

But Swinburne was also an expert in the writings of the Marquis de Sade. In 1862, the year when he published his translations of Baudelaire's *Les Fleurs du mal*, Swinburne read de Sade's *Justine, ou les malheurs de la vertu*. Swinburne may have been disappointed with de Sade, but they shared an obsession with the body which translated in a very literal way into a materiality that was mathematically controlled by parts which added up to wholes, or wholes which can indeed be made 'holey' – and holy – by breaking them again into pieces. In *Justine* human beings are no more and no less than matter and, according to the practitioner in that novel, Clément, the process of breaking up the human body through varieties of abuse and torture is simply one which takes 'a portion of oblong-shaped matter' and transmutes it into 'three or four thousand rounds or squares'.[5]

Like de Sade, Swinburne' s concern is with numbers. Not how many times or in what order, not with size or frequency, but with metric quantity, rhythmic numbers. His poetic measure is always material. When the words 'foot' or 'feet' appear in Swinburne it is always split in meaning, for it suggests both body part and verse, rhythm, metre, poetic number.

So in 'Ave Atque Vale' Swinburne offers to Baudelaire a garland of verse, a 'wreath' of rhyme which is fierce and exotic:

> And full of bitter summer, but more sweet
> To thee than gleanings of a northern shore
> Trod by no tropic feet?

To read this right we must break up the material language of Swinburne's image as he broke up its substantial puns to make it. Swinburne's own 'feet', physically and poetically, are English, therefore of the North, but his spirit is exotic therefore 'tropic' – as in 'tropical' – but also as in a poetic 'trope'. In Swinburne the poetic figure is always both metaphor and matter.

Of course this relates to the many bodies which figure in Swinburne' s verse, but in reading Swinburne's letters and the many references to Sappho which are included there, it is striking to see how his image of her is so physically realised. Just as Sappho is a body (albeit lost and sought) in both Baudelaire and in Swinburne's 'Ave Atque Vale' so she seems always to appear to Swinburne' s imagination clothed in flesh and very little else.

In 1864 after visiting the Uffizi Gallery in Florence Swinburne wrote that he was disappointed with Veronese's *Martyrdom of St Justina* but (and it's an interesting juxtaposition) he goes on to speak of Titian's *Venus of Urbino* which seems to have pleased him more:

> As for Titian' s Venus – Sappho and Anactoria in one – four lazy fingers buried *dans les fleurs de son jardin* – how any creature can be decently virtuous within thirty square miles of it passes my comprehension. I think with her Tannhauser need not have been bored – even till the end of the world; but who knows?[6]

Venus, Sappho, Anactoria. Body, parts, stimulation, response. Measurement in space, time and satisfaction. When Swinburne says Sappho's name, even in the most unlikely circumstances, he says body, sexual parts, and measurement. In a letter to Edmund Gosse about his surprise at Cardinal Newman's attempt to separate 'religion' and 'amorousness' he remarks on various examples of sexualised religious ecstasy and goes on:

> Not to speak of the filthy visions of the rampant and rabid nun who founded the worship of the Sacred Heart (she called it heart – in the phallic processions they called it by a more – and less – proper name), he might have found passages from St. Theresa which certainly justify from a carnal point of view her surname of the Christian Sappho. There is as much detail, if I mistake not (judging by extracts), in her invocations of her Phaon – Jesus

Christ – as in the Ode to Anactoria itself – which, as Byron justly observes, is *not* 'a good example'.[7]

An even more bizarre example of Swinburne's idea of Sappho occurs in a letter written to Dante Gabriel Rossetti in which he discussed Christina Rossetti's imminent publication of her collection *Commonplace and Other Short Stories* in 1870.

> I am delighted to hear of your sister's projects. I read again lately her little story of 'Hero' in the Argosy – and it seems to me, if only from the song there near the end, that she of all living women of genius (or dead for that matter – for I don't imagine the Tenth Muse of Lesbos would have tried her quite-otherwise-employed hand at inditing songs and stories to soothe the cradles of infants to the necessary preliminaries of whose production she held such strong objections) is best qualified and surest to write what will give deep and passionate delight to imaginative children, as well as the more articulate and expressible pleasure of beautiful work to men. (Perhaps I am wrong about Sappho, for she *did* write epithalamiums on friends' nuptials, which was I must say like her Olympian impudence and her Titanic cheek, and might have sung and played to children with the same mouth and the same hand which made music on the Lesbian lyre, and on another feminine organ not necessary to specify.)[8]

One wonders if Dante Gabriel ever conveyed Swinburne's compliments to Christina ... if he showed her the letter? Perhaps not. But Swinburne's lengthy asides – demonstrating where his real interests lie in this discussion of women's writing – give a clear indication of his Sappho who, like Dante Gabriel or Simeon Solomon, is a chum with whom he can indeed say 'I will be naughty' and indulge his love of innuendo.[9]

Swinburne's obsessive return to dissected body parts in his vision of Sappho makes the link between his idea of her and his reading of de Sade. Swinburne himself made the connection – writing to his friend George Powell in 1868 he says that he wished to see him, '1) to see you and cheer and be cheered if ill or worried 2) to satiate my craving (ultra Sapphic and plusquam Sadic) lust after the sea'[10] – and many critics have noted it since though, with the exception of Yopie Prins, only in a generalised way. 'The Sappho of "Anactoria"', says Douglas Bush, 'is not merely the descendant of Libitina and Priapus, she is the daughter of de Sade.'[11] Swinburne's Sadist Sappho is huge, larger than life – 'Olympian' and 'Titanic' as in Swinburne's letter – so that her large body can be spread out across land and sea, available for inspection and division into parts; mouth, and hand, and 'another feminine organ not necessary to specify'.

In this too Swinburne borrows from and recalls Baudelaire's treatment of Sappho. Just as she is the body of the island in 'Lesbos', so in Swinburne's 'Ave Atque Vale' the younger poet imagines the elder in the embrace of that huge woman created by his own vision:

Now all strange hours and all strange loves are over,
    Dreams and desires and sombre songs and sweet,
    Hast thou found place at the great knees and feet
Of some pale Titan-woman like a lover,
    Such as thy vision here solicited,
    Under the shadow of her fair vast head,
The deep division of prodigious breasts,
    The solemn slope of mighty limbs asleep,
    The weight of awful tresses that still keep
The savour and shade of old-world pine-forests
    Where the wet hill-winds weep?[12]

Baudelaire first made Sappho into a landscape where he could intrude himself; he made her body into a fetish which represented the poetic power he desired; he made himself into the singer of Lesbos because Sappho – used in this way – was silenced.

And then Swinburne follows the pattern. Baudelaire, dead, is now – as at the end of Swinburne's memorial poem – a 'silent soul', while Swinburne himself is doing the singing. Baudelaire's is the fetishised body now, existing only as a body of work, and thus desired and taken over by the survivor, 'this shut scroll/ I lay my hand on ... As though a hand were in my hand to hold ...' And Baudelaire, once dead, returns to earth and to the sea, to become like Sappho, like the 'mer/mère' who made him:

    Thin is the leaf, and chill the wintry smell.
And chill the solemn earth, a fatal mother,
    With sadder than the Niobean womb,
    And in the hollow of her breasts a tomb.
Content thee, howsoe'er, whose days are done;
    There lies not any troublous thing before,
    Nor sight nor sound to war against thee more,
For whom all winds are quiet as the sun,
    All waters as the shore.

Of course, in spite of Sappho, in spite of Niobe and the land and sea mother, there is still no woman in this text, any more than there was in Baudelaire. She is 'apparitional' as she is in Gautier, invariably a man in drag playing the part of 'de la mâle Sapho', for this is a society of men, even if they are prepared to cross-dress.

In his retrospective vision of the pre-Raphaelite circle, Max Beerbohm drew one picture of Swinburne reading his Sappho-poem 'Anactoria' to Dante Gabriel and William Michael Rossetti. The sketch is entitled 'The Small Hours in the Sixties at 16, Cheyne Walk. – Algernon reading "Anactoria" to Gabriel and William'. It shows Swinburne tiny, frenetic, his ginger mane illuminated by the candle, sitting at the slippered feet of Dante Gabriel who reclines his huge bulk on a sofa. If Beerbohm had read 'Ave Atque Vale' he may have been inspired by the image of the poet who has found a 'place at the great knees and feet/ Of some pale Titan-woman like a lover'. For in Beerbohm's picture it is Rossetti who cross-dresses, or cross-poses as Sappho, as the sweeping shape of *chaise longue* recalls the Greek curve of the *klismos* chair, and his sumptuous indolence mimics the seductive pose of the odalisque so often employed in Sappho and Sappho-related pictures.[13]

'Anactoria' was Swinburne's most famous Sappho poem, but it was only one of the three Sappho poems which appeared in his first publication *Poems and Ballads* (1866). The other two were 'Satia Te Sanguine' and 'Sapphics'. There is also a mention of Sappho in the 1866 poem 'The Masque of Queen Bersabe'.

Swinburne had read de Sade in 1862 and he had published a translation of Baudelaire's *Les Fleurs du mal* in 1862. In his essay on *Les Fleurs du mal* published in *The Spectator* in September of that year he describes Baudelaire as if he were a disciple of de Sade:

> Not the luxuries of pleasure in their simple first form, but the sharp and cruel enjoyments of pain, and acrid relish of suffering felt or inflicted, the sides on which nature looks unnatural, go to make up the stuff and substance of this poetry. Very good material they make too; but evidently such things are unfit for rapid or careless treatment ...[14]

Swinburne returned often and at length to his sources borrowed from Baudelaire and de Sade and, while he portrayed many rapacious women in his verses, nowhere were these two influences more marked than in Swinburne's invention of Sappho. In 'The Masque of Queen Bersabe', a mock medieval morality play about David and Bathsheba, published in 1866, the prophet Nathan warns David of the harm Bathsheba will bring by parading before him a phantom show of all the wicked women the world has known: Herodias and Cleopatra, Semiramis and Aholah, along with sixteen others, including Sappho, who precedes Messalina:

> I am the queen of Lesbians.
> My love, that had no part in man's,
>   Was sweeter than all shape of sweet.
> The intolerable infinite desire
> Made my face pale like faded fire
>   When the ashen pyre falls through with heat.

My blood was hot wan wine of love,
And my song's sound the sound thereof,
The sound of the delight of it.[15]

This Sappho's 'infinite desire' comes from Baudelaire's 'Delphine et Hippolyte', the first of his 'Femmes Damnées' poems, but the pleasure in bodily pain that translates into singing, sound made on and out of the body, is out of de Sade.

'Satia Te Sanguine'

The inheritance from de Sade is present also in 'Satia Te Sanguine' from *Poems and Ballads* (1866) where the speaker complains of the beloved who tortures him (or her?), breaking up his body into parts as Sappho's is broken and adrift in the sea, even as he simultaneously desires to break up the limbs of the beloved:

If you loved me ever so little,
I could bear the bonds that gall,
I could dream the bonds were brittle;
You do not love me at all.

O beautiful lips, o bosom
More white than the moon's and warm,
A sterile, a ruinous blossom
Is blown your way in a storm.

As the lost white feverish limbs
Of the Lesbian Sappho, adrift
In foam where the sea-weed swims,
Swam loose for the streams to lift,

My heart swims blind in a sea
That stuns me; swims to and fro,
And gathers to windward and lee
Lamentation and mourning, and woe

A broken, an emptied boat,
Sea saps it, and winds blow apart,
Sick, and adrift and afloat,
The barren waif of a heart ...

I wish you were dead, my dear;
I would give you, had I to give,
Some death too bitter to fear;
It is better to die than live.

I wish you were stricken of thunder
  And burnt with a bright flame through
Consumed and cloven in sunder,
  I dead at your feet like you ...[16]

The body in this poem is in pieces, 'cloven in sunder', 'broken', 'blown apart'. The heart of the speaker is swimming 'loose' just as Sappho's limbs in the sea are 'swimming loose', just as they were, according to her own formula, taken apart by love, the 'loosener' of limbs.

But when Swinburne takes Sappho's body apart he also breaks up her corpus. Swinburne's poetry is always ready to recognise a simultaneous relation to the material body and to the spiritual insubstantiality of writing. But in Sappho's case – and it may be one reason why she figures so large in his poetic view – there is an actual body/corpus which is broken, whose textual limbs are ' loosened' and a text/body-of-work which can be cannibalised, incorporated into his own body-of-work.

'Sapphics'

In 'Sapphics' Swinburne sets a scenario where he, the male poet, is Sappho's successor who conjures her up in order to make poetry out of that vision:

All the night sleep came not upon my eyelids,
Shed not dew, nor shook nor unclosed a feather,
Yet with lips shut close and with eyes of iron
  Stood and beheld me.

Then to me so lying awake a vision
Came without sleep over the seas and touched me,
Softly touched mine eyelids and lips; and I too,
  Full of the vision ...[17]

In this poem Swinburne follows the pattern of Baudelaire's 'Lesbos', but the body of Sappho which is envisioned here is not just the 'carrion' which appears in Baudelaire, 'the limitless, nonsensed body, harrowed by a crisis that one might call deeply narcissistic', but the actual body of Sappho's text. Swinburne's vision of Sappho is not 'nonsensed' in this; that he, unlike Baudelaire, has Greek. So Swinburne can usurp her actual poetic body, can take over her form, and the rhythmic shape that fleshes her verse.

In 'Sapphics' Swinburne puns on the idea of both the 'Sapphic' adjective and metre. His subject is sapphic, and his form is Sapphic, for he uses both the form of the strict metre of the Sapphic stanza,

¯ ¯ x ¯ ¯ ¯ ¯ || ^ia hag||
¯ ¯ x ¯ ¯ ¯ ¯ || ^ia hag||
¯ ¯ x ¯ ¯ : ¯ x : ¯ ¯ ¯ |||

and the connective technique of *enjambement*, carrying a thought over from one stanza to the next.[18] Knowing, as he did, all of Sappho's extant fragments in as pure a form as possible for this period, Swinburne mimics Sappho closely. Sappho's Fragment 1 is the so-called ' Ode to Aphrodite'. Here is the Greek, followed by two English versions, one a prose translation (the Loeb edition), the other a poetic translation by Josephine Balmer.

ποικιλόθρον' ἀθανάτ' Ἀφρόδιτα,
παῖ Δίος δολόπλοκε, λίσσομαί σε,
μή μ' ἄσαισι μηδ' ὀνίαισι δάμνα,
πότνια, θῦμον,

ἀλλά τυίδ' ἔλθ', αἴ ποτα κἀτέρωτα
τὰς ἔμας αὔδας ἀίοισα πήλοι
ἔκλυες, πάτρος δὲ δόμον λίποισα
χρύσιον ἦλθες

ἄρμ' ὐπασδεύξαισα· κάλοι δέ σ' ἆγον
ὤκεες στροῦθοι περὶ γᾶς μελαίνας
πύκνα δίννεντες πτέρ' ἀπ' ὠράνωἴθε-
ρος διὰ μέσσω,

αἶψα δ' ἐξίκοντο· σὺ δ', ὦ μάκαιρα,
μειδιαίσαισ' ἀθανάτῳ προσώπῳ
ἤρε' ὄττι δηὖτε πέπονθα κὤττι
δηὖτε κάλημμι,

κὤττι μοι μάλιοτα θέλω γέεσθαι
μαινόλᾳ θύμῳ· τίνα δηὖτε πείθω
ἄψ σ' ἄγην ἐς Ϝὰν φιλότατα; τίς σ', ὦ
Ψάπφ', ἀδικήει;

καὶ γὰρ αἰ φεύγει, ταχέως διώξει·
αἰ δὲ δῶρα μὴ δέκετ', ἀλλὰ δώσει·
αἰ δὲ μὴ φίλει, ταχέως φιλήσει
κωὐκ ἐθέλοισα.

ἔλθε μοι καὶ νῦν, χαλέπαν δὲ λῦσον
ἐκ μερίμναν, ὄσσα δέ μοι τέλεσσαι
θῦμος ἰμέρρει, τέλεσον· σὺ δ' αὔτα
σύμμαχος ἔσσο.

Ornate-throned immortal Aphrodite, wile-weaving daughter of Zeus, I entreat you: do not overpower my heart, mistress, with ache and anguish, but come here, if ever in the past you heard my voice from afar and acquiesced and came, leaving your father's golden house, with chariot yoked: beautiful swift sparrows whirring fast-beating wings brought you above the dark earth down from heaven through the mid-air and soon they arrived; and you, blessed one, with a smile on your immortal face asked what was the matter with me this time and why I was calling this time and what in my maddened heart I most wished to happen to myself: 'Whom am I to persuade this time to lead you back to her love? Who wrongs you, Sappho? If she runs away, soon she shall pursue; if she does not accept gifts, why, she shall give them instead; and if she does not love, soon she shall love even against her will'. Come to me now again and deliver me from oppressive anxieties; fulfil all that my heart longs to fulfil, and you yourself be my fellow-fighter.

Immortal, Aphrodite, on your patterned throne,
daughter of Zeus, guile-weaver,
I beg you, goddess, don't subjugate my heart
with anguish, with grief

but come here to me now, if ever in the past
you have heard my distant pleas
and listened; leaving your father's golden house
you came to me then

with your chariot yoked; beautiful swift sparrows
brought you around the dark earth
with a whirl of wings, beating fast, from heaven
down through the mid-air

to reach me quickly; then you, my sacred goddess,
your immortal face smiling,
asked me what had gone wrong this time and this time
why was I begging

and what in my demented heart, I wanted most:
'Who shall I persuade this time
to take you back, yet once again, to her love;
who wrongs you, Sappho?

For if she runs away, soon she shall run after,
if she shuns gifts, she shall give,
if she does not love you, soon she shall even
against her own will'.

So come to me now, free me from this aching pain,
fulfil everything that
my heart desires to be fulfilled: you, yes you,
will be my ally.[19]

In Sappho's Fragment 1 her method of *enjambement* enacts in verse the passage of the flight of birds bringing Aphrodite in response to Sappho's invocation, by carrying the sense across stanzas 3 to 4. In his 'Sapphics' Swinburne copies Sappho's picture and form, reproducing both.

Then to me so lying awake ...
... and I too,
Full of the vision,

Saw the white implacable Aphrodite,
Saw the hair unbound and the feet unsandalled
Shine as fire of sunset on western waters;
Saw the reluctant

Feet, the straining plumes of the doves that drew her,
Looking always, looking with necks reverted,
Back to Lesbos, back to the hills whereunder
Shone Mitylene; ...[20]

Similarly borrowed from Sappho's Fragment 1, is the address which Swinburne puts into Aphrodite's mouth. In Sappho's original it is the poet who calls on the goddess begging her attention and her assistance. In Swinburne, it is the Goddess who calls to Sappho, so moved by her song that she is translated into the petitioner:

...

Yea, almost the implacable Aphrodite
Paused, and almost wept; such a song was that song.
Yea, by her name too

Called her, saying, 'Turn to me, O my Sappho'; ...

So the goddess departs, returns to Mitylene, to Lesbos. In Swinburne's revision of Sappho's Fragment 1 his Aphrodite now seems to live – not, as in Sappho's original, in an Olympian heaven – but in Sappho's own place, on her own island. From there, in this new version of Sappho's song, the poet (whether Sappho or Swinburne) can call her. But Sappho is now independent of Aphrodite, of the Loves, of the Muses and all the gods. In Swinburne's version Sappho sings her song with, or without, the approval of the old gods who retire to the place which Sappho herself once inhabited.

Swinburne's 'Sapphics' is no programmatic revision of Fragment 1. Others of Sappho's fragments are also alluded to in his poem, most particularly of course that other Sappho poem which was thought to be complete in the nineteenth century, Sappho's Fragment 31. In his stanza 9 Swinburne describes Sappho's body in stress, in the moment of inspiration as she sings her song:

> While the tenth sang wonderful things they knew not.
> Ah the tenth, the Lesbian! the nine were silent,
> None endured the sound for weeping;
>   Laurel by laurel,
>
> Faded all their crowns; but about her forehead,
> Round her woven tresses and ashen temples
> White as dead snow, paler than grass in summer,
>   Ravaged with kisses,
>
> Shone a light of fire as a crown for ever.

The Muses can no longer sing, in this belated scene, but Sappho – whom the ancients called the 'Tenth Muse' – still sings and still is heard, while she herself, in the moment of that passion, is still, as she described herself in Fragment 31, 'paler than grass'.

Sewing Sappho's fragments, or rather his versions, his translations, of those fragments into his own verse, Swinburne takes Sappho's body, makes it the field of his image, and translates her 'loosened limbs', fragments of her verse, into his own poetry. He literally makes of the Lesbian's body the instrument for his singing, for he sees Sappho singing, and she sings her song:

> [I] ...
> Saw the Lesbians kissing across their smitten
> Lutes with lips more sweet than the sound of lute-strings,
> Mouth to mouth and hand upon hand, her chosen,
>   Fairer than all men;
>
> Only saw the beautiful lips and fingers,
> Full of songs and kisses and little whispers,
> Full of music ...

And yet Swinburne's 'Sapphics' is a poem not entirely made out of Sappho, or Sappho's verse, alone. Swinburne's intertextual method of poetry means that he borrows here also from his more immediate mentor, Baudelaire. 'Mouth to mouth and hand upon hand', suggests a memory of 'Femmes Damnées': 'Et leur pieds se cherchant et leurs mains rapproachées/ Ont de douces languers et des frissons amers.' And the conclusion of 'Sapphics' where the song of the 'outcast women' fills the land, where the land is nothing but song, refers back to both Baudelaire's 'Femmes Damnées' poems, and to his 'Lesbos', where Lesbos laments, and the song of torment is all that remains of Sappho:

> All withdrew long since, and the land was barren,
> Full of fruitless women and music only.
> Now perchance, when winds are assuaged at sunset,
>   Lulled at the dewfall,
>
> By the grey sea-side, unassuaged, unheard of,
> Unbeloved, unseen in the ebb of twilight,
> Ghosts of outcast women return lamenting,
>   Purged not in Lethe,
>
> Clothed about with flame and with tears, and singing
> Songs that move the heart of the shaken heaven,
> Songs that break the heart of the earth with pity,
>   Hearing, to hear them.

Jerome McGann has suggested that Swinburne's 'Sapphics' is, in effect, a 'mirror poem' where Sappho's own Fragment 1 is revised and inverted.[21] In the 'Ode to Aphrodite' Sappho invokes the goddess to come to Lesbos; in 'Sapphics' Aphrodite is summoned by the poet away from Lesbos. In the 'Ode to Aphrodite' Sappho calls to the goddess, but in Swinburne the goddess calls to Sappho. And finally, Aphrodite, far from being Sappho's 'ally' as she is petitioned in Fragment 1, in Swinburne she flees from Sappho, repulsed and stricken by her song. Swinburne makes of Sappho's body/corpus a glass to reflect his own image. But Baudelaire showed him the way, and Baudelaire too is inverted, made into a trans-sexualised body of verse in Swinburne's poetic mirror.

'Anactoria'

'Anactoria' is Swinburne's most sustained and monumental version of Sappho, published in *Poems and Ballads: First Series* (1866). The ventriloquism of the performance, where Swinburne performs Sappho, articulates her 'loosened limbs', is suggested by the epigraph

> τίνος αὖ τὺ πειθοῖ
> μὰψ σαγηνεύσας φιλότατα

which, though signed 'Sappho' is in fact Aphrodite speaking in Sappho's Fragment 1 and saying 'Whom am I to persuade this time to lead back to your love?' and continuing 'Who wrongs you Sappho?'[22] As in 'Sapphics', the epigraph is not the only quotation from Sappho to appear in the poem. Her fragments are woven into the verse so that, for instance, Love (or Aphrodite) is seen 'upon her storied seat', she has a 'mind of many colours', she arrives in a train of 'flying feet of fluttered doves' and she twice recites her own words as borrowed from Sappho's Fragment 1:

> ... and she bowed,
> With all her subtle face laughing aloud,
> Bowed down upon me, saying, 'Who doth thee wrong,
> Sappho? ...
>
> Yet the queen laughed from her sweet heart and said:
> 'Even she that flies shall follow for thy sake,
> And she shall give gifts that would not take,
> Shall kiss that would not kiss thee' (yea, kiss me)
> 'When thou wouldst not' – ...[23]

Swinburne's choice of particular quotations here exemplifies the perversity of his monstrous Titan Sappho in 'Anactoria'. In this poem she is indeed the daughter of de Sade, wreaking her power by desiring and taking the unwilling love. A lover, too, who is explicitly female, as she is indeed in Sappho, as she was in the permissions of Gautier and Baudelaire. In 'Anactoria' Sappho is caught in the Sadeian pattern of a rhetoric of excess and denial, of minutely particularised parts and magnified, infinite longing. As in Swinburne's other Sappho poems, there is an obsessive attention to parts of the body, to parts of the broken body: 'thy sharp sighs/ Divide my flesh', 'Severed bones that bleach, the flesh that cleaves'.

Continuing this strand of imagery, and reflecting Swinburne's Sadeian version of Sappho is his drawing on Sappho's own 'limb-loosening' poem, Fragment 130, 'Once again limb-loosening Love makes me tremble, the bitter-sweet irresistible creature.' Thus Anactoria's beauty is

> ... like a beast it bites,
> Stings like an adder, like an arrow smites.
> Ah sweet, and sweet again, and seven times sweet ...

And the poem begins 'My life is bitter with thy love', repeated later in 'Me hath love made more bitter toward thee ...'

Endless frustrated repetitions of the fantasy scene of desire are part of the fretful irritations of Sadeian excess which brings no release in satiation. Last year it was Atthis, this year it is Anactoria, and no matter what Sappho does to her, no relief from the effort of speaking out that desire will ever come. As Sappho is dismembered by desire, so her desire dismembers Anactoria:

> I would my love could kill thee: I am satiated
> With seeing thee live, and fain would have thee dead.
> I would earth had thy body as fruit to eat,
> And no mouth but some serpent's found thee sweet.
> I would find grievous ways to have thee slain,
> Intense device, and superflux of pain;
> Vex thee with amorous agonies, and shake
> Life at thy lips, and leave it there to ache:
> Strain out thy soul with pangs too soft to kill,
> Intolerable interludes, and infinite ill;
> Relapse and reluctation of the breath,
> Dumb tones and shuddering semitones of death.

Sappho's dismembering of Anactoria, her minute piecing of the body into parts, will make the music of her poetry:

> ... but thou – thy body is the song,
> Thy mouth the music; thou art more than I,
> Though my voice die not till the whole world die.

Sappho's desire draws Anactoria's body as if it were a landscape envisioned with a connoisseur's eye, exposed in all its most private parts to view, and she makes her song out of that exhibition:

> Yea, though she scourge thee, sweetest, for my sake,
> Blossom not thorns and flowers not blood should break.
> Ah that my lips were tuneless lips, but pressed
> To the bruised blossom of thy scourged white breast!
> Ah that my mouth for Muses' milk were fed
> On the sweet blood thy sweet small wounds had bled!
> That with my tongue I felt them, and could taste
> The faint flakes from thy bosom to the waist!
> That I could drink thy veins as wine, and eat
> Thy breasts like honey! That from face to feet
> Thy body were abolished and consumed,
> And in my flesh thy very flesh entombed!
> ...
> Would I not plague thee dying overmuch?
> Would I not hurt thee perfectly? not touch
> Thy pores of sense with torture, and make bright

Thine eyes with bloodlike tears and grievous light?
Strike pang from pang as note is struck from note,
Catch the sob's middle music in thy throat,
Take thy limbs living, and new-mould with these
A lyre of many faultless agonies?

In Swinburne's version of Sadeian Sappho, Sappho strings up Anactoria's body to make the Lesbian lyre. Her body is the instrument upon which her (or his) mouth plays. From the first publication of *Poems and Ballads* critics reproved Swinburne for his erotic content, especially in 'Dolores', 'The Garden of Proserpine' and 'Anactoria'. Many writers since have noted the indefinitely prurient tone, not quite convinced by the flowery imagery, elevated diction and poetic diffuseness that obscures the pictures presented there. And nor should they be; for when one puts the image of Sappho's desire ('Ah that my mouth for Muses' milk were fed/ On the sweet blood thy sweet small wounds had bled'), alongside Swinburne's prosaically undressed punning in a private letter ('the same mouth and hand which made music on the Lesbian lyre, and on another feminine organ not necessary to specify'), then his pictures might indeed be pornographic.[24]

But all poetry is about poetry, and even for the man who thrills to dirty puns pronounced in public, this is the case. In the end it is not Anactoria who is dismembered and made into music in this poem, but Sappho. Following Baudelaire's model, Swinburne has literally incorporated her parts. Where, in Baudelaire, his Sappho became 'pâture' – 'fodder' – for the 'brute' who took her apart, in Swinburne she is consumed, absorbed into the body of another, for Sappho's verse is embedded in Swinburne's verse, her fragments are encased in his 'from face to feet' (another pun):

… from face to feet
Thy body were abolished and consumed,
And in my flesh thy very flesh entombed!

Yet this cannibalistic 'entombing' inside another's verse is paradoxically a kind of immortality. For the rest of the long poem of 'Anactoria' Sappho reiterates the song of her own desire which will never cease and, thus unceasing, will make her live forever even while the subjects of her song – Atthis or Anactoria, or all the other unnamed girls – will die.[25]

Yea, thou shalt be forgotten like spilt wine,
Except these kisses of my lips on thine
Brand them with immortality; but me –
…

But in the light and laughter, in the moan
And music, and in grasp of lip and hand
And shudder of water that makes felt on land
The immeasureable tremor of all the sea,
Memories shall mix and metaphors of me.

And the reason Sappho's memory shall survive? Because others will sing her song. It is in the mouths of her successors, Baudelaire, and Swinburne himself of course, that Sappho will survive. There her dissected corpse and corpus will be tortured and twisted into new shapes and galvanised into life:

And they shall know me as ye who have known me here,
... and they shall praise me, and say
'She hath all time as all we have our day,
Shall she not live and have her will?' – even I?
Yea, though thou diest, I say I shall not die.
For these shall give me of their souls, shall give
Life, and the days and loves wherewith I live,
Shall quicken me with loving, fill with breath,
Save me and serve me, strive for me with death.

'On the Cliffs'

Swinburne's last Sappho poem was 'On the Cliffs' which appeared in *Songs of the Springtides* published in 1880. Positioning himself, as Baudelaire had done, in 'Lesbos', and as his many predecessors among the women had done – 'on the cliffs' – Swinburne sings not 'Sappho's Last Song' but an extended hymn to Sappho and a detailed account of his relationship to her textual body.[26]

His chosen epigraph on this occasion is Fragment 136:

ἱμερόφωνος ἀηδών.

In the Loeb translation, 'the lovely voiced nightingale', but in Greek carrying connotations of a voice full of longing, yearning, desire.[27]

On the cliff, caught between sea and sky, between moondawn and sundown, between 'an hour too dim for night or day', the poet listens for a voice carrying to him through the air:

O wind, O wingless wind that walk'st the sea,
Weak wind, wing-broken, wearier wind than we,
Who are yet not spirit-broken, maimed like thee,
Who wail not in our inward night as thou
In the outer darkness now,

What word has the old sea given thee for mine ear
From thy faint lips to hear?
For some word would she send me, knowing not how.

Sent by 'mother Night', and speaking in the wind that comes out of the sea, is 'The same sea's word unchangeable'. In that ancient sea the poet's soul – which is feminine – swims, attempting to come to terms with the voice that has dominated his past:

... and my soul,
Sickening, swam weakly with bated breath
In a deep sea like death,
And felt the wind buffet her face with brine
Hard and harsh thought on thought in long bleak roll
Blown by keen gusts of memory sad as thine
Heap up the weight of pain, and break, and leave
Strength scarce enough to grieve
In the sick heavy spirit, unmanned with strife
Of waves that beat at the tired lips of life.

It transpires – some 140 lines later – that the voice the poet-speaker hears, and has always heard, in the night, in the sea, in the air, is the voice of Sappho. She is it, 'more than man or man's desire,/ Being bird and God in one', who is to have 'Life everlasting of eternal fire' because she is the poet's origin and lead:

The sun whom all our souls and songs call sire,
Whose godhead gave thee, chosen of all our quire,
Thee only of all that serve, of all that sing
Before our sire and king ...
This gift, this doom.[28]

While praising Sappho, setting her above all succeeding poets, Swinburne makes a bid for equality by naming her 'sister' throughout, and insisting that *she* must listen to *him*: 'And yet even so thine ear should hear me – yea,/Hear me this nightfall by this northland bay.' It is he, he argues, and others like him, who have made her vocal, who have permitted her song to be heard. He describes his own experience of the earliest effects of her song in the usual terms of dismemberment as her voice penetrates him:

As brother and sister were we, child and bird.
Since thy first Lesbian word
Flamed on me, and I knew not whence I knew

This was the song that struck my whole soul through
Pierced my keen spirit of sense with edge more keen,
Even when I knew not, – even ere sooth was seen, –
When thou wast but the tawny sweet winged thing
Whose cry was but of spring.

And yet, of course, as ever, it is *Sappho's* textual body that is broken up by *his* singing, for pieces from her Fragment 1 and Fragment 49 are included in 'On the Cliffs' in two different Swinburne translations.[29] Still he turns the facts round, reverses them as if in a mirror, saying that it is the Gods who have decreed their relation, and that 'their will/ Made my song part of thy song'. As the younger poet, he argues, he has had to take Sappho's song, which would otherwise be lost, diffused through nature and time, as Sappho's broken body is consumed by the sea:

As through some strait sea-shell
The wide sea's immemorial song, – the sea
That sings and breathes in strange men's ears of thee
How in her barren bride-bed, void and vast,
Even thy soul sang itself to sleep at last.

Again, inverting Sappho's Fragment 1, the 'Ode to Aphrodite', Swinburne says that the goddess has herself 'wronged' Sappho by failing to ensure that her poetry survived, even though, ironically, of all the many hymns once sung to Aphrodite, only this one of Sappho's still endures:

And now of all songs uttering all her praise,
All hers who had thy praise and did thee wrong,
Abides one song yet of her lyric days,
Thine only, this thy song.

But help is at hand. For 'Man, man at least has heard/... Hath heard or hears, – even Aeschylus as I'. While Sappho was alive, 'when thy name was woman, and thy word/ Human', then – so this story goes – the earth was silent. Field, woodland, lawn and hill were 'Dumb', 'mute', 'tongueless', and only one island heard 'Thrill, but through no bird's throat/ In one strange manlike maiden's godlike note,/ The song of all these as a single bird'. But once Sappho was dead, passing through the 'sea's portal' as a 'funeral gate', then her song came to be heard all over the world, and Sappho was reanimated in the voices of others:

... only then,
When her life's wing of womanhood was furled,

> Their cry, this cry of thine was heard again,
> As of me now, of any born of men,
> Through sleepless clear spring nights filled full of thee,
> Rekindled here …

The moral is clear. Sappho has to be dead to make a poem for her heirs. By taking her apart, Swinburne learnt 'Song, and the secrets of it, and their might'. Just as he images Sappho, her body 'small' and 'dark', as her corpus is fragmented and obscured, requiring interpretation – so he appraises her with the eye of the Sadeian connoisseur, who breaks up the body to get at the parts and the spirit inside:

> I know them since my spirit had first in sight,
> … The small dark body's Lesbian loveliness
> That held the fire eternal.

The body enshrined

Under the heading of '*corps*' Barthes speaks about the relation of the lover to the body of the beloved:

> Sometimes an idea occurs to me: I catch myself carefully scrutinizing the loved body (like the narrator watching Albertine asleep). *To scrutinize* means *to search*: I am searching the other's body, as if I wanted to see what was inside it, as if the mechanical cause of my desire were in the adverse body (I am like those children who take a clock apart in order to find out what time is.) This operation is conducted in a cold and astonished fashion; I am calm, attentive, as if I were confronted by a strange insect of which I am suddenly *no longer afraid*. Certain parts of the body particularly appropriate to this *observation*: eyelashes, nails, roots of the hair, the incomplete objects. It is obvious that I am then in the process of fetishizing a corpse …[30]

Swinburne and Baudelaire subject the body of Sappho to this scrutiny as Gautier's hero subjects the bodies of Rosette and Théodore-Madeleine to his. The parts of the living body, categorised and collected, resemble the treasuring of parts of the dead saint's body, the nails, the hair, the pieces of bone kept in reliquaries jewelled with precious stones. For relics too participate in the metonymy of the part which substitutes for the whole. They signify the entirety of the saint, spirit and flesh, though she has had her flesh torn apart in an attempt to root out the spirit. Which enterprise, of course – as in all narratives of saintly martyrdom – conversely confirms the independence of that spirit. Still, like the witch, or the practitioner of voodoo, or the religious who adores the saint, or the lover who steals the beloved's slippers, he/she/they know that possession of the part is indicative of power over the whole person. More than that, the study of that relic provides the subject with control. He is, in Barthes's words, 'no longer afraid'. Possession of the part means that the beloved can be manipulated where her whole presence would throw the beloved into the chaos of desire. Possession of the part means that sufficient distance and composure can be mustered to allow for a second scrutiny, the cause and spring of the lover's own desire.

Mademoiselle de Maupin is a text which examines the lover's own desire, whether one focuses on d'Albert's story or Madeleine's. The challenges which it presented to the contemporary moralities are there to make sure that there is no resort to romance conventions. It is a text about desire, and to keep that end pure, the sex has to be perverse. The reiterated analysis of the beloved's dress and manner, parts and pieces, allows for this self-absorbed contemplation in just the manner described by Barthes:

> (I was looking at everything in the other's face, the other's body, coldly: lashes, toenail, thin eyebrows, thin lips, the lustre of the eyes, a mole, a way of holding a cigarette; I was fascinated – fascination being, after all, only the extreme of detachment – by a kind of coloured, ceramicized, vitrified figurine in which I could read, without understanding anything about it, *the cause of my desire*.)[31]

In the end, Gautier's reader is also made into an accomplished fetishist, scrutinising the 'two pearls' found by the maid in Rosette's bed and being encouraged thereby to consider the 'cause of his own desire': 'I leave this remark to the sagacity of the reader and leave him to draw what inferences he will.'[32]

The scene which is the centre of that desire – two women in bed – is elusive but it is, in Barthes's sense, the object of fascination in Baudelaire's and Swinburne's poetry. That *Les Fleurs du mal* began with the fugitive title of *Les Lesbiennes*, and that Baudelaire's Sappho poems remained in the collection, signals the connection. That Swinburne returned to Sappho as subject so often (as indeed he used other voracious females, but none so frequently and comprehensively) and quite clearly – from the evidence of his letters – always within a sexualised context, signals the connection. But the thing that is especially curious about this image as an object of desire for these two men is the fact that it is a scene that can never be realised, it can only ever be imagined or imaginary. There is, to be sure, the expedient of cross-dressing, or of 'feigned femininity' as in Baudelaire's 'Lesbos' and in Swinburne's 'Anactoria', but the real thing can never be achieved.

Yet that is the point of the attraction and the reason for the fascination. Lesbian sex here is itself a fetish, one which can be scrutinised, broken into parts and examined without bearing any relation to the real, which facilitates a minute attention to the cause of desire in the self. When Baudelaire's 'Lesbos' fetishises the 'adored cadaver' of Sappho, when Swinburne 'loosens' her limbs, they both play with their own sensitive parts. The tortures imagined on the body of Sappho are designed to pleasure the perpetrator. Here is Barthes again, writing under the heading '*écorche*', flayed:

> The resistance of the wood varies depending on the place where we drive in the nail: wood is not isotropic. Nor am I; I have my 'exquisite points'. The map of these points is known to me alone, and it is according to them that I make my way ... In order to find the grain of the wood ... one need merely drive in a nail and see if it penetrates readily. In order to discover my exquisite points, there exists an instrument which resembles a nail: this instrument is a joke: I do not suffer jokes lightly ... I am cut off from playing: ... [in play I] continuously risk bruising one of my exquisite points ...[33]

When Jean-Paul Sartre was reading Gustave Flaubert's extravagant letters to his male friends on the prodigies of his sex life and the prowess of his performance, Sartre named this phenomenon '*opération miroir*'.[34] Reflected in the account he produced for his friend's eyes Flaubert magnified himself but he also augmented himself. Because he was telling all the story, retailing her mighty orgasms as well as his own, he played both the male and female part. His mistress became only a part of himself, seen back to front, wrong way round, inverted as in a mirror. This ties in with the processes of literary transvestism that mark *Mademoiselle de Maupin*, *Les Fleurs du mal*, and *Poems and Ballads*. It suggests the narcissism involved in all of those texts, but it also illuminates the treatment of lesbianism and of Sappho.

In Baudelaire's vision Lesbos is a world of mirrors:

> Lesbos, terre des nuits chaudes et langoureuses,
> Qui font qu'à leurs miroirs, stérile volupté!
> Les filles aux yeux creux, de leur corps amoureuses,
> Caressent les fruits mûrs de leur nubilité;
> Lesbos, terre des nuits chaudes et langoureuses.[35]

The image of woman with woman is part of Baudelaire's mirror here, as is the masturbatory picture. But the other source of this '*stérile volupté*' is the unproductive or self-reflective intercourse between the imaginary women and the vision of the poet. In Swinburne's poetry this encounter between imaginary woman and poet has still more complicated mirror effects. When Swinburne does sex with Sappho his is an '*opération miroir*', but when he plays the part of Sappho, like Flaubert, he speaks her lines, but he also does a violence to her corpus: he quotes her poems, but he translates them; he reveres her fragments, but he distorts her image; he idolises the scenes of her verse, but he inverts them, turns them inside out. For Swinburne as a Greek scholar, Sappho owns two bodies, a material body of 'loosened limbs' and a textual body of fetishised pieces, and both of these can be possessed in his poetry.

Fallen women

Swinburne was not the only one to make the elision between body and text or to treat of Sappho's works as precious relics which in some way transmuted into 'her'. The classical scholar John Addington Symonds writes of Sappho in his *Studies of the Greek Poets* (1873):

> ... these dazzling fragments, 'Which still, like sparkles of Greek fire,/ Burn on through time and n'er expire', are the ultimate and finished forms of passionate utterance, diamonds, topazes and blazing rubies, in which the fire of the soul is crystallised forever ... Instead of attempting, therefore to interpret for English readers the charm of Sappho's style, it is best to refer to pp. 874–924 of Bergk, where every vestige that is left of her is shrined.[36]

The jewels of Sappho's reliquary text, like the two pearls found in Rosette's bed, are the part that represents the elusive whole.

Yet it is this metonymic insistence which may suggest a reason why Sappho, in the minds of so many late nineteenth century writers and painters, took on the role of a full-blooded daughter of the Decadence. By the end of this period many critics were trying to analyse 'Decadence', and, as Linda Dowling has argued, its key image was an idea to do with language which privileged the parts over the whole. She quotes, for instance, Nietzsche saying that the tendency of the Decadence was ever toward an 'anarchy of atoms'. She also quotes Havelock Ellis bringing the theories of Paul Bourget to an English audience for the first time in 1889:

> A style of decadence is one in which the unity of the book is decomposed to give place to the independence of the page, in which the page is decomposed to give place to the independence of the phrase, and the phrase to give place to the independence of the word.[37]

In this sense *Mademoiselle de Maupin, Les Fleurs du mal* and *Poems and Ballads* are all Decadent texts. They focus on the minute part and they are all ready to subordinate any overall impression to the image of the moment in the extended digression, the sidelining metaphor, the embedded allusion, or the elaborate pun. 'What decadence in literature really means', wrote Arthur Symons in 1897, 'is that learned corruption of language by which style ceases to be organic and becomes, in the pursuit of some new expressiveness or beauty, deliberately abnormal.'[38]

In effect, Decadent writers treat of language as a fetish just as Baudelaire and Swinburne make Sappho a fetish. The 'organic' whole is substituted for the part found in 'some new expressiveness of beauty'. And yet Sappho is peculiarly ripe for such treatment. Both according to the legends and to her few facts, Sappho is thrice over, in pieces: her body is broken by the story of her battering death on the rocks of the sea; her limbs are 'loosened' by the conventions of her description of desire; and her textual body is in tatters. Metaphorically too Sappho is a Decadent: she is, in the legends, a 'fallen' woman, and there too she was indeed 'decadent', falling from the rock of Leucadia.

But there is another link, more abstruse because is it a complicated story of scholarly influence and exchange, but one which explains why the idea of Sappho, especially, was so readily exploited and treasured by writers and artists of the Decadence. Modern critical explanations of what Decadence is – following the contemporary nineteenth century critics who wrote on the subject – have concentrated on the development of language as its characteristic mark. Linda Dowling has set this particular concern into a broader European context, suggesting that it was a profound and, in many ways, destabilising change in the way the Victorians came to regard language, to think about what it was and how it works, that underpinned the literary experiments of Decadence. She argues that the influence of German philologists, and the works of Franz Bopp and Jacob Grimm in particular, which initiated the new linguistic sciences, raised what she calls a 'spectre of autonomous language – language as a system blindly obeying impersonal phonological rules in isolation from any world of human values and experience – that was to eat corrosively away at the hidden foundations of a high Victorian ideal of civilization'. Today, thinking as we are on this side of what Dowling sees as the 'epochal' work of de Saussure, the idea of language as an independent system does not necessarily carry connotations of threat and cultural disintegration. But it did for the Victorians.[39]

Obviously one can see how this leads to the cult, and cultivation, of an ideology of artificiality. If language is mere form, working independently of value, then why connect literature to life? Similarly, one can see how it leads to a moral permissiveness. If language is pure artifice, what duties does it owe in terms of moral responsibility and education? With their primary attention to language, their cultivation of artifice and their moral independence, *Mademoiselle de Maupin*, *Les Fleurs du mal*, and *Poems and Ballads* are all Decadent texts.

But the pervasive influences of advances in German philology had consequences for Sappho too. In the early nineteenth century the sophistication of language studies in Germany meant also that Greek scholarship undertaken by German scholars, was of the first rank. In the eighteenth century Sappho studies were most advanced in France, but in the nineteenth century Germany took the lead with the work of Volger, Welcker and Neue and culminating in the editions of Theodor Bergk published in the middle of the century. Just as the work of the philologists filtered into English writing, so Bergk's influence was felt in England too: Alfred Tennyson owned a copy of his 1843 edition; John Addington Symonds directed his reader to Bergk's collection of Sappho's 'vestiges'; and H.T. Wharton used Bergk as his source in producing his own enshrining volume *Sappho: Memoir, Text, Selected Renderings*.[40]

Bergk's scholarly work was the equivalent of a literary archaeology. It excavated a dead language to piece together the remnants of the past. In doing so it gave new life to words, to phrases, simply because it brought them wilfully back into circulation through the artifice of scholarship. Sappho's was an archaic language, all its native speakers extinct. But scholarship revivified it, made it live a kind of fake life, where it was – like language itself – independent, autonomous, and amoral. Sappho's text, as presented by Bergk, was all of these. Because he had no 'civilized' ideal in mind to distort the clear perception of an independent language, Bergk, for instance, had no scruples about retaining Sappho's feminine pronouns in his edition. In this his Sappho resembled the independence of language as it was itself perceived by his compatriots.

In addition, the very fact of valuing and treasuring a language which was 'dead' had consequences for Decadence. Linda Dowling refers to the literary critical 'commonplace' which associates Decadence with a fashion for 'dead languages'. The criticism began with Haldane MacFall's account of the writings of Aubrey Beardsley who, he says, 'uses his native language as if it were obsolete, a dead language – he is more concerned with dead words than live ... In short, he is a hopeless decadent in art.'[41]

Developments in Greek scholarship were also responsible for another theme that turns Sappho into a Decadent. In his article on the 'Decadent Movement in Literature' Arthur Symons pointed to the 'qualities that mark the end of great periods, the qualities that we find in the Greek, the Latin, decadence: an intense self-consciousness, a restless curiosity in research, an over-subtilizing refinement upon refinement, a spiritual and moral perversity'.[42] The Classical scholar John Addington Symonds was writing from the perspective of a period that considered itself just such one of these, the 'end of a great period', but his account of events in Sappho's Lesbos is remarkably similar and sounds jewelled and flamboyant like the 'Decadent' writings of Walter Pater and Oscar Wilde.

> Nowhere in any age of Greek history, or in any part of Hellas, did the love of physical beauty, the sensibility to radiant scenes of nature, the consuming fervour of personal feeling, assume such grand proportions and receive so illustrious an expression as they did in Lesbos. At first this passion blossomed into the most exquisite lyrical poetry that the world has known: this was the flower-time of the Aeolians, their brief and brilliant spring. But the fruit it

> bore was bitter and rotten. Lesbos became a byword for corruption. The passions which for a moment had flamed into the gorgeousness of Art, burning their envelope of words and images, remained a mere furnace of sensuality, from which no expression of the divine in the human life could be expected ... the motive of enthusiastic passion sufficed to produce a dazzling result. But as soon as its freshness was exhausted there was nothing left for Art to live on, and mere decadence to sensuality ensued.[43]

Corrupted, exhausted, bitter and rotten. Governed – as so many nineteenth century discourses were – by a notion of organic development, they were subject also, especially with the impact of Darwin's work on the processes of natural selection, to concepts of decay and degeneration.[44] Gautier saw himself, as he saw Baudelaire, as a product of an 'advanced and unsound' civilisation with a concomitant taste for the artificial and the degenerate:

> Baudelaire knew how to find the morbidly rich tints of decomposition, the tones of mother-of-pearl which freeze stagnant waters, the roses of consumption, the pallor of chlorosis ... and all that gamut of intensified colours, correspondent to autumn, to the setting of the sun, to over-ripe fruit, and the last hours of civilisation.[45]

Too highly organised to survive, too complex and refined to be successful in the competition of natural selection, too far removed from the 'expression of the divine in human life', Decadence falls into 'mere sensuality'. The 'decomposing' into parts symptomatic of the literature of Decadence, corrupts and rots its subjects – whether its Victorian practitioners, or Sappho herself.

These trends in the late nineteenth century may be seen – by their proponents – as refined and multiple. Oscar Wilde, for instance, declaring that 'Of course Culture has intensified the personality of man. Art has made us myriad-minded', borrowed his epithet from Sappho's invocation to Aphrodite.[46] But for their opponents, Decadent tendencies were amoral and pernicious. As early as 1873 Alfred Tennyson, from his position as Poet Laureate, complained about 'Art – with poisonous honey stolen from the flowers of France', and he soon came to be perceived as the defender of all that was pure and untainted.[47] One reviewer of Arthur Symons's *London Nights* (1895) made the comparison:

> Mr. Symons's Rene, Nora, Lilian, and the rest of them, remind us, in a way, of the figures which meet us in Lord Tennyson's 'Juvenilla' [thus], Eleänore, Isabel, and their fellows. But what a difference! What a descent from the purity and dignity of the elder singer to the unclean and ignominious themes of the new; from the splendour of the one to the tinsel and paint of the other! There is something very repellent about the art of the modern muse; about her

> appeals to the baser passions. The title suggests to the possible purchaser a feast of forbidden things.[48]

In fact, if this reviewer had known a little more about the Sapphic origins of Tennyson's 'Eleänore' he might have thought even her little better than Symons's streetwalkers.[49]

The name of Sappho, partly because of the notoriety of Gautier and Baudelaire, partly because of Swinburne's exposure, insinuated corruption. In 1866, soon after the publication of Swinburne's *Poems and Ballads, First Series*, John Addington Symonds – Greek scholar and pioneer for homosexual rights – was writing to Henry Graham Dakyns about the difficulties associated with the naming of names when prejudice reduced subtle distinctions to a blanket perception of moral degradation:

> You know that I consider the tone of F. Myers to be medically wrong in matters of passion, and that I regret the peculiar colour of A.S.'s erotics, not to speak of the misery wh. I have myself suffered. There, *salve modestia*, are at once three of our University assailed by the same disease. But I found it difficult to express to Percival the exact manner of the evil in this its most subtle manifestation. The grossness of boys is palpable and when observed is easily dealt with. But a man who regards Swinburne as a clear case of lunacy *because* he treats of Sappho cannot readily understand how there is much danger of the best and purest of his pupils idealising the passion of the Phraedrus.[50]

In 1866 'Sappho' spelt depravity and lunacy to the upright schoolmaster in Dr Percival. In 1867 the historian W.H. Lecky reviled 'that lowest abyss of unnatural love' of which he found it difficult to speak. But at the same time the notion of 'inversion' was speaking the unspeakable so that by 1897 Havelock Ellis could introduce the book that he had planned with John Addington Symonds by saying that 'A few years ago ... sexual inversion was scarcely a name. It was a loathsome and nameless vice, only to be touched with a pair of tongs.'[51]

Curiously in accord with this new terminology, it is interesting to note that Sappho – well-known invert – had already had that inverting, mirroring, turning back to fronting, done to her by the literary successors who represented her or usurped her in nineteenth century poetry. Later commentators in the twentieth century felt compelled to defend her against the charge of 'inversion' and the charge of decadence. 'There is nothing here to cause nastiness,' wrote one scholar in 1926, 'nothing that has a nasty flavour, no lilies that fester like weeds.'[52] But for the time being 'Sappho', both woman and poet, had turned into that characteristic emblem of the Decadence, the 'Fatal Book'.

Reading risky things I: 'A Singer Asleep'

The most famous of all 'fatal books' is that presented to Dorian Gray by Lord Henry Wotton. Because it is the quintessential book of the Decadence it possesses a style which is fractured, particularised, learned and precious: 'The style in which it was written was that curious jewelled style, vivid and obscure at once, full of argot and of archaisms, of technical expressions and of elaborate paraphrases ... It was a poisonous book.' Like the language of an unexpurgated Sappho or the works of Gautier and Baudelaire the book entrances because it reveals what was hidden, then decomposes, corrupting the reader:

> It was the strangest book that he had ever read. It seemed to him that in exquisite raiment, and to the delicate sound of flutes, the sins of the world were passing in dumb show before him. Things that he had dimly dreamed of were suddenly made real to him. Things of which he had never dreamed were gradually revealed.

'I thought you would like it', says Lord Henry to Dorian. 'I didn't say I liked it,' replies Dorian, 'I said it fascinated me. There is a great difference.'[53]

The younger generation of poets were similarly fascinated by their own inheritance of 'fatal books'. For Thomas Hardy, Swinburne's *Poems and Ballads, First Series* was just one of these. In 'A Singer Asleep' Hardy positions himself in Swinburne's place, in Sappho's place, 'on the cliffs' – this time at Bonchurch on the Isle of Wight where Swinburne was buried. In this symbolic position, Hardy recalls the publication of *Poems and Ballads*:

> – It was as though a garland of red roses
> Had fallen about the hood of some smug nun
> When irresponsibly dropped as from the sun,
> In fulth of numbers freaked with musical closes,
> Upon Victoria's formal middle time,
> His leaves of rhythm and rhyme.[54]

Hardy relishes the scandal of the episode in its suggestion of perverse sexuality, for the verse is 'freaked' both in form and content, and the 'fulth' of numbers hints at the assonance of 'filth'. Swinburne's volume confronts the bodies of propriety realised in 'some smug nun' and 'Victoria's formal middle'. Hardy recalls the censorious reaction of the public – 'the brabble and the roar/ At those thy tunes' – but, more pertinently still, he recalls the effect of the book on his own youth and his recognition of this 'fatal book':

> O that far morning of a summer day
> When, down a terraced street whose pavements lay

Glassing the sunshine into my bent eyes,
I walked and read with a quick glad surprise
New words, in classic guise.

And then it turns out that Hardy knows that Swinburne's 'classic guise' is not his own. These are the transvestite wrappings borrowed from Sappho, Swinburne's 'music- mother' who – as in Baudelaire – is both mother (*mère*) and identified with the all-surrounding sea (*mer*):

– His singing-mistress verily was no other
Than she the Lesbian, she the music-mother
Of all the tribe that feel in melodies;
Who leapt, love-anguished, from the Leucadian steep
Into the rambling world-encircling deep
Which hides her where none sees.

As she is in the sea, and Swinburne is buried above the sea 'On the Cliffs', Hardy imagines a ghostly tryst seen only by ignorant mariners, 'Unknowing of him or her', which appears to them as 'a dim/ Lone shine upon the heaving hydrosphere'. And at that meeting, unworldly and unhealthily phosphorescent, Hardy endorses the inheritance claimed by both Baudelaire and Swinburne, where the male poet takes on Sappho's mantle, revises her texts, and fleshes a new body of writing to supply the place of her lost corpus:

One dreams him sighing to her spectral form:
'O teacher, where lies hid thy burning line;
Where are those songs, O poetess divine
Whose very orts are love incarnadine?'
And her smile back: 'Disciple true and warm,
Sufficient now are thine'.

The title of Hardy's valedictory poem is 'A Singer Asleep', but the resonances within that title are complex and multiple. Swinburne once envisioned Sappho while he was sleeping in his poem called 'Sapphics', and within all his Sappho poems the poet herself sleeps, requiring animation, like the Sleeping Beauty, through the agency of Swinburne's own vision, poem, kiss. Now it is Swinburne who sleeps – as well as Sappho – and both of their unconscious forms are animated and empowered by the desiring gaze of a later poet, another lover of their textual bodies, who scrutinises their parts to examine the 'cause of his own desire'.

Reading risky things II: *Pagan Poems*

Younger still than Hardy, George Moore found his meeting with Sappho mediated by Baudelaire, and, impressed by the impact of the 'fatal book' on his own youthful imagination, he attempted to produce one of his own.

Moore grew up in the bucolic philistinism of rural Ireland and then studied painting in London and Paris. There, as he tells it at the advanced age of 36, he was intoxicated by the 'poison' or any number of 'fatal books'. He read Gautier singing 'to his antique lyre praise of the flesh and contempt of the soul'. He studied Baudelaire which 'hurried the course of the disease', and later he read Swinburne too. These 'Flowers, beautiful in sublime decay' were the books which made him: 'Never shall I open these books again, but were I to live for a thousand years, their power in my soul would remain unshaken. I am what they made me.' Moore was seduced by the style of Decadence and by that artificial discrimination of parts, and he connected Gautier's writing to the experience of the body. This is indeed the materiality of language that affects and infects the sensuality of the flesh:

> Who has not been, unless some dusty old pedant, thrilled and driven to pleasure by the action of a book that penetrates and speaks to you of your most present and intimate emotions. This is of course pure sensualism ... But there are affinities in literature corresponding to, and very analogous to, sexual affinities – the same unreasoned attractions, the same pleasures, the same lassitudes.[55]

Moore's own attempts at literary seduction have their comic side. But he does know his masters – Gautier, Baudelaire, Swinburne – and he knows Sappho, his 'singing-mistress'. Before he began to write novels Moore published two volumes of verse, both at his own expense. Acknowledging one of his mentors, the title of his first volume was *Flowers of Passion* (1878). When it was unfavourably reviewed Moore withdrew the book on the advice of Mrs William Rossetti, though not before he had sent an inscribed copy to Oscar Wilde. His second go at poetry was *Pagan Poems* (1881) which reproduced some slightly revised verses from *Flowers of Passion* and included many new poems. It met the same fate as its predecessor, and neither volume was ever reprinted.[56]

Flowers of Passion announces itself as a 'fatal book' even before it is opened. The cover in dark green cloth is stamped with a gilded design of an unstringed lyre woven with ivy and supporting a skull wearing a laurel crown and two crossbones. The first poem in the collection is 'Ode to a Dead Body'. The last poem is 'A Sapphic Dream':

> I love the luminous poison of the moon,
> The silence of illimitable seas,
> Vast night, and all her myriad mysteries,

Perfumes that make the burdened senses swoon
And weaken will, large snakes who oscillate
Like lovely girls, immense exotic flowers,
And cats who purr through silk-enfestooned bowers
Where white-limbed women sleep in sumptuous state.

My soul dreams, in such a dream as this is,
Visions of perfume, moonlight and the blisses
Of sexless love, and strange unreachéd kisses.[57]

The snakes, the flowers, the cats, the 'strange unreachéd kisses' are all part of Sappho dreamed through Baudelaire's *Les Fleurs du mal* and Swinburne's 'Anactoria'. The texts of his mentors, like the 'luminous poison' of the moon he loves, are corrupting and exotically other. Moore's shopping list of Decadent props is a succession of fragments, both images borrowed from textual sources and keyhole glimpses of a *fin de siècle* 'what the butler saw' for self-conscious aesthetes. This is indeed a language of parts.

But George Moore's most elaborately realised account of his peculiarly nineteenth century 'Sapphic dream' is in a short, two-part verse drama called 'Sappho' and published in *Pagan Poems* in 1881. The first scene opens on a boudoir straight out of *Mademoiselle de Maupin* taken over by Aubrey Beardsley's Venus:

> An Ionic-columned room, Sappho seated amid her attendants who are engaged in completing her toilette. On one side a porphyry table with silver boxes and vases containing odours, essences, pomatums, pins, depilatories, and the little golden scissors. In the middle of the room a bronze dolphin bestridden by a Cupid, blowing from his nostrils two jets of water, one hot, the other cold, into two oriental alabaster basins, into which the women dip alternately the white sponges. Through the purple-curtained windows, between the tops of the laurels growing at the foot of the court-wall, is seen a strip of azure sky.[58]

The story of Moore's verse drama is briefly told. Hylas is in love with Sappho, wooing her with words reminiscent of Moore's own earlier 'A Sapphic Dream':

I love thee as the drinker loves the wine
That maddens him – I love thee as I love
Sometimes the moon when, like a floating flower,
She swims and swoons, and fills the languid night
With luminous languors and perfumed poison's air,
And sickening ecstasy and maddening dreams
That melt my soul like vapour into air,
And leave me chill of an unreached desire!

But Sappho is not interested: 'Once I might/ Have loved thee; now my love seeks other ends/ Than thee'. Megara, 'fair Samian, Queen of the Hetiries' is the object of Sappho's affections. Megara is announced, bearing rich gifts for Sappho. These, she says, are worthless because Megara's desire is not to please Sappho, but to gain some personal end. Sure enough, Megara confesses that she is in love with Hylas, and she has come to beg Sappho's assistance. Sappho refuses, so Megara tries another ploy. If Sappho will help her to deceive Hylas so that she can enjoy him if only for one night, then she, Megara, will give herself over to the poet's pleasure:

> Here at thy feet, O cruel Sappho! I
> Make unto thee my body full in flower
> And perfect bloom of ripened womanhood,
> As bond-slave bounden to thy plainest will,
> A thing to please the pleasure of thy strange
> Passion, a rose to cherish and to kill
> With kisses keener than the wind on sea,
> And bitter-sweet with aching softness, stung
> With all the sultry perfumes of desire.

Sappho agrees, playing Delphine to Megara's Hippolyte. But there is one condition: Megara must promise to kill Hylas in the morning. Megara pleads with Sappho:

> ... I cannot give to death
> The life that I would consecrate to love!
> I bare my body to thee: there ensheath
> Thy teeth and claws of passion, till I be
> As dead before thee, but O Sappho, spare
> This one sweet life.

Sappho, implacable, declares that Megara's love is 'too pitiful' and presents her with a dagger. Scene II opens:

> The sleeping chamber of Sappho, a marble-walled room divided by an immense richly embroidered curtain hanging by large rings from an iron rod, with bread-fruit ornaments at each end; against the curtain a low couch raised upon lion's claws, upon which Megara sits half reclining, gazing upon Hylas, who lies by her side in a profound slumber. Close by her hand at the head of the couch is a small tripod on cloven feet, upon it an inlaid casket with a jewelled dagger. The floor is of multicoloured marble; on the left, nearly in the middle of the room, placed on a table of precious wood, is a female figure holding in her arms a mirror of polished metal. On the right is a statue of Sappho.

Looking on the sleeping form of Hylas, Megara scrutinises her beloved, as Swinburne imagines Sappho asleep, as Hardy perceives Swinburne in 'A Singer Asleep', as Barthes recognises the analysis of love's particularised gaze, anatomising the parts of the loved one. While Megara praises his beauty, Sappho is heard outside, singing in the dawn and, to this accompaniment, Megara stabs the sleeping youth with the jewelled dagger:

> The measure of thy days is meted out,
> Thy sweet young life is taken as a prey,
> And strangest loves are knelt to and adored
> At Lesbian shrine with thee for sacrifice.
> These lips will give delight to maiden mouth
> No more ...

With its 'one night of love' and cross-sexualities straight out of Gautier, its exotic scents and settings out of Baudelaire, with its Sadeian Sappho out of Swinburne, Moore's 'Sappho' is the perverse product of the *fin de siècle*. Made up out of the parts of other 'fatal books', the texts of both Sappho and Baudelaire are here, quite literally, fatal.

Early on in the verse drama, while plotting the consummation of her desire for Megara, Moore's Sappho sings a version of Fragment 31, done up by Moore into English, but shaped in a Sapphic metre:

> That man, God-like, seems to me sitting by thee,
> Who alone doth draw to him all thy passion,
> Hears thee midwhile whispering tender speaking,
>   Seeing thee smiling;
>
> This is what my shuddering sense tortures,
> Now I see thee, beautiful, gazing on thee,
> All my love-words falter to feeble nothings,
>   Broken in sighings.
>
> Subtle flames stray molten in liquid fires
> Through my blood-ways, blind are my eyes, and dizzy
> Are my stunned ears, deafened with sounds of murmurs
>   Swimming around me.
>
> Chilling dew-damps over my flesh are breaking,
> And a heart born of shivering through me wanders
> I am wan as grass in the summer places,
>   And I am dying.

And, at the end of the verse-drama, as Megara murders Hylas, Sappho sings again. The first three stanzas of her song, with their allusion to the 'high Gods' who give 'longing with loathing', are a version of fragments and phrases drawn from Swinburne, especially his 'Anactoria'. But the rest of the poem is a direct translation. It's a version – again, carefully arranged in Sapphic metre – not of Sappho's own work, but of one her Decadent descendants, Baudelaire's second 'Femmes Damnées' poem:

Have not the high Gods longing with loathing given
And our sleepings woven around with dreamings
And the whole world crowned with a crown of sorrow
    Filling it full with ...

Flowers of passion, weakness, and fervid milking,
Hope, the green shoot grafting of weary grieving,
Love, the sense-smit shuddering of the spirit,
    Weeping and laughter ...

Weary are they, sorrowful are their dreamings
Whom the high Gods stricken with perfect vision
Making soul-will infinite, and the senses
    Mortal and weakling.

This is the song to which the murder is done. Sappho's cruel will is carried out, and Hylas's violent death leads into Sappho's song of triumph and strange vision, which itself is a song of parts, reassembled from Baudelaire's own Sapphic writings:

Megara: Yea, he is dead; I can unveil my face,
He cannot see me now, for he is dead.

Sappho: Through the twilight shadows of fading evening,
By the shore-strand, glimmering in the rays of
Purple sunset, purpling all the ocean
    Cliffs and headlands.

Women dream there, sorrowful women, dreaming,
Gazing sunward whispering sweetest secrets,
Hands on hands laid, shivering with the languors
    Born of their passion.

Others white-robed, sister-like, wander slowly
Through the dark woods filled with the apparitions,
Mixing fearful frothing of pleasure into
    Weeping of torments.

Degenerate, corrupt, made up of textual parts in pieces, Moore's decadent 'Sappho' presents a version of the poetess who enacts on others the dismembering done to her. Sappho herself becomes a holy – and holey – 'writ of beauty'. Her text, like Gautier's, Baudelaire's and Swinburne's, is a new book of Decadence, a book where one may read of 'risky things', a book whose very name gives away the secret of the reader's illicit knowledge.

8
The Island and the Mirror

Dreams of origin

I want to begin with two dreams.

> I dream Joan and Dorothy are arguing. Joan possesses herself of some boxes and jewel-cases of mine: she treats my dream treasures as common property, spreads them out on a table. I am angry at her casual appropriation of my personal belongings. I take up one red-velvet-lined box (actually Bryher had got this for me in Florence) and say passionately, 'Can you understand *nothing*?'. Joan is a tall girl, we stand level, challenging each other. I say, 'Can't you understand. My *mother* gave me this box'. I press this red-velvet-lined red-leather Florentine box against my heart. Actually, physically, my heart is surcharged and beating wildly at the vehemence of my passion.

And this is the second dream.

> I tried desperately to get back to my flat in Sloane Street, London. The flat is at the top of the house. As I enter the downstairs hall, a man and then a rough boy barred my way to the staircase and seemed to threaten me. I did not dare challenge them ... (I could not tell the Professor that this terror was associated in my mind with news of fresh Nazi atrocities.) As I stood threatened and terrified I call, loudly, 'Mother'. I am out on the pavement now. I look up at the window of my flat. It has different curtains or a suggestion of Venetian blinds. A figure is standing there, holding a lighted candle. It is my mother. I was overpowered with happiness and all trace of terror vanished.

Both of these dreams were dreamed and recorded by the American poet Hilda Doolittle, known and published as H.D.[1] She noted these dreams in March 1933 because she was then in Vienna undergoing her first sessions of analysis with

Freud, the 'Professor' to whom she refers in the second extract. They are dreams that suggest symbols associated with loss, misappropriation of that which is your own, exile, absence, banishment, and an ambivalent relation to the mother. During Freud's analysis he 'translated' H.D.'s account of a number of her visions as symptomatic of 'a desire for union with my mother', and he called this her only 'dangerous symptom'.[2]

H.D. knew pretty well why she had come to Freud. He was 77 by this time and had few analysands. The arrangement was effected by an influential friend, and paid for by Bryher, H.D.'s companion, sometime lover, and an immensely wealthy woman who was herself, at this time, closely involved in assisting threatened Jews to flee Austria. H.D.'s presence in Vienna under analysis was a useful cover. War was in H.D.'s mind, and she knew very well what that meant, having lived in London throughout the period of the 1914–18 war. When she took herself to Freud she said:

> I did not specifically realise just what it was I wanted, but I knew that I, like most of the people I knew, in England, America, and the continent of Europe, was drifting. We were drifting. Where? I did not know but at least I accepted the fact that we *were* drifting. At least, I knew this – I would (before the current of inevitable events swept me right into the main stream and so on to the cataract) stand aside, if I could (if it were not already too late), and take stock of my possessions. You might say that I had – yes, I had something that I specifically owned. I *owned* myself. I did not really, of course. My family, my friends, and my circumstances owned me. But I *had* something. Say it was a narrow birch-bark canoe ... With the current gathering force, I could at least pull in to the shallows before it was too late, take stock of my very modest possessions of mind and body, and ask the old Hermit who lived on the edge of this vast domain to talk to me, to tell me, if he would, how best to steer my course.[3]

And so he did tell her. If not of the future course, then of the past. But H.D. did not altogether like what she heard.

> Why had I come to Vienna? The Professor had said in the very beginning that I had come to Vienna hoping to find my mother. Mother? Mamma. But my mother was dead. Anyhow he was a terribly frightening old man, too old and too detached, too wise and too famous altogether, to beat that way with his fist, like a child hammering a porridge-spoon on the table.[4]

H.D.'s image gives her away. Certainly she had come to Vienna looking for an origin, if not for a mother. Sometimes she calls Freud the Professor, or the old Hermit, sometimes he is a 'marvellous old Greek oracle'. 'Back to the womb seems to be my only solution', she wrote when Freud first offered her his interpretation. But if H.D. came looking for a Father, who referred her to a lost Mother, then what she ended up with was a child that made herself into a Mother.

This chapter focusses on H.D.'s mother. Not her real mother, or her phantasy mother, but the mother that was also herself, a mother whom she had inevitably lost, from whose presence she would always be exiled, but whose body – loved, desired, fantasised, despised – represented a lost home, a collection of 'dream treasures' that she might specifically own in owning herself.

That mother was Sappho: a real woman and poet, who did exist and, according to legend, the first woman poet, the mother of lyric poetry, as Homer is the father of epic poetry. The terms of H.D.'s belated relation to Sappho include the same complicated patterns of ambivalent emotion that characterise the relation of any exile to the place which is denied. Whatever the reason for exile, whether it is one of choice on the part of the leaver, or duress either actual or self-imposed, the scene of exile is safer, more congenial and it is actual, while the place lost, the exile's home, is dangerous, difficult, rejected (more or less violently) and imagined. Always it is imagined – possibly it is imaginary – because it is necessarily absent.

Sappho's corpus may have been lost but that has only made it all the more inviting for those followers who scrawled new writings on her blank page. As we have seen, there are two lines of development: one where it is Sappho's life or reputation that attracts the graffitist; and another where is it her text and poetry that matter. In the case of most of the women poets discussed here – Mary Robinson, Letitia Landon, Felicia Hemans, Christina Rossetti – it was Sappho's fame and suffering that drew their attention. But for H.D. – like Michael Field – the draw was her poetry. And – like Michael Field – it was, to begin with, through Henry Thornton Wharton's edition that she knew Sappho. It was Ezra Pound who introduced her to it. They met when she was 15, and when they became engaged a few years later he took on the task of directing her reading and her study in the Classics, in the songs of the Troubadours, and in the pre-Raphaelite and Decadent writers of the *fin de siècle*.[5]

From the very beginnings of H.D.'s creative life, she knew the subjects of Sappho's poems: loss, longing, desire, pain, themes of love and ecstasy, themes of exile, banishment, absence and bereavement. Sappho herself, according to the legends, was at some time exiled to Sicily, away from Lesbos, and it was this fact that Richard Aldington emphasised in the short foreword to his translation of Anyte of Tegea which was published in 1919 along with a translation of Sappho by Edward Storer: 'At some period of her life she was exiled from Lesbos. An inscription in the Parian Chronicle says: "When Aristokles reigned over the Athenians Sappho fled from Mitylene and sailed to Sicily".'[6] The first poem in Edward Storer's translation is a version of Sappho's Fragment 1, the so-called

'Ode to Aphrodite', but the second is a version of Fragment 16, a poem of loss and longing, here re-made into a poem for Atthis:

Atthis has not come back to me: truly I long to die.
Many tears she wept at our parting, saying:
'Sappho, how sad is our fate. I leave you unwillingly.'
To her I answered: 'Go on your way happily and
Do not forget me, for you know how I love you.
But if you should forget, then I will remind you
How fair and good were the things we shared together,
How by my side you wove many garlands of violets
Sweet smelling roses, and made of all kinds of flowers
Delicate necklaces, how many a flask of the finest myrrh
Such as a king might use you poured on your body,
How then reclining you sipped the sweet drinks of your choice.'

The third poem in Storer's translation is based on Fragment 96, made into a another poem of love, loss and longing:

Atthis, whom we both love Mnasidika, dwells
Far away in Sardis, but she often turns
Hither her thoughts to us and to that beautiful life
We lived together when she looked on you
As on some far-famed goddess and
Delighted in your songs especially.

But now among the Lydian women she
Shines as sometimes the rosy-fingered moon
Shines after dark above the stars and pours
Over salt sea and myriad-flowered earth her light,
While the fair dew is shed upon the roses and
Delicate anthrisks and the blossoming melilote.

How many restless thoughts recall to me
The sterile Atthis and I long for the slender one.
Sadness devours my soul. From far there comes to us
The sound of her sharp cry, and it is not
Unheard, for night the many-eared carries it
To us across the sea that flows between.

There follow various fragments and then poem XV which is Sappho's minute Fragment ... 'I loved you once, Atthis, long ago.' But curiously, Storer gives the fragment an interpolated title which turns even this little piece into a poem of exile, for that title is 'IN SICILY?'[7]

Storer's versions of Sappho would have been well known to all the circle: H.D., Ezra Pound and, obviously to Richard Aldington himself. The focus for all of them was not the two most famous Fragments – 1 and 31 – but these other poems of distance and desire. Aldington did not make a complete translation of Sappho, but in 1912 he had transcribed her Fragment 16 and turned it – again – into an exile poem:

> Atthis, far from me and dear Mnasidika,
> Dwells in Sardis;
> Many times she was near us
> So that we lived life well
> Like the far-famed goddess
> Whom above all things music delighted.
>
> And now she is first among the Lydian women
> As the mighty sun, the rosy-fingered moon,
> Beside the great stars.
> And the light fades from the bitter sea
> And in like manner from the rich-blossoming earth;
> And the dew is shed upon the flowers,
> Rose and soft meadow-sweet
> And many-coloured melilote.
> Many things told are remembered of sterile Atthis.
>
> I yearn to behold thy delicate soul
> To satiate my desire ...[8]

From 1911 when H.D. first came to England, she shared a close interest in Sappho and in all things Classical with Ezra Pound and with Richard Aldington. They were all to go on to use Sappho in their work, but as this was the period when H.D. was becoming a poet – 'H.D. Imagiste' – Sappho was most important to her and in the development of her poetic life.

The creative and artistic centre for these young people at this time was the British Museum. H.D. sat in the Reading Room of the British Library copying out the extracts of Sappho then being published in the *Classical Review*. She was doing this work because Aldington, at 19, was too young to get a ticket. At the end of the day they all three would meet in the British Museum tea room. And so it was that here, in August 1912, H.D. showed Pound her earliest poems, 'Priapus' and 'Hermes of the Ways'. Pound took the sheets of paper. He read. Then he took a pen and scribbled 'cut this out, shorten this line'. Pound 'slashed' – H.D.'s own word describing the scene in retrospect – *slashed* the typescript with 'his creative pencil' and 'scratched' – again, H.D.'s own word – *scratched* 'H.D. Imagiste' at the bottom of the page.[9]

Later, Pound would send the poems to Harriet Monroe for publication. So, H.D.'s entry into creative life was a curious one: her influences and sources were Greek, specifically Sapphic, but her signature was written by someone else – Ezra Pound – and her poems were birthed by someone else – Pound again, under the name he'd given her.

If that experience in the British Museum was alienating, worse was to come. Over the next years Pound and H.D. split up, H.D. married Aldington, war broke out, Aldington enlisted, and H.D. miscarried a daughter when she heard the news of the sinking of the *Lusitania*. Aldington began a series of frenetic affairs conducted in his intermittent leaves from France, H.D. had an affair – platonic or not – with D.H. Lawrence, she visited Cornwall with another man, the musician Cecil Gray, and she became pregnant again – by whom, she would never say – and she fell victim to the influenza then sweeping Europe. As she approached her confinement H.D. expected to die, and her baby with her. But then she was rescued by Bryher, a young woman who'd fallen in love with her and who was wealthy enough to look after her. H.D. survived. She called the baby Perdita.

H.D. herself described these years, from 1910 to 1920, as the 'lost' years of her life. They were, she said, 'forgotten, suppressed, repressed', and it was the 'fear of losing them, forgetting them, or just giving then up as neurotic fantasies, residue of the war, confinement and the epidemic, that drives me on to begin again and again a fresh outline'.[10] The fresh outline began with that analysis with Freud and manifested itself in a novel in many drafts, *Paint It Today*.

Exile was a key idea for H.D. at this time – as it was too for many others and, as such, it has been read as one of the definitions of Modernism. In Paris the expatriate community that consisted of Americans like Gertrude Stein, Sylvia Beach, Natalie Barney, Djuna Barnes, as well as others like Pound, Hemingway and James Joyce, all felt themselves part of the diaspora created by the war. They fantasised collectively about a lost home, a lost ideal of civilisation and order, and Greece, in particular, became the focus for these dreams of a past and a place of safety. The dancer Isadora Duncan and the poet Renée Vivien actually took themselves off to Greece: Duncan to build a house outside Athens, Vivien to buy a villa on Lesbos. Others saw Paris itself as a shelter, a shared community which might repair the damage and make a new world, as in Pound's poem 'The Island of Paris' or his 'Exile's Letter' translated from the notes of Fenollosa. In 1923 Bryher published a poem called 'In Exile' and Richard Aldington wrote in 'Exile and Other Poems',

> Let us shade our eyes from the sun
> And gaze through the leaves,

Far, most far –
Shall we see her hill
And the marble front of her house
And herself standing calm
Many coloured, triumphant, austere ...[11]

It is an invocation of Greece – the sun, the marble house – and to Sappho, or perhaps to poetry itself represented by a woman, far distant and 'many coloured', the epithet Sappho herself uses for Aphrodite in her Fragment 1.

At this time Aldington used Sappho as a place of refuge in a very curious way. One of his oddest ventures is a volume called *The Love of Myrrhine and Konallis* published in 1917 and again in 1926. It is, first of all, a long sequence of flowery lesbian love poems telling the story of how Konallis the goat girl loved Myrrhine the 'beautiful-fingered *hetaira*'. This is followed up by a group of crude, bitter, realistic and angry poems written directly out of his war experiences. It is as though Sappho and her all female world, lost and desired, provides a refuge from the harsh facts of war. And yet this Sapphic world is one from which Aldington must always be exiled, always denied, simply by virtue of being a man who can never experience directly the scenes of woman-to-woman desire that he imagines.[12]

At the same time, during the war years, H.D. edited the series of anthologies that identified the 'school' of 'Imagism' in the work of Pound, Aldington, H.D., D.H. Lawrence and Amy Lowell. Writing about this group in 1915 O.W. Firkins said:

> The loneliness in which [the Imagists] dwell is almost polar; they are exiles who have actually accomplished the traditionally impossible feat of fleeing from themselves ... The solitude above described is not restricted to the observer; the object likewise is a drifting, homeless, expatriated thing. It is destitute alike of a place in a charted globe and a function in a civilized order. It has no history, no prospects, no causes, no sequels, no association, no cognates, no allies ... As the man is abridged into mere vision, the object contracts into pure visibility.
>
> The psychology of Imagism ... contains matter of undoubted interest. Not the least conspicuous of its traits is the supineness or passivity of the attitudes which the faithful assume in relation to the overshadowing or incumbent universe. [The Imagists] have the air of patients, of people under treatment; they *undergo* the things which other men observe or contemplate.[13]

This theme of the patient, so close in a sense to H.D.'s own assessment of her psychoanalytic vulnerability, was taken up by other critics too, who saw the Imagists' skewed vision as a kind of illness. William Ellery Leonard wrote:

1. The Imagists can't see straight.
2. The Imagists can't feel straight.
3. The Imagists can't think straight.
4. The Imagists can't talk straight.[14]

Well no more they could. H.D. saw herself 'adrift', floating on a current in a 'birchbark canoe'. She was indeed, as far as her retrospect at this period was concerned, 'fleeing herself', and yet seeking an image, a symbol, a metaphor or other object in poetry that could become a 'land', a place where she might 'pull into the shallows', where she might be 'at home'.

'The Islands'

This is the quest in her poem 'The Islands'.

1.

What are the islands to me,
what is Greece,
what is Rhodes, Samos, Chios,
what is Paros facing west,
what is Crete?

What is Samothrace,
rising like a ship,
what is Imbros, rending the storm-waves
with its breast?

What is Naxos, Paros, Milos,
what is the circle about Lycia,
what, the Cyclades'
white necklace?

What is Greece –
Sparta, rising like a rock,
Thebes, Athens,
what is Corinth?

What is Euboia
with its island-violets,
what is Euboia spread with grass,
set with swift shoals,
what is Crete?

What are the islands to me,
what is Greece?

2.

What can love of land give to me
that you have not –
what do the tall Spartans know,
and gentler Attic folk?

What has Sparta and her women
more than this?

What are the islands to me
if you are lost –
what is Naxos, Tinos, Andros,
and Delos, the clasp
of the white necklace?

3.

What can love of land give to me
that you have not,
what can love of strife break in me
that you have not?

Though Sparta enter Athens,
Thebes wrack Sparta,
each changes as water,
salt, rising to wreak terror
and fall back.

4.

'What has love of land given to you
that I have not?'

I have questioned Tyrians
where they sat
on the black ships,
weighted with rich stuffs,
I have asked the Greeks
from the white ships,
and Greeks from ships whose hulks
lay on the wet sand, scarlet
with great beaks,
I have asked bright Tyrians
and tall Greeks –
'what has love of land given you?'
And they answered – 'peace'.

5.

But beauty is set apart,
beauty is cast by the sea,
a barren rock,
beauty is set about
with wrecks of ships,
upon our coast, death keeps
the shallows – death waits,
clutching toward us
from the deeps.

Beauty is set apart;
the winds that slash its beach,
swirl the coarse sand
upward toward the rocks.

Beauty is set apart
from the islands
and from Greece.

6.

In my garden,
the winds have beaten
the ripe lilies;
in my garden, the salt
has wilted the first flakes
of young narcissus
and the younger hyacinth,
and the salt has crept
under the leaves of the white hyacinth.

In my garden,
even the wind-flowers lie flat,
broken by the wind at last.

7.

What are the islands to me
if you are lost,
what is Paros to me
if your eyes draw back,
what is Milos
if you take fright of beauty,
terrible, tortuous, isolated,
a barren rock?

What is Rhodes, Crete,
what is Paros, facing west,
what, white Imbros?

What are the islands to me
if you hesitate,
what is Greece, if you draw back
from the terror
and cold splendour of song
and its bleak sacrifice?[15]

The islands here are a list of names, a litany, a chant, the repetition designed to make them happen, to conjure up their solid existence in the shifting sea. Samothrace is indeed 'like a ship' rising up, to be clung to as it 'rides the storm waves' and makes a place of haven. Sparta too rises up 'like a rock' becoming an eternal certainty to be clung to. And yet these islands, these broken-up pieces, dissected by the sea, represent a kind of body, a woman's body made up of the 'breast' of Imbros, a girdle – 'the circle about Lydia' – and the Cyclades's 'white necklace'. Even Euboia seems dressed 'spread with grass and island-violets' in stanza 5. The answer to the question 'What are the islands to me?' is unspoken. It is for us to work out that the answer is Land, as in 'Landed' and 'homeland', and *matria* as in 'motherland', the body of the mother being evoked by the map of Greece.

That this is a loved and desired land is taken for granted in the beginning of the next section: 'What can love of land give to me/ That you have not?' It is an exile's question. If you are always at home, if all the loved shapes are gathered in one place, there is no need to set love of land against any other love. But here the question we must ask is who is this 'you' that is suddenly introduced into the poem? It is – and again we have to infer this – a something, a someone, loved as much, perhaps loved more, than the body of the nurturing islands invoked in the incantation of the first section. Of course it is an internal 'you', a you that has to be given a home, a you that can be 'lost' as in stanza 3 of section 2, and a 'you' that can 'break' and destroy the speaking 'I' in the poem, as in stanza 1 of section 3.

Then that 'you' answers the question, and becomes 'I' – 'What has love of land given to you/ That I have not?' The answer, at the end of this section, given to the speaker by the ordinary inhabitants of this land, the Tyrians and the Greeks, is 'Peace'. So love of land, being at home, having a home, as expressed so lyrically across the black, white and red images in this section, brings 'Peace' while – by implication – the 'you' of the first two sections, now become 'I', does *not* bring peace. That this is the trend of the argument of the poem is confirmed by fact that the next section opens with a contradiction 'But …'

I would suggest that the 'you' and the 'I' in the poem are both H.D. in different voices. The first 'I' is a general self; while the 'you' or the second 'I' is her poetic self, her *writing* self, maybe *poetry itself*, poetry equated in section 5 with 'beauty'. But this is a threatening beauty. Notice the violences in this section: the barren rock, the wrecks of ships, the death waiting, clutching towards us, the winds that slash – and 'slash' remember is a potent word for H.D., the 'slash' of Pound's creative pen at the moment when she was made into a poet. So – in the last stanza of section 5 – 'Beauty is set apart/ from the islands/ and from Greece.' To be a poet means that you are always in exile, always set apart, and away from the islands, from the Greece that is home and brings 'Peace'.

Then in section 6, 'in my garden', in the poet's place that makes her a poet, there is only devastation: 'the winds have beaten/ the ripe lilies', the salt has wilted the narcissus and the hyacinth, 'the wind-flowers lie flat/ broken by the wind at last ...' Broken by the poetic wind of inspiration borrowed from Keats, from Shelley, from the troubadours to whom Pound had introduced her. And then – in the conclusion – which pulls this together and takes us to the answer: to poetry. The islands, the fantasised motherland, the idea of home, is nothing if it means loss of 'beauty' – which is poetry and poetic inspiration. 'Love and land' and 'home' both have to be given up if they in any way oppose 'the terror/ and cold splendour of song/ and its bleak sacrifice'.

The indented coastline

In 1920 after this long, ten-year period of disintegration and loss, H.D. did go to Greece for the first time. 'If I got well', she wrote, 'she [Bryher] would herself see that the baby was protected and cherished and she would take me to a new world, a new life, to the land, spiritually of my predilection, geographically of my dreams. We would go to Greece.'[16] This was to be part of her recuperation, and H.D. travelled there aboard a ship belonging to Bryher's father. On board were Bryher, H.D.'s daughter, Bryher's parents, a man named Peter Rodeck and Havelock Ellis, invited by Sir John Ellerman, Bryher's father, who did not believe that women should travel unchaperoned. And on board H.D. had another dream:

> I climbed the now level flight of steps to the upper deck ... We were crossing ... the line ... Perhaps it was more than a few minutes, but we were crossing something 'the line'? What line? We were coasting along in the Bay ... there was a violet light over the sea ... I must get Bryher I thought; Bryher must not miss this, but as I am about to turn back I see Mr Van Eck standing by the deck rail to my *right* ... Well, he sees me ... I notice to my surprise that he is somewhat taller than myself ... He is taller than I thought him. I must not stare at Mr Van Eck. I am always afraid that he will catch my eyes unfocussed, in some uncontrollable fascination, on that curious deep scar over his left eyebrow ... he is taller. He is older – no, he must be younger ... On his right

> as he stands there there is an indented coastline. 'Land' I said. I did not in my thought realise that land, were there land, would be on the other side of the boat. Or had the boat turned round? Or were these some off-lying islands of which I in my ignorance knew nothing? There were dolphins, yes, there were dolphins ... The dolphins are joined by other dolphins; they make curiously unconvincing pattern, leaping in rhythmic order like crescent moons or half moons out of the water, a flight or a dance or dolphins. Yet they are dolphins.[17]

This passage is one of the visions that went over and over again into H.D.'s fictions – that was a conflation of versions written up in *Advent* where Peter Rodeck has become Mr Van Eck – and it was one of the key dreams that she discussed later with Freud in 1933. This Mr Van Eck I should say was, in the dream, not Peter Rodeck, but – as H.D. realises – some unknown or other man, possibly D.H. Lawrence, possibly her own father? – '[H]e is older ... no he must be younger' – who really was the possessor of that deep scar above his eyebrow. But it's the sighting of the imaginary, phantasised 'land' here that I want to emphasise, 'land' or islands ... conjoined with the idea of a pattern, or a rhythmic order that the dolphins make. H.D. was, after all, on her way to Greece, to the islands, to the home that was and was not poetry.

In a note on her early poetry written in 1937, H.D. said that her use of a Greek context in that work had a specific purpose. 'It is nostalgia for a lost land. I call it Hellas. I might, psychologically just as well, have listed the Casco Bay islands off the coast of Maine ...'[18] She might have done, but she didn't. She listed Greek islands and, as Rachel Blau DuPlessis points out, to 'call it Hellas' means 'it' – this special source of writing – is going by a version of her mother's name, which was Helen. In 1920 H.D. visited Greece with Bryher. In 1923 H.D. may actually have visited Lesbos itself with her mother. There's some debate about whether or not this trip took place, but if it didn't, it should have done.

For Sappho was H.D.'s poetic mother, and though the condition of exile expressed in her poem 'The Islands' was conceived as necessary to her role as poet, nonetheless, Greece, the islands of Greece, were the place H.D. envisaged as home. A Greece that could not, she said, be lost, because Greece was a spirit. H.D. is a highly allusive poet, and her references to other poets are multiple, her intertextuality elaborate. Because it is so fitting that Sappho should figure in this enterprise, a great deal of attention has already been given to this inheritance, but much criticism does tend to simplify H.D.'s relation to Sappho as one where the antique poet can function as a role model, permitting H.D. licence to write, a freedom to speak out as a woman, and a pattern for her bisexuality or her lesbianism, or just her feminism, depending on the position of whichever critic is making the comparison. Eileen Gregory, and other writers too, express some surprise that Sappho is not more fully acknowledged in H.D.'s writings. 'Unlike her male predecessors and peers,' says Gregory, 'and indeed unlike her female predecessors such as Michael Field and Renée Vivien, H.D. chooses to abstain completely from public intercourse with the textual body of the Mitylenean.'[19]

In fact, much as one might well understand this reluctance in the light of Freud's analysis, even in Gregory's own account of Sappho in H.D.'s work, this simply isn't true. Sappho's vocabulary, and her imagery are everywhere in H.D. absorbed, as Gregory says, perhaps more tellingly than she knows, 'at the preverbal level'. In H.D.'s many novels Sappho is referred to or her poems quoted; in her collection *Hymen* published in 1921 H.D. included one poem alluding to Sappho entitled 'Fragment 113' and with the first line 'Neither honey nor bee for me'; in her next collection *Heliodora*, which appeared in 1924, she published four more poems entitled 'Fragment 36', 'Fragment 40', 'Fragment 41' and 'Fragment 68', each one prefaced by a quotation from Sappho.[20]

Then in the 1920s H.D. reviewed a new edition of Sappho produced by Edward Marion Cox, and she wrote an essay called 'The Wise Sappho'. In this essay H.D. tries to characterise and to come to terms with the poetry of Sappho, with what Sappho means and with what she might mean. She begins with colours, white, scarlet, scarlet and purple especially, then gold:

> 'Little, but all roses'. I think, though the stains are deep on the red and scarlet cushions, on the flaming cloak of love, it is not warmth we look for in these poems, not fire nor sunlight ... but another element containing all these, magnetic vibrant ... white, unhuman element, containing fire and light and warmth, yet in its essence differing from all these, as if the brittle crescent moon gave heat to us, or some splendid scintillating star turned warm suddenly in our hand like a jewel sent by the beloved.
>
> I think of the words of Sappho as these colours or states rather ... to the superficial lover – truly – roses ...

Then H.D. goes on to expand her reverie and corrects herself, deciding that neither roses, nor colours, nor jewels will do:

> Yet not all roses – not roses at all ... but reading deeper we are inclined to visualise these broken sentences and unfinished rhythms as rocks – perfect rock shelves and layers of rock between which flowers by some chance may grow but which endure when the staunch blossoms have perished.
>
> Not flowers at all, but an island with innumerable, tiny, irregular bays and fjords and little straits between which the sun lies clear (fragments cut from a perfect mirror of iridescent polished silver or of the bronze reflecting richer tints), or breaks, wave upon destructive passionate wave.

> Not roses, but an island, a country, a continent, a planet, a world of emotion ... not a woman, not a goddess even, but a song or the spirit of a song.[21]

Here are all the many things that Sappho is in H.D.'s imagination. Flowers, colours, a jewel sent by the beloved, rock, an island, a mirror, or rather fragments of a mirror, a country, a continent, a song and the spirit of song. Of all these there are three in particular that are regularly associated in H.D.'s mind with Greece and with poetry and with her own (and Freud's) analysis of her mental perspective. The 'innumerable, tiny, irregular bays and fjords and little straits' of the 'island' that is Sappho resembles the 'indented coastline' of the land H.D. saw in her dream on board the cruise ship in the Aegean sea. The 'mirror' or the 'fragments cut from a perfect mirror' in this passage from 'The Wise Sappho' is similar to the mirroring or reversal that took place in that dream – 'I did not in my thought realise that land, were there land, would be on the other side of the boat. Or had the boat turned round?' And the island and the mirror are both there in Sappho's text, literally there, because H.D. would have known what the papyrus scraps of her text looked like. Photographs of them – torn and tattered, and looking much like an island with a raggedly indented coastline – were published in Wharton's edition, which H.D. knew well, as well as in that Edwin Marion Cox edition that she reviewed in the same year as she wrote 'The Wise Sappho'.[22] Of all the writers and artists I have discussed in this book H.D. is one of the first to understand thoroughly the terms on which Sappho's oeuvre existed and to imaginatively respond to the remnants, the 'fragments' of a 'perfect mirror' that those papyri represented.

The jewel box

Now I want to take up the third image: the image of the jewel, the 'fragments of a perfect mirror' and also to take you back to that dream with which I began, the dream of the red-velvet-lined jewel box that contained H.D.'s 'dream treasures' and that, in the dream (though not in fact) had belonged to her mother. To do that, we must first recall the particular status of Sappho's textual body at the beginning of the twentieth century. In Chapter 1 I explained how the single most important development in Sappho scholarship came at the end of the nineteenth and beginning of the twentieth century when Grenfell and Hunt began their excavations in Oxyrhynchus under the aegis of the Egypt Exploration Society. Most of their papyrus finds dated from the Egyptian Hellenistic period of the first to the third century AD and consisted of bills, laundry lists, agreements and other ephemera. But there were also longer versions of poems known to be by Sappho, and inscriptions on these scraps – even where they had been overwritten or torn into strips to wrap around mummified bodies – could be discerned and recorded. As a result, major new poems such as that on the wedding of Hector and Andromache were discovered, and Sappho's oeuvre almost doubled.

H.D. knew all about this and at the end of 'The Wise Sappho' she wrote:

> The roses Meleager saw as 'little' have become in the history not only of literature but of nations ... a great power ... each fragment witness to the love of some scholar or hectic antiquary searching to find a precious inch of palimpsest among the funereal glories of the sand-strewn Pharoahs.

H.D. was not the only woman to have her imagination fired by this image of Sappho's fragments returning, of Sappho becoming undead and released into new life, her dismembered corpus wrapped around other corpses. Some of the reactions to this romance were amusing; others were peculiar. In Paris in January 1907 the French writer Colette and her lover the Marquise de Belbeuf, known as 'Missy', caused a riot and very nearly got themselves arrested when they enacted a music hall tableau called 'Rêve d'Egypte'. Their mime portrayed an Egyptian mummy – played by Colette – being woken from her eternal sleep by the kiss of her archeologist lover – played by Missy in a suit, as 'he' stripped off her wrappings down to a jewelled bra. As Colette was part of the contemporary lesbian scene in Paris – one that included avowed Sappho fans such as Renée Vivien and Natalie Barney – I'm sure that the scene owed something to the facts of Sappho's scholarly reconstruction at the time, as well as to the fictions of her *amours*.[23]

Perhaps more curious still, one of the most extraordinary finds that took place slightly later in the twentieth century was that of an early potsherd dating from the third century BC discovered at Oxyrhynchus by the Italian papyrologist Medea Norsa. The shard, which is now in the Uffizi in Florence, had a large part of a poem scratched on it – a poem attributed to Sappho because a few lines of it were quoted by the ancient writer Hermogenes in his *Kinds of Style*. This shard, so comparatively close in time to the real life of Sappho – only dating from some three hundred years after her death – seemed so much the substance, the real body of Sappho, that Norsa came first to believe that it was the body of Sappho, and then, in a bizaare twist, that the potsherd was her own body, or that she was the potsherd.[24]

I am not suggesting that H.D. ended up anywhere quite so dotty, but her psychic relation to Sappho and her treatment of Sappho – poetry, persona and image – was closely connected to the fact of Sappho's existence as, in, through, fragments.

H.D.'s imagination is, characteristically, interested in *remnants*, in precious fragments embedded or contained within a box, a cocoon, or some other enclosing shape or body. This is why she maintains the image of the palimpsest – which is actually the title of one of her books – and the focus of much of her poetic imagining. In *The Walls Do Not Fall* she writes:

I know, I feel
the meaning that words hide;
they are anagrams, cryptograms,
little boxes, conditioned
to hatch butterflies.

Shari Benstock points to the way that H.D.'s language 'exploit[s] the language of enclosure (employing images of shells, cocoons, boxes, cryptograms)' and she suggests that this is to do with H.D. recognising a truth of female experience encoded, and embedded within a larger public expression of a male truth.[25] But I don't think that is all.

H.D. loved museums. For her, the museum was a big cocoon or jewel box holding precious items. And she wanted to get at those precious things because sometimes, so often in her imagination, they belonged to her. Long before she left America as a young woman she had a dream – again – about a motif of a thistle and a serpent. When she visited the Louvre in Paris for the first time, there it was – an ancient signet ring incised with the thistle and the serpent. In the British Museum H.D. read Sappho. In the British Museum tea room H.D. became a poet when she too became a broken thing – but precious – when she was 'slashed' into being by Ezra Pound. This is how she put it in her novel *Paint It Today*:

> She had parted with the youth, having gained nothing from him but a feeling that someone had tampered with an oracle, had banged on a temple door, had dragged out small, curious, sacred ornaments, had not understood their inner meaning, yet with a slight sense of their inner value, their perfect tint and carving, had not stolen them, but left them, perhaps worse, exposed by the roadside, reft from their shelter and their holy setting.[26]

Although this is painful – this looting, this violence, this exposure of internal objects, hidden inside another body – it is, in H.D.'s imagination, the process that *made her* into a poet. And it is the process that made another poet – Sappho – into her.

In her brief note on the poems published in *Heliodora* – which included the four specific Sappho poems, as well as number of more indirectly referential ones – H.D. says that the fragments of Sappho are 'freely translated'.[27] So they are. Sappho has been treated very freely – so freely that she is hardly recognisable. Rather, she has been raided, mutilated, her box rifled, her jewels treated as common property. In these poems H.D. emphasises the mutilated state of Sappho's corpus, insisting in her titles on 'Fragments'. More, she mutilates Sappho still further for even when she is dealing with the larger poems, she cuts them down, chops them up, into smaller pieces. And H.D. recognises her own processes, for in each of these four cases – that she titles Fragment 36, 40, 41 and 68 – her version of Sappho's poems are about some threatened violence, some splitting of self, or selves.

Fragment Forty-one
... thou flittest to Andromeda.
SAPPHO

1.

Am I blind alas,
am I blind?
I too have followed
her path.
I too have bent at her feet.
I too have wakened to pluck
amaranth in the straight shaft,
amaranth purple in the cup,
scorched at the edge to white.

Am I blind?
am I the less ready for her sacrifice?
am I the less eager to give
what she asks,
she the shameless and radiant?

Am I quite lost,
I towering above you and her glance,
walking with swifter pace,
with clearer sight,
with intensity
beside which you two
are as spent ash?

Nay, I give back to the goddess the gift
she tendered me in a moment
of great bounty.
I return it. I lay it again
on the white slab of her house,
the beauty she cast out
one moment, careless.

Nor do I cry out:
'why did I stoop?
why did I turn aside

one moment from the rocks
marking the sea-path?
Aphrodite, shameless and radiant,
have pity, turn, answer us.'

Ah no – though I stumble toward
her altar-step,
though my flesh is scorched and rent,
shattered, cut apart,
slashed open;
though my heels press my own wet life
black, dark to purple,
on the smooth rose-streaked
threshold of her pavement.

2.

Am I blind alas, deaf too
that my ears lost all this?
nay, O my lover,
shameless and still radiant,
I tell you this:

I was not asleep,
I did not lie asleep on those hot rocks
while you waited.
I was not unaware when I glanced
out toward the sea
watching the purple ships.

I was not blind when I turned.
I was not indifferent when I strayed aside
or loitered as we three went
or seemed to turn a moment from the path
for that same amaranth.
I was not dull and dead when I fell
back on our couch at night.
I was not indifferent when I turned
and lay quiet.
I was not dead in my sleep.

3.

Lady of all beauty,
I give you this:
say I have offered small sacrifice,
say I am not unworthy your touch,

but say not:
'she turned to some cold, calm god,
silent, pitiful, in preference.'

Lady of all beauty,
I give you this:
say not:
'she deserted my altar-step,
the fire on my white hearth
was too great,
she fell back at my first glance.'

Lady, radiant and shameless,
I have brought small wreaths,
(they were a child's gift,)
I have offered myrrh-leaf,
crisp lentisk,
I have laid rose-petal
and white rock-rose from the beach.

But I give now a greater,
I give life and spirit with this.
I render a grace
no one has dared to speak,
lest men at your altar greet him
as slave, callous to your art;
I dare more than the singer
offering her lute,
the girl her stained veils,
the woman her swathes of birth,
or pencil and chalk,
mirror and unguent box.

I offer more than the lad
singing at your steps,
praise of himself,
his mirror his friend's face,
more than any girl,
I offer you this:

(grant only strength
that I withdraw not my gift,)
I give you my praise and this:
the love of my lover
for his mistress.

She was a dark lady

Here is another one of H.D.'s dreams recorded during her psychoanalysis.

> She was a dark lady. She wore a clear-coloured robe, yellow or faint-orange. It was wrapped round her as in one piece, like a sari worn as only a high caste Indian lady could wear it. But she is not Indian, she is Egyptian. She appears at the top of a long staircase; marble steps lead down to a river. She wears no ornament, no circlet or sceptre shows her rank, but anyone would know this is a Princess. Down the steps she comes ... There is no detail. The steps are geometrical, symmetrical and she is as abstract as a lady could be yet she is a real entity, a real person. I, the dreamer, wait at the foot of the steps. I have no idea who I am or how I got there. There is no before or after, it is a perfect moment in time or out of time. I am concerned about something, however. I wait below the lowest step. There, in the water beside me, is a shallow basket, or ark or box or boat. There is, of course, a baby nested in it. The Princess must find the baby. I know that she will find this child. I know that the baby will be protected and sheltered by her and that is all that matters.[28]

When H.D. offered this dream to Freud he recognised the allusion to Moses from the book of Exodus, as she did also, and H.D. herself was able to add to that the conviction that her view was partly coloured by her own memories of Gustave Doré's illustrations to the Bible (published 1875–76). The story of a mother – who is not a mother – and the hidden baby, the secret treasure shut up in a box is one that goes far beyond H.D.'s image of Miriam. As is the way with dreams, the punning connections suggest more than they say. But will the Princess – who might be an Egyptian mummy, who might be 'mummy', who might be a resurrected Sappho – will that 'Sappho' be protected by H.D. – who might be the nested baby inside 'the basket, or ark, or box'; or the 'birch-bark canoe'.

My own analysis of H.D.'s dreaming poems is Kleinian rather than Freudian, with two sidelights from Winnicott and Lacan. The Sappho that H.D. inherited was by no means any pure Sappho, nor could she offer any uncomplicated idea of home. H.D. did read Greek, but she also read Wharton's edition of Sappho which included many other versions, and she also – and especially – knew the savage and destructive *femmes-fatales*-type Sapphos that inhabited the poems of nineteenth century writers like Baudelaire – who had also figured Sappho as island and mirror – and Swinburne, who did the same. And then, because of the highly particularised state of Sappho scholarship in the early twentieth century and because of the resultant knowledge of broken potsherds and torn papyrus strips, H.D. appreciated the violence done to Sappho's corpus. If we look now for images of restitution in that process of Greek scholarship and archaeology, it reminds us too of the violence of dismemberment that put Sappho there, that reduced her to that fragmented state.

Sappho then, is not any comfortable role model for H.D. When H.D. makes her into a mirror, she makes her into shards, 'fragments cut from a perfect mirror'. So, to compare this with Lacan's 'mirror stage', as Jacqueline Rose explains, the mirror does not – any more than the mother does – 'mirror the child to itself; she grants an image to the child, which her presence instantly deflects. Holding the child is, therefore, to be understood not only as containing, but also replicates a process of referring, which fractures the unity it seems to offer'.[29] So Sappho 'contains' H.D. She is the mother who will birth H.D. by containing her no longer, but her presence in H.D.'s imagination also deflects the wholeness of the Sappho/H.D. dyad and a fracture appears. Sameness becomes difference.

Part of that fracture takes place, as in Kleinian theory, because of the interplay of love and hate in the relations between mother and infant child. The child envies the mother's breast and its creativity – as H.D. envies Sappho, and she too, like the child who fantasises the mother's destruction, might be *pleased* with the mutilation of Sappho's corpus. 'Trying', as Klein says, 'to destroy its mother by every method at the disposal of its sadistic trends – with its teeth, nails, and excreta and with the whole of its body, transformed in a phantasy into all kinds of dangerous weapons.'[30] And why? Because the child fantasises internal objects which it desires and then it fantasises a possibility of attacking, sublimating, tearing out of the mother's body in order to consume them, whether in hatred or in envy, or desire. This is the attack that H.D. makes on Sappho's corpus in the 'paranoid-schizophrenic' position where the mother is not – as Sappho is not – a whole object, but part objects, fragments then, both external and internal. But then follows a 'depressive position' when the child recognises the mother as a whole person, stops perceiving her as an array of parts and split objects. 'Now', as Hanna Segal says in summarising Klein,

> the predominant fear is that of the loss of the loved object in the external world and in his own inside. The infant at that stage is still under the sway of uncontrollable greedy and sadistic impulses. In phantasy his love object is still attacked in greed and hatred, is destroyed, torn into pieces and fragments; and not only is the external object so attacked but also the internal one, and then the whole internal world feels destroyed and shattered as well. Bits of the destroyed object may turn into persecutors and there is a fear of internal persecution as well as a pining for the lost loved object and guilt for the attack. The memory of the good situation, where the infant's ego contained the whole loved object, and the realisation that it has been lost through his own attacks, gives rise to an intense feeling of loss and guilt and to the wish to restore and recreate the lost love object outside and within the ego.[31]

Sappho is the mother H.D. attacks and repairs. She is the home H.D. fantasises and denies. She is the jewel box full of fragments and precious ornaments that H.D. would possess, yet sees scattered, profaned and treated as 'common property'. The fragments of the poems themselves representing, as they do, only a fragment of the lost mother's body, body of work, are transitional objects: a snuggy, a comforter, a *schmusediche*, a red blanket with the right smell, a red-velvet-lined box which represents the desired body of the love object and the treasures it contains.

And, if you look, that transitional object appears over and over again. In 'The Wise Sappho' one of Sappho's manifestations is 'the red and scarlet cushions, on the flaming cloak of love', a cloak which is warm in the 'The Wise Sappho' because, of course, it is a body, it is alive. It is Sappho's verse, body, body of work. And in H.D.'s novel *Paint It Today* there it is again:

> You might think the light was very shallow in this forest. Shallow – that is quite an idea. The word shallow came of itself just as my lover slides of himself, without being called, without being expected, around a pillar or out of a door when I am just going to sleep on a whortleberry-coloured blanket ... The light is very warm ... I will not tell you exactly what my lover looks like nor what he wears for you would laugh and say you thought it very like a cheap steel engraving of an idealised eighteenth-century portrait of Catullus. My description would give that idea. But if you say Catullus, Catullus, Catullus often enough like a charm (though I don't think my lover is Catullus), you will get some idea of the colour of the things he wears.
>
> This colour does not match nor does it clash with the whortle-berry blanket.[32]

'Though I don't think my lover is Catullus'. Throughout *Paint It Today* H.D. uses typical Sapphic imagery and, in many places, direct allusions to Sappho's work. In some ways her naming of Catullus here is a game with that Sapphic inheritance, because behind Catullus lies Sappho, said but not said, in that the Roman poet was the one who re-made Sappho in his 'Lesbia' poems and who re-wrote her Fragment 31 in his famous poem 'Ille mi par esse deo videtur'. This naming which appropriates and denies both Sappho and Catullus ('I don't think my lover is Catullus') raises a last point about naming in the work of H.D. If, to the puzzlement of some modern critics, she does not often (or at least comparatively rarely) name the name of Sappho, H.D. often *names herself*. Her initials are encoded in titles like *Heliodora* where the title poem itself is a poem about naming, self-assertion and sexual contest.[33] Other examples might be *Hedylus* or *Her* and even in *Helen in Egypt* which points to her mother's name, and all the names in her novels – and often in her poems – are coded versions of real names, and especially her own name or names.

This tendency connects to Kristeva's suggestion in *Desire in Language* that part of the entry into syntax constitutes a 'first victory' over the mother. She describes how the

> discourse of a two year old girl demonstrated what I think is the psychoanalytical underpinning of the archaic naming of referential space by demonstratives. Each time she organised the space of the room in which we played together by means of demonstratives or shifters (*c'est, ici, la, haut, bas, ceci, cela*), she felt obliged to 'analyze' that place (those places) thus fragmented by giving them a person's name; 'mamma', or the mother's first name ...[34]

This is what the name of 'Greece' meant to H.D. Or the name Sappho, or Lesbos, or 'the Myrtilenean', or for that matter, Catullus, or the whortle-berry blanket, or the rose, or the island, or the mirror. It named a space which names H.D.'s poetic mother and one that H.D. would both possess and destroy as she made herself into a poet. The poetic process was much the same as that through which Tennyson or Baudelaire exploited Sappho, but H.D.'s psychoanalytic knowledge meant that her enterprise was more aware, if it was also more fragmented and opaque. 'Greece' named a place that she longed for, and to which she could never return.

In an article on the world's love affair with the *Venus de Milo*, Peter Fuller quotes the Marxist art historian Arnold Hauser:

> The delight in ruins, torsos, sketches, so characteristic of the second half of the eighteenth century and the subsequent period is a symptom of the romantic mood, which has now taken hold of the Western world. It is only within this frame of mind that the whole psychic mechanism of frustration, retaliation, compensation, a sense of guilt, and anxiety for restitution as psychoanalysis describes it, becomes operative and creative in art; it is only from that time on that a torso ... a fragment ... is felt to be more suggestive and expressive than an unmutilated work of art.
>
> It is since romanticism that art has become a quest for a home that the artist believes he possessed in his childhood, and which assumes in his eyes the character of a Paradise lost through his own fault.[35]

This was the trauma H.D. wished to discuss with Freud. It was the one that she rehearsed in her work throughout her whole life. But it was also the split self, travelling on through desire and loss and back again, that made her into a poet, made her into an island and a mirror, so that when she died in 1961 Ezra Pound could write to her daughter Perdita, '... algae of long past sea currents are moved'.[36]

And finally, one last dream, from June 1941 this time, just after the British Museum had been hit in the Blitz. Much of the British Library's collection was destroyed on this occasion but, for H.D., given that this was where she had read Sappho and where she had been 'slashed' into poetry, much more was lost. On this occasion H.D. dreamt again of a lady, a lady who was 'wise' (like H.D.'s own 'The Wise Sappho') and a lady for whom she wrote 'stalactite-shape running verse' (like Sappho's own papyrus fragments):

> Who is this lady? Yes, it is part of myself, I conclude, that had died ... now it is projected out ... She was wise ... she was not so much arrogant in her wisdom, as lost. She had only this peculiar garment of my own body to live in. It must have been a burden to her. There were very few occasions when she could express herself, sometimes I wrote for her, stalactite-shape running verse ... broken ... frozen.
>
> I am free of her, she is dead. She died the night of June 20th 1941, I think after mid-night, yes, surely it must have been just before dawn.[37]

9
Epilogue: Virginia's Sapphists

Virginia Woolf knew that there were many Sapphos. Like the writers and artists whose readings of Sappho are presented in this book, Woolf re-invented 'Sappho' as a muse, as a poet, as an icon, as a feminist, and as a friend and lover of women. Each one of them are, in their different ways, Sapphists.

When she first met and became enthralled with Vita Sackville-West, Woolf wrote: 'These Sapphists *love* women; friendship is never untinged with amorosity.'[1] As a sapphist, a lover of Sappho and of her poetry, Woolf also looked at the Greek poet's incarnations with 'amorosity'. There is a certain erotic tone that colours Woolf's frequent brief allusions to her precursor. It connects to professional and political strands in her life, but there were two women in particular whom Woolf linked with Sappho.

The first was Jane Harrison, the Classical scholar, and a 'learned Lady' whom she met at Cambridge in 1904 and with whom Woolf studied Greek.[2] Woolf could never think of Harrison – or of Greek – without that hint of sexual intrigue. In 1919 the Woolfs printed a 'very obscure, indecent, and brilliant poem' by Hope Mirrlees, Jane's 'favourite pupil' and companion,[3] and later in the year when she was reviewing Mirrlees' *Madeleine: One of Love's Jansenists* for the *Times Literary Supplement* Woolf wrote to Clive Bell that 'It's all sapphism so far as I've got – Jane and herself.'[4] In 1921 James Strachey came to visit, 'leapt on to my bed, directly I had left it, & lay reading Jane's pamphlet' [*Epilegomena to the Study of Greek Religion* (1921)]. Directly afterwards a conversation with Lytton Strachey turned to 's——y' where they agree that 'the b's are all namby pambies & sentimentalists'.[5]

The other woman was Vita herself, who became Woolf's friend and lover. When Virginia watched Vita dozing on a train journey she said she looked like 'Sappho asleep by [Frederic] Leighton' and when Woolf planned *Orlando*, her 'love letter' to Vita, there was Sappho again:

> Suddenly, between twelve & one I conceived a whole fantasy to be called 'The Jessamy Brides' – why, I wonder? I have rayed round it several scenes. Two women, poor, solitary at the top of a house. One can see anything (for this is all fantasy) the Tower Bridge, clouds, aeroplanes. Also some men listening in the room over the way. Everything is to be tumbled, pall mall. It is to be written as I write letters at the top of my speed: the ladies of Llangollen; on Mrs Fladgate; on people passing. No attempt is to be made to realise the character. Sapphism is to be suggested. Satire is to be the main note – satire & wildness. The Ladies are to have Constantinople in view. Dreams of golden domes. My own lyric vein to be satirised. Everything mocked. And it is to end with three dots ... For the truth is I feel the need of an escapade ... I want to kick up my heels & be off. I want to embody all those innumerable ideas & tiny stories which fly into my mind at all seasons ...[6]

In this case its not just Sappho's sexual proclivities that are relevant. The fact of the fragmentary character of her work suggests to Woolf an appropriate literary form, fit for an 'escapade'. She notes her own 'lyric vein' which is to be satirised even though, later on in 1937, Woolf declared herself 'satisfied with my share of the compliment' when the young Christopher Isherwood said 'I'll come out with it then Mrs Woolf – you see, I feel you're a poetess.' [7]

But it was Sappho's role as woman writer that allowed Woolf to use her in a polemical argument. In 1920 she cited her Greek precursor in a famous exchange with Desmond MacCarthy on 'The Intellectual Status of Women'. In a review of Arnold Bennett's *Our Women* published in the *New Statesman* MacCarthy, writing as 'Affable Hawk', had made a number of derogatory remarks about the capacities and abilities of women and Woolf rose to the challenge. She named many women of achievement (including Jane Harrison) and ended with the example of Sappho:

> ... if Affable Hawk sincerely wishes to discover a great poetess, why does he let himself be fobbed off with a possible authoress of the Odyssey? Naturally I cannot claim to know Greek as Mr Bennett and Affable Hawk know it, but I have often been told that Sappho was a woman, and that Plato and Aristotle placed her with Homer and Archilochus among the greatest of their poets. That Mr Bennett can name fifty of the male sex who are indisputably her superiors is therefore a welcome surprise, and if he will publish their names I will promise, as an act of that submission which is so dear to my sex, not only to buy their works but, so far as my faculties allow, to learn them by heart.

When 'Affable Hawk' remained unconvinced, arguing that many underprivileged men had still succeeded where women had failed, Woolf took him on again:

> Sir, – To begin with Sappho. We do not, as in the hypothetical case of Burns suggested by 'Affable Hawk', judge her merely by her fragments. We supplement our judgment by the opinions of those to whom her works were known in their entirety. It is true that she was born 2,500 years ago. According to 'Affable Hawk' the fact that no poetess of her genius has appeared from 600 B.C. to the eighteenth century proves that during that time there were no poetesses of potential genius. It follows that the absence of poetesses of moderate merit during that period proves that there were no women writers of potential mediocrity. There was no Sappho; but also, until the seventeenth or eighteenth century, there was no Marie Corelli and no Mrs Barclay.
>
> To account for the complete lack not only of good women writers but also of bad women writers I can conceive of no reason unless it be that there was some external restraint upon their powers. For 'Affable Hawk' admits that there have always been women of second or third rate ability. Why, unless they were forcibly prohibited, did they not express these gifts in writing, music, or painting? The case of Sappho, though so remote, throws, I think, a little light upon the problem. I quote J.A. Symonds:
>
> 'Several circumstances contributed to aid the development of lyric poetry in Lesbos. The customs of the Aeolians permitted more social and domestic freedom than was common in Greece. Aeolian women were not confined to the harem like Ionians, or subjected to the rigorous discipline of the Spartans. While mixing freely with male society, they were highly educated and accustomed to express their sentiments to an extent unknown elsewhere in history – until, indeed, the present time'.
>
> And now to skip from Sappho to Ethel Smyth ... It seems to me indisputable that the conditions which make it possible for a Shakespeare to exist are that he shall have had predecessors in his art, shall make one of a group where art is freely discussed and practised, and shall himself have the utmost freedom of action and experience. Perhaps in Lesbos, but never since, have these conditions been the lot of women ...[8]

'Affable Hawk' gave in, or rather simply desisted with bad grace – 'If the freedom and education of women is impeded by the expression of my views, I shall argue no more' he said. Virginia Woolf, however, was encouraged to think out her own ideas on women and writing and they eventually found expression in *A Room of One's Own* (1928).

In 1930 Woolf replied to an American correspondent who admired that work:

> It is very good of you to write and tell me that you like my book A room of ones Own. It was the product of a highly unscientific mind, and I am therefore glad that you still find something true in it.

> My knowledge of Greek history is small; but I suppose that writing poetry was, in one island and for a certain group of women, the habit at a certain period, and that Sappho was not a unique writer but supported by many other poetesses. That I think until the late eighteenth century was never the case in England. Why Sappho and the others were allowed to write, I do not of course presume to say. Historians perhaps might help.[9]

It is a double myth of origin. Once upon a time in Sappho's day, women were able to write and work within a supportive female community. Once upon a time in the late eighteenth century, women began again to enjoy those freedoms. However historically dubious either of these claims may be in terms of their facts, there is no doubt that both these scenes of origin worked vividly in the imaginations of women writers from Mary Robinson, through the Michael Fields to H.D. and Woolf herself. For Virginia Woolf, as for all of those of her predecessors that figure in this book, Sappho – in her many shapes whether literary, political or personal – was the mother, the mirror and the model.

Virginia Woolf did write one Sapphic fiction. It is 'A Society', a short story published in 1921 in her collection entitled *Monday or Tuesday*. Cassandra – named for the prophetess who speaks the truth but who is never believed – is surrounded by a group of women, much as Sappho was surrounded by her girls. This 'Society' agrees to go out into the world of men and ask questions in an attempt to discover whether or not men are as truly admirable as they had all been brought up to believe. Furthermore the girls all agree that, until they have the answer, they will all remain 'chaste'. It's a delicious extended riposte to MacCarthy who would have recognised himself:

> 'Of course they despise us' said Eleanor. 'At the same time how do you account for this – I made enquiries among the artists. Now no woman has ever been an artist, has she Poll?'
>
> 'Jane-Austen-Charlotte-Bronte-George-Eliot,' cried Poll, like a man crying muffins in a back street.
>
> 'Damn the woman!' someone exclaimed. 'What a bore she is!'
>
> 'Since Sappho there has been no female of first rate – ' Eleanor began, quoting from a weekly newspaper.[10]

But this story is not just a play with Woolf's own contemporary engagement with feminist politics. Sure enough, the important institutions the women visit and the questions they ask there, poke fun at the Navy, the academic life, the law, the Royal Academy, the Army and the business world. But the range of reference suggests that Woolf was also up to date with the state of Sappho scholarship in the early twentieth century. Castalia sets herself up in Oxbridge to ask questions of Professor Hobkin, and she discovers that his 'life work' is an edition of Sappho:

> It's a queer looking book, six or seven inches thick, not all by Sappho. Oh no. Most of it is a defence of Sappho's chastity, which some German had denied, and I can assure you the passion with which these two gentlemen argued, the learning they displayed, the prodigious ingenuity with which they disputed the use of some implement which looked to me for all the world like a hairpin astounded me; especially when the door opened and Professor Hobkin himself appeared. A very nice, mild, old gentleman, but what could *he* know about chastity?

Sue decides that Castalia has 'made some mistake. Probably Professor Hobkin was a gynaecologist', but Woolf herself is not in error. In 1913 the German scholar Ulrich von Wilamowitz-Moellendorf had published *Sappho und Simonides: Untersuchungen uber griechische Lyriker* which argued that Sappho was chaste. Her imagination was not fired by men, he said, and her only interest in girls was academic, in that she ran a school. When he tried to explain this theory to the British composer Ethel Smyth – a lesbian, and an admirer of Virginia Woolf – she was not convinced: 'I dismissed this depressing view of "burning Sappho" from my mind.' But Wilamowitz-Moellendorf was not the only proponent of this theory. This image of Sappho was also promoted by J.M.F. Bascoul, a Frenchman, a medical doctor and amateur scholar living in Algiers, who published two pamphlets – one on Fragment 31 (1911) and one on Fragment 1 (1913) – both with the overall title of *La Chaste Sappho* and both designed to show that it was only a salacious conspiracy that made these into poems about love. They were, in fact, the record of Sappho's defence of her own role as the leading poet of the day against her rival Stesichore. It may be that Bascoul and his arguments is the original for Professor Hobkin. And as to the 'implement which looked to me for all the world like a hairpin' – who knows? It could be a plectrum, or is it some contraceptive device (as Sue seems to imply), or a sex toy? I suspect that it's a hairpin.

Woolf's short story is a larger sending up of all the serious Sappho questions and all the assumptions that men make about women. Everything is turned on its head. Here are Sappho's girls, given names, just like the Greek girls in the poet's circle, but they are modern names: Poll, Jane, Clorinda, Rose, Fanny, Helen, Castalia, Sue, Cassandra, Moll, Judith, Jill, Eleanor, Ruth and Liz. Or are they? And are any of them 'chaste'? – that Victorian ideal of 'the Angel in House' that, in Woolf's view, so hampered the ambitions of the woman writer. In legend Clorinda dressed in man's clothes, then there was Fanny Hill, Helen who ran off with Paris, Sue Bridehead, an unmarried mother, Judith who seduced Holofernes with wine, Jill who went with Jack, Ruth who pledged herself to Naomi. Perhaps these names aren't quite as innocent as they might seem.

Even Cassandra herself is not so 'chaste'. When Castalia returns from three months' worth of further investigations, Cassandra says 'I don't know what it was in the look of her that so moved me; but I could not restrain myself, and dashing across the room, I clasped her in my arms. Not only was she very beautiful; she seemed also in the highest spirits.' Castalia – who turns out to be pregnant – points out Cassandra's lapse:

'If you'd been a chaste woman yourself you would have screamed at the sight of me – instead of which you rushed across the room and took me in your arms. No, Cassandra. We are neither of us chaste.' Three times the word 'queer' is used in this story, Woolf was knowing enough to include both meanings.

Even the whole of English literature is reduced in this story to a succession of fragmentary lines in a send-up of the state of Sappho's own oeuvre. Helen goes to the Royal Academy to conduct her research into the question of why men are to be admired but when asked to deliver her findings, recites from a 'pale blue volume':

> O for the touch of a vanished hand and the sound of a voice that is still. Home is the hunter, home from the hill. He gave his bridle reins a shake. Love is sweet, love is brief. Spring, the fair spring, is the year's pleasant King. O! to be in England now that April's there. Men must work and women must weep. The path of duty is the way to glory ...

But it's with the conclusion of her story that Woolf makes a Sapphic reference that looks back a few years to an event in the Greek poet's afterlife, and that looks forward to what will happen – and has happened – to Sappho.

Castalia gives birth to a girl, Ann, war is declared, waged and concluded, and the women agree to disband their group and abandon their quest:

> 'My cook will have bought the Evening News' said Castalia 'and Ann will be spelling it out over her tea. I must go home.'
>
> 'It's no good – not a bit of good' I said. 'Once she knows how to read there's only one thing you can teach her to believe in – and that is herself.'
>
> 'Well that would be a change,' said Castalia.
>
> So we swept up the papers of our Society, and though Ann was playing with her doll very happily, we solemnly made her a present of the lot and told her we had chosen her to be President of the Society of the future – upon which she burst into tears, poor little girl.

The allusion is to the dedication Pierre Louys printed in his Sapphic book of poems called *Chansons de Bilitis* (1894): 'This little book of antique love is respectfully dedicated to the young daughters of a future society.'[11]

Woolf's Sapphic fiction looks forward, as she looks forward also in *A Room of One's Own*, to the day in an imagined future when the woman writer will not be hampered by the constraints of social expectation and assumption. Woolf's vision was prophetic. Now, at the beginning of the twenty-first century, young women writers, coming into their own, can work without constraint.

This is why this book ends here. Woolf, through Sappho, fantasised about a world in the past where the woman writer was as free as the man. Then she imagined a place where that liberation would come again. Since the time of Woolf's writing a great number of women and men have gone on with the project of re-inventing Sappho.[12] For them, as for the lovers of Sappho that are discussed in this book, she will continue as muse, mother, mirror, mine, model, motive. But the first idea for this study came out of my reading Jeanette Winterson's Sappho in her *Art & Lies*, and it began with my work on Mary Robinson and the Victorian women poets. It seems appropriate to end with another intellectual woman who used Sappho not only to look back, but also to look forward.

Notes

1. Introduction

1. *Greek Lyric I, Sappho and Alcaeus*, Loeb Classical Library, ed. David A. Campbell (Harvard University Press, Cambridge Mass., 1982), pp. 78–81. All translations in this section are taken from Josephine Balmer, trans., *Sappho: Poems and Fragments* (Brilliance Books, London, 1984), reissued (Bloodaxe, Newcastle upon Tyne, 1992).
2. For discussions on the context of Fragment 31 see Page Dubois, *Sappho is Burning* (University of Chicago Press, Chicago, 1995), pp. 64–75; Margaret Williamson, *Sappho's Immortal Daughters* (Harvard University Press, Cambridge Mass., 1995), pp. 154–60; Giuliana Lanata, trans. William Robins, 'Sappho's Amatory Language', Mary R. Leftokowitz, 'Critical Stereotypes and the Poetry of Sappho', Charles Segal 'Eros and Incantation: Sappho and Oral Poetry', Jack Winkler, 'Gardens of Nymphs: Public and Private in Sappho's Lyrics', Judith P. Hallett, 'Sappho and her Social Context: Sense and Sensuality', and Margaret Williamson, 'Sappho and the Other Woman' – all in *Reading Sappho: Contemporary Approaches*, ed. Ellen Greene (University of California Press, Berkeley and Los Angeles, 1995); Jane McIntosh Snyder, *Lesbian Desire in the Lyrics of Sappho* (Columbia University Press, New York, 1997), pp. 27–38; Lyn Hatherly Wilson, *Sappho's Sweet Bitter Songs: Configurations of Female and Male in Ancient Greek Lyric* (Routledge, London and New York, 1996), pp. 55–64; Jesper Svenbro, 'Death by Writing: Sappho, the Poem, and the Reader' in *Phrasikleia: An Anthropology of Reading in Ancient Greek*, trans. Janet Lloyd (Cornell University Press, Ithaca, New York, 1993), pp. 152–61; Thomas McEvilley, 'Sappho, Fragment 31: The Face Behind the Mask', *Phoenix* 32 (1978), pp. 1–18; and George Devereux, 'The Nature of Sappho's Seizure in Fragment 31 as Evidence of her Inversion', *Classical Quarterly* 20 (1970), pp. 17–31.
3. Margaret Williamson, *Sappho's Immortal Daughters* (Harvard University Press, Cambridge Mass., 1996), pp. 75–84.
4. Margaret Williamson, *Sappho's Immortal Daughters* (Harvard University Press, Cambridge Mass., 1996), p. 38.
5. Aelian, quoted by Stobaeus in his *Anthology*. See *Test.* 10 in *Greek Lyric I, Sappho and Alcaeus*, Loeb Classical Library, ed. David A. Campbell (Harvard University Press, Cambridge Mass., 1982), pp. 12–13.
6. Josephine Balmer, trans., *Sappho: Poems and Fragments* (Brilliance Books, London, 1984), reissued (Bloodaxe, Newcastle upon Tyne, 1992); Mary Barnard, trans., *Sappho* (University of California Press, Berkeley and Los Angeles, 1958), reissued (Shambhala Press, Boston and London, 1994); David Constantine, *Watching for Dolphins* (Bloodaxe, Newcastle upon Tyne, 1983); Guy Davenport, *Seven Greeks* (New Directions Publishing Corporation, New York, 1995); Diane Rayor, trans., *Sappho's Lyre: Archaic Lyric and Women Poets of Ancient Greece* (University of California Press, Berkeley and Los Angeles, 1991). Ellen Greene, 'Apostrophe and Women's Erotics in the Poetry of Sappho', *Transactions of the American Philological Association* 124 (1994), pp. 41–56; Judith P. Hallett, 'Sappho and her Social Context: Sense and Sensuality', *Signs*, 4 (1979), pp. 447–64, both reprinted in *Reading Sappho: Contemporary Approaches*, ed. Ellen

Greene (University of California Press, Berkeley and Los Angeles, 1995); John J. Winkler, *The Constraints of Desire: The Anthropology of Sex and Gender in Ancient Greece* (Routledge, New York and London, 1990); Charles Segal 'Eros and Incantation: Sappho and Oral Poetry', in *Reading Sappho: Contemporary Approaches*, ed. Ellen Greene (University of California Press, Berkeley and Los Angeles, 1996), pp. 58–78; and André Lardinois, 'Who Sang Sappho's Songs?' in *Reading Sappho*, ed. Ellen Greene (University of California Press, Berkeley and Los Angeles, 1996), pp. 150–74; Leslie Kurke, 'The Strangeness of "song culture": Archaic Greek Poetry' in *Literature in the Greek and Roman Worlds: A New Perspective*, ed. Oliver Taplin (Oxford University Press, Oxford, 2000), pp. 58–87.

In fact, the question of the ancient audience for Greek literature has become increasingly significant in recent Classical scholarship. That is: who the audiences were; the circumstances of performance; how audiences reacted; and how works were created with a consciousness of the audience. See Oliver Taplin, 'The Spring of the Muses: Homer and Related Poetry' in *Literature in the Greek and Roman Worlds: A New Perspective*, ed. Oliver Taplin (Oxford University Press, Oxford, 2000), pp. 22–57 and *passim*. See also Oliver Taplin's 1999 address to the Classical Society, *Greek with Consequence* (The Classical Association, Alresford Hants., 1999) on the importance of new reception studies.

7. For an account of the papyrus discoveries at Oxyrhynchus in the early twentieth century see Margaret Williamson, *Sappho's Immortal Daughters* (Harvard University Press, Cambridge Mass., 1996), pp. 46–9 and Margaret Reynolds, *The Sappho Companion* (Chatto and Windus, London, 2000), pp. 19–20. Early twentieth century editions of Sappho include Edwin Marion Cox, *The Poems of Sappho* (Williams and Norgate Ltd, London, 1925), John Maxwell Edmonds, *Lyra Graeca* (London, 1922) reprinted (Heinemann and Putnams, London and New York, 1928), C.R. Haines, *Sappho: The Poems and Fragments* (George Routledge and Sons Ltd, London, 1926). These were superseded by *Poetarum Lesbiorum Fragmenta*, eds Edgar Lobel and Denys Page (Clarendon Press, Oxford, 1955). The most up-to-date scholarly editions of Sappho are Eva Maria Voigt, *Sappho et Alcaeus: Fragmenta* (Amsterdam-Polak and Van Gennep, Amsterdam, 1971) and the Loeb Classical Library, *Greek Lyric I: Sappho and Alcaeus*, ed. David A. Campbell (Harvard University Press, Cambridge Mass., 1982).
8. Alcaeus, Testimonia 22, *Greek Lyric I, Sappho and Alcaeus*, Loeb Classical Library, ed. David A. Campbell (Harvard University Press, Cambridge Mass., 1982), pp. 228–9.
9. Christopher Stray, *Classics Transformed: Schools, Universities, and Society in England, 1830–1960* (Clarendon Press, Oxford, 1998); *Poetarum Lesbiorum Fragmenta*, eds Edgar Lobel and Denys Page (Clarendon Press, Oxford, 1955); Denys Page, *Sappho and Alcaeus: an Introduction to the Study of Ancient Lesbian Poetry* (Clarendon Press, Oxford, 1955); Richard Jenkyns, *Three Classical Poets: Sappho, Catullus and Juvenal* (Duckworth, London, 1982); Joan DeJean, *Fictions of Sappho: 1546–1937* (University of Chicago Press, Chicago, 1989); Margaret Williamson, *Sappho's Immortal Daughters* (Harvard University Press, Cambridge Mass., 1995); Page DuBois, *Sappho is Burning* (University of Chicago Press, Chicago, 1995); Lyn Hatherly Wilson, *Sappho's Sweet Bitter Songs: Configurations of Female and Male in Ancient Greek Lyric* (Routledge, London and New York, 1996); and Jane McIntosh Snyder, *Lesbian Desire in the Lyrics of Sappho* (Columbia University Press, New York, 1997).
10. Joan DeJean, *Fictions of Sappho: 1546–1937* (University of Chicago Press, Chicago, 1989).
11. Yopie Prins, *Victorian Sappho* (Princeton University Press, Princeton, 1999).

12. Lucian *Imagines. 18*, quoted in *Greek Lyric I: Sappho and Alcaeus*, Loeb Classical Library, ed. David A Campbell (Harvard University Press, Cambridge Mass., 1982), p. 3.
13. Late sixth century BC vase in the Czartoryski collection, 142333 in the National Museum, Warsaw, Poland. Red figure *hydria* dating from the mid to late fifth century BC showing Sappho seated with one of her pupils holding a lyre in the National Museum, Athens, Greece, NM 1260.
14. The ancient sources for Sappho's legends are in the *Testimonia* included in David A. Campbell's Loeb Classical Library edition, *Greek Lyric I: Sappho and Alcaeus* (Harvard University Press, Cambridge Mass., 1982), pp. 2–51. See also Margaret Williamson, *Sappho's Immortal Daughters* (Harvard University Press, Cambridge Mass., 1995), pp. 5–33, and Margaret Reynolds, *The Sappho Companion* (Chatto and Windus, London, 2000), pp. 67–78.
15. Henry Thornton Wharton, *Sappho: Memoir, Text, Selected Renderings and a Literal Translation* (David Stott, London, 1885). In the preface to the second edition (David Stott, London, 1887) Wharton mentions the work of the Egypt Exploration Fund. By the time of the third (John Lane, London, 1895) he writes 'I would fain have enriched this edition of my *Sappho* with some new words of the poetess ... but, to the world's sorrow, that pleasure has been denied me.'
16. Mary Robinson, *Sappho and Phaon in a Series of Legitimate Sonnets, with Thoughts on Poetical Subjects and Anecdotes of the Grecian Poetess* (London, 1796), pp. 25–6. Alfred Lord Tennyson, *The Princess* (1847), II, lines 355–7, in *The Poems of Tennyson*, ed. Christopher Ricks (Longmans, London, 1969), p. 769. John Addington Symonds, *Studies of the Greek Poets, First Series* (Smith, Elder and Co., London, 1873), pp. 139–40.
17. Tennyson, *The Princess* (1847), II, lines 353–7 in *The Poems of Tennyson*, ed. Christopher Ricks (Longmans, London, 1969), p. 769.
18. John Addington Symonds, *Studies of the Greek Poets, First Series* (Smith, Elder and Co., London, 1873), pp. 139–40.
19. Angela Carter, in John Haffenden, *Novelists in Interview* (Methuen, London and New York, 1985), pp. 76–96. Claudine Herrmann, *Les voleuses de langue* (Editions des femmes, Paris, 1976).

    For the 'unwritten novel' Elizabeth Wanning Harries quotes a review by Stephen Koch published in the *New York Times Book Review* (4 October 1981). 'The twentieth century has witnessed the emergence of a potent – and, I think, possibly even new – literary form, which we might dub, informally, the unwritten novel. The unwritten novel is a book, however polished, that seems a compilation of fragments. A typical example looks like a salad of autobiography, notebook ecstasies, diaristic confessions, prose poems, epigrams, meditations, shafts of critical discourse. Yet these scattered works are not mere pastiches. They *do* have a unity; but theirs is the coherence of a unifying refusal, an energizing denial ...': Elizabeth Wanning Harries, *The Unfinished Manner: Essays on the Fragment in the Later Eighteenth Century* (University Press of Virginia, Charlottesville and London, 1994), p. 176. It is hardly surprising to me that the book Koch happens to be reviewing here is Marguerite Yourcenar's *Fires* (1981) which raids various Greek myths for its sources and ends with an extended meditation on Sappho.

    Peter Ackroyd was the author who began the fashion for combining biographical fact with literary fiction in his *Dickens* (Sinclair Stevenson, London, 1990). Many others have followed, but none so successfully.

    The art of the twentieth century has certainly been marked by a taste for the 'incidental' qualities of collage and found objects. It is a theme that begins early on, but is still continued in the recent work of, for example, Tracey Emin or Damian

Hirst. Their work, along with much produced by their contemporaries as well as older artists, almost invariably relies for its effect on some conspiracy with the viewer. Examples might include the reflecting and reflective sculptures of Anish Kapoor, or the large structures of Louise Bourgeouis which require the viewer to climb them and insert themselves into the perspective.

In fact, our contemporary fascination with the idea of the fragment underlies many movements in art, in science, and in social phenomena. The human genome project captures the imagination because it confronts a fundamental observation common to us all: that we are all different, and yet all the same. Each one of us is a fragment, a small piece of a larger pattern, whether God's or biology's. Mapping genes brings our fragmented individuation closer to the larger self. And yet, at the same time, in art and in life, we privilege the functions of accident. Fragments and ruins remind us that chance and time rule our lives. We plan, but are subject to the coincidental. We live each moment in a false expectation of our own immortality, even while we know that time writes over us and death may come at any moment. I do not think it too wild a proposition to suggest that the popularity of lotteries in all the nation states of Europe, as well as the popularity of detective stories and psychological thrillers, is not unrelated to our valorisation of the fragment. The lottery ticket is the infinitesimal part that might represent the untold wealth of the whole. The structure of the thriller concentrates on clues and scraps of evidence, but it builds up to a complete picture. Thus, in both cases, we are invited to contemplate the unpalatable facts of our contingent existence while, at the same time, we are comforted by the duality that the fragment represents. The broken-off part allows us to confront the haphazard, while permitting us the consolation of the implied whole.

20. See Elizabeth Wanning Harries, *The Unfinished Manner: Essays on the Fragment in the Later Eighteenth Century* (University Press of Virginia, Charlottesville and London, 1994); Anne Janowitz, *England's Ruins: Poetic Purpose and the National Landscape* (Basil Blackwell, Oxford, 1990) and Anne Janowitz, 'The Romantic Fragment' in *A Companion to Romanticism*, ed. Duncan Wu (Basil Blackwell, Oxford, 1998), pp. 442–51; Thomas McFarland, *Romanticism and the Forms of Ruin: Wordsworth, Coleridge and Modalities of Fragmentation* (Princeton University Press, Princeton New Jersey, 1981); Balachandra Rajan, *The Form of the Unfinished: English Poetics from Dryden to Blake* (Princeton University Press, Princeton New Jersey, 1985); Marjorie Levinson, *The Romantic Fragment Poem: A Critique of a Form* (University of North Carolina Press, Chapel Hill, 1986).
21. Elizabeth Wanning Harries, *The Unfinished Manner: Essays on the Fragment in the Later Eighteenth Century* (University Press of Virginia, Charlottesville and London, 1994, pp. 12–33. On the importance of the Renaissance technologies of the book see Lisa Jardine, *Worldly Goods: A New History of the Renaissance* (Macmillan, London, 1996), and Adrian Jones, *The Nature of the Book: Print and Knowledge in the Making* (University of Chicago Press, Chicago, 1998).
22. See Christopher Charles Parslow, *Re-Discovering Antiquity: Karl Weber and the Excavation of Herculaneum, Pompeii and Stabiae* (Cambridge University Press, Cambridge, 1998).
23. Camilla Paderni, in an open letter to the Royal Society of London (18 October 1754), quoted in Christopher Charles Parslow, *Re-Discovering Antiquity: Karl Weber and the Excavation of Herculaneum, Pompeii and Stabiae* (Cambridge University Press, Cambridge, 1998), p. 103.
24. Etienne Lantier, *Voyages d'Antenor en Grèce et en Asie* (Paris, 1797). *The Travels of Antenor in Greece and Asia from a Greek Manuscript Found at Herculaneum: Including Some Account of Egypt* (T.N. Longman and O. Rees, London, 1799), pp. iv–v, 249–322.

25. Jean Jacques Barthélemy, *Voyage du jeune Anacharsis en Grèce dans le milieu du quatrième siècle avant l'ère Vulgaire* (du Bure, Paris, 1788). *Travels of Anacharsis the Younger in Greece during the Middle of the Fourth Century before the Christian Era* (J. Mawman etc., London, 1817), Vol. II, pp. 53–4. Joan DeJean includes some discussion of Barthélemy, Imperiale, Grainville, Verri and Lantier in her *Fictions of Sappho: 1546–1937* (Chicago University Press, Chicago, 1989). Extracts from Lantier, Barthélemy and Verri are included in my *The Sappho Companion* (Chatto and Windus, London, 2000), pp. 165–88.
26. Franz von Kleist, *Sappho: Ein dramatisches Gedicht* (In der Voffischen Buchhandlung, Berlin, 1793). Maggs sale catalogue reference 1992.
27. See Ruth Vanita, *Sappho and the Virgin Mary: Same Sex Love and the English Literary Imagination* (Columbia University Press, New York, 1996) pp. 49–61. The Eton College textbook that Shelley would have used is the 1806 edition of *Poetae Graeci: Sive Selecta ex Homerii etc* (Etonae, ex Officini M. Pote et E. Williams, 1806). I am much indebted to Michael Meredith for this reference.
28. See Elisabeth Vigée-LeBrun, *Souvenirs de Madame Louise-Elisabeth Vigée-LeBrun* (Librairie de H. Fournier, Paris, 1835) and *Souvenirs*, ed. Claudine Herrmann, (editions des femmes, Paris, 1984), Vol. I, pp. 85–8. See also Mary D. Sheriff, *The Exceptional Woman: Elisabeth Vigée-LeBrun and the Cultural Politics of Art* (University of Chicago Press, Chicago and London, 1996), pp. 47–8 and Angelica Goodden, *The Sweetness of Life: A Biography of Elisabeth Louise Vigée-LeBrun* (Andre Deutsch, London, 1997), pp. 38–40.
29. Mary Shelley, *The Last Man* (1826), ed. Morton D. Paley (World's Classics, Oxford University Press, Oxford, 1994), pp. 5, 6–7.
30. Paul the Silentiary, *The Greek Anthology*. From *Select Epigrams from the Greek Anthology*, ed. J.W. MacKail (Longmans, Green and Co., London, 1906), p. 73. A modern translation by Andrew Miller is more explicitly erotic:

    Soft are Sappho's kisses,
    soft, under silken skin,
    those snowy arms – but hard
    as stone what lies within.

    She opens honeyed lips
    to speak what Love himself,
    brazen, would blush to hear.
    She opens nothing else.

    He who endures long nights
    beside those limbs of snow
    learns to envy the thirst
    of Tantalus below.

    The Greek Anthology and Other Ancient Epigrams, ed. Peter Jay (Penguin, Harmondsworth Middlesex, 1981), p. 344.
31. Giuseppe Mazzotta, 'The *Canzoniere* and the Language of the Self', *Studies in Philology* 75 (1978), p. 294.
32. Mel Steel, 'Butch Muse', *Guardian* (13 May 2000).
33. Jeanette Winterson, *Art & Lies* (Jonathan Cape, London, 1994), p. 51.

2. Mary Robinson's Attitudes

1. Johann Wolfgang von Goethe, *Italienische Reise* (1786–88), translated as *Italian Journey* by W.H. Auden and Elizabeth Mayer (1962: Penguin, London, 1970), p. 315.
2. Letters numbered 137 and 142 in A. Morrison, 'Catalogue of the Collection of Autograph Letters and Historical Documents found between 1865 and 1882 by A. Morrison'. The Hamilton and Nelson Papers, I: nos 1–301; II: nos 302–1067, combined and annotated under the direction of A.W. Thibideau (London, 1893–94).
3. Johann Wolfgang von Goethe, *Italienische Reise* (1786–88), translated as *Italian Journey* by W.H. Auden and Elizabeth Mayer (1962: Penguin, London, 1970), p. 208.
4. *Memoires de la Comtesse de Boigne*, ed. M. Charles Nicoullard, Vol. 1781–1814 (Paris, 1907), pp. 114–5. Tommaso Piroli, after Friedrich Rehberg *Drawings Faithfully Copied from Nature at Naples and with Permission Dedicated to the Right Honourable Sir William Hamilton* (1794). This set of Attitudes included two Christian subjects (Mary Magdalen and Saint Rosa) but the rest were drawn from Classical sources, including one representing the Sybil and another (where the pose may have been borrowed from one of Sir William's antique vases) which showed Emma seated pensively on a *klismos* chair.

   Piroli's engravings are reproduced in K.G. Holmstrom's *Monodrama, Attitudes, Tableaux Vivants: Studies on Some Trends of Theatrical Fashion 1770–1815* (Almquist and Wiksell, Stockholm, 1967), pp. 122–5. They are very much posed and static in comparison with other drawings made – for instance those by Pietro Novelli or William Artaud, which attempt to convey the kinetic quality of the swiftly varying Attitudes. A few of Piroli's prints as well as some of Novelli's and Artaud's drawings appear in *Vases and Volcanoes: Sir William Hamilton and his Collection*, eds Ian Jenkins and Kim Sloan (British Museum Press, London, 1996), pp. 259–61. Hugh Douglas Hamilton's triple portrait of Emma Hamilton is in the Hamilton Collection, Lennoxlove, East Lothian, Scotland.
5. William Artaud to his father, May 1796; see A.C. Sewter, 'The Life, Work and Letters of William Artaud' (MA thesis, University of Manchester, 1951), p. 115. Elisabeth Vigée LeBrun, *Souvenirs* (Paris, 1835), Vol. II, pp. 90–1. Conte della Torre di Rezzonico, 1789; see *Opere della Cavaliere Carlo Gastone, Conte della Torre Rezzonico, VII: Giornale del Viaggio di Napoli negli Anni 1789 e 1790*, ed. F. Mocchetti (Como, 1819), pp. 246–7. Horace Walpole, *The Yale Edition of Horace Walpole's Correspondence*, ed. W.S. Lewis (Yale University Press, New Haven and London, 1937–38), Vol. IX, p. 349. Emma Hamilton, in A. Morrison, 'Catalogue of the Collection of Autograph Letters and Historical Documents found between 1865 and 1882 by A. Morrison'. The Hamilton and Nelson Papers, I: nos 1–301; II: nos 302–1067, combined and annotated under the direction of A.W. Thibideau (London, 1893–94), no. 150.
6. *Memoirs of Mary Robinson 'Perdita'*, from the edition compiled by her daughter (1803), with introduction and notes by J. Fitzgerald Molloy (J.B. Lippincott, Philadelphia, 1894), pp. 69–70, 164, ix. See also Stanley Makower, *Perdita: A Romance in Biography* (Hutchinson and Co., London, 1908), and Robert Bass, *The Green Dragoon: The Lives of Banastre Tarleton and Mary Robinson* (Alvin Redman, London, 1957).
7. Mary Robinson, *Sappho and Phaon, In a Series of Legitimate Sonnets with Thoughts on Poetical Subjects and Anecdotes of the Grecian Poetess* (printed for the author by S. Gosnell, London, 1796), p. 5. The sequence has recently been reprinted, edited by Terence Hoagwood and Rebecca Jackson (Delmar Scholars' Facsimiles and Reprints, New York, 1995).

8. Luce Irigaray, 'Ce sexe qui n'en pas un' (1977) translated as 'This sex which is not one' by Claudia Reeder in *New French Feminisms*, eds Elaine Marks and Isabelle de Courtivron (Harvester, Brighton, 1985), p. 101. Goethe tells a story about Emma Hamilton attempting to buy an enslaved Moorish girl captured by the captain of a Christian vessel and brought into the bay of Naples which suggests that Emma was all too painfully aware of her own position; *Italian Journey* (Penguin, London, 1962), p. 354.
9. The repeated posturing, posing, trying out ideas of psychological positions, roles and experiences that takes place in the scenes Robinson imagines for her Sappho, in many ways looks forward to the experimental series of self images created by modern photographers such as Jo Spence, Rosy Martin or Mary Duffy. Using themselves as the model, using costumes and settings and props, Spence's *Narratives of Dis-ease* (1986) or Duffy's *Stories of a Body* (1990) explore their own experiences and emotions, tell themselves the story of their stories. See Lynda Nead, *The Female Nude* (Routledge, London, 1992), pp. 78–81.
10. Jerome McGann also emphasises Robinson's treatment of the aesthetic; see 'Mary Robinson and the Myth of Sappho' in *The Poetics of Sensibility: A Revolution in Literary Style* (Clarendon Press, Oxford, 1996), pp. 94–116. For other recent work on Mary Robinson see Sharon Setzer, 'Mary Robinson's Sylphid Self: The End of Feminine Self-Fashioning', *Philological Quarterly* 75:4 (Fall 1996), pp. 501–20, and Chris Cullens, 'Mrs. Robinson and the Masquerade of Womanliness' in *Body and Text in the Eighteenth Century*, eds Veronica Kelly and Dorothea von Mucke (Stanford University Press, Stanford CA, 1994), pp. 266–89.
11. *The Poetical Works of the Late Mrs Mary Robinson, Including Many Pieces Never Before Published* (printed for Richard Phillips, London, 1806), Vol. III, pp. 226–7. Lesbia was the name Catullus gave to the mistress to whom he wrote a number of licentious poems, including 'Ille mi par esse', his famous re-writing of Sappho's Fragment 31.
12. As well as *Sappho and Phaon* she wrote, among other things, a version of Fragment 31 in 'Stanzas' (1791), 'To a False Friend, in Imitation of Sappho', and another entitled 'Sappho and Bacchus', as well as several 'Lesbia' poems.
13. See Longinus, *On the Sublime*, translated with a commentary by James A. Arieti and John M. Crossett (The Edwin Mellen Press, New York and Toronto, 1985), and Longinus, *On Great Writing*, translated with an introduction by G.M.A. Grube (Hackett Publishing Company, Indianapolis and Cambridge, 1991). A selection of eighteenth century writings on the sublime is in *The Sublime: A Reader in British Eighteenth Century Aesthetic Theory*, eds Andrew Ashfield and Peter de Bolla (Cambridge University Press, Cambridge, 1996). For critical writings on the sublime see Samuel H. Monk, *The Sublime: A Study of Critical Theories in XIII-Century England* (Modern Language Association of America, 1935: University of Michigan Press, Ann Arbor, 1960), Thomas Weiskel, *The Romantic Sublime: Studies in the Structure and Psychology of Transcendence* (Johns Hopkins University Press, Baltimore and London, 1976), Peter de Bolla, *The Discourse of the Sublime: Readings in History, Aesthetics and the Subject* (Basil Blackwell, Oxford, 1989), Terry Eagleton, *The Ideology of the Aesthetic* (Basil Blackwell, Oxford, 1990), and Frances Ferguson, *Solitude and the Sublime: Romanticism and the Aesthetics of Individuation* (Routledge, London and New York, 1992).
14. *Dionysius Longinus on the Sublime Translated from the Greek, with Notes and Observations, and Some Account of the Life, Writings, and Character of the Author.* By William Smith, the second edition corrected and improved (J. Watts, London, 1739). Compare G.M.A. Grube's modern translation of this passage:

> Let us now consider whether we can point to any other factor which can make writing great. There are, in every situation, a number of features which combine to make up the texture of events. To select the most vital of these and to relate them to one another to form a unified whole is an essential cause of Great writing. One writer charms the reader by the selection of such details, another by the manner in which he presses them into close relationship.
>
> Sappho, for example, selects on each occasion the emotions which accompany the frenzy of love. She takes these from life. How does she excel? In her skilful choice of the most important and intense details and in relating them to one another ... [Fragment 31] ... Do you not marvel how she seeks to make her mind, her body, ears, tongue, eyes and complexion, as if they were scattered elements strange to her, join together in the same moment of experience? In contradictory phrases she describes herself as hot and cold at once, rational and irrational, at the same time terrified and almost dead, in order to appear afflicted not by one passion but by a swarm of passions. Lovers do have all those feelings, but it is, as I said, her selection of the most vital details and her working them into one whole which produce the outstanding quality of the poem.

Ruth Vanita points out that William Smith's translation established the use of the word 'sublime' (as opposed to 'loftiness' or 'height') and remained the standard text of Longinus for some time: see *Sappho and the Virgin Mary: Same-Sex Love and the English Literary Imagination* (Columbia University Press, New York, 1996), pp. 41–4.

15. Edmund Burke, *A Philosophical Enquiry into the Origin of our Ideas of the Sublime and Beautiful* (1757, revised and expanded 1759). Edited with an Introduction and Notes by Adam Phillips (Oxford University Press, Oxford and New York, 1990), pp. 1, 12, 24.
16. See *Women in the Eighteenth Century: Constructions of Femininity*, ed. Vivien Jones (Routledge, London and New York, 1990), pp. 2–6; Anne Mellor, *Romanticism and Gender* (Routledge, London and New York, 1993), pp. 85–6, 107–9; and Tom Furniss *Edmund Burke's Aesthetic Ideology* (Cambridge University Press, Cambridge, 1993), pp. 34–7.
17. Thomas Weiskel, *The Romantic Sublime: Studies in the Structure and Psychology of Transcendence* (Johns Hopkins University Press, Baltimore and London, 1976), p. 3.
18. Joseph Addison, 'The Pleasures of the Imagination', *The Spectator*, 21 June–3 July 1712; in *Critical Essays from The Spectator*, ed. Donald F. Bond (Clarendon Press, Oxford, 1970), p. 178.
19. *The Poetical Works of the Late Mrs Mary Robinson* (Richard Phillips, London, 1806), pp. II, 198–9. This is another case where Robinson's poem refers to a real Sappho poem 'Dead you shall lie there' (Fragment 55 in modern editions), where Sappho gloats over her own certain immortality while the person she addresses will lie dead and forgotten for eternity.
20. Mary Robinson, *Sappho and Phaon in a Series of Legitimate Sonnets* (London, 1796), p. 70. The bee was an emblem associated with Sappho in the eighteenth century and often appears on gems carved with her profile. It may refer to her fragments – 130 and 146 in modern editions – which describe, or seem to describe, desire as a 'sting'.
21. Anne Frances Randall, *A Letter to the Women of England, on the Injustice of Mental Subordination with Anecdotes* (T.N. Longman and O. Rees, London, 1799), p. 1. One of the things that Robinson complains of in this letter is the neglect of the claims of her own countrywomen: 'They must fly to foreign countries for celebrity, where talents are admitted to be of no SEX, where genius, whether it be concealed beneath the form of a Grecian Venus, or that of a Farnese Hercules, is still honoured *as* GENIUS,

one of the best and noblest gifts of THE CREATOR.' In a footnote she adds: 'Lady Hamilton, and Helen Maria Williams, are existing proofs, that an English woman, like a prophet, is never valued in her own country. In Britain they were neglected, and scarcely *known*; on the continent, they have been nearly IDOLIZED!' Robinson's attempts to raise the status of women in England went into practical projects too. She collaborated with the artist Maria Cosway and the engraver Caroline Watson to produce a poem, *The Wintry Day* (London, 1803) illustrated with twelve prints; 'The superior taste and talents which have been displayed by the females of the present age in the various departments of the Fine Arts is universally admitted. To exhibit one proof of superiority so honourable to the sex and country, this series of prints is respectfully submitted to the attention of the public.'

22. *Memoirs of Mary Robinson 'Perdita'*, from the edition compiled by her daughter (1803), with introduction and notes by J. Fitzgerald Molloy (J.B. Lippincott, Philadelphia, 1894), p. 131.
23. There are a few traces that suggest a memory of Robinson's work. In Felicia Hemans's poem 'The Last Song of Sappho' published some forty years after Robinson's death, the younger poet has Sappho address her sea grave to say, 'Bury my anguish, my renown,/ With *hidden wrecks, lost gems*, and wasted gold' (my emphasis), which may be a reference to one of Robinson's prefaces in *Sappho and Phaon* where she states: 'In examining the curiosities of antiquity, we look to the perfections, and not to the magnitude of those reliques, which have been preserved amidst the wrecks of time: as the smallest gem that bears the fine touches of a master, surpasses the loftiest fabric reared by the labours of false taste, so the precious fragments of the immortal Sappho, will be admired, when the voluminous productions of inferior poets are mouldered to dust.' And, oddly enough, one phrase from Robinson's *Letter to the Women of England* survived. 'Their proper sphere' reappeared in the title of Mary Ann Stodart's 1842 handbook on *Female Writers: Their Proper Sphere and Powers of Usefulness*. Unfortunately by then, according to Stodart's own reckoning, that sphere only extended as far as the boudoir and the nursery.
24. Erasmus Darwin, *A Plan for the Conduct of Female Education in Boarding Schools* (Dublin, 1798), p. 3. Quoted in Nancy Armstrong, 'The Rise of the Domestic Woman' in *The Ideology of Conduct: Essays in Literature and the History of Sexuality*, eds Nancy Armstrong and Leonard Tennenhouse (Methuen, New York and London, 1987), p. 119. Armstrong has suggested that increasingly, from the latter part of the eighteenth century on, definitions of 'femininity' were used to promote the politicised dominance of 'masculinity'; see *Desire and Domestic Fiction: A Political History of the Novel* (Oxford University Press, Oxford, 1987), pp. 3–27. For gender-policing reaction to the French Revolution see Vivian Cameron, 'Political Exposures: Sexuality and Caricature in the French Revolution' in *Eroticism and the Body Politic*, ed. Lynn Hunt (Johns Hopkins University Press, Baltimore, 1991), pp. 90–107.
25. *The Collected Letters of Samuel Taylor Coleridge*, ed. E.L. Griggs (Oxford University Press, 1956–71), Vol. I, p. 562. Coleridge may have sent Robinson a manuscript copy of 'Kubla Khan', and in the first volume of his biography of Coleridge Richard Holmes suggests that it may have been a laudanum experience of Mary Robinson's that gave Coleridge the idea for the waking dream that inspired his famous poem: *Coleridge: Early Visions* (Flamingo, London, 1990), p. 257. He doesn't follow this up in the second volume, but Holmes is clearly thinking of Robinson's story about the composition of 'The Maniac' which appears in *Memoirs of Mary Robinson 'Perdita'*, from the edition compiled by her daughter (1803), with introduction and notes by J. Fitzgerald Molloy (J.B. Lippincott, Philadelphia, 1894), pp. 218–19.

26. *The Poetical Works of the Late Mrs Mary Robinson* (Richard Phillips, London, 1806), Vol. II, pp. 226–9. The concluding section of the poem is as follows:

> And now with lofty tones inviting,
> Thy NYMPH, her dulcimer swift smiting,
> Shall wake me in ecstatic measures!
> Far, far remov'd from mortal pleasures!
> In cadence rich, in cadence strong,
> Proving the wondrous witcheries of song!
> I hear her voice! thy *sunny dome,*
> Thy *caves of ice,* loud repeat,
> Vibrations, madd'ning sweet,
> Calling the visionary wand'rer home.
> She sings of THEE, O favour'd child
> Of *Minstrelsy,* SUBLIMELY WILD!
> Of thee, whose soul can feel the tone
> Which gives to airy dreams *a magic* ALL THY OWN!

27. *The Poems of Samuel Taylor Coleridge*, ed. E.H. Coleridge (Oxford University Press, Oxford, 1935), pp. 350–2. Coleridge's poem takes its title and theme from Robinson's earlier poem, where she imagines the landscape of his home in the Lake district and repeats 'Skiddaw's heights sublime' or 'thy mountain haunts sublime', or 'NATURE's book sublime' five times. 'Accept a STRANGER's song', she wrote, 'An untaught Minstrel joys to sing of thee!'
28. *The Complete Poems of Samuel Taylor Coleridge*, ed. E.H. Coleridge (Oxford University Press, Oxford, 1935), p. 353.
29. *The Poetical Works of the Late Mrs Mary Robinson* (Richard Phillips, London, 1806), Vol. I, pp. 3–42.
30. In an unpublished letter (in the Bodleian) Robinson wrote a long, jokey verse story of domestic matters which ends: 'This is *quite* an *Extempore*, therefore pray keep it;/ For with nonsense congenial, to *times* pinion will sweep it,/ To darkest oblivion; where folly shall borrow/ Her feeblest Ideas from "rhyme spinning Laura"'. Her writing, her self-construction, her self-naming here is so haphazard, so improvisatory, so multiple, that she does not know whether this literary creation should live or die, and even the rhyme (borrow/Laura) is dissonant, doesn't quite work the way it should. Ms. letter dated 'Salthill Octr. 1st 99' – tipped in *Poems* by Mrs M. Robinson (London, 1791). Bodleian pressmark, Vet. A5 e 549.
31. Anonymous (James Gillray?), *Drawings faithfully copied from Nature at Naples and with permission dedicated to the Right Honourable Sir William Hamilton, A new edition considerably enlarged and humbly dedicated to all admirers of the grand and sublime* (Hannah Humphrey, London, 1807). Plate 6, *The Muse of Dance* is reproduced in *Vases and Volcanoes: Sir William Hamilton and his Collection*, eds Ian Jenkins and Kim Sloan (British Museum Press, London, 1996), p. 303.

3. Picturing Sappho

1. Felicia Hemans, 'The Last Song of Sappho' and Caroline Norton, 'The Picture of Sappho' in *Victorian Women Poets: An Anthology*, eds Angela Leighton and Margaret Reynolds (Basil Blackwell, Oxford, 1995), pp. 4 and 136. George Eliot, *The Mill on the*

Floss, ed. Carol Christ (1860: W.W. Norton and Co., New York, 1994), p. 270. Virginia Woolf, 30 June 1927, in *The Diary of Virginia Woolf*, ed. Anne Olivier Bell assisted by Andrew McNeillie (The Hogarth Press, London, 1980), Vol. III, p. 142.

2. See Jacques Lacan, 'The subversion of the subject and the dialectic of desire in the Freudian unconscious' in *Ecrits: A Selection*, trans. Alan Sheridan (Norton, New York, 1977), pp. 292–325. See also definitions by Juliet Flower MacCannell, 'Jouissance' in *Feminism and Psychoanalysis: A Critical Dictionary*, ed. Elizabeth Wright (Basil Blackwell, Oxford, 1992), pp. 185–7; Bruce Fink, *A Clinical Introduction to Lacanian Psychoanalysis, Theory and Technique* (Harvard University Press, Cambridge Mass., 1977), pp. 207–26; and Bice Benvenuto and Roger Kennedy, *The Works of Jacques Lacan: An Introduction* (Free Association Books, London, 1986), pp. 189–93. See also Judith Butler, *Bodies That Matter: On the Discursive Limits of 'Sex'* (Routledge, London, 1993).
3. Judith Stein's unpublished thesis 'The Iconography of Sappho 1775–1875' (University of Pennsylvannia, 1981) gives by far the most comprehensive account of the range of images of Sappho. Peter Tomory's article 'The Fortunes of Sappho' in *Re-discovering Hellenism: The Hellenic Inheritance and the English Imagination*, eds G.W. Clarke and J.C. Eade (Cambridge University Press, Cambridge, 1989), pp. 121–35 also discusses some late eighteenth and early nineteenth images. Otherwise for statues, see Adolf Michaelis, *Ancient Marbles in Great Britain* (Cambridge University Press, Cambridge, 1882), pp. 60–1, 114, 269; for coins see Warwick Wroth, *Catalogue of the Greek Coins of Troas, Aeolis and Lesbos* (British Museum, London, 1894) and L. Forer, 'Les Portraits de Sapho sur Les Monnaies', *Revue Belge de Numismatique* 57 (1901), pp. 413–25; for vases see J.D. Beazley *Greek Vases in Poland* (Clarendon Press, Oxford, 1928); for some medieval illuminations see Patricia M. Gathercole, 'Illuminations on the French Manuscripts of Boccaccio's *De Claris Mulieribus*', *Italia* XLII (1965), p. 217; and for other images see Helga von Heintze, *Das Bildnis der Sappho* (Florian Kupferberg, Mainz, 1966), Karl Schefold, *Die Bildnisse der Antiken Dichter* (Benno Schwabe, Basel, 1943) and ' Sappho in Ulm', *Antike Kunst* III (1960), p. 89 and Horst Rudiger *Sappho ihr Ruf und Ruhm bei der Nachwelt* (Dieterich, Leipzig, 1933). Some images are reproduced in *The Sappho Companion* edited and introduced by Margaret Reynolds (Chatto and Windus, London, 2000).

   The department of Prints and Drawings at the British Museum holds prints by Bartolozzi, Cipriani, Kauffmann and Antonio Zucchi as well as drawings by Giuseppe Bossi and Sir William Beechey, editions of the suites of engravings by Tresham and Girodet-Trioson. See also C.H.S. John, *Bartolozzi, Zoffany and Kauffmann with other Foreign Members of the Royal Academy 1768–1792* (Frederick A. Stokes, New York, n.d.); for Kauffmann's wall painting at 12 Grosvenor Square see Frances A. Gerard *Angelica Kauffmann* (Ward and Downey, London, 1893), p. 412; for Fragonard see Georges Wildenstein, *The Paintings of Fragonard* (Phaidon, London, 1960), pp. 291–3; for Ingres' 1809 drawing traditionally called 'Sappho' see Agnes Mongan's essay on the Forsythe Wickes Collection of the Museum of Fine Art in Boston in *Great Private Collections*, ed. Douglas Cooper (Macmillan, New York, 1963), p. 149; Antonio Canova's statue *Saffo* or *Terpsichore* is in the Museum of Art, Cleveland Ohio, and another is in the Museo Civico, Turin; Joseph Chinard's 1802–08 bust of Sappho is in the Collection of Major General Sir Harold Wernher, Luton, Bedfordshire, and his terracotta group 'Sappho and Phaon' (*c.* 1800–10) is in the Arthur M. Sackler Foundation, New York; Johann Dannecker's *Sappho* (1797–1802) is in the Staats-gallerie, Stuttgart; for Wedgwood's Sappho-related designs, see Wolf Mankowitz, *Wedgwood* (Batsford, London, 1953), pp. 218, 223, 254. Interestingly, the British Library's copy of Henry Tresham's 1784 suite of aquatints, *Le avventure di Saffo*, bears Josiah Wedgwood's bookplate.

4. The portrait tondo of a bust called 'Sappho' was discovered in 1759 (along with a companion tondo of a man) in a room in the Cuomo property on the Royal Road in Pompeii. See Christopher Charles Parslow's *Rediscovering Antiquity: Karl Weber and the Excavation of Herculaneum, Pompeii, and Stabiae* (Cambridge University Press, Cambridge, 1998), p. 203.
5. Maria Cosway's pen-and-ink drawing of 'Sappho' is now in the Collection of Andrew Wilton, New Haven, Connecticut. She was a friend of Mary Robinson's and she may have known Henry Tresham, for with her husband, Richard Cosway, these artists were all part of the Fuseli circle in Rome; see Nancy Pressly, *The Fuseli Circle in Rome: Early Romantic Art of the 1770's* (Yale Center for British Art, 1979), pp. 114–15. Nanine Vallain exhibited *Sappho Singing a Song to Love* (now lost) in the Paris Salon of 1806. Mlle Rivière's *Portrait of Josephine Budaevskaya* (1806) is in the Pushkin State Museum of Fine Arts in Moscow. Vigée-LeBrun's portrait of Madame de Stael 'en Corinne' is in the Musée d'Art d'Histoire in Geneva, and a prettified copy is in the Collection Château de Coppet. Marie Guillaume Benoist (1768–1826) exhibited a 'Sappho' (now lost) in the Paris Salon of 1795, and she also seems to have sketched, if not painted, a scene of Sappho's death in 1791; see Marie-Juliette Ballot, *Une Elève de David, La Comtesse Benoist* (E. Plon, Paris, 1914), p. 115. Marianne Birch Lamartine, the English wife of the poet Alphonse de Lamartine included a portrait of Sappho in a wall painting *The Apotheosis of Homer* which she executed for her home at the Château Saint Point; see E. Abry et al., *Les Grands Ecrivains de France* (Didier, Paris, 1946), Vol. II, p. 1225.
6. Mario Praz, *On NeoClassicism* (1940), translated from the Italian by Angus Davidson (Thames and Hudson, London, 1969), p. 259. Praz lists some fourteen examples of 'lady with the lyre' pictures.
7. Francesco Bartolozzi, 'Sappho' (June 1793). Stipple engraving published by A.C. de Poggi. The Department of Prints and Drawings, British Museum. The fragment quoted is from Francis Fawkes's 1760 translation.
8. Anne-Louis Girodet Trioson and M. Coupin, *Recueil de Compositions dessinées par Girodet ... avec la traduction en vers par Girodet de quelques-uns des poésies de Sapho* (Paris, 1827). Department of Prints and Drawings, British Museum.
9. Jean-Jacques Rousseau, *Emile, or On Education*, trans. by Allan Bloom (Penguin, Harmondsworth Middlesex, 1991), pp. 368–9. Sigmund Freud, 'Femininity' (1933) in *The Standard Edition of the Complete Psychological Works of Sigmund Freud*, trans. and ed. James Strachey (Hogarth Press, London, 1964), Vol. XXII, p. 132.
10. Angelica Kauffmann, *Sappho and Love* (1775) in the John and Mable Ringling Museum of Art, Sarasota, Florida. This painting was engraved by the Facius Brothers in 1778, Department of Prints and Drawings, British Museum.
11. Vigée-LeBrun's *Self-Portrait with Julie* or *Self-Portrait à la Grecque* is in the Louvre, Paris. See Mary D. Sheriff, *The Exceptional Woman: Elisabeth Vigée-LeBrun and the Cultural Politics of Art* (University of Chicago Press, Chicago and London, 1996), pp. 43–52. See also Angelica Goodden, *The Sweetness of Life: A Biography of Elisabeth Vigée-LeBrun* (Andre Deutsch, London, 1997).
12. Angelica Kauffmann's *The Artist in the Character of Design Listening to the Inspiration of Poetry* (1782) is in the Iveagh Bequest, Kenwood House, London; her *Self-Portrait Hesitating Between the Arts of Painting and Music* (1794) is in the Collection of the Winn family and the National Trust. In another 'Self Portrait' (1787) in the Uffizi Gallery in Florence Kauffmann holds her sketchbook on her knee in a manner reminiscent of her *Sappho*, and the Classical references are multiplied by a broad belt which secures her Grecian drapery with a cameo clasp representing Apollo and a Muse playing a

lyre. Richard Samuel's *The Nine Living Muses of Great Britain* (1779) is in the National Portrait Gallery in London.

13. See Mary D. Sheriff, *The Exceptional Woman: Elisabeth Vigée-LeBrun and the Cultural Politics of Art* (University of Chicago Press, Chicago and London, 1996), pp. 72–3.
14. Vigée-LeBrun's portrait of Laure de Bonneuil (1773) is now lost. Mario Praz may have seen it, for he describes her seated in a grotto, playing a lyre and dressed in a red peplum over a yellow robe; see Mario Praz, *On NeoClassicism* (1940), translated from the Italian by Angus Davidson (Thames and Hudson, London, 1969), p. 259. He also describes François Gérard's *Portrait of Madame de la Pleigne* as showing her 'in a sacred wood, beneath a grey sky, playing upon the lyre'. A. Evariste Fragonard's *Madame Récamier en Sapho* (*c.* 1830s) was formerly at St Malo in France, but was destroyed during the Second World War; see Edouard Herriot, *Madame Recamier* (G.P. Putnam and Sons, New York, 1906). Antonio Zucchi's picture (1774, whereabouts unknown) is now generally called *Homer Inspired by Calliope* but it has also been called *Homer Conversing with Sappho* or *History and Music*. It was engraved by Angelica Kauffmann and Giuseppe Zucchi and published by Boydell in 1781. A copy of the engraving is in the Gemeindenmuseum, Schwarzenberg. Kauffmann herself was once supposed to have been the model for 'Sappho'. Angelica Kauffmann also painted an oval *Portrait of a Girl* (*c.* 1770, private collection) who wears a turban head-dress, looks over her left shoulder, and holds a pen in her right hand. This picture has also been called *Sappho*. See Bettina Baumgartel, *Angelica Kauffmann: Herausgegein und Scarbertet* (Kunstmuseum Dusseldorf and Verlag Gerd Hatje, Ostfildern-Ruit, 1999), pp. 156–7 and 242–5.
15. Westall's *Portrait of the Artist's Wife as Sappho* is in the Walker Art Gallery, Liverpool. It was engraved by John Sartain in a print dated 1 January 1802, and this was reproduced as the frontispiece to Robert Bell's *Early Ballads* (London, 1862). This is only one of at least three Sappho pictures painted by Westall. The other two are *Sappho in the Lesbian Shades Chanting a Hymn to Love* (1796) and *Sappho's Leucadian Leap* (before 1836) which shows her in a state of *déshabillé*, about to leap off the cliff while a crowd below in boats waits to rescue her. It may be based on a scene from Lantier's *Voyages d'Antenor* (1797).
16. Germaine de Stael, *De la litterature* in *Oeuvres complètes* (Paris, 1838), Vol. I, p. 212.
17. For Marie Antoinette see Lynn Hunt, 'The Many Bodies of Marie Antoinette: Political Pornography and the Problem of the Feminine in the French Revolution' in *Eroticism and the Body Politic*, ed. Lynn Hunt (Johns Hopkins University Press, Baltimore and London, 1991), pp. 108–30. For Marie Antoinette's varied history as a fantasy heroine for lesbians see Terry Castle, 'Marie Antoinette Obsession' in *The Apparitional Lesbian: Female Homosexuality and Modern Culture* (Columbia University Press, New York, 1993), pp. 107–49. For Eleanor Butler and Sarah Ponsonby see Elizabeth Mavor, *The Ladies of Llangollen: A Study in Romantic Friendship* (Michael Joseph, London, 1971); for Miss Woods and Miss Pirie, see Lillian Fadermann, *Surpassing the Love of Men: Romantic Friendship and Love Between Women* (William Morrow and Co. Inc., New York, 1981), pp. 147–54.
18. Germaine de Stael, *De la litterature* in *Oeuvres completes* (Paris, 1838), Vol. I, p. 214.
19. William King, *The Toast. An Heroick Poem in four books originally written in Latin by Frederick Scheffer: now done into English, and illustrated with Notes and Observations by Peregrine O'Donald* (Dublin, 1736). In June 1773 the *Covent Garden Magazine; or, Amorous Reppository* published a dialogue between the souls of Sappho and the seventeenth century French courtesan Ninon de L'Enclos where the two women discuss Sappho's activities with the Lesbian maids. Anon., *The Sappho-An. An Heroic*

poem of three cantos, in the Ovidian stile, describing the pleasures which the fair sex enjoy with each other ... found among the papers of a lady of quality ... (C. Brasier, London, 1740). This volume was clearly read – by men – and may have been on display in public places, because the University of Kansas has a copy which is annotated with an address in Covent Garden, 'Tom's Coffee House, April 10, 1749'. Anon., *A Sapphick Epistle from Jack Cavendish to the Honourable and Most Beautiful Mrs. D—* (London, *c.* 1782?): 'She was the first Tommy the world has upon record; but to do her justice, though there hath been many more Tommies since, yet we never had but one Sappho'; see Rictor Norton, *Mother Clap's Molly House: The Gay Sub-Culture 1700–1830* (GMP, London, 1992), pp. 234–36.

20. Anon., *La Nouvelle Sapho, ou histoire de la secte anandryne,* also called *Histoire d'une jeune fille* and *Anandria, la jolie t----* (tribade?) (London, 1780s). *La Nouvelle Sapho* was reprinted in the 1790s and under the title of *Anandria, ou confession de Mlle Sapho avec la clef* this was also reprinted at least twice in about the 1860s with illustrations by the famous French pornographer Félicien Rops.
21. Nicolai Abildgaard *Sappho and the Lesbian Maid* (1809) in the Statens Museum fur Kunst, Copenhagen. For his other sketches see Bente Skovgaard, *Catalogue of Abildgaard's Drawings,* Kobberstiksamling-ens 110, 11, 113 billedhefter 4 (The Royal Museum of Fine Arts, Copenhagen, 1978). Abildgaard was also part of Henry Fuseli's circle in Rome. Fuseli was the friend of Mary Wollstonecraft, and he completed at least one almost-erotic drawing that quoted Sappho (illustrated in Tomory, see note 3 above), as well as being the centre of a circle that included a number of artists who produced Sappho or Sappho-related pictures, among them, Henry Tresham, Hugh Douglas Hamilton, George Romney and Richard Cosway, husband of Maria.
22. Anne-Louis Girodet Trioson and M. Coupin, *Recueil de compositions dessinées par Girodet ... avec la traduction en vers par Girodet de quelques-uns des poésies de Sapho* (Paris, 1827). Department of Prints and Drawings, British Museum.
23. Jacques Louis David, *Sappho and Phaon* (1809) in the Hermitage Museum, St Petersburg. A sketch for the painting is in an undated sketchbook in the Palais des Beaux Arts, Lille. The picture was commissioned by Prince Youssopoff; see Brooks Adams, 'Painter to Patron: David's Letters to Youssopoff about the "Sappho, Phaon and Cupid"', *Marsyas* XIX (1977–78), pp. 29–36. David's painting *Paris and Helen* (1789) is similar in theme and treatment and the two pictures have often been muddled up. Paris plays a lyre and a bed figures also; now in the Louvre, Paris.
24. Henry Tresham, *Le avventure di Saffo* (Rome, 1784). Tresham's plates were based on the story taken from Alessandro Verri's novel of the same name published in Rome in 1780. For the creation of 'proto-Napoleonic' stories about Sappho, see Joan DeJean, *Fictions of Sappho: 1546–1937* (Chicago University Press, Chicago, 1989), pp. 167–76.
25. François Gérard *Corinne at Cape Miseno* (1821) in the Musée des Beaux Arts, Lyons. Ingres's *Sappho or Corinne* (1809) is in the Forsythe Wickes Collection at the Boston Museum of Fine Arts. Joseph Marie Vien's *Sapho chantant ses vers s'accompagnant de la lyre,* exhibited at the Paris Salon in 1789, is now lost. Louis Ducis's *Sappho Recalled to Life by the Charm of Music* (1811) is in the Norton Simon Museum, Pasadena, California. Pierre Antoine Augustin Vafflard's *Sapho retirée de l'eau par les soins d'un étranger* exhibited at the Paris Salon (1819) is now lost. Antoine Jean Gros's *Sappho* (1801) is in the Musée des Beaux Arts, Bayeux. Gerard's head of Sappho engraved by J. Reverdin is now lost. Charles Meynier's *Sappho and Cupid* or *Erato and her Muse, Cupid* (1802) was engraved by Normand for C.P. Landon's *A Collection of Etchings* (1821).
26. Nancy Armstrong, *Desire and Domestic Fiction: A Political History of the Novel* (Oxford University Press, Oxford, 1987), pp. 3–27. For Madame de Stael, see Avriel H.

Goldenberger's introduction to Germaine de Stael, *Delphine* (Northern Illinois University Press, De Kalb, 1995); and Madelyn Gutwirth, *Madame de Stael, Novelist: The Emergence of the Artist as Woman* (University of Illinois Press, Urbana, 1978).

27. Christopher Prendergast argues that in many paintings, but particularly in Baron Gros's *Napoleon visitant le champ de la bataille d'Eylau* (1808), Napoleon is privileged as the controlling figure who sees and interprets all the chaos of the battlefield where everyone else involved is subject to reaction and feeling. See Christopher Prendergast, *Napoleon and History Painting: Antoine-Jean Gros's 'Le Bataille d'Eylau'* (Oxford University Press, Oxford, 1997), pp. 156–78.
28. Sir William Beechey's (n.d.) pen-and-ink sketch is in the British Museum, Department of Prints and Drawings. Jacob Asmus Carsten's Sappho sketch is in a sketchbook (*c.* 1792–98) (folio 31, verso) in the collection at Stadel, Frankfurt am Main, Germany; see Stadelsches Kunstinstitut, *Katalog der deutschen Zeichnungen: Alte Meister*, eds Schilling and Schwarz-weller (1972), no. 622. Stein (see note 3 above) also mentions sketches by the Swedish admiral Carl August Ehrensvard (1745–1800) who did a pen-and-wash drawing of 'Sappho's Leap' in a sketchbook dated *c.* 1797, now in the Statens Konstmuseer, Stockholm, Sweden, and another jokey portrait sketch of her leap by Per G. Wickenberg entitled *Sappho sorjer Faons obestandighet* (1834, or 1843), now also in the Statens Konstmuseer, Stockholm, Sweden. Johann August Nahl produced an engraving *Sappho's Leucadian Leap* (1799), now in the Albertina, Vienna, and this image was discussed by Goethe in '*Sappho sich vom leucabischen Selsen sturzend*', in *Propylaen* II, no. 1 (Tubingen, 1799), pp. 135–6. Sappho is also shown in a headlong fall in an illustration by Pierre Choffard for Adrien Blin de Sainmore's French translation of Ovid's *Lettre de Sapho à Phaon* (1766) and in another by Charles Eisen to Moutonnet de Clairfons's French translation *Anacreon, Sapho, Bion et Moschus* (1773). G.B. Cipriani and F. Bartolozzi produced a stipple engraving *Sappho Throwing herself from the Rock* (London, 1782) now in the New York Public Library, and this image was used as the frontispiece to an edition of William Beckford's *Dreams, Waking Thoughts, and Incidents in a Series of Letters from Various Parts of Europe* (J. Johnson, P. Elmsley, London, 1783). Richard Westall's *Sappho's Leucadian Leap* was reproduced in *The Poet and the Painter* (1868). Stein (see Note 3 above) gives a list of several paintings on the theme of Sappho's leap exhibited at the Paris Salon, in Rome and Madrid from 1795 to 1873 including pictures by Taurel, Dantan, Ansiaux, Vafflard, Lafond, Agnemi, Dugasseau, Aznar Garcia, Bertrand and Gastaldi. There was also a 'Sappho and Phaon' exhibited at the Paris Salon in 1833, and doubtless many more; see Gen Doy, *Women and Visual Culture in Nineteenth Century France, 1800–1852* (Leicester University Press, London and New York, 1998), pp. 148, 157.
29. Honoré Daumier, 'Sapho' in *Histoire ancienne* (Paris, 1842), p. 49. Anon. (D.K. Sandford?), 'Greek Authoresses', *The Edinburgh Review* 4 (April 1832), p. 187.
30. Ary Renan's oil on wood *Sappho at the Bottom of the Sea* is in the Musée de Luxembourg, Paris. It is described in Bram Djkstra's *Idols of Perversity: Fantasies of Feminine Evil in Fin de Siècle Culture* (Oxford University Press, Oxford, 1986), p. 87. Théodore Chasseriau's watercolour and black pencil *Sapho* (1849) is in the Louvre, Paris. His oil on wood *Sapho prête à se précipiter du rocher du Leucade* (*c.* 1849, exhibited at the Paris Salon 1850–51) is in the Musée d'Orsay, Paris. Chasseriau also made three minor studies of Sappho, see Charles Sterling, *Chasseriau* (Orangeries, Paris, 1933), no. 13, and L. Benedite *Théodore Chasseriau* (Dezarrois, Paris, 1932), Vol. I, p. 186. Leopold Burthe's *Sapho jouant à la lyre* (1849) is in the Musée des Beaux Arts, Carcassone. James Pradier's silvered bronze and gilt *Standing Sappho* (1848–51) is in the Van Gogh Museum, Amsterdam, and his marble *Sapho* (1852) is in the Musée d'Orsay, Paris.

Clesinger seems to have produced some seven different works with a Sappho theme including at least one jewelled and polychromed version, see *A. Estignard Clesinger: sa vie, ses oeuvres* (Paris, 1900), p. 75. Gustave Moreau made some twelve paintings on Sappho in the period 1846–93, see P. Mathieu, *Gustave Moreau* (New York Graphics Society, Boston, 1976). Among them are three oils *La Mort de Sapho* in the Musée Gustave Moreau in Paris, an oil *The Death of Sappho* sold at Sotheby's London in June 1995, and *Sappho* (n.d., *c.* 1880s), a watercolour in the Victoria and Albert Museum, London. Hector LeRoux painted a *Sappho* (n.d.) which shows her standing on a cliff with her lyre propped on a rock behind her and a city in the background. An engraving by Erdes appeared in Jean Richepin, *Sapphô* in *Les Grandes Amoureuses* series (C. Marpon and E. Flammarion, Paris, 1884). He also seems to have painted a *Sappho's School* with her standing in front of a building about to perform on her lyre.

31. Richard Poirier, *The Performing Self: Compositions and Decompositions in the Languages of Contemporary Life* (Oxford University Press, Oxford and New York, 1971), p. 87, quoted in Edward Said, *Musical Elaborations* (Vintage, London, 1991), pp. 2–7.
32. Janet Bezier, *Ventriloquized Bodies: Narratives of Hysteria in Nineteenth Century France* (Cornell University Press, Ithaca and London, 1994), p. 240. See also Elisabeth Bronfen, *The Knotted Subject: Hysteria and Its Discontents* (Princeton University Press, Princeton New Jersey, 1998), pp. 176–90.
33. For works by Chasseriau, Moreau, Girodet Trioson, Renan and Carsten see notes 28 and 30 above. Corot's lithograph *Sappho* (1871) shows her seated in a landscape with cliffs behind. Heinrich Dreber's *Sappho* (1864–70) is in the Schack Gallery in Munich.
34. See Mary D. Sheriff, *The Exceptional Woman: Elisabeth Vigée-LeBrun and the Cultural Politics of Art* (Chicago University Press, Chicago and London, 1996), and Gen Doy, *Women and Visual Culture in Nineteenth Century France, 1800–1852* (Leicester University Press, London and New York, 1998), pp. 95–120.
35. Joseph Addison, 'The Pleasures of the Imagination', *The Spectator* (412) 21 June to 3 July 1712. Edmund Burke, *A Philosophical Enquiry into the Origin of Our Ideas of the Sublime and the Beautiful* (1757/59), ed. James T. Boulton (Routledge, Kegan Paul, London, 1958), p. 136.
36. Susan Griffin, *Pornography and Silence: Culture's Revenge Against Nature* (The Women's Press, London, 1981), p. 66.
37. There was a widespread debate on the subject of the prostitute and the prevalence of prostitution in the mid-nineteenth century, typical publications in Britain and France included Alexis-Jean-Baptiste Parent-Duchatelet's *De la prostitution dans la ville de Paris* (Paris, 1837), James Beard Talbot's *The Miseries of Prostitution* (London, 1844), and Michael Ryan's *Prostitution in London* (London, 1839). All these books were reviewed by William Rathbone Greg in *The Westminster Review* 53 (1850), pp. 448–79. Lynda Nead, *Myths of Sexuality: Representations of Women in Victorian Britain* (Basil Blackwell, Oxford, 1988), pp. 62–7 and 91–109. Elisabeth Bronfen, *Over her Dead Body: Death, Femininity and the Aesthetic* (Manchester University Press, Manchester, 1992). George Cruikshank, 'The Drunkard's Children', plate VIII. The caption reads: 'The maniac father and the convict mother are gone – The poor girl, homeless, penniless, deserted, destitute and gin-mad, commits self-murder.'
38. Arsène Houssaye, *Les Confessions: souvenirs d'un demi-siècle, 1830–1880* (1885–1891), Vol. III (Slatkine Reprints, Geneva, 1971), p. 13. Joan DeJean gives a full account of the publications that contributed to Sappho's French reputation as a lesbian in *Fictions of Sappho: 1546–1937* (Chicago University Press, Chicago, 1989). The first was J.-B. Chaussard's *Fêtes et courtisanes de la Grèce* where a long section appears under 'S' for Sappho. The second was Allier de Hauteroche's 1822 article 'Notice sur la courtisane

Sapho, née à Eresos, dans l'ile de Lesbos' where he resurrected an old story from the ancient writer Aelian that there were two Sapphos of Lesbos; one from Mytilene who was a respected poetess, and the other from Eresus who was a notorious courtesan. These publications emphasised Sappho's heterosexual credentials, but during the 1830s and through the 1840s and 1850s there grew up in Paris a distinct fashion for lesbianism – both as actual sexual experience, and as a literary and artistic theme. Lesbians were all the rage, appearing in fictions like Théophile Gautier's *Mademoiselle de Maupin* (1835), Honoré de Balzac's *La Fille aux yeux* d'or (1835) and *Seraphitus-Seraphita* (1854), and in Charles Baudelaire's *Les Fleurs du mal* (1857). They appeared in salacious pictures like Gustave Courbet's *Sleep* (1862), and Sappho, inevitably, was one of them. Bram Dijkstra includes a section on 'The Lesbian Glass' in his *Idols of Perversity: Fantasies of Feminine Evil in Fin de Siècle Culture* (Oxford University Press, Oxford, 1986), pp. 147–59.

39. Engraving after James Pradier's silvered bronze and gilt statuette of 'Sappho' in *l'Illustration* 11 (1848). This image is reproduced in Janis Bergman-Carton's *The Woman of Ideas in French Art, 1830–1848* (Yale University Press, New Haven, 1995), p. 182. Parian figures of 'Sappho' were produced by the Worcester, Minton and Copeland factories in the nineteenth century. Pradier's 1852 marble was reproduced (with slight modifications) in Parian by Minton in 1858; see *The Parian Phenomenon*, ed. Paul Atterbury (Richard Dennis, Shepton Beauchamp, London, 1989), fig. 112. For Louise Colet as the model for Pradier's later marble *Sappho* see Francine du Plessix Gray, *Rage and Fire: A Life of Louise Colet, Pioneer Feminist, Literary Star, Flaubert's Muse* (Hamish Hamilton, London, 1994), pp. 230, 281. Arsène Houssaye reports a conversation between James Pradier and Rachel the *tragédienne* about antiquity and her roles in representing its heroines, 'Oh, Rachel', said Pradier, 'it is you who have discovered Herculaneum'; see Arsène Houssaye, *Behind the Scenes of the Comédie Française and Other Recollections*, trans. and ed. Albert Vandam (Chapman and Hall, London, 1889), p. 335. While Pradier was fascinated by Sappho, he was also clearly intrigued – like so many of his contemporaries – with the idea of lesbianism and its pornographic possibilities. One of his last works was a small marble sculpture of 'two girls in the very act'.
40. This marble model was sold at auction by Phillips in Edinburgh in October 1995. It is illustrated in *Country Life*, 2 November 1995, p. 69. William Theed's marble *Sappho* (*c.* 1848) was shown at the Great Exhibition in London in 1851 and it was purchased by Prince Albert. It is still in the royal collection at Buckingham Palace. Theed's statue was reproduced in (clothed) miniature by Copeland in 1851 and 1869; see *The Parian Phenomenon*, ed. Paul Atterbury (Richard Dennis, Shepton Beauchamp London, 1989), fig. 522.
41. Alphonse Daudet, *Sappho: Parisian Manners: A Realistic Novel,* English translation (Vizetelly and Co., London, 1886), p. 61. *Sappho, or The Idol of an Hour* by G.G. Collingham was a play based on Daudet's novel performed at the Shakespeare Theatre, Clapham in 1898. In this version Fanny is called 'Francine' throughout, and though she writes a letter of farewell to her young lover, as in the novel, he here finds her dead at the close of the play. *Sapho, pièce en cinq actes* by Alphonse Daudet and Adolphe Belot (Paris, 1893) was translated into English and licensed for performance at the Garrick Theatre, London in April 1895. In this version Fanny leaves Gaussin as in the original. Jules Massenet's opera with libretto by Henry Cain and Arthur Bernède was premiered in Paris in November 1897.
42. With reference to Lamartine, Gabriele D'Annunzio's poem 'Four Nude Studies' from the collection *Intermezzo di rime* (Sommaruga, Rome, 1883) included the lines, 'Feline

haunches in whose furrows my musician's fingers rise rhythmically as on the strings of a lyre'; see Phillippe Jullian, *D'Annunzio*, trans. Stephen Hardman (The Pall Mall Press, London, 1972), p. 53. A selection of representative siren pictures where they play on a suggestive lyre includes W.E. Frost's *The Syrens* (1849) and E.J. Poynter's *The Siren* (1864), both reproduced in Alison Smith, *The Victorian Nude: Sexuality, Morality and Art* (Manchester University Press, Manchester and New York, 1996), pp. 91, 107. Charles Gleyre's *Le Coucher de Sapho* (1868) is in the Musée Cantonal des Beaux Arts, Lausanne. Felix Joseph Barrias's *Sapho d'Ereze* (1847), whereabouts unknown, is reproduced in a photograph in A. Cipollini, *Saffo* (Fratelli Dumolard, Milan, 1890), p. 421.

43. Simeon Solomon's *Sappho and Erinna in the Garden of Mytilene* (1864) is in the Tate Gallery, London. Charles Mengin's *Sappho* (1877) is in the Manchester City Art Gallery. Frederic Leighton's *The Tragic Poetess* (*c.* 1890) is in a private collection in Japan. Leighton's *Summer Moon* (*c.* 1872) is one of his many paintings showing two (or more) sleeping women wrapped in each others' arms. William Reynolds Stephens's *Summer* (1891), painted for the Refreshment Room of the exhibition galleries at the Royal Academy, shows five girls lying about in a languid state, and one is toying with a lyre. Albert Moore produced any number of pictures of lazy girls in Greek drapery, posed alone or in groups, including *Yellow Marguerites* (*c.* 1880), *The Dreamers* (1882) and *Beads* or *The Fan* (*c.* 1880). Moore's favourite punningly suggestive prop – and it appears in all three of these pictures – is the fan. In a large marble statue of *Sappho* (1895) by Prosper d'Epinay, now in the Metropolitan Museum of Art, New York, the poet leans back in her chair and looks abstractedly down, her left hand holds the lyre and laurel wreath down by her side, while her right hand clutches at her breast.
44. Algernon Charles Swinburne to Dante Gabriel Rossetti, 22 February 1870. *The Swinburne Letters*, Vol. II. Félicien Rops's frontispiece to Stéphane Mallarmé's *Les Poésies* (Paris, 1891) shows a naked woman seated on a throne over a pile of skulls while disembodied hands play the strings of her lyre and she caresses its frame to make it grow in her hands. This image is reproduced in my *The Sappho Companion* (Chatto and Windus, London, 2000), p. 239.
45. Hector LeRoux's *Sappho à Mitylene* (*c.* 1860's) is in the Musée de la Princerie, Verdun. Alma Tadema's *Sappho* (1881) is in the Walters Art Gallery, Baltimore. Sappho has actually been thoroughly cleaned up by Alma Tadema's representation: not only is she shown as schoolmistress, but she has put aside her laurel wreath, and is docilely listening to the male poet perform. Oscar Wilde took the painter to task over this picture when he pointed out that some of the Greek names on the benches are actually boy's names. Frederick Dudley Walenn (fl. 1894–1930) *Famous Women of Antiquity: Miriam, Rebecca, Semiramis, Penelope, Sappho, Cleopatra, Cornelia, Phyrne, Aspasia, Helen, Atalanta, Imogen and Boadicea*, sold at auction by Mallett and Son Antiques Ltd, Bridgeman Art Library. *Catalogue of an Exhibition of Engraved Portraits of Women Writers from Sappho to George Eliot at the Grolier Club, New York* (The Gilliss Press, New York, 1895), p. 20. There were five images of Sappho in this exhibition including an engraving by Fontana of Raphael's portrait in the Vatican, and an engraving by Worlidge of a cornelian gem. Though most images of Sappho through the nineteenth century were produced by men she was still an attractive subject for women artists. Two of the most interesting examples are an etching by Queen Victoria dated 1841 and reproduced in Christian Brinton's article 'Queen Victoria as Etcher' in *The Critic* (June 1900), pp. 501–10 and in Yopie Prins, *Victorian Sappho* (Princeton University Press, Princeton, New Jersey, 1999), p. 187. Victoria's interest may have been sparked by Pacini's opera *Saffo* (premiered in Naples in November 1840, it was performed in

London in 1841). Queen Victoria's etching shows the poet kneeling on a cliff looking resignedly into the sunset, but, intriguingly, Sappho herself closely resembles portraits of the young queen. The other curious woman-artist's image is a photograph from 1870 by Julia Margaret Cameron where she posed her servant Mary Hillier as 'Sappho', in profile, with a Grecian hair do, and wearing an oriental embroidered blouse and bold jewellery; see Nicholas Mirzoeff, *Bodyscape: Art, Modernity and the Ideal Figure* (Routledge, London, 1995), p. 125.

46. Sarah Baylis, pen-and-ink illustrations to *Sappho: Poems and Fragments*, trans. Josephine Balmer (Brilliance Books, London, 1984). Gillian Ayres (b. 1930), *Sappho* (1988), Bridgeman Art Library. Rose Frain, *Sappho Fragments* (1989), one of two copies of an Artist's Book, in the Special Collections, National Art Library, Victoria and Albert Museum.
47. Rachilde, *Monsieur Venus* ([1884] Flammarion, Paris, 1926), p. 90. I am grateful to Lisa Downing for this reference.

4. Fragments of an elegy

1. *Greek Lyric I, Sappho and Alcaeus*, Loeb Classical Library, ed. and trans. David A. Campbell (1982: Harvard University Press, Cambridge Mass. and London, 1990), pp. 78–81. *Sappho: Poems and Fragments*, trans. Josephine Balmer (1984: Bloodaxe Books, Newcastle-upon-Tyne, 1992), p. 38.
2. Roland Barthes, *A Lover's Discourse: Fragments*, trans. Richard Howard (1977: Penguin, Harmondsworth Middlesex, 1990), pp. 155–6, 10. As Sappho's Fragment 31 stands at the head of all love lyrics, all written expression of desire in language, so it also lies behind many more of Barthes's headings including the first 'I am engulfed, I succumb':

   'I am engulfed, I succumb ...'
   s'abimer/ to be engulfed
   Outburst of annihilation which affects the amorous subject in
   despair or fulfilment ...

   ... This is how it happens sometimes, misery or joy engulfs me, without any particular tumult ensuing: nor any pathos: I am dissolved, not dismembered; I fall, I flow, I melt ... (p. 3)

3. Marilyn Hacker, *Love, Death and the Changing of the Seasons* (Onlywomen Press, London, 1987), p. 22.
4. Ambrose Phillips, *The Works of Anacreon and Sappho, Done from the Greek, by several hands* (London, 1715), pp. 61–75. Joseph Addison's praise for Phillips's translation meant that it remained a highly influential version for some time: see *The Spectator*, no. 223, 15 November and 27 November, 1711.

   Catullus's poem is 'Ille mi par esse': see Loeb Classical Library, *Catullus, Tibullus, Pervigilium Veneris*, ed. G.P. Goold (Harvard University Press, Cambridge Mass., 1988), pp. 58–61. Ovid's is one of his *Heroides*, 'Letters of the Heroines', XV, 'Sappho to Phaon': see Loeb Classical Library, *Ovid I: Heroides and Amores*, trans. Grant Showerman, second edition, revised by G.P. Goold (Harvard University Press, Cambridge Mass., 1977), pp. 180–97. For Nicolas Boileau, see *Oeuvres completes* (Gallimard-Pleiade, Paris, 1966), pp. 356–7. John Donne's poem 'Sapho to Philaenis', along with Sidney's, Smollett's, Shelley's and other versions of Fragment 31 are included in Margaret Reynolds, *The Sappho Companion* (Chatto and Windus, London,

2000), pp. 38–44. Other versions of Fragment 31 are also to be found in *Sappho Through English Poetry*, eds Peter Jay and Caroline Lewis (Anvil Press, London, 1996).

5. In Catullus's version he makes himself the speaker addressing his mistress Lesbia. Ovid has Sappho writing to Phaon though she does acknowledge her old lesbian *amours*. It is sometimes said that Sappho does not become a lesbian Lesbian until the nineteenth century. But in fact John Donne's poem has his Sappho rejecting Phaon in favour of a new girlfriend, Philaenis, and some early translations, like that by John Addison of 1735, make it clear that Fragment 31 is addressed by a woman to a woman.

   Much scholarly argument has gone on over *chlorotera* but relates usually to its meaning, 'greener', and few now dispute that its ending is feminine. Recently however, Germaine Greer has taken further the questioning that used to go on over the gender of the speaker in the poem to suggest that there is another 'feminine signature' in Fragment 31 in the word *idros*. It is usually translated as 'sweat' but has been a source of embarrassment to many writers and commentators from Boileau – who left it out on the grounds that 'le mot sueur en français ne peut jamais être agréable, et laisse une vilaine idée à l'ésprit' – to Phillips, who transformed it to the rather more polite 'dewy damps'. According to Greer *idros* suggests 'oozing', and Sappho's speaker, dissolving like a lovesick teenager or an overawed child when addressed by a beloved mentor, has wet herself: Germaine Greer, *Slipshod Sibyls: Recognition, Rejection and the Woman Poet* (Viking, Harmondsworth Middlesex and London, 1995), p. 113.

   Without calling Sappho's continence into question, it is certain that whatever is suggested here (and of course the Greek text is corrupt) the oozing in Sappho's poem generally either disappears altogether in later versions (as in Catullus), or is modified in some way into general bodily fluids, sweat or tears, or shifted altogether out of the physical-specific into the metaphoric applications of water as, for instance, in 'swimming' eyes or roaring 'waves' in the ears.

6. See Joan DeJean, *Fictions of Sappho* (University of Chicago Press, Chicago and London, 1989), pp. 49–50; George Devereux, 'The Nature of Sappho's Seizure in Fragment 31 as Evidence of her Inversion', *Classical Quarterly* 20 (1970), pp. 17–31; and Thomas McEvilley, 'Sappho, Fragment 31: The Face Behind the Mask', *Phoenix* 32 (1978), pp. 1–18.

7. Margaret Williamson, *Sappho's Immortal Daughters* (Harvard University Press, Cambridge Mass. and London, 1995), p. 157. See also John Winkler, *The Constraints of Desire: The Anthropology of Sex and Gender in Ancient Greece* (Routledge, New York and London, 1990), pp. 178–80. Page DuBois, *Sappho is Burning* (The University of Chicago Press, Chicago and London, 1995), pp. 72–5, quoting Bruno Snell, *The Discovery of the Mind: The Greek Origins of European Thought*, trans. T.G. Rosenmeyer (Harvard University Press, Cambridge Mass. and London, 1953), p. 8. Charles Segal, 'Eros and Incantation: Sappho and Oral Poetry', *Arethusa* (1974), pp. 139–57. Jesper Svenbro, 'Death by Writing: Sappho, the Poem, and the Reader' in *Phrasikleia: An Anthropology of Reading in Ancient Greek*, trans. Janet Lloyd (Cornell University Press, Ithaca New York, 1993), p. 152.

8. The poet's water metaphor also appears translated into 'swell', 'eddies' and the 'swimming' senses. In fact, this water imagery, like much else in his poem, is probably derived from Phillips's translation of Fragment 31; compare 'tumults', 'in transport tost' and 'my dim eyes' which also appear in Phillips.

9. For the text of Arthur Hallam's poem, 'To the Loved One' see *The Writings of Arthur Hallam: Now First Collected and Edited by T.H. Vail Motter* (Oxford University Press and the Modern Language Association of America, Oxford and New York, 1943), pp. 93–4.

The poem was first published in *Remains in Verse and Prose of Arthur Henry Hallam*, ed. Henry Hallam (W. Nichol, London, 1834), pp. 64–9.

10. Robert Bernard Martin, *Tennyson: The Unquiet Heart* (Clarendon Press, Oxford, 1980), p. 29. When James Murray was working on the OED in 1884 he asked Tennyson about his use of the compound 'balm-cricket' in 'A Dirge' (1830), and the poet replied that it came out of his memory of Dalzel's edition of poems by Theocritus. See Peter Levi, *Tennyson* (Macmillan, London, 1993), pp. 29–30. For Tennyson's copy of Dalzel see *Tennyson in Lincoln: A Catalogue of the Collections in the Research Centre* compiled by Nancie Campbell (Tennyson Research Centre, Lincoln, 1971), Vol. I, p. 7, entry 93. I am grateful to Edith Hall for her comments on Tennyson's Greek.
11. Frederick Tennyson, *The Isles of Greece: Sappho and Alcaeus* (Macmillan and Co., London, 1890), p. v. The book Frederick Tennyson refers to is Jean François Boissonade's *Lyrici Graeci* (Lefevre, Paris, 1825). For Alfred Tennyson's copy of Boissonade see *Tennyson in Lincoln: A Catalogue of the Collections in the Research Centre*, compiled by Nancie Campbell (Tennyson Research Centre, Lincoln, 1971), Vol. I, p. 33, entry 582. A 'weird little volume' it may be, but Boissonade represented, at the time, a relatively high standard of Sappho scholarship, and Boissonade was also one of the significant nineteenth century commentators to acknowledge Sappho's homosexuality; see Joan DeJean, *Fictions of Sappho: 1546–1937* (Chicago University Press, Chicago and London, 1989), pp. 231–2.
12. Theodor Bergk, *Poetae Lyrici Graeci* (Leipzig, 1843). Bergk was to go on to produce the most comprehensive and reliable editions of Sappho published before the papyrus discoveries of the late nineteenth century, most notably in his *Anthologia Lyrica* (Leipzig, 1854). *Tennyson in Lincoln: A Catalogue of the Collections in the Research Centre*, compiled by Nancie Campbell (Tennyson Research Centre, Lincoln, 1971), Vol. I, p. 31, entry 512.
13. Fitzgerald actually quoted three Sappho fragments in a letter to Tennyson. His letter is lost, but Tennyson's reply survives and on this Fitzgerald noted a line from Sappho's Fragment 105a 'on the sweetapple'. See Alfred Tennyson to Edward Fitzgerald, 12 November 1846, in *The Letters of Alfred Lord Tennyson*, eds Cecil Y. Lang and Edgar F. Shannon Jr. (Oxford University Press, Oxford, 1982), Vol. I, p. 26. The book to which Tennyson refers is F.G. Schneidewin, *Delectus Poesis Graecorum Elegiacae, Iambicae, Melicae: Sapphonis Mitylenaeae Carmina* (Gottingen, 1838), pp. 289–322.
14. The most circumstantial account of Tennyson's debt to Sappho is in Linda H. Peterson, 'Sappho and the Making of Tennysonian Lyric', *English Literary History*, Vol. 61 (1994), pp. 121–37. See also John Churton Collins, *Illustrations of Tennyson* (Chatto and Windus, London, 1891), Wilfred P. Mustard, *Classical Echos in Tennyson*, (1904: Haskell House Publishers, New York, 1971), W.D. Paden, *Tennyson in Egypt* (1942: Octagon Books, New York, 1971), Robert Pattison, *Tennyson and Tradition* (Harvard University Press, Cambridge Mass. and London, 1979), Stephen C. Allen, 'Tennyson, Sappho, and "The Lady of Shalott"', *Tennyson Research Bulletin*, 2 (1975), pp. 171–2, and Peter Levi, *Tennyson* (Macmillan, London, 1993). A great number of Tennyson's classical allusions are recorded and suggested in Christopher Ricks's edition of *The Poems of Tennyson* (Longman's, London, 1969). This edition is referred to for the rest of this chapter as Ricks (1969).

The poem 'And ask ye why these sad tears stream?' which was published in *Poems by Two Brothers* (1827) appeared with an epigraph from Ovid's *Heroides* XV, 'Sappho to Phaon'. On the evidence of a shared stock of images, or of shared vocabulary, the fragments of Sappho which feed most regularly into Tennyson's later verse would seem to be Fragment 1, with its epithet of 'many-minded' or 'myriad-minded' which appears in 'Ode to Memory', and with its form of invocation which appears throughout Tennyson; Fragment 2 (thought to be two separate poems in the nineteenth century) which gives a garden topos such as that in 'Youth' (written 1833) where 'I heard Spring laugh in hidden rills,/ Summer through all her sleepy leaves/ Murmured ...' is borrowed from Sappho; Fragment 31 which is discussed here; Fragment 46 'I will lay down my limbs on soft cushions' which crops up in Tennyson's 'Eleanore'; Fragment 47 'Love shook my heart' which is in Tennyson's 'Fatima'; Fragment 49 'I loved thee once, Atthis, long ago'; Fragment 52 'I do not expect to touch the sky (with my two arms?)' which may be in Tennyson's 'This Earth is Wondrous' (written *c.* 1833); Fragment 102 'Truly, sweet mother, I cannot weave my web for I am overcome with desire for a boy because of slender Aphrodite' which may be in the background to 'The Lady of Shalott'; Fragment 104 on the evening star which is mentioned in 'Leonine Elegiacs' (originally 'Elegiacs') and in 'Locksley Hall Sixty Years After'; Fragment 105a about the sweet-apple which may be in 'The Hesperides' and which Tennyson recognised in his 1846 letter to Fitzgerald; Fragment 123, among others, which describe 'golden-sandalled Dawn' which Tennyson uses in 'Oenone' among other poems; Fragment 130 'Once again limb-loosening love ... the bitter-sweet irresistible creature' which gives both 'limb-loosening', which is suggested in both 'Eleänore' and 'Fatima', and 'bitter-sweet', which is in 'Love, Pride and Forgetfulness', 'A Dream of Fair Women' and in *In Memoriam* XV, as well as in other poems; and Fragment 168B 'The moon has set and the Pleiades ... and I lie alone' which is referenced in both 'Mariana' and 'Mariana in the South' as well as in 'Over the dark world flies the wind' (written 1833), and the bridal poems regretting 'single sleep', 'The Bridesmaid' and 'Move Eastward, happy earth ...'.

15. The collaborative poem was 'To Poesy' which appears in both the Allen notebook at Trinity College Cambridge and in the Heath Commonplace Book in the Fitzwilliam Museum. Both sources note that the poem was a joint composition, and in the Allen notebook, where it is written out in Hallam's hand, Hallam has written: 'N.B. I had some hand in the worst part of this.' In the Heath Commonplace Book the scribe has dated the poem 1827 and 1832 and crossed both dates out. Hallam's modern editor T. Vail Motter suggests a date early in their acquaintance, 1828, as noted in the Allen manuscript. See *The Writings of Arthur Hallam*, ed. T. Vail Motter (Oxford University Press and Modern Language Association of America, Oxford and New York, 1943), p. 46. The poem is printed in *The Poems of Tennyson*, ed. Christopher Ricks (Longmans, London, 1969), pp. 168–9 where Ricks also draws attention to a similar poem of Tennyson's with the same title and date, 'O God, make this age great', pp. 167–8.
16. See *The Writings of Arthur Hallam*, ed. T. Vail Motter (Oxford University Press and the Modern Language Association of America, Oxford and New York, 1943). See also *Remains, in Verse and Prose of Arthur Henry Hallam*, ed. Henry Hallam (W. Nichol, London, 1834), pp. xxxvii–xxxviii, where Henry Hallam says that a 'considerable portion' of Hallam's poems were to have been published with the work of 'his intimate friend Mr. Alfred Tennyson. They were however withheld from the publisher at the request of the Editor.'
17. The poem they argued over was 'The Lover's Tale'. See Ricks (1969), p. 299.
18. *The Letters of Arthur Henry Hallam*, ed. Jack Kolb (Ohio State University Press, Columbus, 1981), pp. 401–2. Arthur Hallam to William Bodham Donne, 13 February 1831.
19. This 1825 copy of the *Epigrammata* is in the Tennyson collection at Lincoln. See *Tennyson in Lincoln: A Catalogue of the Collections in the Research Centre*, compiled by Nancie Campbell, (Tennyson Research Centre, Lincoln, 1971), Vol. I, p. 54, entry 1053.

20. *Remains, in Verse and Prose of Arthur Hallam*, ed. Henry Hallam (W. Nichol, London, 1834), p. xxix.
21. Ricks (1969), pp. 367–71.
22. It also suggests Keats's 'Ode to a Nightingale' and 'Ode on a Grecian Urn'. Both those poems have a distinctly Sapphic background so it is hardly surprising that Tennyson should also make connections which link his allusions to Keats with his Sappho versions.
23. Ricks (1969), pp. 382–4. The title 'Fatima' was added when the poem was published in *Poems* (1842) and it supplies the typically oriental setting that Tennyson associates with Sappho. His tendency to merge Eastern themes with the lyric character of her work is emphasised by the addition of the second stanza in 1842 which refers to the story of Jemily, set in a harem, and drawn from Tennyson's memories of C.E. Savary's *Letters on Egypt*. See W.D. Paden, *Tennyson in Egypt: A Study of the Imagery in his Early Work* (1942: Octagon Books, New York, 1971), pp. 32–41.
24. The other two Sappho references are to Fragment 168B (in modern editions) which was attributed to Sappho by Arsenius (*c.* 1500) and was known as Fragment 111 in the nineteenth century. The attribution is now rejected by modern editors: 'The moon has set/ and the Pleiades;/ it is midnight,/ and time goes by,/ and I lie alone'. And there is a second Sappho reference at the end of the first stanza. In Tennyson, 'Lo, falling from my constant mind,/ Lo, parched and withered, deaf and blind,/ I whirl like leaves in roaring wind ...'; in Sappho, Fragment 47 (in modern editions), 'Love shook my heart like a wind falling on oaks on a mountain'.
25. Ricks (1969), p. 1787. J.M. Heath's Commonplace Book is now in the Fitzwilliam Museum at Cambridge. The fragment of 'Love and Friendship' was first published by Sir Charles Tennyson in *The Cornhill*, cliii (1936), pp. 444–5 where the editor says that the piece is 'reminiscent ... of "The Lover's Tale" and no doubt composed at about the same time'.
26. Sigmund Freud, *Civilization and its Discontents* (1930), *Standard Edition of the Complete Psychological Works of Sigmund Freud*, trans. James Strachey (Hogarth Press, London, 1953–74), Vol. 21, p. 99. Jacqueline Rose, *Sexuality in the Field of Vision* (Verso, London and New York, 1986), p. 227.
27. Matthew Rowlinson, *Tennyson's Fixations: Psychoanalysis and the Topics of the Early Poetry* (University of Virginia Press, Charlottesville, 1994), pp. 60–3. Revealingly, Tennyson used to say that he would, as a child, work himself into a trance by repeating his own name over and over.
28. Peter Brooks, *Body Work: Objects of Desire in Modern Narrative* (Harvard University Press, Cambridge Mass. and London, 1993), p. xiii.
29. Except – and it's quite a big except – that there is still the secret possibility of Tennyson, the male poet, being no more than a female impersonator here, trying on Sappho's own clothes, masquerading in femininity. And, if so, then the poet is still the Subject, and Sappho-Fatima no more than the Object of his gaze.
30. Jacques Lacan, 'Desire, Life and Death' in *The Seminar of Jacques Lacan, Book II, The Ego in Freud's Theory and in the Technique of Psychoanalysis 1954–1955*, ed. Jacques-Alain Miller, trans. Sylvana Tomaselli (Cambridge University Press, Cambridge, 1988), p. 223.
31. The biographical facts of their entwining lives over the four years of their friendship is well known. What is less well-known is how closely their literary lives, especially around the period from mid-1830 to 1832, were bound up in each other. Hallam and Tennyson do in fact appear together in one volume, just as they had planned, for their mutual Cambridge friend J.M. Heath copied out not only Tennyson's drafts into

his Commonplace Book (now in the Fitzwilliam Museum in Cambridge), but some of Hallam's too. Tennyson and Hallam shared ideas; a cursory glance at modern editions of their collected works shows how often one borrows phrases from the other, both mutually during these early years and later, when Tennyson seems to have remembered, or even re-read poems by Hallam. For instance, 'lavish lights' which appears in Tennyson's 'Eleänore', appears as 'lavish light' in Hallam's poem 'To Two Sisters' which dates from February 1831. See Ricks (1969), p. 367; and *The Writings of Arthur Hallam*, ed. T. Vail Motter (Oxford University Press and Modern Language Association of America, Oxford and New York, 1943), p. 95.

In this context, Tennyson's poem 'O Darling Room' – so ridiculed by Tennyson's contemporaries, so knowingly deconstructed by modern critics – stages a sacred primal space where Tennyson, Hallam and Sappho met. Of course it is a nursery because it is at the beginning of poetry and the beginning of the world; of course it is 'warm and bright' because it is where Tennyson and Hallam found mother-Sappho, her outdoor garden world transferred to an indoor Victorian domestic setting; of course here are two couches, both sensually enticing and innocent, both 'soft' and 'white', because they hint at the moment of transference which takes place in this room, from childish attachment to mature knowledge. Tennyson's biographer R.B. Martin wonders if Tennyson feared he had said too much. He had. But the only thing we actually *know* that happens in this enchanted space is reading and, crucially, writing.

32. Julia Kristeva, *Tales of Love*, trans. Leon S. Roudiez (Columbia University Press, New York, 1987), 21.
33. Jonathan Wordsworth in the introduction to a facsimile reprint of Alfred Tennyson, *Poems, Chiefly Lyrical, 1830* (Woodstock Books, Oxford and New York, 1991), p. v, and Alan Sinfield, *Alfred Tennyson* (Basil Blackwell, Oxford, 1986), p. 134.
34. The flourishing of the Don Juan myth coincides with the rise of democracy, and the doctrine of liberality, and Roy Porter argues that Enlightenment ideas about nature, the body, sex and medicine gave rise to a 'common ideological currency' which recognised 'a libertinism based on instinct, freedom, and the pursuit of pleasure under the aegis of a benevolent Nature ...' See Roy Porter, 'Libertinism and Promiscuity' in *The Don Giovanni Book*, ed. Jonathan Miller, (Faber and Faber, London, 1990), p. 12. While Narcissism is a charge often levelled against homosexuality, Michael Warner points out that the most common figure of Narcissism in erotic encounters is that within heterosexuality where the presence of the woman is used to confirm the identity/existence of the (male) self and where that is her primary function, denying her individuality. See Michael Warner, 'Homo-Narcissism, or, Heterosexuality' in *Engendering Men: The Question of Male Feminist Criticism*, eds Joseph A. Boone and Michael Cadden (Routledge, London and New York, 1990), pp. 190–206.
35. Ricks (1969), p. 181.
36. While on an extended tour to Italy in 1827 Hallam wrote poems to a picture of the Madonna, to Nina, to 'A.R.' and to Anna. And it continued from there. Soon after he had met Tennyson, Hallam wrote a poem 'Lines Addressed to Alfred Tennyson' while he was at Malvern in September 1829. The poem was certainly addressed to Tennyson – 'Alfred, hadst thou been there' – but it is about a mad girl shut up in an asylum, whom Hallam describes while trying to imagine Alfred also looking at the girl and the effect that 'vision' might have had on him. So this girl's story was written by Arthur for Alfred as Alfred's later girl-poems were written by Alfred for Arthur.
37. Arthur Hallam, 'On Some of the Characteristics of Modern Poetry', *Englishman's Magazine*, August 1831, in *Victorian Scrutinies*, ed. Isobel Armstrong (Athlone, London, 1972), p. 99.

38. Teresa de Lauretis, *Alice Doesn't: Feminism, Semiotics, Cinema* (Indiana University Press, Bloomington, 1984), p. 13.
39. Ricks (1969), p. 298.
40. Sigmund Freud, 'Jokes and Their Relation to the Unconscious' in *The Complete Psychological Works of Sigmund Freud*, trans. James Strachey (Hogarth Press, London, 1953–1974), Vol. VII, pp. 97–102.
41. Eve Kosofsky Sedgwick, *Between Men: English Literature and Male Homosocial Desire* (Columbia University Press, New York, 1985). René Girard's work on erotic triangles in the European novel emphasises the dominance of the relation between two men, where the woman is only the cipher through which their desire for each other passes. See René Girard, *Deceit, Desire and the Novel: Self and the Other in Literary Structure*, trans. Yvonne Freccero (1961: Johns Hopkins University Press, Baltimore, 1965). For a criticism of Girard which puts the woman back into the story, see Toril Moi, 'The Missing Mother: The Oedipal Rivalries of René Girard', *Diacritics*, 12:2 (1982), pp. 21–31.
42. Tennyson did, at one time, write a poem about a triangle. It was 'The Lover's Tale' based on a story from Boccaccio about Julian, who was 'supposed himself to be a poet', his foster-sister Camilla and his friend and rival, Lionel. Camilla, married to Lionel, dies, but is rescued from the tomb by Julian and brought back to life. Although he still loves her, Julian gives her back to Lionel, standing before her own portrait and under strict injunction of silence, as an earnest of his own relation to the other man. Tennyson planned to publish part of it in 1832, but he withdrew it, much to Hallam's sorrow – this was the poem he tried to save. Tennyson concluded the poem only in 1869, and though he eventually published all four parts he never completed it to his own satisfaction. It may be relevant that while Tennyson's first surviving son was named Hallam, his second was named Lionel.
43. Ricks (1969), pp. 210–14.
44. See Isobel Armstrong, *Victorian Poetry: Poetry, Poetics and Politics* (Routledge, London and New York, 1993), Angela Leighton, *Victorian Women Poets: Writing Against the Heart* (Harvester, Hemel Hempstead, 1992) and Jerome McGann, *The Poetics of Sensibility* (Clarendon Press, Oxford, 1996).
45. See particularly Tennyson's poems 'Check every outflash, every ruder sally' and 'In the Valley of Cauteretz': Ricks (1969), pp. 297, 1123.
46. Alan Sinfield, *Alfred Tennyson* (Basil Blackwell, Oxford, 1986), p. 152.
47. See Jeffrey Weeks, *Coming Out: Homosexual Politics in Britain from the Nineteenth Century to the Present* (Quartet Books, London and New York, 1977), pp. 51, 14. Symonds was convinced that his chapter on Greek love published in his *Studies of the Greek Poets* (1876) lost him the chair in Poetry at Oxford. He later privately printed a larger consideration of the subject in *A Problem in Modern Ethics* (1891). See also Linda Dowling, *Hellenism and Homosexuality in Victorian Oxford* (Cornell University Press, Ithaca and London, 1994).
48. Roland Barthes, *A Lover's Discourse: Fragments*, trans. Richard Howard (1977: Penguin Books, Harmondsworth Middlesex, 1990), pp. 13–14.
49. Ricks (1969), p. 1424. Jeff Nunokowa takes an evolutionary model to argue that Tennyson (and his contemporaries) saw homosexuality as a phase of immaturity through which the subject would develop into an evolved heterosexual paterfamilias. His reading of *In Memoriam* traces this growth to adulthood as expressed in Tennyson's version(s) of his love for Hallam. See Jeff Nunokowa, '*In Memoriam* and the Extinction of the Homosexual' in *Tennyson*, ed. Rebecca Stott (Longman, London and New York, 1996), pp. 197–209. Michel Foucault, *History of Sexuality, An Introduction*, Vol. I (Penguin, Harmondsworth Middlesex, 1984), p. 59. See also Allon

White's argument that reading poetry became 'a case of looking through the semi-transparency of the words to the "real origin" which was the psycho-physiology of the author', in Allon White, *The Uses of Obscurity* (Routledge, London and New York, 1981), pp. 46–7.

50. The Labouchère amendment was introduced at the very time, as Alan Sinfield points out, when Tennyson was writing 'Locksley Hall Sixty Years After' where he altered the line 'As our greatest is man-woman, so was she the woman-man' to the more politically correct (for the time) sexual integration which allowed the woman to acquire masculine characteristics, but not the man, feminine: 'She with all the charm of woman, she with all the breadth of man.' This was also, as we have seen, the moment when Sappho became anonymous when Tennyson revised her to 'the poet'. Théophile Gautier's novel *Mademoiselle de Maupin* (1835), Charles Baudelaire's *Les Fleurs du mal* (1857), Swinburne's 'Anactoria' (1866) and Pierre Louys's *Les Chansons de Bilitis* (1895), respectively excoriated, banned and reviled, all contributed to Sappho's declining reputation.
51. Ricks (1969), p. 926. *In Memoriam*, LXXVII.
52. His own brother Frederick, spurred on by the finds, wrote a version of Sappho's story *The Isles of Greece: Sappho and Alcaeus* (Macmillan and Co., London, 1890); an American admirer, J. Easby-Smith, presented his *The Songs of Sappho* (Georgetown University, Washington DC, 1891) 'To Alfred, Lord Tennyson, Poet Laureate, with compliments'; see *Tennyson in Lincoln: A Catalogue of the Collections in the Research Centre*, compiled by Nancie Campbell (Tennyson Research Centre, Lincoln, 1971), Vol. I, p. 90, entry 1937. H. Montagu Butler, 'Recollections of Tennyson' in *Tennyson and His Friends*, ed. Hallam Tennyson (Macmillan, London, 1911), p. 216.
53. Hallam Tennyson to the Duke of Argyll, 24 October 1892: 'His last words were calling out to me "Hallam – Hallam" and to my mother whispering, "God bless you, my joy"'. Quoted in *The Letters of Alfred Lord Tennyson*, eds Cecil Y. Lang and Edgar F. Shannon Jr (Oxford University Press, Oxford, 1982), p. xix. The editors remark on Tennyson's reported words: 'If *In Memoriam* is indeed, as Tennyson said, "a sort of Divine Comedy", it is tempting to put a different construction on these words, but it is a temptation that scholarship must resist.'
54.

Far-far-away

What sight so lured him through the fields he knew
As where earth's green stole into heavens own hue,
Far-far-away?

What sound was dearest in his native dells?
The mellow lin-lan-lone of evening bells
Far-far-away.

What vague world-whisper, mystic pain or joy,
Through those three words would haunt him when a boy,
Far-far-away?

A whisper from his dawn of life? a breath
From some fair dawn beyond the doors of death
Far-far-away?

Far, far, how far? from o'er the gates of Birth,
The faint horizons, all the bounds of earth,
Far-far-away?

What charm in words, a charm no words could give?
O dying words, can Music make you live
Far-far-away?

Ricks (1969), pp. 1405–6. The poem was published in *Demeter and Other Poems* (1889). Manuscript versions of the poem (at Harvard) include two discarded stanzas. See Ricks (1969), p. 1406.

(i) That weird soul-phrase of something half-divine,
In earliest youth, in latest age is mine,
Far-far-away.
(Harvard A)
(ii) Ghost, do the men that walk this planet seem
[Ghost, can you see us, hear us, do we seem] [1st reading]
Far, far away, a truth and yet a dream,
Far-far-away?
(Harvard B)

5. The woman poet sings Sappho's last song

1. See Joan DeJean, *Fictions of Sappho: 1546–1937* (University of Chicago Press, Chicago and London, 1989), p. 201. For various treatments of the reception of Sappho see Susan Gubar, 'Sapphistries', *Signs* 10 (1984), pp. 43–62; Lawrence Lipking, *Abandoned Women and Poetic Tradition* (Chicago University Press, Chicago and London, 1988); Angela Leighton, *Victorian Women Poets: Writing Against the Heart* (Harvester, Hemel Hempstead, 1992), pp. 35–6, 60–1, 143–4, and 228–32; *Re-Reading Sappho: Reception and Transmission*, ed. Ellen Greene (University of California Press, Berkeley and Los Angeles, 1996); and Yopie Prins, *Victorian Sappho* (Princeton University Press, Princeton New Jersey, 1999).
2. A version of this chapter was first published in *Victorian Women Poets: A Critical Reader*, ed. Angela Leighton (Basil Blackwell, Oxford, 1996), pp. 277–306. Yopie Prins has since taken up – and contradicted – some of my arguments in her chapter 'P.S. Sappho' in *Victorian Sappho* (Princeton University Press, Princeton New Jersey, 1999), pp. 174–245.
3. *Lady Blessington's Conversations of Lord Byron*, ed. Ernest J. Lovell (Princeton University Press, Princeton New Jersey, 1969), p. 26. Byron's long-term mistress Teresa Guiccioli was very fond of de Stael's *Corinne*, and Byron blamed some of her emotional extravagance on her taste for the novel. See Joanne Wilkes, *Lord Byron and Madame De Stael: Born for Opposition* (Ashgate Publishing Ltd, Aldershot, 1999), pp. 10–11, 45–7. Ellen Moers in *Literary Women* (The Women's Press, London, 1978) was the first to draw attention to the wide-ranging influence of de Stael's writings and to the powerful 'myth of Corinne' in Victorian women's writing both in Britain and America.
4. Elizabeth Barrett to Benjamin Robert Haydon, 1 January 1844: in Elizabeth Barrett Browning and Robert Browning, *The Brownings' Correspondence*, eds Philip Kelley, Ronald Hudson and Scott Lewis (Wedgestone Press, Winfield Kansas, 1984–), Vol. VIII, p. 128.
5. Sara Coleridge, *Memoir and Letters of Sara Coleridge, Edited by her Daughter* (London, 1873), Vol. II, p. 447.
6. For accounts of these editions see Joan DeJean, *Fictions of Sappho: 1546–1937* (University of Chicago Press, Chicago and London, 1989), pp. 117–201; Ruth Vanita,

Sappho and the Virgin Mary: Same-Sex Love and the English Literary Imagination (Columbia University Press, New York, 1996), pp. 41–51; and Margaret Reynolds, *The Sappho Companion* (Chatto and Windus, London, 2000), pp. 149–200. English translations published and widely used during this period include Ambrose Phillips, *The Works of Anacreon and Sappho. Done from the Greek by several hands* (London, 1715); John Addison, *The Works of Anacreon translated into English verse ... To which are added the Odes, Fragments and Epigrams of Sappho* (London, 1735); Francis Fawkes, *The Works of Anacreon, Sappho, Bion, Moschus and Museaus* translated into English by a Gentleman of Cambridge (London, 1760); E. Burnaby Greene, *The Works of Anacreon and Sappho* (London, 1768); and Edward Du Bois, *The Wreath: Composed of Selections from Sappho etc ...* (London, 1799).

7. Mary Ann Stodart, *Female Writers: Thoughts on Their Proper Sphere and on Their Powers of Usefulness* (London, 1842), p. 88. Algernon Charles Swinburne, *The Living Age* 280 (1914), pp. 817–18.
8. Hemans's note reads, 'Suggested by a beautiful sketch, the design of the younger Westmacott. It represents Sappho sitting on a rock above the sea, with her lyre cast at her feet. There is a desolate grace about the whole figure, which seems penetrated with the feeling of utter abandonment.' I discuss this headnote briefly in Chapter 3 'Picturing Sappho' on the pictures and sculptures of Sappho. Richard Westmacott the younger was the son of the eminent sculptor of the same name, and was also best known for his statues. I have been unable to identify the sketch to which Hemans refers. Hemans's headnotes should generally be read as part of her poem. Her related poem 'Corinne at the Capitol' begins with a quotation from Madame de Stael: 'Les femmes doivent penser qu'il est dans cette carrière bien peu de sorte qui puissent valoir la plus obscure vie d'une femme aimée et d'une mère heureuse.' Her poem 'A Parting Song' also quotes from Corinne: '"O mes amis! Rapellez-vous quelquefois mes vers! Mon ame y 'est empreinte" – Corinne'. Yopie Prins takes up my suggestions here to argue that many of the 'picture of Sappho' poems popular with the Victorian women poets become, in effect, mirrors reflecting each other, 'a picture of the picture of the picture of Sappho'; see Yopie Prins, *Victorian Sappho* (Princeton University Press, Princeton New Jersey, 1999), p. 216.
9. Letitia Elizabeth Landon, *The Poetical Works of Letitia Elizabeth Landon* (Longman, Orme, Brown, Greene and Longman, London, 1839), Vol. I, pp. 8–11.
10. Caroline Norton, *The Undying One and Other Poems* (London, 1830), p. 39. Most of the poems cited here are included in *Victorian Women Poets: An Anthology*, eds Angela Leighton and Margaret Reynolds (Basil Blackwell, Oxford, 1995). On Caroline Norton's poetry see Yopie Prins, *Victorian Sappho* (Princeton University Press, Princeton New Jersey, 1999), pp. 209–25. For Elizabeth J. Eames see *The American Female Poets*, ed. Caroline May (Philadelphia, 1848).
11. Christina Rossetti, *The Complete Poems of Christina Rossetti*, ed. R.W. Crump (Louisiana State University Press, Baton Rouge and London, 1990), Vol. III, pp. 266–8.
12. Angela Leighton, *Victorian Women Poets: Writing Against the Heart* (Harvester, Hemel Hempstead, 1992), p. 62. Leighton makes the speaker of Rossetti's poem male, but she also suggests that Rossetti is echoing and remembering the courtly love terms of L.E.L.'s poem *The Improvisatrice*.
13. Adrienne Rich, *Snapshots of a Daughter-in-Law: Poems 1954–1962* (Norton, New York, 1963), pp. 22–3.
14. Christina Rossetti, *The Complete Poems of Christina Rossetti*, ed. R.W. Crump (Louisiana State University Press, Baton Rouge and London, 1990), Vol. III, p. 464.

15. Because femininity is often associated with imagery in Western culture, while masculinity is associated with either the artist-producer of the image, or the viewer-consumer of the art, then concepts of the production and value of the art-object itself become entangled with the ideological effects of sexual difference. See, for instance, John Berger, *Ways of Seeing* (Penguin, London and Harmondsworth, 1972), and Teresa de Lauretis, *Alice Doesn't: Feminism, Semiotics, Cinema* (Indiana University Press, Bloomington Indiana, 1984). Other theorists writing on the assumptions of heterosexuality in the conceptualising of art practice have shown how women artists can use themselves as both subjects and objects in order to undermine these apparent givens. See particularly Lynda Nead, *The Female Nude: Art, Obscenity and Sexuality* (Routlege, London, 1992). The self-reflexive strategies in the work of the Victorian women poets pre-figures these twentieth century practices.
16. Lawrence Lipking, 'Donna Abandonata' in *The Don Giovanni Book: Myths of Seduction and Betrayal*, ed. Jonathan Miller (Faber and Faber, London, 1990), p. 41.
17. Christina Rossetti, 1881, in *The Family Letters of Christina Georgina Rossetti*, ed. William Michael Rossetti (Brown, Langham, London, 1908), p. 95. Rossetti's capacity for self-irony and her resistance to the pretty 'poetess' model is what Max Beerbohm satirised in his famous cartoon where the caption reads:

    > Rossetti, having just had a fresh consignment of 'stunning fabrics' from that new shop in Regent Street, tries hard to prevail on his younger sister to accept at any rate one of these and have a dress made of it from designs to be furnished by himself.
    >
    > D.G.R. 'What *is* the use, Christina, of having a heart like a singing bird and a water-shoot and all the rest of it, if you insist on getting yourself up like a pew-opener?'
    >
    > C.R. 'Well, Gabriel, I don't know – I'm sure you yourself always dress very quietly.'

    Max Beerbohm, *Rossetti and His Circle* (William Heinemann, London, 1922), p. 12. The same self-consciousness about the power of the gaze is in Christina Rossetti's poems – mostly notably in 'In An Artist's Studio', but it is also readily found in the work of the other women poets. Compare Lizzie Siddal's 'The Lust of the Eyes', May Probyn's 'The Model' and Constance Naden's 'The Two Artists', all in *Victorian Women Poets: An Anthology*, ed. Angela Leighton and Margaret Reynolds (Basil Blackwell, Oxford, 1995).
18. Letitia Elizabeth Landon, *The Poetical Works of Letitia Elizabeth Landon* (Longman, Orme, Brown, Greene and Longman, London, 1839), Vol. IV, pp. 89–90, 114.
19. Elizabeth Barrett Browning, *Aurora Leigh* Book II, lines 56–63, ed. Margaret Reynolds (Norton, New York, 1996), pp. 40–1.
20. See Angela Leighton on how the unstoppable flow of the improvising woman poet can be interpreted as unstructured Romantic excess: *Victorian Women Poets: Writing Against the Heart* (Harvester, Hemel Hempstead, 1992), pp. 58–62.
21. Angela Leighton, *Victorian Women Poets: Writing Against the Heart* (Harvester, Hemel Hempstead, 1992), p. 143.
22. George Eliot, 'Armgart' (1870) in *The Legend of Jubal and Other Poems* (William Blackwood and Sons, Edinburgh and London, 1874), pp. 75–148.
23. Elizabeth Barrett Browning, 'A Vision of Poets' (1844); *The Poetical Works of Elizabeth Barrett Browning* (Houghton Mifflin Co., Boston, 1974), p. 132.
24. William Mure, *A Critical History of the Language and Literature of Ancient Greece* (London, 1850), Vol. III, pp. 280–9.

25. Catherine Clément, *Opera: The Undoing of Women*, trans. Betsy Wing (1988: Virago, London, 1989), p. 78, quoting Søren Kierkegaard, *Diary of a Seducer*, trans. Gerd Gillhoff (Unger, Stockholm, 1966).
26. Catherine Clément, *Opera: The Undoing of Women*, trans. Betsy Wing (1988: Virago, London, 1989), p. 79.
27. Compare Hélène Cixous: 'Personally, when I write fiction, I write with my body. My body is active, there is no interruption between the work that my body is actually performing and what is going to happen on the page. I write very near my body and my pulsions ...' See 'Difficult Joys' in *The Body and the Text: Hélène Cixous, Reading and Teaching*, eds Helen Wilcox, Keith McWatters, Ann Thompson and Linda R. Williama (Harvester, Hemel Hempstead, 1990), p. 27.
28. Catherine Clément, *Opera: The Undoing of Women* trans. Betsy Wing (1988: Virago, London, 1989), p. 38. The bravery of the leap is also discussed in relation to the Sublime in my Chapter 2 'Mary Robinson's Attitudes' and in Chapter 3 'Picturing Sappho'.
29. Lawrence Lipking, 'Donna Abandonata' in *The Don Giovanni Book: Myths of Seduction and Betrayal*, ed. Jonathan Miller (Faber and Faber, London, 1990), pp. 37–8. Catherine Clément, *Opera: The Undoing of Women*, trans. Betsy Wing (1988: Virago, London, 1989), pp. 81–2.
30. Elisabeth Bronfen, *Over Her Dead Body: Death, Femininity and the Aesthetic* (Manchester University Press, Manchester, 1992), pp. 142–3.
31. Mary Robinson, *Sappho and Phaon* (London, 1796), p. 18.
32. Roland Barthes, *A Lover's Discourse: Fragments* (1978: Penguin, Harmondsworth, 1990), p. 157.
33. All of these poems are in *Victorian Women Poets: An Anthology*, eds Angela Leighton and Margaret Reynolds (Basil Blackwell, Oxford, 1995), pp. 19, 60, 68, 377.
34. *The Complete Poems of Christina Rossetti*, ed. R.W. Crump (Louisiana State University Press, Baton Rouge and London, 1979–90), Vol. I, p. 58.
35. David M. Robinson, *Sappho and Her Influence* (George G. Harrap, London, 1925), p. 150. Other editions were also available and known, for instance, to writers like Alfred Tennyson, who possessed copies of a French edition by Boissonade (1825) as well as copies of editions by Bergk and others. See my Chapter 4 'Fragments of an Elegy'.
36. Henry Thornton Wharton, *Sappho: Memoir, Text, Selected Renderings with a Literal Translation* (David Stott, London, 1885). This was followed by a second edition (David Stott, London, 1887) and third (John Lane, London, 1895) – with a new cover designed by Aubrey Beardsley. In the new preface to the second edition Wharton discussed the recent publication of the so-called 'Fayum fragment', a parchment unearthed in Egypt some years previously and housed in the collection of the Imperial Egyptian Museum in Berlin. He mentioned the work of the Egypt Exploration Fund and he noted that 'Since the years now and then bring to light some fresh verses of Sappho's, there is still a faint hope that more may still be found. The rich store of parchments and papyri discovered in the Fayum has not all been examined yet.' In 1895, by the time of his third edition, Wharton wrote that he regretted that no more discoveries had yet been made, but he persists in his optimism by citing the fact that in 1890 a manuscript of the hitherto unknown *Mimiambi* of Herondas was discovered on a papyrus roll used to stuff an Egyptian mummy-case. Yopie Prins's first chapter in her *Victorian Sappho* considers the critical approach adopted by Wharton and outlines the influence of his work. See *Victorian Sappho* (Princeton University Press, Princeton New Jersey, 1999), pp. 52–73. Wharton's book was widely read and became the key Sappho text for many English writers. Thomas Hardy bought a copy of the

book, and it was this volume that the young Ezra Pound read in America. See Margaret Reynolds, *The Sappho Companion* (Chatto and Windus, London, 2000), p. 309.

37. After the Fayum Fragment came to public attention through its publication by Friedrich Blass in the *Rheinisches Museum* Vol. XXXV (1880), pp. 287–90 and Wharton's description of it in the second edition of his *Sappho* (David Stott, London, 1887) the Egypt Exploration Fund was set up and Bernard Grenfell and Arthur Hunt, two young scholars from Queen's College, Oxford set out for Egypt in 1895. They eventually settled on a site just outside Oxyrhynchus – now called Behnasa – a town about 120 miles south of Cairo. Large mounds around this town turned out to be rubbish heaps dating from about the fifth century AD but much of the refuse dated from two hundred years earlier, about the third century AD. Over the years they sent back crates of scraps of papyrus to the Ashmolean in Oxford and some of their finds still lie, unsorted and awaiting publication, in the basement of the museum. So far, the finds have been published in 66 volumes under the auspices of what is now called the Egypt Exploration Society. See Margaret Williamson, *Sappho's Immortal Daughters* (Harvard University Press, Cambridge Mass., 1996), pp. 46–9 and Margaret Reynolds, *The Sappho Companion* (Chatto and Windus, London, 2000), pp. 19–20. One of the more romantic papyrus finds were strips used to wrap an Egyptian mummy – strips which turned out to have writing on them which gives us the text for Stesichoros 6 – and the metaphoric implications of torn fragments of ancient lyric writings having been used to preserve a corpse have had a certain imaginative currency for some later writers. See Diane Rayor, *Sappho's Lyre: Archaic Lyric and Women Poets of Ancient Greece* (University of California Press, Berkeley and Los Angeles, 1991), p. 3 and Jeannette H. Foster, *Sex Variant Women in Literature* (Frederick Muller, London, 1958), pp. 19–20.
38. Elizabeth Barrett Browning learned Greek because as a child she insisted upon sharing her brother's lessons with his tutor. She later set herself to study informally with a neighbour at Hope End, the blind Greek scholar Hugh Stuart Boyd. George Eliot taught herself to read Greek as a young adult. As training at the great public schools of the nineteenth century was largely based on tuition in Latin and Greek, education for middle and upper class boys differed widely from the meagre curricula on offer (at home or at school) to their sisters. An awareness of having been denied access to the Classics meant that the intellectual woman of the late nineteenth century almost always aspired to learn Latin and Greek. See Christopher Stray, *Classics Transformed: Schools, Universities, and Society in England, 1830–1960* (Clarendon Press, Oxford, 1998), pp. 46–7, 74, 80–2. For Michael Field see Chris White, 'The Tiresian Poet: Michael Field' in *Victorian Women Poets: A Critical Reader*, ed. Angela Leighton (Basil Blackwell, Oxford, 1996), pp. 148–61, and Chris White '"Poets and Lovers Evermore": Interpreting Female Love in the Poetry and Journals of Michael Field', *Textual Practice*, Vol. 4 (1990), pp. 197–212. See also Yopie Prins, *Victorian Sappho* (Princeton University Press, Princeton New Jersey, 1999), pp. 74–94.
39. Angela Leighton, *Victorian Woman Poets: Writing Against the Heart* (Harvester, Hemel Hempstead, 1992), pp. 202–3.
40. Medea Norsa published her findings on the third century BC potsherd in 'Dai papiri della Societa Italiana: Versi di Saffo in un ostrakon del sec. II a C' in *Annali della Schuola Normale Superiore di Pisa* (1937), pp. 8–15. For modern editions of Fragment 2 see *Sappho et Alcaeus: Fragmenta*, ed. Eva Maria Voigt (Athenaeum-Polak and Van Gennep, Amsterdam, 1971), and the Loeb Classical Library *Greek Lyric I: Sappho and Alcaeus* ed. David A. Campbell (Harvard University Press, Cambridge Mass., 1992).
41. Richard Jenkyns, *Three Classical Poets: Sappho, Catullus and Juvenal* (Duckworth, London, 1982), p. 32.

42. Michael Field, *Long Ago* (George Bell and Sons, London, 1889), pp. 68–69. See Yopie Prins, *Victorian Sappho* (Princeton University Press, Princeton New Jersey, 1999), pp. 94–111.
43. Michael Field, *Long Ago* (George Bell and Sons, London, 1889), p. 130. The artefacts to which the Fields refer are a vase painting dating from the late sixth century BC which is now in the Czartoryski Collection 142333 in the National Museum, Warsaw, and a red figure *hydria* dating from the mid to late fifth century BC now in the National Museum in Athens, NM 1260. These images are reproduced in my *The Sappho Companion* (Chatto and Windus, London, 2000), pp. 67, 75.
44. John Addington Symonds, *The Letters of John Addington Symonds* eds Herbert M. Schueller and Robert L. Peters (Wayne State University Press, Detroit, 1967–69), Vol. II, p. 683.
45. John Addington Symonds, *The Letters of John Addington Symonds*, eds Herbert M. Schueller and Robert L. Peters (Wayne State University Press, Detroit, 1967–69), Vol. III, pp. 108–9.
46. Agnes Mary Robinson (later Darmesteter, later Duclaux), *The Collected Poems, Lyrical and Narrative of Mary Robinson* (T. Fisher Unwin, London, 1902), pp. 19–20.
47. Mary Coleridge, *Poems* (London, 1908), p. 210. See also poems such as:

    CLVIII
    The sum of loss I have not reckoned yet,
    I cannot tell.
    For ever it was morning when we met,
    Night when we bade farewell!

    Poems (London, 1908), p. 154. For William Cory, see *Victorian Women Poets: An Anthology*, eds Angela Leighton and Margaret Reynolds (Basil Blackwell, Oxford, 1995), p. 610. Mary Coleridge's annotated Philoctetes and her Antigone – with notes taken down from Cory's instruction are both in the Eton College Library. I am grateful to Michael Meredith for this reference.
48. Mary Robinson, *Sappho and Phaon* (London, 1796). See my Chapter 2 'Mary Robinson's Attitudes'. See also Jerome McGann, *The Poetics of Sensibility* (Clarendon Press, Oxford, 1995), pp. 64–5. Rather ironically Elizabeth Wanning Harries makes the point that Petrarch was one of the first writers of the Renaissance to experiment with the idea of the deliberately contrived fragment in his *'rime sparsi'*, scattered rhymes. See *The Unfinished Manner: Essays on the Fragment in the Later Eighteenth Century* (University Press of Virginia, Charlottesville and London, 1994), pp. 14–20.
49. See my Chapter 8 on H.D. 'The Island and the Mirror'. For a selection of works by Agnes Mary Robinson, Mary Coleridge, May Probyn and Charlotte Mew see *Victorian Women Poets: An Anthology*, eds Angela Leighton and Margaret Reynolds (Basil Blackwell, Oxford, 1995).
50. Mary Coleridge, *The Collected Poems of Mary Coleridge*, ed. Theresa Whistler (Hart Davis, London, 1954), pp. 176–7. Michael Field, *Wild Honey from Various Thyme* (T. Fisher Unwin, London, 1908), p. 41.
51. Michael Field, *Long Ago* (George Bell and Sons, London, 1889), p. vii. The translations are from H.T. Wharton, *Sappho: Memoir, Text, Selected Renderings with a Literal Translation* (John Lane, London, 1887), pp. 77, 48.
52. H.T. Wharton, *Sappho: Memoir,Text, Selected Renderings with a Literal Translation* (David Stott, London, 1887), p. 106.
53. Michael Field, *Long Ago* (George Bell and Sons, London, 1889), p. 3.

54. Michael Field, *Long Ago* (George Bell and Sons, London, 1889), p. 127.
55. Chris White, '"Poets and Lovers Evermore": Interpreting Female Love in the Poetry and Journals of Michael Field', *Textual Practice*, Vol. 4 (1990), p.201.
56. Agnes Mary Robinson (later Darmesteter, later Duclaux), *The Collected Poems, Lyrical and Narrative of Mary Robinson* (T. Fisher Unwin, London, 1902), pp. 20–1.
57. See my Chapter 8 on H.D. 'The Island and the Mirror'. For the kinds of 'collaborative' Sapphic fictions that were developed in France and England in the early part of the twentieth century see Margaret Reynolds, *The Sappho Companion* (Chatto and Windus, London, 2000), pp. 289–306.
58. Michael Field, *Underneath the Bough* (George Bell and Sons, London, 1893), p. 51. After the first edition 'An Invitation' was omitted from later editions of the collection. 'A Girl' also appeared in *Underneath the Bough*, p. 88, and 'A Palimpsest' was published in *Wild Honey from Various Thyme* (T. Fisher Unwin, London, 1908), p. 180. Both are included in *Victorian Women Poets: an Anthology*, eds Angela Leighton and Margaret Reynolds, (Basil Blackwell, Oxford, 1995), pp. 495, 504.
59. Michael Field, *Wild Honey from Various Thyme* (T. Fisher Unwin, London, 1908), p. 166.

6. Poisonous honey

1. *Pall Mall Gazette*, 11 October 1889. Charles Louis Napoleon Bonaparte (1808–1873) was elected president of the republican government of France after the revolution of 1848. In 1851 he staged a *coup d'état*, ratified retrospectively by plebiscite, and in 1852 he brought about the restoration of Empire and declared himself Emperor Napoleon III. After a series of parliamentary crises the Second Empire came to an end and the Third Republic was proclaimed in 1870. Louis Napoleon and his wife the Empress Eugenie (1825–1920) fled into exile and his last years were spent in England.
2. Charles Baudelaire, *Les Fleurs du mal* (1857), ed. Antoine Adam (Classiques Garnier, Paris, 1994), p. 3.
3. *Charles Baudelaire: His Life by Théophile Gautier* (1868), translated into English with selections from his poems, and an essay on his influence by Guy Thorne (Greening and Co., London, 1915). *Les Fleurs du mal and Other Studies* by Algernon Charles Swinburne, ed. Edmund Gosse (printed for private circulation, London, 1913). 'Ave Atque Vale' was published in Swinburne's *Poems and Ballads, Second Series* (1878). Algernon Charles Swinburne to E.C. Stedman, 21 January 1874, in *The Swinburne Letters*, ed. Cecil Y. Lang, 6 vols (Yale University Press and Oxford University Press, New Haven and London, 1962), Vol. II, p. 270.
4. Algernon Charles Swinburne, *Poems and Ballads, Second Series* (1878), in *The Complete Works of Algernon Charles Swinburne*, eds Edmund Gosse and T.J. Wise, 20 vols (William Heineman, London, 1925), Vol. 3, p. 60.
5. The book given to Dorian Gray is generally thought to be based upon J.K. Huysman's *A Rebours* (1884), but as it is a book where the life of the senses was described in terms of mystical philosophy any number of influential books might be a source for Wilde's inspiration. Wilde, along with the rest of his generation, certainly knew *Mademoiselle de Maupin* well and there is a curious passage in Gautier's novel concerning d'Albert's worship of beauty which may even suggest the germ of the idea for *The Picture of Dorian Gray*: see Théophile Gautier, *Mademoiselle de Maupin* (1835) trans. G.F. Monkshood and Ernest Tristan (Greening and Co., London, 1917?), pp. 92–3. This work is referred to for the rest of this chapter as Gautier (1835).
6. Gautier (1835), pp. 127–8, 137.

7. Gautier (1835), pp. 176–7.
8. Gautier (1835), pp. 292, 294–5. Although Gautier's version of the young girl disguised as a page in order to follow her lord (as she appears to be) is used first of all for it's voyeuristic possibilities here, the motif was one widely used by women writers of the period to fantasise a means of escaping the restrictions of sex and gender conventions. Mary Shelley wrote a short story on this theme in 'The False Rhyme: A Tale' in *The Keepsake* (London, 1830), pp. 265–8. Elizabeth Barrett Browning entertained as a child the dream of running away to be Byron's page and in adulthood used the theme to make a pointed criticism of the separate spheres of masculine and feminine in 'The Romaunt of the Page', *Finden's Tableaux* (London, 1839).
9. Gautier, (1835), pp. 302–3, 309.
10. Gautier (1835), p. 311.
11. Gautier (1835), pp. 312, 314.
12. Gautier (1835), pp. 236, 144, 151.
13. Gautier (1835), pp. 151, 155, 131, 133, 136, 134.
14. Gautier (1835), pp. 152, 131, 148–9, 163.
15. Gautier (1835), pp. 89, 90, 142.
16. Gautier (1835), pp. 152, 151, 258.
17. Terry Castle, *The Apparitional Lesbian: Female Homosexuality and Modern Culture* (Columbia University Press, New York, 1993), pp. 35–6. Castle's chapter on Marie Antoinette in the same volume (pp. 107–49) suggests another connection. Among the many scurrilous accusations levelled against Marie Antoinette in the years leading up to the French Revolution and her eventual execution, one rumour was that she was a lover of women and that the Duchess of Polignac, in particular, was her *paramour*. See Lynn Hunt, 'The Many Bodies of Marie Antoinette: Political Pornography and the Problem of the Feminine in the French Revolution' in *Eroticism and the Body Politic*, ed. Lynn Hunt (Johns Hopkins University Press, Baltimore, 1991), pp. 108–30. This gossip was widespread and long-lived, along with other well-known tales of trysts in the Trianon. In *Mademoiselle de Maupin* the scene between Madeleine and Rosette set in a rustic garden pavilion may well have triggered these associations for Gautier's contemporary audience.
18. For a brief summary of the numerous lesbian-themed fictions of the early nineteenth century see Jeanette H. Foster, *Sex Variant Women in Literature: A Historical and Quantitative Survey* (Frederick Muller Ltd, London, 1958), pp. 51–68. In France such titles included: Philip Cuisin, *Clementine: Orpheline et Androgyne* (1819); Henri de Latouche, *Fragoletta* (1829), which presented a scene between Queen Caroline of Naples, Marie Antoinette's sister, and Emma Hamilton taking place in a marble bath; Honoré de Balzac, *La Fille aux yeux d'or* (1835) and *Seraphitus-Seraphita* (1854); and Céleste Venard, comtesse de Chabrillon, *La Sapho* (1858). On the more specifically Sappho-themed fictions and dramas from the French tradition including those by Arsène Houssaye and Philoxène Boyer, see Joan DeJean, *Fictions of Sappho 1546–1937* (Chicago University Press, Chicago and London, 1989), pp. 266–9.
19. Charles Baudelaire, *Correspondence*, ed. Claude Pichois (Gallimard, Bibliothèque de la Pleide, Paris, 1973), Vol. I, p. 378. Joan DeJean *Fictions of Sappho, 1546–1937* (University of Chicago Press, Chicago and London, 1989), p. 269.
20. Joan DeJean, *Fictions of Sappho, 1546–193* (University of Chicago Press, Chicago and London, 1989), p. 268. The poet Théodore de Banville was also one of those promoting an artistic interest in Sappho during this period; he collaborated with Boyer on his 1850 play, wrote an influential review of the work which pronounced that 'the novel of Sapho is our history ... Monsieur Philoxène Boyer's Sapho, like that

of Pradier, like that of Clesinger, is a profoundly contemporary work', and he wrote a poem 'Erinna' which was influenced by Baudelaire' s lesbian-themed poems and which, when published in his volume *Les Exiles* (1861) concludes what DeJean calls 'this extended group': DeJean (1989), *Fictions of Sappho*, p. 268.

21. See Jean Richter, 'Restitution à Gautier du Texte "Sapho"', *Bulletin de la Société Théophile Gautier*, Vol. 7 (1985), pp. 163–8.
22. F.W. Leakey suggests that during the period 1845–47 when Baudelaire was still working with the projected title of *Les Lesbiennes*, he intended to create an eponymous first section incorporating the three surviving lesbian poems into a longer type of verse-novel. For a variety of reasons Baudelaire's collection took a long time in preparation and it was only toward the end of 1856 that he found a publisher for his new title of *Les Fleurs du mal* in Poulet-Malassis. By this time Baudelaire was aware, especially in view of the contemporary trial for indecency of Flaubert's novel *Madame Bovary*, that the repressive moral regime of the Second Empire was not likely to look with favour on his own work. In a futile attempt to ward off accusations of indecency Baudelaire included the famous initial address to the reader 'Au Lecteur' which implicates the audience in his subjects and their treatment, and, very late on during the publication process, he added the condemning last five stanzas to the poem 'Delphine et Hippolyte'. See F.W. Leakey, *Baudelaire: Les Fleurs du mal* (Cambridge University Press, Cambridge, 1992), pp. 3, 5, 10.
23. Charles Baudelaire, *Les Fleurs du mal*, ed. Antoine Adam (Classiques Garnier, Paris, 1994), pp. 166–9. All translations are mine unless otherwise stated.
24. See Jean Léon Gérôme's painting of 'Phryné' (date unknown).
25. Joan DeJean, *Fictions of Sappho, 1546–1936* (University of Chicago Press, Chicago and London, 1989), pp. 271–2. Walter Benjamin, *Charles Baudelaire: A Lyric Poet in the Era of High Capitalism* (1969), trans. Harry Zohn (New Left books, London, 1973), pp. 90–4.
26. Charles Baudelaire, 'Femmes Damnées', in *Les Fleurs du mal*, ed. Antoine Adam (Classiques Garniers, Paris, 1994), pp. 131–2.
27. Charles Baudelaire, 'Delphine et Hippolyte', in *Les Fleurs du mal*, ed. Antoine Adam (Classiques Garniers, Paris, 1994), pp. 169–72.
28. Charles Baudelaire (attributed), 'Sapho', see Baudelaire: *The Complete Verse*, Vol. I, with an introduction and translations by Francis Scarfe (Anvil Press Poetry, London, 1986), pp. 379–80.
29. Julia Kristeva, 'Baudelaire, or Infinity, Perfume and Punk' in *Tales of Love*, trans. Leon S. Roudiez (Columbia University Press, New York, 1987), p. 328. George Blin was the author of *Le Sadisme de Baudelaire* (Corti, Paris, 1948).
30. See Lyn Hatherly Wilson, *Sappho's Sweet Bitter Songs: Configurations of Female and Male in Ancient Greek Lyric* (Routledge, London, 1996), pp. 60–2, 66–7. Wilson argues that the aggressively violent characterisation of Sappho's image of Eros is also found in Homer's *Odyssey* as well as in the works of Archilochus. On Sappho's Fragment 130 see also Jane McIntosh Snyder, *Lesbian Desire in the Lyrics of Sappho* (Columbia University Press, New York, 1997), pp. 22–3. *Greek Lyric I: Sappho and Alcaeus*, Loeb Classical Library, ed. and trans. David A. Campbell (1982: Harvard University Press, Cambridge Mass. and London, 1990), pp. 146–7, *Sappho: A New Translation*, trans. Mary Barnard (University of California Press, Berkeley, Los Angeles and London, 1958), p. 53, *Sappho: Poems and Fragments*, trans. Josephine Balmer (Bloodaxe Books, Newcastle-upon-Tyne, 1992), p. 32. *Sappho's Lyre: Archaic Lyric and Women Poets of Ancient Greece*, trans. Diane Rayor (University of California Press, Berkeley, Los Angeles and Oxford, 1991), p. 62.

31. John Winkler, 'Double Consciousness in Sappho's Lyrics' in *The Constraints of Desire: The Anthropology of Sex and Gender in Ancient Greece* (Routledge, New York and London, 1990), pp. 162–87.
32. *Greek Lyric I: Sappho and Alcaeus*, Loeb Classical Library, ed. and trans. David A. Campbell (1982: Harvard University Press, Cambridge Mass. and London, 1990), pp. 78–81. Lyn Hatherly Wilson, *Sappho's Sweet Bitter Songs: Configurations of Female and Male in Ancient Greek Lyric* (Routledge, London, 1996), pp. 60–2.
33. Charles Baudelaire, 26 December 1853, *Dernières Lettres inédities à sa mère* (Crepet, Paris, 1926), pp. 44–5.
34. Walter Benjamin, *Charles Baudelaire: A Lyric Poet in the Era of High Capitalism*, trans. Harry Zohn (1969: New Left Books, London, 1973), p. 97.
35. See Patricia Clements, *Charles Baudelaire and the English Tradition* (Princeton University Press, Princeton New Jersey, 1985), pp. 106–7. The intertextuality of Baudelaire's poetry works both in terms of his influence on later poets, and in his use of earlier poets, as I argue here in relation to Sappho. See Jonathan Culler, 'Intertextuality and Interpretation: Baudelaire's *Correspondances*', in *Nineteenth-Century French 'Poetry: Introductions to Close Reading*, ed. Christopher Prendergast (Cambridge University Press, Cambridge, 1990), pp. 118–37.
36. Julia Kristeva, ' Baudelaire, or Infinity, Perfume and Punk' in *Tales of Love*, trans. Leon S. Roudiez (Columbia University Press, New York, 1987), p. 338.
37. Joan Rivière, 'Womanliness as Masquerade' (1929), in *Formations of Fantasy*, eds Victor Burgin, James Donald and Cora Kaplan (Methuen, London and New York, 1986), pp. 35–44. Simone de Beauvoir, *The Second Sex* (1949), trans. H.M. Parshley (Vintage, New York, 1974).
38. Charles Baudelaire, 'Fusées', in *Oeuvres complètes* (Bibliothèque de la Pleide, Gallimard, Paris, 1975), Vol. I, pp. 652, 659.
39. Angela Carter, *The Sadeian Woman: An Exercise in Cultural History* (Virago, London, 1979). Angela Carter, *'The Bloody Chamber' and Other Stories* (1979: London, 1995), p. 15. 'He stripped me, gourmand that he was, as if he were stripping the leaves off an artichoke ... He approached this familiar treat with a weary appetite. And when nothing but my scarlet, palpitating core remained, I saw, in the mirror, the living image of an etching by Rops ... the child with her sticklike limbs, naked but for her button boots, her gloves, shielding the last repository of her modesty; and the old, monocled lecher who examined her, limb by limb. He in his London tailoring; she, bare as a lamb chop. Most pornographic of all confrontations.'
40. See Nancy Vickers, 'The Body Re-Membered: Petrarchan Lyrics and the Strategies of Description', in *Mimesis: From Mirror to Method, Augustine to Descartes*, eds J.D. Lyons and S.G. Nichols (University Press of New England, Hanover New Hampshire, 1982), pp. 100–9.
41. See Peter Fuller, 'The Venus and "Internal Objects"' in *Art and Psychoanalysis* (Writers and Readers, London, 1980), pp. 71–129; Diana Fuss, *Essentially Speaking: Feminism, Nature and Difference* (Routledge, London, 1989); Naomi Wolf, *The Beauty Myth* (Chatto and Windus, London, 1990), and Lynda Nead, *The Female Nude: Art Obscenity and Sexuality* (Routledge, London, 1992).
42. Elaine Showalter, *Sexual Anarchy: Gender and Culture at the Fin De Siècle* (Bloomsbury, London, 1991), pp. 128–33, and Elisabeth Bronfen, *Over Her Dead Body: Death, Femininity and the Aesthetic* (Manchester University Press, Manchester, 1992), pp. 200–2. The artist Elisabeth Vigée-LeBrun inspected an array of anatomical Venuses at the workshop of Felice Fontana in Florence during her visit to Italy in 1792. She was impressed by these productions but also disturbed by them, especially those

which unveiled the flesh of the wax woman to reveal the intricacies of the internal organs: 'Fontana told me to approach this figure, then, raising a kind of cover, he offered to my regard all the intestines, turned as in our bodies. This sight made such an impression on me that I sensed myself near to being sick.' Later she said, 'it was impossible to distract myself from it to the point that I could not see a [woman] without mentally stripping her of her clothing and of her skin which put me into a deplorable nervous state': Elisabeth Vigée-LeBrun, *Souvenirs*, ed. Claudine Herrmann (Des Femmes, Paris, 1986), quoted in Mary D. Sherriff, *The Exceptional Woman: Elisabeth Vigée-LeBrun and the Cultural Politics of Art* (University of Chicago Press, Chicago and London, 1996), pp. 17–18.

43. Maxime Du Camp, *Les Convulsions de Paris* (Hachette, Paris, 1889), Vol. II, pp. 189–90, quoted in Elaine Showalter, *Sexual Anarchy: Gender and Culture at the Fin de Siècle* (Bloomsbury, London, 1990), p. 147. Courbet's *L'Origine du monde* is now in the Musée d'Orsay in Paris.
44. Bram Dijkstra, *Idols of Perversity: Fantasies of Feminine Evil in Fin de Siècle Culture* (Oxford University Press, Oxford, 1986). Elaine Showalter, *Sexual Anarchy: Gender and Culture in the Fin de Siècle* (Bloomsbury, London, 1990). Elisabeth Bronfen, *Over Her Dead Body: Death, Femininity and the Aesthetic* (Manchester University Press, Manchester, 1992). Linda Dowling, *Language and Decadence in the Victorian Fin de Siècle* (Princeton University Press, Princeton New Jersey, 1986). Rebecca Stott, *The Fabrication of the Late Victorian Femme Fatale* (Macmillan, London, 1992).
45. Sigmund Freud, 'Fetishism' (1927), in *The Standard Edition of the Complete Psychological Works of Sigmund Freud*, trans. James Strachey (Hogarth Press, London, 1953–74), Vol. XXI, pp. 149–57. However unstable and suspect Freud's theory may be – and the fantasy of the 'phallic mother' has been particularly subject to criticism – Freud is often useful in reading nineteenth century texts because his world view came out of those same texts. In effect, Freud's thinking shares a particularised historical moment with many texts of the period.
46. Théophile Gautier, *Charles Baudelaire: His Life*, trans. Guy Thorne (Greening and Co., London, 1915), pp. 31–2.
47. Théophile Gautier, *Mademoiselle de Maupin* (1835), trans. G.F. Monkshood and Ernest Tristan (Greening and Co., London, 1917?), p. 89.
48. Compare Mark Simpson's reading of another transvestite text, Neil Jordan's film *The Crying Game* (1992) in 'A Crying Shame: Transvestism and Misogyny in "The Crying Game"', in *Male Impersonators: Men Performing Masculinity* (Cassell, London, 1994), pp. 164–76.

7. Sappho's fatal book

1. Algernon Charles Swinburne, *Poems and Ballads, Second Series* (1878: Chatto and Windus, London, 1887), pp. 71–83.
2. See *Swinburne: The Critical Heritage*, ed. Clyde K. Hyder (Routledge Kegan Paul, London, 1970), pp. 100–18.
3. Robert Buchanan, 'The Fleshly School of Poetry' in *The Contemporary Review* (1871), quoted in *The Victorian Poet: Poetics and Persona*, ed. Joseph Bristow (Croom Helm, London, 1987), pp. 139–45.
4. See Yopie Prins, *Victorian Sappho* (Princeton University Press, Princeton New Jersey, 1999), pp. 112–73. Camille Paglia and Catherine Maxwell have also written on Swinburne's intertextual relation with Sappho's work, and Maxwell also makes the link

via Swinburne's interest in and admiration for the work of Charles Baudelaire. See Camille Paglia, *Sexual Personae: Art and Decadence From Nefertiti to Emily Dickinson* (Yale University Press, New Haven and London, 1990), pp. 460–88 and Catherine Maxwell, *The Female Sublime from Milton to Swinburne: Bearing Blindness* (Manchester University Press, Manchester, 2001), pp. 31–46, 178–221.

5. *Justine*, 1st edn, in *Oeuvres complètes*, ed. Jean-Jacques Pauvert (Paris, 1955–70), Vol. III, p. 91. Swinburne wrote to Richard Monckton Milnes, 'I have just read "Justine ou les Malheurs de la Vertu"', 18 August 1862: see *The Swinburne Letters* ed. Cecil Y. Lang (Yale University Press, New Haven and London, 1959–62), Vol. I, p. 53. Cecil Lang says that on this occasion Swinburne actually read the revised version of 1797 entitled *La Nouvelle Justine de Sade.*
6. Algernon Charles Swinburne to Lord Houghton, 31 March 1864. *The Swinburne Letters*, ed. Cecil Y. Lang (Yale University Press, New Haven and London, 1959–62), Vol. I, p. 98.
7. Algernon Charles Swinburne to Edmund Gosse, 14 January 1876. *The Swinburne Letters*, Vol. III, pp. 116–17. His reference is to Byron's *Don Juan* (1819):

   Ovid's a rake, as half his verses show him,
   Anacreon's morals are a still worse sample,
   Catullus scarcely had a decent poem,
   I don't think Sappho's Ode a good example,
   Although Longinus tells us there is no hymn
   Where the sublime soars forth on wings more ample.

8. Algernon Charles Swinburne to Dante Gabriel Rossetti, 22 February 1870. *The Swinburne Letters*, Vol. II, p. 101.
9. Swinburne's letters to George Powell and to Simeon Solomon are full of sexual wordplay, much of it unremarked and unannotated by his editor. For example, see his letter to George Powell of 26 April 1871 where he is much amused by an erroneous description of the novel *Mrs St Clair's Son* (1868) by Lady Blake:

   > I wrote yesterday to Simeon to tell him a truly shocking thing – I have seen advertised for sale or hire (Oh Monsieur!) 'Mrs. Sinclair's Daughter by Lady Blake'!!! This is tribadism in excelsis. Even the immortal foundress of Lesbianism is not recorded to have begotten children on Atthis, Anactoria, or Cydro, and then let them out to hire!
   >
   > I wish you well through your bother with that wretched boy whom I would commend to the notice of Father Clement did I know his address. Dean Buggeridge, I hear, is now in town – he has taken lodgings for the season in Quimlico.

   The Swinburne Letters, Vol. II. pp. 140–1. 'Father Clement' is a reference to *Justine*. 'Dean Buggeridge' and 'Quimlico' are slang jokes.
10. Algernon Charles Swinburne to George Powell, 28 July 1868. *The Swinburne Letters*, Vol. I, p. 305.
11. See Yopie Prins, *Victorian Sappho* (Princeton University Press, Princeton New Jersey, 2000), pp. 112–73. See also Catherine Maxwell, *The Female Sublime from Milton to Swinburne: Bearing Blindness* (Manchester University Press, Manchester, 2001), pp. 31–46, 178–221; Margot K. Louis *Swinburne and His Gods: The Roots and Growth of an Agnostic Poetry* (McGill-Queens University Press Montreal and London, 1990), pp.

20–3, and Douglas Bush, *Mythology and the Romantic Tradition in English Poetry* (Harvard University Press, Cambridge Mass., 1937), p. 351.

12. Algernon Charles Swinburne, 'Ave Atque Vale' in *Poems and Ballads: Second Series* (1878: Chatto and Windus, London, 1887), pp. 74–5.
13. Max Beerbohm, *Rossetti and His Circle* (William Heinemann, London, 1922), p. 11. Rossetti's sofa includes a visual memory of Juliette Récamier's sofa in Jacques Louis David's famous portrait. Beerbohm turns Rossetti's sofa into a running joke throughout *Rossetti and His Circle* for it – or a glimpse of it along with the slippered feet – appears also in 'A Man from Hymettus' portraying Frederic Leighton haranguing Rossetti (p. 19), and in 'Quis Custodiet Ipsum Custodem?' where Theodore Watts is shown forbidding Hall Caine to read Rossetti for fear of the work giving him nightmares (p. 20).
14. Algernon Charles Swinburne, *'Les Fleurs du mal' and Other Studies*, ed. Edmund Gosse (printed for private circulation, London, 1913), p. 8.
15. Algernon Charles Swinburne, 'The Masque of Queen Bersabe', in *Poems and Ballads, First Series* (1866: Chatto and Windus, London, 1887), p. 263.
16. Algernon Charles Swinburne, 'Satia Te Sanguine' in *Poems and Ballads, First Series* (1866: Chatto and Windus, London, 1887), pp. 96–7.
17. Algernon Charles Swinburne, 'Sapphics' in *Poems and Ballads, First Series* (1866: Chatto and Windus, London, 1887), pp. 232–5.
18. See M.L. West, *Introduction to Greek Metre* (Clarendon Press, Oxford, 1987), p. 34.
19. *Greek Lyric I, Sappho and Alcaeus*, Loeb Classical Library, trans. D.A. Campbell (Harvard University Press, Cambridge Mass., 1982), pp. 52–5. *Sappho: Poems and Fragment*, trans. Josephine Balmer (Bloodaxe Books, Newcastle-upon-Tyne, 1992), p. 66.
20. Algernon Charles Swinburne, 'Sapphics', *Poems and Ballads, First Series* (1866: Chatto and Windus, 1887), p. 232.
21. Jerome McGann, *Swinburne: An Experiment in Criticism* (University of Chicago Press, Chicago and London, 1972), p. 115.
22. *Greek Lyric I, Sappho and Alcaeus*, Loeb Classical Library, trans. D.A. Campbell (1982: Harvard University Press, Cambridge Mass. and London, 1990), pp. 52–5.
23. Algernon Charles Swinburne, 'Anactoria', *Poems and Ballads, First Series* (1866: Chatto and Windus, London, 1887), pp. 64–74.
24. Delighting, as Swinburne did, in both his letters and his poetry, in risking saying that which should not be said, especially about the body, it is interesting that his elaborately obscuring poetic image here flirts with a reference to menstruation.
25. The notion of the death and subsequent anonymity of Sappho's girls – as opposed to Sappho's own literary immortality – draws on Swinburne's knowledge of another two of Sappho's Fragments: 32 and 68 in Wharton, and 55 and 147 in Loeb. 'But when you die you will lie there, and afterwards there will never be any recollection of you or any longing for you since you have no share in the roses of Pieria: unseen in the house of Hades also, flown from our midst, you will go to and fro among the shadowy corpses': Loeb translation, and 'Someone, I say, will remember us in the future': Loeb translation. See *Greek Lyric I: Sappho and Alcaeus*, Loeb Classical Library, ed. David A. Campbell (1982: Harvard University Press, Cambridge Mass., 1990), pp. 99, 159.
26. See my Chapter 5, 'The Woman Poet Sings Sappho's Last Song', in this volume.
27. *Greek Lyric I: Sappho and Alcaeus*, Loeb Classical Library, ed. David A. Campbell (1982: Harvard University Press, Cambridge Mass. and London, 1990), pp. 152–3.
28. Algernon Charles Swinburne, 'On the Cliffs', *Songs of the Springtides* (1880). In Algernon Charles Swinburne, *Selected Poems*, ed. L.M. Findlay (Carcanet, Manchester, 1982), pp. 185–96.

29. At lines 299–306 of 'On the Cliffs' Swinburne includes repeated fragments translated from Sappho's Fragment 1, the so-called 'Ode to Aphrodite', marked out in italics:

> *O thou of divers-coloured mind, O thou*
> *Deathless, God's daughter subtle-souled* – lo, now,
> Now too the song above all songs, in flight
> Higher than the day-star's height,
> And sweet as sound from the moving wings of night!
> *Thou of the divers-coloured seat* – behold,
> Her very song of old! –
> *O deathless, O God's daughter subtle-souled!*

Swinburne demonstrates his Greek scholarship here, by included both 'divers-coloured mind' and 'divers-coloured seat', both of which are readings derived from the word *poikilothron* or *poikilotron* in Sappho which, depending on the edition, is variously recorded and translated as 'many-coloured throne' or 'many-coloured mind'. At lines 333–5 of 'On the Cliffs' Swinburne returns again to Fragment 1 offering yet another English translation:

> *Child of God, close craftswoman, I beseech thee,*
> *Bid not ache nor agony break nor master,*
> *Lady, my spirit.*

At lines 325–9 he similarly offers versions in English of Sappho's Fragment 49 which, in the Loeb translation, is 'I loved you, Atthis, once long ago':

> *I loved thee,* – hark, one tenderer note than all –
> *Atthis, of old time, once* – one low long fall,
> Sighing – one long low lovely loveless call,
> Dying – one pause in song so flamelike fast –
> *Atthis, long since in old time overpast* –
> One soft first pause and last.

30. Roland Barthes, *A Lover's Discourse: Fragments* (1977), trans. Richard Howard (Penguin, London, 1990), p. 71. The allusion to Albertine refers to an episode in Marcel Proust's *A la récherche du temps perdu.*
31. Roland Barthes, *A Lover's Discourse: Fragments* (1977), trans. Richard Howard (Penguin, London, 1990), p. 72.
32. Théophile Gautier, *Mademoiselle de Maupin* (1835), trans. G.F. Monkshood and Ernest Tristan (Greening and Co., London, 1917), p. 311.
33. Roland Barthes, *A Lover's Discourse: Fragments* (1977), trans. Richard Howard (Penguin, London, 1990), pp. 95–6.
34. Jean Paul Sartre, *l'Idiot de la famille* (Gallimard, Paris, 1971), 2 vols. Gustave Flaubert actually did steal the slippers of his mistress Louise Colet in the early days of their liaison, as well as a bloodstained handkerchief and various other personal items. Sartre concludes that Flaubert, like any fetishist, preferred this 'denoted object of absence' to the real thing because it allowed him 'an erection in the void'.
35. Charles Baudelaire, 'Lesbos' in *Les Fleurs du mal* (1857), ed. Antoine Adam (Classiques Garnier, Paris, 1994), p. 167.
36. John Addington Symonds, *Studies of the Greek Poets: First Series* (Smith, Elder and Co., London, 1873), pp. 139–40.

37. Linda Dowling, *Language and Decadence in the Victorian Fin de Siècle* (Princeton University Press, Princeton, 1986), pp. 133, 135, quoting Friedrich Nietzsche, *Der Fall Wagner* (1888), and Havelock Ellis, 'A Note on Paul Bourget' (1889) in *Views and Reviews: A Selection of Uncollected Articles 1884–1932*, First and Second series (Houghton and Mifflin, Boston and New York, 1932), p. 52.
38. Arthur Symons, 'A Note Upon George Meredith', in *Studies in Prose and Verse* (E.P. Dutton, New York, 1922), p. 149. Arthur Symons had already written a well-known analysis of Decadence in 'The Decadent Movement in Literature', *Harper's New Monthly Magazine*, Vol. 87 (November 1893).
39. Linda Dowling, *Language and Decadence in the Victorian Fin de Siècle* (Princeton University Press, Princeton New Jersey, 1986), p. xii.
40. Heinrich Friedrich Magnus Volger, *Sapphus Lesbiae Carmina et Fragmenta recensuit, comentario illustravit, schemata musica adjecit, et indices confecit Henr. Frid. Magnus Volger* (Leipzig, 1810); Friedrich Gottlieb Welcker, *Sappho von einem herrschenden Vorurtheil befreyt* (Gottingen, 1816); Christian Friedrich Neue, *Sapphonis Mytilenaeae Fragmenta: Specimen operae in omnibus artis graecorum Lyricae reliquiis excepto Pindaro collocandae* (Berlin, 1827); Theodor Bergk, *de Aliquot fragmentis Sapphonis et Alcaei, Rheinisches Museum fur Philologie* (Bonn, 1835); Theodor Bergk, *Anthologia Lyrica* (Leipzig, 1854), Theodor Bergk; *Poetae Lyrici Graeci* (Leipzig, 1843). Henry Thornton Wharton used the 1882 fourth edition of Bergk's *Poetae Lyrici Graeci* as the basis for his Sappho texts in *Sappho: Memoir, Text, Selected Renderings with a Literal Translation* (John Lane, London, 1895). On the importance and influence of Wharton's book, see Yopie Prins, *Victorian Sappho* (Princeton University Press, Princeton New Jersey, 2000).
41. Haldane MacFall, *Aubrey Beardsley: The Man and His Work* (John Lane, London, 1928), pp. 80, 83, quoted in Linda Dowling, *Language and Decadence in the Victorian Fin de Siècle* (Princeton University Press, Princeton New Jersey, 1986), p. 148.
42. Arthur Symons, 'The Decadent Movement in Literature', *Harper's New Monthly Magazine*, Vol. 87 (November, 1893), pp. 859–60.
43. John Addington Symonds, *Studies of the Greek Poets: First Series* (Smith Elder and Co., London, 1873), pp. 136–7.
44. See particularly Gillian Beer, *Darwin's Plots: Evolutionary Narrative in Darwin, George Eliot and Nineteenth Century Fiction* (Routledge, London, 1982).
45. Théophile Gautier, *Charles Baudelaire: His Life by Théophile Gautier*, trans. Guy Thorne (Greening and Co., London, 1915), pp. 35–6.
46. Oscar Wilde, *De Profundis* (1905), in *The Complete Works of Oscar Wilde* with an introduction by Vyvyan Holland (Collins, London, 1988), p. 926. In spite of his education in the Classics, Wilde does not often refer to Sappho except in a very general sense as the first woman poet. As a young man, writing in a friend's autograph album, Wilde answered the question 'Your favourite poetesses?' with 'Sappho and Lady Wilde' (Album of Adderley Millar Howard, 1877. Sold at Christie's, London, May 1997). In his poetry, Sappho appears as the representative of early lyric poetry whose role has been taken over by the latter-day male poet. See, for instance, his poem 'Charmides', section 3, stanza 6: '... and bid thy lay/ Sleep hidden in the lyre's silent strings/ Till thou hast found the old Castalian rill,/ Or from the Lesbian waters plucked the drowned Sappho's golden quill'. See also 'The Grave of Keats', 'O sweetest lips since those of Mitylene!', and 'Ravenna', section 4, 'Byron, thy crowns are ever fresh and green:/ Red leaves of rose from Sapphic Mitylene/ Shall bind thy brows ...'
47. Matthew Sturgis, *Passionate Attitudes: The English Decadence of the Eighteen Nineties* (Macmillan, London, 1995), p. 45.
48. Review of *London Nights* (1895) published in the *Westminster Gazette* and reprinted with other press notices in Arthur Symons's *Amoris Victima* (Leonard Smithers,

London, 1897), p. v. Symons's *London Nights* was advertised as 'the most discussed of any recently issued volume of verse'.

49. See my Chapter 4 on Tennyson, 'Fragments of an Elegy', in this volume.
50. John Addington Symonds to Henry Graham Dakyns, 22 August 1866, in *The Letters of John Addington Symonds*, eds Herbert M. Schueffer and Robert L. Peters (Wayne State University Press, Detroit, 1967), Vol. I, pp. 666–7. Dr Percival was the headmaster of Clifton College in Bristol. F.W.H. Myers and Arthur Sidgewick were friends of Symonds's.
51. For an account of the conception and publication of Havelock Ellis's *Sexual Inversion* (1897) see Jeffrey Weeks, *Coming Out: Homosexual Politics in Britain from the Nineteenth Century to the Present* (1977: Quartet Books, London and New York, 1990), pp. 47–67. Weeks makes the point that *Sexual Inversion* was designed to present the case for homosexuality. Sappho was listed by Ellis as one of the 'homosexuals of note' along with Christopher Marlowe, Erasmus, Francis Bacon, Oscar Wilde and Walt Whitman.
52. C.R. Haines, ed., *Sappho: The Poems and Fragments* (George Routledge and Sons Ltd, London, 1926), p. 35.
53. Oscar Wilde, *The Picture of Dorian Gray* (1890), in *The Complete Works of Oscar Wilde* with an introduction by Vyvyan Holland (Collins, London, 1988), pp. 101–2. The skewed Victorian notion of Hellenism in the background to *The Picture of Dorian Gray* has often been noticed, but I would like to note the Greek reference in Dorian's own name, and the multiple allusions which surround Sybil who is not only given the name of that 'intellectual woman' but who is also a performer. That Dorian's first ecstatic account of Sybil should be the result of her playing the part of Rosalind in *As You Like It* points also to the homosexual subtext and to Wilde's inheritance from Gautier's *Mademoiselle de Maupin*.
54. Thomas Hardy, 'A Singer Asleep (Algernon Charles Swinburne, 1837–1909)', which was published in *Poems of the Past and the Present* (1902). In the same volume Hardy included his poem called 'Sapphic Fragment'. Hardy referred to Sappho in *The Hand of Ethelberta*, and in *The Well-Beloved*. The epigraph to part III of *Jude the Obscure* is Sappho's Fragment 113 drawn from H.T. Wharton's *Sappho: Memoir, Text and Selected Renderings* (John Lane, London, 1895). It was in writing about this book that Hardy said, 'I have made myself a present of Wharton's Sappho – a delightful book. How I love her – how many man have loved her! – more than they had Christ I fear.' See Thomas Hardy to Florence Henniker, 4 August 1895, in *One Rare Fair Woman: Thomas Hardy's Letters to Florence Henniker 1983–1922*, eds Evelyn Hardy and F.B. Pinion (Macmillan, London, 1972), p. 42.
55. George Moore, *Confessions of a Young Man* (1886), ed. Susan Dick (McGill-Queen's University Press, Montreal, 1972), pp. 85, 80, 99.
56. Edwin Gilcher, *A Bibliography of George Moore* (Northern Illinois University Press, De Kalb, 1970), pp. 2, 4, 5.
57. George Moore, 'A Sapphic Dream' in *Flowers of Passion* (Provost and Co., London, 1878), p. 114.
58. George Moore, 'Sappho', in *Pagan Poems* (Newman and Co., London, 1881), p. 27.

8. The island and the mirror

1. H.D., *Tribute to Freud, Writing on the Wall, Advent* (David R. Godine, Boston, 1974), pp. 135, 174–5. H.D.'s 'Tribute to Freud' was written in 1944 but not published until after her death. A great deal of excellent critical work on H.D. has been published

recently including Diana Collecott, *H.D. and Sapphic Modernism 1910–1950* (Cambridge University Press, Cambridge, 1999) which carries a comprehensive account of H.D.'s debt to Sappho. Other works include Eileen Gregory, *H.D. and Hellenism* (Cambridge University Press, Cambridge, 1997); Cassandra Laity, *H.D. and the Victorian Fin de Siècle: Gender, Modernism and Decadence* (Cambridge University Press, Cambridge, 1997); *Agenda: H.D. Special Issue*, ed. Diana Collecott (1988); *Signets: Reading H.D.*, eds Susan Stanford Friedman and Rachel Blau DuPlessis (The University of Wisconsin Press, Madison Wisconsin, 1990); Susan Stanford Friedman, 'Exile in the American Grain: H.D.'s Diaspora', in *Women's Writing in Exile*, eds Mary Lynn Broe and Angela Ingram (University of North Carolina Press, Chapel Hill and London, 1989), pp. 87–112; Rachel Connor, 'Textu(r)al Braille: Visionary (Re)Readings of H.D.', in *Body Matters: Feminism, Textuality, Corporeality*, eds Avril Horner and Angela Keane (Manchester University Press, Manchester, 2000), pp. 199–208; Norman Kelvin 'H.D. and the Years of World War I', in *Victorian Poetry*, Vol. 38, part 1 (Spring, 2000), pp. 170–96. Other important critical readings include Angela DiPace Fritz, *Thought and Vision: A Critical Reading of H.D.'s Poetry* (Catholic University of America Press, Washington DC, 1988); Susan Stanford Friedman, *Penelope's Web: Gender, Modernity H.D.'s Fiction* (Cambridge University Press, Cambridge, 1990); Rachel Blau DuPlessis, *H.D. The Career of That Struggle* (Harvester, Brighton, 1986); and Susan Stanford Friedman, '"I Go Where I Love": An Intertextual Study of H.D. and Adrienne Rich', in *Signs: The Lesbian Issue* (University of Chicago Press, Chicago, 1985).

2. See Janice S. Robinson, *H.D.: The Life and Work of An American Poet* (Houghton Mifflin Company, Boston, 1982), p. 247.
3. H.D., *Tribute to Freud, Writing on the Wall, Advent* (David R. Godine, Boston, 1974), p. 13.
4. H.D., *Tribute to Freud, Writing on the Wall, Advent* (David R. Godine, Boston, 1974), p. 43.
5. See Janice S. Robinson, *H.D.: The Life and Work of An American Poet* (Houghton Mifflin Company, Boston, 1982), pp. 10–11.
6. *The Poems of Anyte of Tegea translated by Richard Aldington and Poems and Fragments of Sappho translated by Edward Storer* (The Egoist Press, London, 1919), p. 12.
7. *The Poems of Anyte of Tegea translated by Richard Aldington and Poems and Fragments of Sappho translated by Edward Storer* (The Egoist Press, London, 1919), pp. 13–14, 14–15, 17. On the intimate textual relationship between Sappho, Pound, Aldington and H.D. see Hugh Kenner, *The Pound Era* (1971: Pimlico, London, 1991), pp. 54–75.
8. Richard Aldington, 'Atthis', in *Des Imagistes* (The Egoist Press, London, 1914), p. 14.
9. 'I was 21 when Ezra left and it was some years later that he scratched "H.D. Imagiste," in London, in the Museum tea room, at the bottom of a typed sheet, now slashed with his creative pencil, "Cut this out, shorten this line." H.D. – Hermes – Hermeticism and all the rest of it.' H.D., *End to Torment* (New Directions, New York, 1979), p. 40.
10. H.D., *Tribute to Freud, Writing on the Wall, Advent* (David R. Godine, Boston, 1974), p. 153.
11. Ezra Pound, 'Exile's Letter', *Poetry* (March 1915), p. 261, and Ezra Pound, 'The Island of Paris: A Letter', *The Dial* (September 1920), p. 406; Winifred Ellerman, 'Bryher', *Arrow Music* (London, 1922), p. 12; Richard Aldington, *Exile and Other Poems* (George Allen and Unwin Ltd, London, 1923), p. 14.
12. Richard Aldington, *The Love of Myrrhine and Konallis, and Other Prose Poems* (The Clerk's Press, Cleveland, 1917), later reprinted (Pascal Covici, Chicago, 1926). Aldington wrote a number of other 'Sappho'-related poems including 'At Mitylene' and 'Lesbia'. See Richard Aldington, *The Complete Poems of Richard Aldington* (Allan Wingate,

London, 1948), pp. 26, 28. For accounts of his character and interests written by his contemporaries see, *Richard Aldington: An Intimate Portrait*, eds Alister Kershaw and F.-J. Temple (Southern Illinois University Press, Carbondale and Edwardsville, 1965).

13. O.W. Firkins, 'The New Movement in Poetry', *The Nation* (14 October, 1915), pp. 458–61, quoted in Glenn Hughes, *Imagism and the Imagists: A Study in Modern Poetry* (Stanford University Press, and Oxford University Press, Palo Alto and London, 1931), pp. 60–1.
14. William Ellery Leonard, 'The New Poetry – A Critique', *Chicago Evening Post* (18 and 25 September, 2 and 9 October, 1915), quoted in Glenn Hughes, *Imagism and the Imagists: A Study in Modern Poetry* (Stanford University Press, and Oxford University Press, Palo Alto and London, 1931), p. 65.
15. H.D., 'The Islands', *Selected Poems* (Grove Press, New York, 1957), pp. 30–4.
16. H.D., *Tribute to Freud, Writing on the Wall, Advent* (David R. Godine, Boston, 1974), pp. 40–1.
17. H.D., *Tribute to Freud, Writing on the Wall, Advent* (David R. Godine, Boston, 1974), pp. 157–8.
18. H.D., 'A Note on Poetry' in *The Oxford Anthology of American Literature*, eds William Rose Benet and Norman Holmes Pearson (Oxford University Press, Oxford and New York, 1938), Vol. II, pp. 1287–8.
19. Eileen Gregory, *H.D. and Hellenism: Classic Lines* (Cambridge University Press, Cambridge, 1997), p. 151. Diana Collecott's recent work, in particular, shows that this is not so. See Diana Collecott, *H.D. and Sapphic Modernism* (Cambridge University Press, Cambridge, 1999). See also Eileen Barrett's essay in *Virginia Woolf: Lesbian Readings*, eds Eileen Barrett and Patricia Cramer (New York University Press, New York, 1997).
20. H.D., *Heliodora and Other Poems* (Jonathan Cape, London, 1924), pp. 44–7, 57–60, 70–5, 81–4. The numbering of Sappho's fragments refers to Henry Thornton Wharton's edition, *Sappho: Memoir, Text, Selected Renderings and a Literal Translation* (David Stott, London, 1885).
21. H.D., *Notes on Thought and Vision and The Wise Sappho* (1919 and 1925), ed. Albert Gelpi (Peter Owen, London, 1988), pp. 57–9.
22. Edwin Marion Cox, *The Poems of Sappho* (Williams and Norgate Ltd, London, 1925).
23. See Judith Thurman, *Colette: A Biography* (Chatto and Windus, London, 2000), pp. 171–3.
24. Medea Norsa, 'Dai papiri della Societa Italiana: Versi di Saffo in un ostrakon del sec. II a C' in *Annali della Schuola Normale Superiore di Pisa* (1937), pp. 8–15.
25. Shari Benstock, *Women of the Left Bank, Paris 1900–1940* (University of Texas Press, Austin, 1986), p. 350.
26. H.D., *Paint It Today*, Beinecke Library, Yale University; chapter 1, p. 7.
27. H.D., *Heliodora* (Jonathan Cape, London, 1924), pp. 70–5.
28. H.D., *Tribute to Freud, Writing on the Wall, Advent* (David R. Godine, Boston, 1974), pp. 36–7.
29. Jacqueline Rose, *Sexuality in the Field of Vision* (Verso, London and New York, 1986), p. 53.
30. Melanie Klein quoted in Susan Edmonds, 'Stealing from "Muddies Body": H.D. and Melanie Klein' in *H.D. Newsletter*, ed. Eileen Gregory, Vol. 4, part 2 (Winter, 1991), pp. 17–30. See also Isobel Armstrong, 'So What's All This About the Mother's Body? The Aesthetic, Gender and the Polis' in *Textuality and Sexuality: Reading Theories and Practices*, eds Judith Still and Michael Worton (Manchester University Press, Manchester, 1993), pp. 218–36.

31. Hanna Segal, quoted in Peter Fuller, 'The Venus and "Internal Objects"' in *Art and Psychoanalysis* (Writers and Readers, London, 1980), p. 65.
32. H.D., *Paint It Today*, ed. Cassandra Laity (New York University Press, New York, 1992), pp. 53–4.
33. H.D., *Heliodora* (Jonathan Cape, London, 1924), pp. 18–23.
34. Julia Kristeva, *Desire in Language: A Semiotic Approach to Literature and Art*, ed. Leon S. Roudiez, trans. Thomas Gora, Alice Jardine and Leon S. Roudiez (Blackwell, Oxford, 1981), pp. 288–9.
35. Hauser quoted in Peter Fuller, 'The Venus and "Internal Objects"' in *Art and Psychoanalysis* (Writers and Readers, London, 1980), p. 67.
36. Ezra Pound to Perdita Schaffner, 1960. See Perdita Schaffner, 'Merano, 1962', in *Paideuma* 4, nos. 2, 3 (1975), p. 514.
37. H.D., 'She Is Dead' in 'Twelve Short Stories', Beinecke Library, Yale; pp. 2–3. Quoted in Janice S. Robinson, *H.D.: The Life and Work of An American Poet* (Houghton Mifflin Company, Boston, 1982), p. 307.

9. Epilogue

1. 21 December 1925, *The Diary of Virginia Woolf*, ed. Anne Olivier Bell (The Hogarth Press, London, 1982), Vol. III, pp. 51–2.
2. Virginia Woolf to Violet Dickinson, 22 October 1904, *The Letters of Virginia Woolf, 1888–1941*, eds Nigel Nicolson and Joanne Trautmann (The Hogarth Press, London, 1975–80), Vol. I, pp. 144–5.
3. The poem was *Paris.* Virginia Woolf to Margaret Llewelyn Davies, 17 August 1919, *The Letters of Virginia Woolf, 1888–1941*, ed. Nigel Nicolson and Joanne Trautmann (The Hogarth Press, London, 1975–1980), Vol. II, pp. 384–5.
4. Virginia Woolf to Clive Bell, 24 September 1919, *The Letters of Virginia Woolf, 1888–1941*, eds Nigel Nicolson and Joanne Trautmann (The Hogarth Press, London, 1975–80), Vol. II, p. 391.
5. 12 September 1921, *The Diary of Virginia Woolf*, ed. Anne Olivier Bell (The Hogarth Press, London, 1982), Vol. II, p. 136.
6. 14 March 1927, *The Diary of Virginia Woolf*, ed. Anne Olivier Bell (The Hogarth Press, London, 1982), Vol. III, p. 131.
7. 21 February 1927, *The Diary of Virginia Woolf*, ed. Anne Olivier Bell (The Hogarth Press, London, 1982), Vol. V, p. 59.
8. Virginia Woolf, 'The Intellectual Status of Women', *New Statesman* (9 October 1920 and 16 October 1920).
9. Virgina Woolf to Dorothy Tyler, 1 January 1930, *The Letters of Virginia Woolf, 1888–1941*, eds Nigel Nicolson and Joanne Trautmann (The Hogarth Press, London, 1975–80), Vol. IV, p. 123.
10. Virginia Woolf, 'A Society', from *Monday or Tuesday* (The Hogarth Press, London, 1921).
11. Woolf was not the only writer to note and use the dedication. The American poet and adventurer Natalie Barney dedicated her *Cinq petits dialogues grecs* (1902) 'a Monsieur Pierre Louys par "une jeune fille de la Société future"'.
12. For some of these twentieth century versions of Sappho see Diana Collecott, *H.D. and Sapphic Modernism 1910–1950* (Cambridge University Press, Cambridge, 1999); ed. Ellen Greene, *Re-Reading Sappho: Reception and Transmission* (University of California Press, Berkeley and Los Angeles, 1996); Judy Grahn, *The Highest Apple: Sappho and the Lesbian Poetic Tradition* (Spinsters, Ink, San Francisco, 1985); Susan

Gubar, 'Sapphistries' in *Signs* 10 (Autumn, 1984), pp. 43–62; Peter Jay and Caroline Lewis, eds. *Sappho Through English Poetry* (Anvil Press, London, 1996); Jane McIntosh Snyder, *Lesbian Desire in the Lyrics of Sappho* (Columbia University Press, New York. 1997); Ruth Vanita, *Sappho and the Virgin Mary: Same Sex Love and the English Literary Imagination,* (Columbia University Press, New York, 1996); Margaret Reynolds, *The Sappho Companion* (Chatto and Windus, London, 2000).

Bibliography

Primary sources

Addison, John, *The Works of Anacreon translated into English verse ... To which are added the Odes, Fragments and Epigrams of Sappho* (London, 1735).

Addison, Joseph, *The Spectator*, No. 223, November 15, 1711 and No. 233, November 27, 1711 (London, 1711).

Addison, Joseph, 'The Pleasures of the Imagination', *The Spectator*, 21 June–3 July 1712; in *Critical Essays from The Spectator*, ed. Donald F. Bond (Clarendon Press, Oxford, 1970).

Aldington, Richard, *Des Imagistes*, ed. Ezra Pound (The Egoist Press, London, 1914).

Aldington, Richard, *The Love of Myrrhine and Konallis, and Other Prose Poems* (The Clerk's Press, Cleveland, 1917), later reprinted (Pascal Covici, Chicago, 1926).

Aldington, Richard, trans., *The Poems of Anyte of Tegea translated by Richard Aldington and Poems and Fragments of Sappho translated by Edward Storer* (The Egoist Press, London, 1919).

Aldington, Richard, *Exile and Other Poems* (George Allen and Unwin Ltd, London, 1923).

The Complete Poems of Richard Aldington (Allan Wingate, London, 1948).

Richard Aldington: An Intimate Portrait, eds Alister Kershaw and F.-J. Temple (Southern Illinois University Press, Carbondale and Edwardsville, 1965).

Anon., *The Sappho-An. An Heroic poem of three cantos, in the Ovidian stile, describing the pleasures which the fair sex enjoy with each other, found among the papers of a lady of quality* (C. Brasier, London, 1740).

Anon., 'A dialogue between the souls of Sappho and the seventeenth century French courtesan Ninon de L'Enclos', *The Covent Garden Magazine*; or, *Amorous Repository* (London, June 1773).

Anon., *A Sapphick Epistle from Jack Cavendish to the Honourable and most beautiful Mrs. D—* (London, *c.* 1782?).

Anon. (James Gillray?), *Drawings faithfully copied from Nature at Naples and with permission dedicated to the Right Honourable Sir William Hamilton, A new edition considerably enlarged and humbly dedicated to all admirers of the grand and sublime* (Hannah Humphrey, London, 1807).

Anon., *La Nouvelle Sapho, ou Histoire de la Secte Anandryne*, also called *Histoire d'une Jeune Fille* and *Anandria, La Jolie T----* (tribade?) (London, *c.*1780s). Reprinted, at least twice in the second half of the nineteenth century under the title of *Anandria, ou Confession de Mlle Sapho avec la clef* and with illustrations by Félicien Rops (London, *c.* 1860s).

Anon. (D.K. Sandford?) 'Greek Authoresses', *The Edinburgh Review* (January July 1832), pp. 182–208.

Anon., 'Review of London Nights' (1895) published in the *Westminster Gazette* and reprinted with other press notices in Arthur Symons's *Amoris Victima* (Leonard Smithers, London, 1897).

Anyte of Tegea, *The Poems of Anyte of Tegea translated by Richard Aldington and Poems and Fragments of Sappho translated by Edward Storer* (The Egoist Press, London, 1919).

Barrett Browning, Elizabeth, 'A Vision of Poets' (1844); *The Poetical Works of Elizabeth Barrett Browning* (Houghton Mifflin Co., Boston, 1974).

Barrett Browning, Elizabeth, *Aurora Leigh* (Chapman and Hall, London, 1857), ed. Margaret Reynolds (Norton, New York, 1996).

Barrett Browning, Elizabeth and Robert Browning, *The Brownings' Correspondence*, eds Philip Kelley, Ronald Hudson and Scott Lewis (Wedgestone Press, Winfield Kansas, 1984–).

Barthélemy, Jean Jacques, *Voyage du Jeune Anacharsis en Grèce dans le milieu du quatrième siècle avant l'ère Vulgaire* (du Bure, Paris, 1788).

Barthélemy, Jean Jacques, *Travels of Anacharsis the Younger in Greece during the Middle of the Fourth Century before the Christian Era* (J. Mawman etc., London, 1817).

Baudelaire, Charles, *Les Fleurs du mal* (Paris, 1857).

Baudelaire, Charles, *Les Fleurs du mal* (1857), ed. Antoine Adam (Classiques Garnier, Paris, 1994).

Charles Baudelaire: His Life by Théophile Gautier (1868), translated into English with selections from his poems ... and an essay on his influence by Guy Thorne (Greening and Co., London, 1915).

Beckford, William, *Dreams, Waking Thoughts, and Incidents in a Series of Letters from Various Parts of Europe* (J. Johnson, P. Elmsley, London, 1783).

Beerbohm, Max, *Rossetti and His Circle* (William Heinemann, London, 1922).

Bell, Robert, *Early Ballads* (London, 1862).

Bergk, Theodor, *de Aliquot fragmentis Sapphonis et Alcaei, Rheinisches Museum fur Philologie* (Bonn, 1835).

Bergk, Theodor, *Poetae Lyrici Graeci* (Leipzig, 1843).

Bergk, Theodor, *Anthologia Lyrica* (Leipzig, 1854).

Blass, Friedrich, *Rheinisches Museum*, Vol. XXXV (1880), pp. 287–90.

Lady Blessington's Conversations of Lord Byron, ed. Ernest J. Lovell (Princeton University Press, Princeton New Jersey, 1969).

Boileau, Nicolas, *Oeuvres complètes* (Gallimard-Pleiade, Paris, 1966).

Boissonade, François, *Lyrici Graeci* (Lefevre, Paris, 1825).

Brinton, Christian, 'Queen Victoria as Etcher', *The Critic* (June 1900), pp. 501–10.

'Bryher' (Winifred Ellerman), *Arrrow Music* (J. & E. Bumpus, London, 1922).

Burke, Edmund, *A Philosophical Enquiry into the Origin of Our Ideas of the Sublime and the Beautiful* (1757; revised edition 1759), ed. James T. Boulton (Routledge, Kegan Paul, London, 1958).

Burke, Edmund, *A Philosophical Enquiry into the Origin of our Ideas of the Sublime and Beautiful* (1757, revised and expanded 1759). Edited with an Introduction and Notes by Adam Phillips (Oxford University Press, Oxford and New York, 1990).

Burnaby Greene, E. , *The Works of Anacreon and Sappho* (London, 1768).

Byron, George Gordon, *Don Juan* (London, 1820).

Catullus, 'Ille mi par esse': see Loeb Classical Library, *Catullus, Tibullus, Pervigilium Veneris*, ed. G.P. Goold (Harvard University Press, Cambridge Mass. and London, 1988).

Chaussard, J.-B. *Fêtes et courtisanes de la Grèce: Supplément aux Voyages d'Anacharsis et d'Antenor* (Paris, 1801).

Cipollini, A., *Saffo* (Fratelli Dumolard, Milan, 1890).

Coleridge, Mary, *Poems* (London, 1908).

Coleridge, Mary, *The Collected Poems of Mary Coleridge*, ed. Theresa Whistler (Hart Davis, London, 1954).

Coleridge, Sara, *Memoir and Letters of Sara Coleridge, Edited by her Daughter* (London, 1873), Vol. II, p. 447.

Collingham, G.G., *Sappho, or The Idol of an Hour,* a play based on Alphonse Daudet's novel, performed at the Shakespeare Theatre, Clapham in 1898 (Lord Chamberlain's Collection, the British Library).

Cory, William, *Ionica* (George Allen, London, 1891).
d'Annunzio, Gabriele, 'Four Nude Studies', *Intermezzo di rime* (Sommaruga, Rome, 1883).
Darwin, Erasmus, *A Plan for the Conduct of Female Education in Boarding Schools* (Dublin, 1798).
Daudet, Alphonse, *Sappho: Parisian Manners: A Realistic Novel*, English translation (Vizetelly and Co., London, 1886).
Daudet, Alphonse and Adolphe Belot, *Sapho, piece en cinq actes* (Paris, 1893), translated into English and licensed for performance at the Garrick Theatre London in April 1895 (The Lord Chamberlain's Collection, the British Library).
Daumier, Honoré, 'Sapho', *Histoire Ancienne* (Paris, 1842).
de Balzac, Honoré, *La Fille aux yeux d'or* (Paris, 1835).
de Balzac, Honoré, *Seraphitus-Seraphita* (Paris, 1854).
de la Boigne, Comtesse , *Memoires de la Comtesse de Boigne*, ed. M. Charles Nicoullard, Vol. 1781–1814 (Paris, 1907).
de Vere Stacpoole, H. , *Sappho: A New Rendering* (Hutchinson and Co., London, n.d.).
H.D. (Hilda Doolittle), *Heliodora and Other Poems* (Jonathan Cape, London, 1924).
H.D., *Tribute to Freud, Writing on the Wall, Advent* (David R. Godine, Boston, 1974).
H.D., *Selected Poems* (Grove Press, New York, 1957).
H.D., 'A Note on Poetry' in *The Oxford Anthology of American Literature*, eds William Rose Benet and Norman Holmes Pearson (Oxford University Press, Oxford and New York, 1938), Vol. II, pp. 1287–8.
H.D., *Notes on Thought and Vision and The Wise Sappho* (1919 and 1925), ed. Albert Gelpi (Peter Owen, London, 1988).
H.D., *Paint It Today*, Beinecke Library, Yale University, and in ed. Cassandra Laity (New York University Press, New York, 1992).
H.D., *End to Torment* (New Directions, New York, 1979).
H.D., 'She Is Dead' in 'Twelve Short Stories', Beinecke Library, Yale.
Du Camp, Maxime, *Les Convulsions de Paris* (Hachette, Paris, 1889).
Du Bois, Edward, *The Wreath: Composed of Selections from Sappho etc. ...* (London, 1799).
Eliot, George, 'Armgart' (1870) in *The Legend of Jubal and Other Poems* (William Blackwood and Sons, Edinburgh and London, 1874).
Ellerman, Winifred, 'Bryher', *Arrrow Music* (London, 1922).
Fawkes, Francis, *The Works of Anacreon, Sappho, Bion, Moschus and Museaus* translated into English by a Gentleman of Cambridge (London, 1760).
Field, Michael, Manuscript copies of poems and letters in the Bodleian Library, Oxford.
Field, Michael, Manuscript copies of poems and the Journal 'Works and Days' in the British Library.
Field, Michael, *Long Ago* (George Bell and Sons, London, 1889).
Field, Michael, *Underneath the Bough* (George Bell and Sons, London, 1893).
Field, Michael, *Wild Honey from Various Thyme* (T. Fisher Unwin, London, 1908).
Finch, Anne, *Countess of Winchelsea, Miscellany Poems on Several Occasions* (London, 1713).
Frain, Rose, *Sappho Fragments* (1989), one of two copies of an Artist's Book, in the Special Collections, National Art Library, Victoria and Albert Museum.
Gautier, Théophile, *Mademoiselle de Maupin* (Paris, 1835).
Gautier, Théophile, *Mademoiselle de Maupin* (1835), trans. G.F. Monkshood and Ernest Tristan (Greening and Co., London, 1917?).
Gautier, Théophile, *Charles Baudelaire: His Life by Théophile Gautier* (1868), translated into English with selections from his poems ... and an essay on his influence by Guy Thorne (Greening and Co., London, 1915).

Girodet Trioson, Anne-Louis, and M. Coupin, *Recueil de compositions dessinées par Girodet avec la traduction en vers par Girodet de quelques-uns des poésies de Sapho* (Paris, 1827).

Goethe, Johann Wolfgang von, *Italienische Reise* (1786–88), translated as *Italian Journey* by W.H. Auden and Elizabeth Mayer (1962: Penguin, London, 1970).

Goethe, Johann Wolfgang von, 'Sappho sich vom leucabischen Selsen sturzend', *Propylaen*, Vol. II, No. 1 (Tubingen, 1799).

Greg, William Rathbone, review article of books by Parent-Duchatelet, Ryan, and Talbot in *The Westminster Review*, Vol. 53 (1850), pp. 448–79.

The Grolier Club, *Catalogue of an Exhibition of Engraved Portraits of Women Writers from Sappho to George Eliot* at the Grolier Club, New York (The Gilliss Press, New York, 1895).

Hacker, Marilyn, *Love, Death and the Changing of the Seasons* (Onlywomen Press, London, 1987).

Hall, John, trans., *Longinus Peri Hypsous, On the Sublime* (London, 1652).

Hallam, Arthur, 'On Some of the Characteristics of Modern Poetry', *Englishman's Magazine*, August 1831; in *Victorian Scrutinies*, ed. Isobel Armstrong (Athlone, London, 1972).

Hallam, Arthur, *The Writings of Arthur Hallam: Now First Collected and Edited by T.H. Vail Motter* (Oxford University Press and the Modern Language Association of America, Oxford and New York, 1943).

Hallam, Arthur, *Remains in Verse and Prose of Arthur Henry Hallam*, ed. Henry Hallam (W. Nichol, London, 1834).

Hallam, Arthur, *The Letters of Arthur Henry Hallam*, ed. Jack Kolb (Ohio State University Press, Columbus, 1981).

'The Hamilton and Nelson Papers', in A. Morrison, *Catalogue of the Collection of Autograph Letters and Historical Documents found between 1865 and 1882 by A. Morrison*. The Hamilton and Nelson Papers, I: nos 1–301, II: nos 302–1067, combined and annotated under the direction of A.W. Thibideau (London, 1893–94).

Hardy, Thomas, *Poems of the Past and the Present* (Macmillan, London, 1902).

Hardy, Thomas, *The Complete Poems* (Macmillan, London, 1981).

Hauteroche, L. Allier de, 'Notice sur la courtisane Sapho, née à Eresos, dans l'ile de Lesbos' (Dondey-Dupre, Paris, 1822).

Housman, A.E., *More Poems* (London, 1936).

Houssaye, Arsène, *Les Confessions: souvenirs d'un demi-siècle, 1830–1880*, 4 vols (Dentu, Paris, 1885–91: Slatkine Reprints, Geneva, 1971).

Howard, Adderley Millar, Album, 1877. Sold at Christie's, London (May 1997).

Hunter, Anne, *Poems* (London, 1802).

King, William, *The Toast. An Heroick Poem in four books originally written in Latin by Frederick Scheffer: now done into English, and illustrated with Notes and Observations by Peregrine O'Donald* (Dublin, 1736).

Landon, Letitia Elizabeth, *The Poetical Works of Letitia Elizabeth Landon*, 4 vols (Longman, Orme, Brown, Greene and Longman, London, 1839).

Lantier, Etienne, *Voyages d'Antenor en Grèce et en Asie* (Paris, 1797).

Lantier, Etienne, *The Travels of Antenor in Greece and Asia from a Greek Manuscript found at Herculaneum: including some account of Egypt* (T.N. Longman and O. Rees, London, 1799).

LeBrun, Elisabeth Vigée, *Souvenirs de Madame Louise-Elisabeth Vigée-Lebrun* (Librairie de H. Fournier, Paris, 1835), and *Souvenirs*, ed. Claudine Herrmann (Editions des femmes, Paris, 1984).

Longinus, Dionysius, *On the Sublime, Translated from the Greek, with Notes and Observations, and some account of the Life, Writings, and Character of the author. By William Smith, the second edition corrected and improved* (J. Watts, London, 1739).

Longinus, *On the Sublime*, translated with a commentary by James A. Arieti and John M. Crossett (The Edwin Mellen Press, New York and Toronto, 1985).

Longinus, *On Great Writing*, translated with an introduction by G.M.A. Grube (Hackett Publishing Company, Indianapolis and Cambridge, 1991).

MacFall, Haldane, *Aubrey Beardsley: The Man and His Work* (John Lane, London, 1928).

Mallarmé, Stéphane, *Les Poésies* (Paris, 1891).

Massenet, Jules, *Sapho*, opera with libretto by Henry Cain and Arthur Bernède, premiered in Paris, November 1897 (Lord Chamberlain's Collection, the British Library).

May, Caroline, *The American Female Poets* (Philadelphia, 1848).

Merivale, John Herman, *Collections from the Greek Anthology*, by the late Rev. Robert Bland and others (London, 1833).

Mocchetti, F. *Opere della Cavaliere Carlo Gastone, Conte della Torre Rezzonico, VII: Giornale del Viaggio di Napoli negli Anni 1789 e 1790* (Como, 1819).

Moore, George, *Flowers of Passion* (Provost and Co., London, 1878).

Moore, George, 'Sappho', in *Pagan Poems* (Newman and Co., London, 1881).

Moore, George, *Confessions of a Young Man* (1886), ed. Susan Dick (McGill-Queen's University Press, Montreal, 1972).

Moore, Thomas, *Evenings in Greece* (London, 1825).

Mure, William, *A Critical History of the Language and Literature of Ancient Greece* (London, 1850).

Neue, Christian Friedrich, *Sapphonis Mytilenaeae Fragmenta: Specimen operae in omnibus artis graecorum Lyricae reliquiis excepto Pindaro collocandae* (Berlin, 1827).

Norton, Caroline, *The Undying One and Other Poems* (London, 1830).

Ovid, Heroides, Letters of the Heroines, XV, Sappho to Phaon; Loeb Classical Library, *Ovid I: Heroides and Amores*, trans. Grant Showerman, second edition, revised by G.P. Goold (Harvard University Press, Cambridge Mass., 1977).

Pacini, Giovanni, 'Saffo' to a libretto by Salvatore Cammarano, premiered in Naples in November 1840, was performed in London in 1841.

Pall Mall Gazette, 11 October 1889 (London).

Parent-Duchatelet, Alexis-Jean-Baptiste, *De la prostitution dans la ville de Paris* (Paris, 1837).

Phillips, Ambrose, *The Works of Anacreon and Sappho. Done from the Greek by several hands* (London, 1715).

Piroli, Tommaso, after Friedrich Rehberg, *Drawings faithfully copied from Nature at Naples and with permission dedicated to the Right Honourable Sir William Hamilton* (1794).

Poetae Graeci: Sive Selecta ex Homerii etc. (Etonae, ex Officini M. Pote et E. Williams, 1806).

Pound, Ezra, 'Exile's Letter', *Poetry* (March 1915).

Pound, Ezra, *Lustra* (Elkin Mathews, London, 1916).

Pound, Ezra, 'The Island of Paris: A Letter', *The Dial* (September 1920), p. 406.

Pound, Ezra, to Perdita Schaffner, 1960. See Perdita Schaffner, 'Merano, 1962', *Paideuma* 4, nos 2, 3 (1975), p. 514.

Rachilde, *Monsieur Venus* (1884; Flammarion, Paris, 1926).

Randall, Anne Frances, (pseudonym for Mary Robinson), *A Letter to the Women of England, on the Injustice of Mental Subordination with Anecdotes* (T.N. Longman and O. Rees, London, 1799).

Rich, Adrienne, *Snapshots of a Daughter-in-Law: Poems 1954–1962* (Norton, New York, 1963).

Richepin, Jean, 'Sapphô' in the series *Les Grandes Amoureuses* (C. Marpon and E. Flammarion, Paris, 1884).

Robinson, Agnes Mary (later Darmesteter, later Duclaux), *The Collected Poems, Lyrical and Narrative of Mary Robinson* (T. Fisher Unwin, London, 1902).

Robinson, Mary, Ms. Letter dated 'Salthill Octr. 1st 99', tipped into a copy of Mary Robinson's *Poems* (1791), Bodleian pressmark, Vet. A5 e 549.

Robinson, Mary, *Poems by Mrs. M. Robinson* (London, 1791).

Robinson, Mary, *Sappho and Phaon in a Series of Legitimate Sonnets, with Thoughts on Poetical Subjects and Anecdotes of the Grecian Poetess* (London, 1796).

Robinson, Mary, *The Wintry Day*, illustrated with twelve prints drawn by Maria Cosway and engraved by Caroline Watson (London, 1803).

Robinson, Mary, *Memoirs of Mary Robinson, 'Perdita'*, from the edition compiled by her daughter (1803), with introduction and notes by J. Fitzgerald Molloy (J.B. Lippincott, Philadelphia, 1894).

Robinson, Mary, *The Poetical Works of the late Mrs Mary Robinson, including many pieces never before published* (printed for Richard Phillips, London, 1806).

Robinson, Mary, under the pseudonym of Anne Frances Randall, *A Letter to the Women of England, on the Injustice of Mental Subordination with Anecdotes* (T.N. Longman and O. Rees, London, 1799).

Rossetti, Christina, *The Complete Poems of Christina Rossetti*, ed. R.W. Crump (Louisiana State University Press, Baton Rouge and London, 1990).

Rossetti, Christina, *The Family Letters of Christina Georgina Rossetti*, ed. William Michael Rossetti (Brown, Langham, London, 1908).

Rossetti, Dante Gabriel, *The Collected Works of Dante Gabriel Rossetti* (Ellis and Elvey, London, 1888).

Rousseau, Jean Jacques, *Emile, or On Education* (1762), trans. Allan Bloom (Penguin, Harmondsworth Middlesex, 1991).

Ryan, Michael, *Prostitution in London* (London, 1839).

Schneidewin, F.G., *Delectus Poesis Graecorum Elegiacae, Iambicae, Melicae: Sapphonis Mitylenaeae Carmina* (Gottingen, 1838).

Shelley, Mary, *The Last Man* (1821), ed. Morton D. Paley (World's Classics, Oxford, 1994).

Smollett, Tobias, *The Adventures of Roderick Random* (London, 1748).

Stael, Germaine de, *Corinne, ou, Italie*, (1807). English translation by Isabel Hill, with verse translations by Elizabeth Letitia Landon (Richard Bentley, London, 1847).

Stael, Germaine de, *Delphine* (1802), ed. Avriel H. Goldenberger (Northern Illinois University Press, De Kalb, 1995).

Stael, Germaine de, *De la litterature*, in *Oeuvres complètes* (Paris, 1838).

Stodart, Mary Ann, *Female Writers: Thoughts on Their Proper Sphere and on Their Powers of Usefulness* (London, 1842).

Storer, Edward, *The Poems and Fragments of Sappho, with The Poems of Anyte of Tegea translated by Richard Aldington* (The Egoist Press, London, 1919).

Swinburne, Algernon Charles, *Songs of the Springtides* (London, 1880).

Swinburne, Algernon Charles, *Poems and Ballads, First Series* (1866: Chatto and Windus, London, 1887).

Swinburne, Algernon Charles, *Poems and Ballads, Second Series* (1878: Chatto and Windus, London, 1887).

Swinburne, Algernon Charles, *The Complete Works of Algernon Charles Swinburne*, eds Edmund Gosse and T.J. Wise, 20 vols (William Heineman, London, 1925), Vol. 3.

Les Fleurs du mal and Other Studies by Algernon Charles Swinburne, ed. Edmund Gosse (printed for private circulation, London, 1913).

Swinburne, Algernon Charles, *The Living Age* 280 (1914).

Swinburne, Algernon Charles, *The Swinburne Letters*, ed. Cecil Y. Lang, 6 vols (Yale University Press and Oxford University Press, New Haven and London, 1962).

Swinburne, Algernon Charles, *Selected Poems*, ed. L.M. Findlay (Carcanet, Manchester, 1982), pp. 185–96.
Symonds, John Addington, *Studies of the Greek Poets, First Series* (Smith, Elder and Co., London, 1873).
Symonds, John Addington, *A Problem in Greek Ethics, being an Inquiry into the Phenomenon of Sexual Inversion, addressed especially to Medical Psychologists and Jurists* (1883: privately printed, London, 1901).
Symonds, John Addington, *A Problem in Modern Ethics, being an Inquiry into the Phenomenon of Sexual Inversion addressed especially to Medical Psychologists and Jurists* (privately printed, London, 1896).
Symonds, John Addington, *The Letters of John Addington Symonds*, eds Herbert M. Schueller and Robert L. Peters (Wayne State University Press, Detroit, 1967–69).
Symons, Arthur, 'The Decadent Movement in Literature', *Harper's New Monthly Magazine*, Vol. 87 (November 1893).
Symons, Arthur, 'A Note Upon George Meredith', in *Studies in Prose and Verse* (E.P. Dutton, New York, 1922).
Talbot, James Beard, *The Miseries of Prostitution* (London, 1844).
Tennyson, Alfred, Manuscript copies of poems in the Allen notebook at Trinity College Cambridge.
Tennyson, Alfred, Manuscript copies of poems in the Heath Commonplace Book in the Fitzwilliam Museum, Cambridge.
Tennyson, Alfred, *Poems, Chiefly Lyrical* (London, 1830).
Tennyson, Alfred, *The Letters of Alfred Lord Tennyson*, eds Cecil Y. Lang and Edgar F. Shannon Jr. (Oxford University Press, Oxford, 1982).
Tennyson, Frederick, *The Isles of Greece: Sappho and Alcaeus* (Macmillan and Co., London, 1890).
Tresham, Henry, *Le avventure di Saffo* (Rome, 1784).
Volger, Heinrich Friedrich Magnus, *Sapphus Lesbiae Carmina et Fragmenta recensuit, comentario illustravit, schemata musica adjecit, et indices confecit Henr. Frid. Magnus Volger* (Leipzig, 1810).
Walhouse, Moreton John, 'The Nine Greek Lyric Poets', *The Gentleman's Magazine* (April 1877), pp. 433–51.
Walpole, Horace, *The Yale Edition of Horace Walpole's Correspondence*, ed. W.S. Lewis (Yale University Press, New Haven and London, 1937–38).
Welcker, Friedrich Gottlieb, *Sappho von einem herrschenden Vorurtheil befreyt* (Gottingen, 1816).
Wharton, H.T., *Sappho: Memoir, Text, Selected Renderings with a Literal Translation* (David Stott, London, 1885).
Winterson, Jeanette, *Art & Lies* (Jonathan Cape, London, 1994).
Woolf, Virginia, 'A Society' in *Monday or Tuesday* (Hogarth Press, London, 1921).
Woolf, Virginia, *The Diary of Virginia Woolf 1915–1941*, eds Anne Olivier Bell and Andrew McNeillie, Vols I–V (The Hogarth Press, London, 1977–84).
Woolf, Virginia, *The Letters of Virginia Woolf, 1888–1941*, eds Nigel Nicolson and Joanne Trautmann (The Hogarth Press, London, 1975–80).

Secondary sources

Abry, E., et al, *Les Grands Ecrivains de France* (Didier, Paris, 1946).
Adams, Brooks, 'Painter to Patron: David's Letters to Youssopoff about the "Sappho, Phaon and Cupid"', *Marsyas* XIX (1977–78), pp. 29–36.

Allen, Stephen C., 'Tennyson, Sappho, and "The Lady of Shalott"', *The Tennyson Research Bulletin* 2 (1975), pp 171–2.

Armstrong, Isobel, *Victorian Poetry: Poetry, Poetics and Politics* (Routledge, London and New York, 1993).

Armstrong, Isobel, 'So What's All This About the Mother's Body? The Aesthetic, Gender and the Polis' in *Textuality and Sexuality: Reading Theories and Practices*, eds Judith Still and Michael Worton (Manchester University Press, Manchester, 1993), pp. 218–36.

Armstrong, Nancy, *Desire and Domestic Fiction: A Political History of the Novel* (Oxford University Press, Oxford, 1987).

Armstrong, Nancy, 'The Rise of the Domestic Woman' in *The Ideology of Conduct: Essays in Literature and the History of Sexuality*, eds Nancy Armstrong and Leonard Tennenhouse (Methuen, New York and London, 1987).

Ashfield, Andrew, and Peter de Bolla, eds, *The Sublime: A Reader in British Eighteenth Century Aesthetic Theory* (Cambridge University Press, Cambridge, 1996).

Atterbury, Paul, ed., *The Parian Phenomenon: A Survey of Victorian Parian Porcelain, Statuary and Busts* (Richard Dennis, Shepton Beauchamp, 1989).

Bachofen, J.J., *Myth, Religion and Mother Right: Selected Writings of J.J. Bachofen*, trans. Ralph Manheim (Routledge Kegan Paul, London, 1967).

Bagg, Robert, 'Love, Ceremony and Daydream in Sappho's Lyrics', *Arion* 3 (1964), pp. 44–82.

Ballot, Marie-Juliette, *Une elève de David, la Comtesse Benoist* (E. Plon, Paris, 1914).

Balmer, Josephine, trans., *Sappho: Poems and Fragments* (Brilliance Books, London, 1984), reissued (Bloodaxe, Newcastle upon Tyne, 1992).

Barnard, Mary, trans., *Sappho* (University of California Press, Berkeley and Los Angelos, 1958), reissued (Shambhala Press, Boston and London, 1994).

Barrett, Eileen and Patricia Cramer, *Virginia Woolf: Lesbian Readings* (New York University Press, New York, 1997).

Battistini, Yves, trans. *Poétesses grecques: Sappho, Corinne, Anyte etc.* (Imprimerie Nationale Editions, Paris, 1998).

Barthes, Roland, *A Lover's Discourse: Fragments* (1978: Penguin, Harmondsworth, 1990).

Bascoul, Jean Marie François, *La Chaste Sappho de Lesbos et le mouvement feministe à Athenes au Ive siècle avant Jesu Christe* (Librairie Universitaire, Paris, 1911).

Bascoul, Jean Marie François, *La Chaste Sappho de Lesbos et Stesichore* (Librairie Universitaire, Paris, 1913).

Bass, Robert, *The Green Dragoon: The Lives of Banastre Tarleton and Mary Robinson* (Alvin Redman, London, 1957).

Baudelaire, Charles, *Les Fleurs du mal*, ed. Antoine Adam (Classiques Garnier, Paris, 1994).

Baudelaire, Charles, *The Complete Verse*, with an introduction and translations by Francis Scarfe (Anvil Press Poetry, London, 1986).

Baudelaire, Charles, *Correspondence*, ed. Claude Pichois (Gallimard, Bibliothèque de la Pleide, Paris, 1973).

Baudelaire, Charles, *Dernières lettres inédities à sa mère* (Crepet, Paris, 1926).

Baumgartel, Bettina, *Angelica Kauffmann: Herausgegein und Scarbertet* (Kunstmuseum Dusseldorf and Verlag Gerd Hatje, Ostfildern-Ruit, 1999).

Beazley, J.D., *Greek Vases in Poland* (Clarendon Press, Oxford, 1928).

Beer, Gillian, *Darwin's Plots: Evolutionary Narrative in Darwin, George Eliot and Nineteenth Century Fiction* (Routledge, London, 1982).

Benjamin, Walter, *Charles Baudelaire: A Lyric Poet in the Era of High Capitalism* (1969) trans. Harry Zohn (New Left Books, London, 1973).

Benstock, Shari, *Women of the Left Bank, Paris 1900–1940* (University of Texas Press, Austin Texas, 1986).

Benvenuto, Bice and Roger Kennedy, *The Works of Jacques Lacan: An Introduction* (Free Association Books, London, 1986).

Berger, John, *Ways of Seeing* (Penguin, London and Harmondsworth, 1972).

Bergman-Carton, Janis, *The Woman of Ideas in French Art, 1830–1848* (Yale University Press, New Haven, 1995).

Bezier, Janet, *Ventriloquized Bodies: Narratives of Hysteria in Nineteenth Century France* (Cornell University Press, Ithaca and London, 1994).

Blankley, Elyse, 'Return to Mytilene: Renée Vivien and the City of Women' in *Women Writers and the City*, ed. Susan Merrill Squier (University of Tennessee Press, Knoxville Tennessee, 1984), pp. 45–67.

Blin, George, *Le Sadisme de Baudelaire* (Corti, Paris, 1948).

Boehringer, Sandra, *Dika, élève de Sappho* (Autrement, Paris, 1999).

Bremmer, Jan, ed., *From Sappho to de Sade: Moments in the History of Sexuality* (Routledge, London and New York, 1989).

Bronfen, Elisabeth, *Over her Dead Body: Death, Femininity and the Aesthetic* (Manchester University Press, Manchester, 1992).

Bronfen, Elisabeth, *The Knotted Subject: Hysteria and Its Discontents* (Princeton University Press, Princeton New Jersey, 1998).

Brooks, Peter, *Body Work: Objects of Desire in Modern Narrative* (Harvard University Press, Cambridge Mass. and London, 1993).

Brown, Susan, 'A Victorian Sappho: Agency, Identity, and the Politics of Poetics', *English Studies in Canada*, 20:2 (June 1994), pp. 205–25.

Burnett, Anne Pippin, 'Desire and Memory (Sappho Fragment 94)', *Classical Philology* 74 (1979), pp. 16–27.

Burnett, Anne Pippin, *Three Archaic Poets: Archilochus, Alcaeus, Sappho* (Harvard University Press, Cambridge Mass., 1983).

Buchanan, Robert, 'The Fleshly School of Poetry', *The Contemporary Review* (1871), quoted in *The Victorian Poet: Poetics and Persona*, ed. Joseph Bristow (Croom Helm, London, 1987).

Bush, Douglas, *Mythology and the Romantic Tradition in English Poetry* (Harvard University Press, Cambridge Mass., 1937).

Butler, Judith, *Bodies That Matter: On the Discursive Limits of 'Sex'* (Routledge, London, 1993).

Butler, H. Montagu, 'Recollections of Tennyson' in *Tennyson and His Friends*, ed. Hallam Tennyson (Macmillan, London, 1911).

Cameron, Vivian, 'Political Exposures: Sexuality and Caricature in the French Revolution' in *Eroticism and the Body Politic*, ed. Lynn Hunt (Johns Hopkins University Press, Baltimore, 1991), pp. 90–107.

Campbell, David A., ed., *Greek Lyric 1: Sappho and Alcaeus* (Loeb Classical Library, Harvard University Press, Cambridge Mass., 1982).

Campbell, Nancie, *Tennyson in Lincoln: A Catalogue of the Collections in the Research Centre* (Tennyson Research Centre, Lincoln, 1971).

Carman, Bliss, *Sappho: One Hundred Lyrics* (Florence Press, Chatto and Windus, London, 1910).

Carson, Anne, *Eros the Bittersweet: An Essay* (Princeton University Press, Princeton New Jersey, 1986).

Castle, Terry, *The Apparitional Lesbian: Female Homosexuality and Modern Culture* (Columbia University Press, New York, 1993).

Carter, Angela, *The Sadeian Woman: An Exercise in Cultural History* (Virago, London, 1979).
Carter, Angela, *The Bloody Chamber and Other Stories* (1979: London, 1995)
Chandler, Robert, ed. and trans., *Sappho* (J.M. Dent, London, 1998).
William Christie, *Paucae Micae (A Few Crumbs)*, (The Castlelaw Press, West Linton Peebleshire, 1971).
Clément, Catherine, *Opera: The Undoing of Women*, trans. Betsy Wing (1988: Virago, London, 1989).
Clements, Patricia, *Charles Baudelaire and the English Tradition* (Princeton University Press, Princeton New Jersey, 1985).
Cixous, Hélène, 'Difficult Joys' in *The Body and the Text: Hélène Cixous, Reading and Teaching*, eds Helen Wilcox, Keith McWatters, Ann Thompson and Linda R. Williams (Harvester, Hemel Hempstead, 1990).
Coleridge, Samuel Taylor, *The Poems of Samuel Taylor Coleridge*, ed. E.H. Coleridge (Oxford University Press, Oxford, 1935).
Coleridge, Samuel Taylor, *The Collected Letters of Samuel Taylor Coleridge*, ed. E.L. Griggs (Oxford University Press, 1956–71).
Collins, John Churton, *Illustrations of Tennyson* (Chatto and Windus, London, 1891).
Collecott, Diana, *H.D. and Sapphic Modernism 1910–1950* (Cambridge University Press, Cambridge, 1999).
Collecott, Diana, ed., *Agenda: H.D. Special Issue* (1988).
Connor, Rachel, 'Textu(r)al Braille: Visionary (Re)Readings of H.D.', in *Body Matters: Feminism, Textuality, Corporeality*, eds Avril Horner and Angela Keane (Manchester University Press, Manchester, 2000), pp. 199–208.
Constantine, David, *Watching for Dolphins* (Bloodaxe, Newcastle-upon-Tyne, 1983).
Cox, Edwin Marion, *The Poems of Sappho* (Williams and Norgate Ltd, London, 1925).
Cox, Edwin Marion, *Sappho: The Text Arranged with Translations an Introduction and Notes* (The Boar's Head Press, Manaton, Devon, 1932).
Cullens, Chris, 'Mrs. Robinson and the Masquerade of Womanliness', in *Body and Text in the Eighteenth Century*, eds Veronica Kelly and Dorothea von Mucke (Stanford University Press, Stanford California, 1994), pp. 266–89.
Culler, Jonathan, 'Intertextuality and Interpretation: Baudelaire's *Correspondances*', in *Nineteenth-Century French Poetry: Introductions to Close Reading*, ed, Christopher Prendergast (Cambridge University Press, Cambridge, 1990).
Dalven, Rae, *Daughters of Sappho: Contemporary Greek Women Poets* (Fairleigh Dickinson University Press, Rutherford, 1994).
Davenport, Guy, *Seven Greeks* (New Directions Publishing Corporation, New York, 1995).
de Beauvoir, Simone, *The Second Sex* (1949), trans. H.M. Parshley (Vintage, New York, 1974).
de Bolla, Peter, *The Discourse of the Sublime: Readings in History, Aesthetics and the Subject* (Basil Blackwell, Oxford, 1989).
Dehler, Johanna, *Fragments of Desire: Sapphic Fictions in Works by H.D., Judy Grahn, and Monique Wittig* (P. Lang, Frankfurt am Main and New York, 1999).
DeJean, Joan, *Fictions of Sappho: 1546–1937* (Chicago University Press, Chicago, 1989).
de Lauretis, Teresa, *Alice Doesn't: Feminism, Semiotics, Cinema* (Indiana University Press, Bloomington, 1984).
Devereux, George, 'The Nature of Sappho's Seizure in Fragment 31 as Evidence of her Inversion', *Classical Quarterly* 20 (1970), pp. 17–31.
Djkstra, Bram, *Idols of Perversity: Fantasies of Feminine Evil in Fin de Siècle Culture* (Oxford University Press, Oxford, 1986).

Dowling, Linda, *Language and Decadence in the Victorian Fin de Siècle* (Princeton University Press, Princeton New Jersey, 1986).

Dowling, Linda, *Hellenism and Homosexuality in Victorian Oxford* (Cornell University Press, Ithaca and London, 1994).

Doy, Gen, *Women and Visual Culture in Nineteenth Century France, 1800–1852* (Leicester University Press, London and New York, 1998).

Duban, Jeffrey M., *Ancient and Modern Images of Sappho: Translations and Studies in Archaic Greek Love Lyric* (University Press of America, Washington DC, 1983).

DuBois, Page, *Sappho is Burning* (University of Chicago Press, Chicago and London, 1995).

DuPlessis, Rachel Blau, *H.D. The Career of That Struggle* (Harvester, Brighton, 1986).

Eagleton, Terry, *The Ideology of the Aesthetic* (Basil Blackwell, Oxford, 1990).

Edmonds, Susan, 'Stealing from "Muddies Body": H.D. and Melanie Klein', *H.D. Newsletter*, ed. Eileen Gregory, Vol. 4, part 2 (Winter, 1991).

Fadermann, Lillian, *Surpassing the Love of Men: Romantic Friendship and Love Between Women* (William Morrow and Co. Inc., New York, 1981).

Ferguson, Frances, *Solitude and the Sublime: Romanticism and the Aesthetics of Individuation* (Routledge, London and New York, 1992).

Fink, Bruce, *A Clinical Introduction to Lacanian Psychoanalysis, Theory and Technique* (Harvard University Press, Cambridge Mass., 1977).

Firkins, O.W., 'The New Movement in Poetry', *The Nation* (14 October, 1915), pp. 458–61, quoted in Glenn Hughes, *Imagism and the Imagists* (1931: Humanities Press, New York, 1969), pp. 60–1.

Forer, L., 'Les Portraits de Sapho sur Les Monnaies', *Revue Belge de Numismatique*, Vol. 57 (1901).

Foster, Jeanette H., *Sex Variant Women in Literature: A Historical and Quantitative Survey* (Frederick Muller Ltd, London, 1958).

Foucault, Michel, *History of Sexuality, An Introduction*, Vol. I (Penguin, Harmondsworth Middlesex, 1984).

Freud, Sigmund, 'Fetishism' (1927), in *The Standard Edition of the Complete Psychological Works of Sigmund Freud*, ed. and trans. James Strachey (The Hogarth Press, London, 1953–74), Vol. XXI, pp. 149–57.

Freud, Sigmund, 'Femininity' (1933) in *The Standard Edition of the Complete Psychological Works of Sigmund Freud*, ed. and trans. James Strachey (The Hogarth Press, London, 1953–74), Vol. XXII, pp. 112–35.

Freud, Sigmund, 'Jokes and Their Relation to the Unconscious', in *The Standard Edition of the Complete Psychological Works of Sigmund Freud*, ed. and trans. James Strachey (The Hogarth Press, London, 1953–74), Vol. VII, pp. 97–102.

Friedman, Susan Stanford, '"I Go Where I Love": An Intertextual Study of H.D. and Adrienne Rich', in *Signs: The Lesbian Issue* (University of Chicago Press, Chicago, 1985).

Friedman, Susan Stanford, 'Exile in the American Grain: H.D.'s Diaspora', in *Women's Writing in Exile*, eds Mary Lynn Broe and Angela Ingram (University of North Carolina Press, Chapel Hill and London, 1989), pp. 87–112.

Friedman, Susan Stanford, *Penelope's Web: Gender, Modernity H.D.'s Fiction* (Cambridge University Press, Cambridge, 1990).

Friedman, Susan Stanford and Rachel Blau DuPlessis, eds, *Signets: Reading H.D.* (University of Wisconsin Press, Madison Wisconsin, 1990).

Fritz, Angela DiPace, *Thought and Vision: A Critical Reading of H.D.'s Poetry* (Catholic University of America Press, Washington D.C., 1988).

Fuller, Peter, 'The Venus and "Internal Objects"' in *Art and Psychoanalysis* (Writers and Readers, London, 1980).

Furniss, Tom, *Edmund Burke's Aesthetic Ideology* (Cambridge University Press, Cambridge, 1993).

Fuss, Diana, *Essentially Speaking: Feminism, Nature and Difference* (Routledge, London, 1989).

Gathercole, Patricia M., 'Illuminations on the French Manuscripts of Boccaccio's *De Claris Mulieribus*', *Italia* XLII (1965).

Gerard, Frances A., *Angelica Kauffmann* (Ward and Downey, London, 1893).

Gilcher, Edwin, *A Bibliography of George Moore* (Northern Illinois University Press, De Kalb, 1970), pp. 2, 4, 5.

Girard, René, *Deceit, Desire and the Novel: Self and the Other in Literary Structure*, trans. Yvonne Freccero (1961: Johns Hopkins University Press, Baltimore, 1965).

Goodden, Angelica, *The Sweetness of Life: A Biography of Elisabeth Louise Vigée-LeBrun* (Andre Deutsch, London, 1997).

Grahn, Judy, *The Highest Apple: Sappho and the Lesbian Poetic Tradition* (Spinsters, Ink, San Francisco, 1985).

Gray, Francine du Plessix, *Rage and Fire: A Life of Louise Colet, Pioneer Feminist, Literary Star, Flaubert's Muse* (Hamish Hamilton, London, 1994).

Greene, Ellen, 'Apostrophe and Women's Erotics in the Poetry of Sappho', *Transactions of the American Philological Association* 124 (1994), pp. 41–56;

Greene, Ellen, ed., *Reading Sappho: Contemporary Approaches* (University of California Press, Berkeley and Los Angeles, 1995).

Greene, Ellen, ed., *Re-Reading Sappho: Reception and Transmission* (University of California Press, Berkeley and Los Angeles, 1996).

Greer, Germaine, 'The Enigma of Sappho' in *Slipshod Sibyls: Recognition, Rejection and the Woman Poet* (Viking Penguin, London, 1995).

Gregory, Eileen, *H.D. and Hellenism* (Cambridge University Press, Cambridge, 1997)

Griffin, Susan, *Pornography and Silence: Culture's Revenge Against Nature* (The Women's Press, London, 1981).

Groden, Suzy Q., *Arion*, Vol. 3, part 3 (Autumn, 1964).

Gubar, Susan, 'Sapphistries', *Signs* 10 (Autumn, 1984), pp. 43–62.

Gutwirth, Madelyn, *Madame de Stael, Novelist: The Emergence of the Artist as Woman* (University of Illinois Press, Urbana Illinois, 1978).

Haffenden, John, *Novelists in Interview* (Methuen, London and New York, 1985).

Haines, C.R., *Sappho: The Poems and Fragments* (George Routledge and Sons, London, 1926).

Hallett, Judith P., 'Sappho and her Social Context: Sense and Sensuality', *Signs* 4 (1979), pp. 447–64, reprinted in *Reading Sappho: Contemporary Approaches*, ed. Ellen Greene (University of California Press, Berkeley and Los Angeles, 1995).

Hallett, Judith P., 'Beloved Cleis', *Quaderni Urbinati di Cultura Classica* 10 (1982), pp. 21–31.

Hardy, Thomas, *One Rare Fair Woman: Thomas Hardy's Letters to Florence Henniker 1983–1922*, eds Evelyn Hardy and F.B. Pinion (Macmillan, London, 1972).

Harries, Elizabeth Wanning, *The Unfinished Manner: Essays on the Fragment in the Later Eighteenth Century* (University Press of Virginia, Charlottesville and London, 1994).

Harvey, Elizabeth, 'Ventriloquizing Sappho, or the Lesbian Muse' in *Ventriloquized Voices: Feminist Theory and English Renaissance Texts* (Routledge, London and New York, 1992), pp. 116–39.

Hawley, Richard and Barbara Levick, *Women in Antiquity: New Assessments* (Routledge, London and New York, 1995).

Heintze, Helga von, *Das Bildnis der Sappho* (Florian Kupferberg, Mainz, 1966).

Herriot, Edouard, *Madame Recamier* (G.P. Putnam and Sons, New York, 1906).

Herrmann, Claudine, *Les voleuses de langue* (Editions des femmes, Paris, 1976).

Holmes, Richard, *Coleridge: Early Visions* (Flamingo, London, 1990).

Holmes, Richard, *Coleridge: Darker Reflections* (Flamingo, London, 1998).

Holmstrom, K.G., *Monodrama, Attitudes, Tableaux Vivants: Studies on Some Trends of Theatrical Fashion 1770–1815* (Almquist and Wiksell, Stockholm, 1967).

Hughes, Glenn, *Imagism and the Imagists: A Study in Modern Poetry* (Stanford University Press and Oxford University Press, Palo Alto and London, 1931).

Hunt, Lynn, 'The Many Bodies of Marie Antoinette: Political Pornography and the Problem of the Feminine in the French Revolution', in *Eroticism and the Body Politic*, ed. Lynn Hunt (Johns Hopkins University Press, Baltimore and London, 1991), pp. 108–30.

Hyder, Clyde K., ed., *Swinburne: The Critical Heritage* (Routledge Kegan Paul, London, 1970).

Irigaray, Luce, 'Ce sexe qui n'en pas un' (1977) translated as 'This sex which is not one' by Claudia Reeder in *New French Feminisms*, eds Elaine Marks and Isabelle de Courtivron (Harvester, Brighton, 1985).

Janowitz, Anne, *England's Ruins: Poetic Purpose and the National Landscape* (Basil Blackwell, Oxford, 1990).

Janowitz, Anne, 'The Romantic Fragment' in *A Companion to Romanticism*, ed. Duncan Wu (Basil Blackwell, Oxford, 1998), pp. 442–51.

Jardine, Lisa, *Worldly Goods: A New History of the Renaissance* (Macmillan, London, 1996).

Jay, Peter and Caroline Lewis, eds, *Sappho Through English Poetry* (Anvil Press, London, 1996).

Jenkins, Ian and Kim Sloan, eds, *Vases and Volcanoes: Sir William Hamilton and his Collection* (British Museum Press, London, 1996).

Jenkyns, Richard, *Three Classical Poets: Sappho, Catullus and Juvenal* (Duckworth, London, 1982).

John, C.H.S., *Bartolozzi, Zoffany and Kauffmann with other Foreign Members of the Royal Academy 1768–1792* (Frederick A. Stokes, New York, n.d.).

Jones, Adrian, *The Nature of the Book: Print and Knowledge in the Making* (The University of Chicago Press, Chicago, 1998).

Jones, Vivien, ed., *Women in the Eighteenth Century: Constructions of Femininity* (Routledge, London and New York, 1990).

Jullian, Phillippe, *D'Annunzio*, trans. Stephen Hardman (The Pall Mall Press, London, 1972).

Kelvin, Norman, 'H.D. and the Years of World War I', *Victorian Poetry*, Vol. 38, part 1 (Spring, 2000), pp. 170–96.

Kenner, Hugh, *The Pound Era* (1971: Pimlico, London, 1991).

Kierkegaard, Søren, *Diary of a Seducer*, trans. Gerd Gillhoff (Unger, Stockholm, 1966).

Kristeva, Julia, *Tales of Love*, trans. Leon S. Roudiez (Columbia University Press, New York, 1987).

Kurke, Leslie, 'The Strangeness of "Song Culture": Archaic Greek Poetry' in *Literature in the Greek and Roman Worlds: A New Perspective*, ed. Oliver Taplin (Oxford University Press, Oxford, 2000), pp. 58–87.

Lacan, Jacques, 'The Subversion of the Subject and the Dialectic of Desire in the Freudian Unconscious' in *Ecrits: A Selection*, trans. Alan Sheridan (Norton, New York, 1977).

Lacan, Jacques, 'Desire, Life and Death' in *The Seminar of Jacques Lacan, Book II, The Ego in Freud's Theory and in the Technique of Psychoanalysis 1954–1955*, ed. Jacques-Alain Miller, trans. Sylvana Tomaselli (Cambridge University Press, Cambridge, 1988).

Laity, Cassandra, *H.D. and the Victorian Fin de Siècle: Gender, Modernism and Decadence* (Cambridge University Press, Cambridge, 1997).

Lanata, Giuliana, trans. William Robins, 'Sappho's Amatory Language', in *Reading Sappho: Contemporary Approaches*, ed. Ellen Greene (University of California Press, Berkeley and Los Angeles, 1995).

Lardinois, André, 'Lesbian Sappho and Sappho of Lesbos' in *From Sappho to de Sade: Moments in the History of Sexuality*, ed. Jan Bremmer (Routledge, London and New York, 1989), pp. 15–35.

Lardinois, André, 'Who Sang Sappho's Songs?' in *Reading Sappho*, ed. Ellen Greene (University of California Press, Berkeley and Los Angeles, 1996), pp. 150–74.

Larnac, Jean and Robert Salmon, *Sappho* (Les Editions Rieder, Paris, 1934).

Lasserre, François, *Sappho, une autre lecture* (Antenore, Padua, 1989).

Leakey, F.W., *Baudelaire: Les Fleurs du mal* (Cambridge University Press, Cambridge, 1992).

Leftokowitz, Mary R., 'Critical Stereotypes and the Poetry of Sappho', *Greek, Roman and Byzantine Studies* 14 (1973), pp. 113–23 and in *Reading Sappho: Contemporary Approaches*, ed. Ellen Greene (University of California Press, Berkeley and Los Angeles, 1995).

Leighton, Angela, *Victorian Women Poets: Writing Against the Heart* (Harvester, Hemel Hempstead, 1992).

Leighton, Angela and Margaret Reynolds, eds, *Victorian Women Poets: An Anthology* (Basil Blackwell, Oxford, 1995).

Leonard, William Ellery, 'The New Poetry – A Critique', *Chicago Evening Post* (18 and 25 September, 2 and 9 October, 1915), quoted in Glenn Hughes, *Imagism and the Imagists* (1931: Humanities Press, New York, 1960).

Levi, Peter, *Tennyson* (Macmillan, London, 1993).

Levinson, Marjorie, *The Romantic Fragment Poem: A Critique of a Form* (University of North Carolina Press, Chapel Hill, 1986).

Lipking, Lawrence, *Abandoned Women and Poetic Tradition* (Chicago University Press, Chicago, 1988).

Lipking, Lawrence, 'Donna Abandonata' in *The Don Giovanni Book: Myths of Seduction and Betrayal*, ed. Jonathan Miller (Faber and Faber, London, 1990).

Lloyd, A.T., *Sappho: Life and Work* (Arthur Humphreys, London, 1910).

Lobel, Edgar and Denys Page, eds, *Poetarum Lesbiorum Fragmenta* (Clarendon, Oxford University Press, Oxford, 1955).

Louis, Margot K., *Swinburne and His Gods: The Roots and Growth of an Agnostic Poetry* (McGill-Queen's University Press, Montreal and London, 1990).

Lowell, Robert, 'Three Letters to Anaktoria' in *Imitations* (Faber and Faber, London, 1962).

MacCannell, Juliet Flower, 'Jouissance' in *Feminism and Psychoanalysis: A Critical Dictionary*, ed. Elizabeth Wright (Basil Blackwell, Oxford, 1992).

McEvilley, Thomas, 'Sappho, Fragment 31: The Face Behind the Mask', *Phoenix* 32 (1978), pp. 1–18.

McFarland, Thomas, *Romanticism and the Forms of Ruin: Wordsworth, Coleridge and Modalities of Fragmentation* (Princeton University Press, Princeton New Jersey, 1981).

McGann, Jerome, *Swinburne: An Experiment in Criticism* (University of Chicago Press, Chicago and London, 1972).

McGann, Jerome, *The Poetics of Sensibility* (Clarendon Press, Oxford, 1995).

McLellan, Diana, *The Girls, Sappho goes to Hollywood* (Robson, London, 2001).

Makower, Stanley, *Perdita: A Romance in Biography* (Hutchinson and Co., London, 1908).

Mankowitz, Wolf, *Wedgwood* (Batsford, London, 1953).

Marcus, Jane, 'Sapphistory: The Woolf and the Well' in *Lesbian Texts and Contexts: Radical Revisions* (Onlywomen, London, 1992), pp. 164–80.

Martin, Robert Bernard, *Tennyson: The Unquiet Heart* (Clarendon Press, Oxford, 1980).

Mavor, Elizabeth, *The Ladies of Llangollen: A Study in Romantic Friendship* (Michael Joseph, London, 1971).

Maxwell, Catherine, 'Engendering Vision in the Victorian Male Poet' in *Writing and Victorianism*, ed. J.B. Bullen (Longman, London and New York, 1997), pp. 73–103.

Maxwell, Catherine, *The Female Sublime from Milton to Swinburne: Bearing Blindness* (Manchester University Press, Manchester, 2001).
Mazzotta, Giuseppe, 'The *Canzoniere* and the Language of the Self', *Studies in Philology* 75 (1978).
Mellor, Anne, *Romanticism and Gender* (Routledge, London and New York, 1993).
Michaelis, Adolf, *Ancient Marbles in Great Britain* (Cambridge University Press, Cambridge, 1882).
Miller, Marion Mills, *The Songs of Sappho: Including the Recent Egyptian Discoveries*, ed. and trans. David M. Robinson (Frank-Maurice, New York, 1925).
Mirzoeff, Nicholas, *Bodyscape: Art, Modernity and the Ideal Figure* (Routledge, London, 1995).
Moers, Ellen, *Literary Women* (The Women's Press, London, 1978).
Moi, Toril, 'The Missing Mother: The Oedipal Rivalries of Rene Girard', *Diacritics* 12:2 (1982), pp. 21–31.
Mongan, Agnes, 'The Forsythe Wickes Collection of the Museum of Fine Art in Boston', *Great Private Collections*, ed. Douglas Cooper (Macmillan, New York, 1963).
Monk, Samuel H., *The Sublime: A Study of Critical Theories in XIII-Century England* (Modern Language Association of America, 1935: University of Michigan Press, Ann Arbor, 1960).
Mora, Edith, *Sappho: histoire d'un poète* (Flammarion, Paris, 1966).
Mustard, Wilfred P., *Classical Echoes in Tennyson* (1904: Haskell House Publishers, New York, 1971).
Nead, Lynda, *Myths of Sexuality: Representations of Women in Victorian Britain* (Basil Blackwell, Oxford, 1988).
Nead, Lynda, *The Female Nude: Art, Obscenity and Sexuality* (Routledge, London, 1992).
Nims, John Frederick, *Poems in Translation: Sappho to Valery* (University of Arkansas Press, Arkansas, 1990).
Norsa, Medea, 'Dai papiri della Societa Italiana: Versi di Saffo in un ostrakon del sec. II a C' in *Annali della Schuola Normale Superiore di Pisa* (1937), pp. 8–15.
Norton, Rictor, *Mother Clap's Molly House: The Gay Sub-Culture 1700–1830* (GMP, London, 1992).
Nunokowa, Jeff, '*In Memoriam* and the Extinction of the Homosexual', in *Tennyson*, ed. Rebecca Stott (Longman, London and New York, 1996), pp. 197–209.
O'Connell, Richard, *Sappho* (Atlantis Editions, Philadelphia, 1975).
Osborn, Percy, *The Poems of Sappho* (Elkin Mathews, London, 1909).
Paden, W.D., *Tennyson in Egypt* (1942: Octagon Books, New York, 1971).
Page, Denys, *Sappho and Alcaeus* (Clarendon Press, Oxford, 1955).
Paglia, Camille, *Sexual Personae: Art and Decadence From Nefertiti to Emily Dickinson* (Yale University Press, New Haven and London, 1990).
Parker, Holt, 'Sappho Schoolmistress', *Transactions of the American Philological Association* 123 (1993), pp. 309–51.
Parslow, Christopher Charles, *Re-Discovering Antiquity: Karl Weber and the Excavation of Herculaneum, Pompeii and Stabiae* (Cambridge University Press, Cambridge, 1998).
Pattison, Robert, *Tennyson and Tradition* (Harvard University Press, Cambridge Mass. and London, 1979).
Peterson, Linda H., 'Sappho and the Making of Tennysonian Lyric', *English Literary History*, Vol. 61 (1994).
Poirier, Richard, *The Performing Self: Compositions and Decompositions in the Languages of Contemporary Life* (Oxford University Press, Oxford and New York, 1971).
Porter, Roy, 'Libertinism and Promiscuity', in *The Don Giovanni Book*, ed. Jonathan Miller (Faber and Faber, London, 1990).
Powell, Jim, *Sappho: A Garland* (Farrar Straus Giroux, New York, 1993).

Praz, Mario, *On NeoClassicism* (1940), translated from the Italian by Angus Davidson (Thames and Hudson, London, 1969).

Prendergast, Christopher, *Napoleon and History Painting: Antoine-Jean Gros's 'Le Bataille d'Eylau'* (Oxford University Press, Oxford, 1997).

Pressly, Nancy, *The Fuseli Circle in Rome: Early Romantic Art of the 1770's* (Yale Center for British Art, 1979).

Prins, Yopie, 'Elizabeth Barrett, Robert Browning, and the Difference of Translation', *Victorian Poetry*, Vol. 29, part 4 (Winter 1991), pp. 435–51.

Prins, Yopie and Maeera Schreiber, eds, *Dwelling in Possibility: Women Poets and Critics on Poetry* (Cornell University Press, Ithaca and London, 1997).

Prins, Yopie, *Victorian Sappho* (Princeton University Press, Princeton New Jersey, 1999).

Rajan, Balachandra, *The Form of the Unfinished: English Poetics from Dryden to Blake* (Princeton University Press, Princeton New Jersey, 1985).

Rayor, Diane, trans. *Sappho's Lyre: Archaic Lyric and Women Poets of Ancient Greece* (University of California Press, Berkeley and Los Angeles, 1991).

Reynolds, Margaret, 'The Woman Poet Sings Sappho's Last Song' in *Victorian Women Poets: A Critical Reader*, ed. Angela Leighton (Blackwell, Oxford, 1996).

Reynolds, Margaret, *The Sappho Companion* (Chatto and Windus, London, 2000).

Richter, Jean, 'Restitution à Gautier du texte "Sapho"', *Bulletin de la Société Théophile Gautier*, Vol. 7 (1985), pp. 163–8.

Rissman, Leah, *Love as War: Homeric Allusion in the Poetry of Sappho* (Hain, Konigstein Texas, 1983).

Rivière, Joan, 'Womanliness as Masquerade' (1929), in *Formations of Fantasy*, eds Victor Burgin, James Donald and Cora Kaplan (Methuen, London and New York, 1986).

Robinson, David M., *Sappho and Her Influence* (George Harrap and Co. Ltd, London, 1925).

Robinson, Janice S., *H.D.: The Life and Work of An American Poet* (Houghton Mifflin Company, Boston, 1982).

Rose, Jacqueline, *Sexuality in the Field of Vision* (Verso, London and New York, 1986).

Rowlinson, Matthew, *Tennyson's Fixations: Psychoanalysis and the Topics of the Early Poetry* (University of Virginia Press, Charlottesville, 1994).

Rudiger, H., *Sappho: Ihr Ruf und Ruhm bei der Nachwelt* (Dieterich, Leipzig, 1933).

Saake, Helmut, *Sapphostudien: Forschungsgeschichte, biografische und literarische Untersuchungen* (Schoningh, Munich, 1972).

Said, Edward, *Musical Elaborations* (Vintage, London, 1991).

Sappho, trans. J. Easby-Smith, *The Songs of Sappho* (Georgetown University, Washington DC, 1891).

Sappho, ed. Henry Thornton Wharton, *Sappho: Memoir, Text, Selected Renderings, with a Literal Translation* (David Stott, London, 1885).

Sappho, trans. H. de Vere Stacpoole, *Sappho: A New Rendering* (Hutchinson and Co., London, n.d.).

Sappho, trans. Percy Osborn, *The Poems of Sappho* (Elkin Mathews, London, 1909).

Sappho, trans. Renée Vivien, *Sapho et huit poétesses grecques* (Alphonse, Lemerre, Paris, 1909).

Sappho, ed. Edwin Marion Cox, *The Poems of Sappho* (Williams and Norgate Ltd, London, 1925).

Sappho, trans. Edwin Marion Cox, *Sappho: The Text Arranged with Translations and Introduction and Notes* (The Boar's Head Press, Manaton Devon, 1932).

Sappho, trans. C.R. Haines, *Sappho: The Poems and Fragments* (George Routledge and Sons, London, 1926).

Sappho, eds Edgar Lobel and Denys Page, *Poetarum Lesbiorum Fragmenta* (Clarendon, Oxford University Press, Oxford, 1955).
Sappho, trans. Marion Mills Miller and ed. David M. Robinson, *The Songs of Sappho: Including the Recent Egyptian Discoveries* (Frank-Maurice, New York, 1925).
Sappho, *The Songs of Sappho: Sappho in English Translation by Many Poets* (The Peter Pauper Press, Mount Vernon, New York, 1942).
Sappho, trans. Mary Barnard, *Sappho* (University of California Press, Berkeley and Los Angelos, 1958), reissued (Shambhala Press, Boston and London, 1994).
Sappho, trans. Suzy Q. Groden, *Arion*, Vol. 3, part 3 (Autumn, 1964).
Sappho, ed. Eva-Maria Voigt, *Sappho et Alcaeus: Fragmenta* (Amsterdam-Polak and Van Gennep, Amsterdam, 1971).
Sappho, trans. Richard O'Connell, *Sappho* (Atlantis Editions, Philadelphia, 1975).
Sappho, ed. and trans. David A. Campbell, *Greek Lyric 1: Sappho and Alcaeus* (Loeb Classical Library, Harvard University Press, Cambridge Mass., 1982).
Sappho, *The Poems of Sappho of Lesbos, the Greek Text edited and translated* with an introduction and notes by Terence DuQuesne with original illustrations by Dwina Murphy-Gigg (Darengo in association with Prebenal, Thame, 1989).
Sappho, trans. Josephine Balmer, *Sappho: Poems and Fragments* (Brilliance Books, London, 1984), reissued (Bloodaxe, Newcastle-upon-Tyne, 1992).
Sappho, trans. Diane Rayor, *Sappho's Lyre: Archaic Lyric and Women Poets of Ancient Greece* (University of California Press, Berkeley and Los Angeles, 1991).
Sappho, trans. D.W. Myatt, *Sappho: Lesbian Fragments* (Thormynd, York, 1991).
Sappho, trans. Jim Powell, *Sappho: A Garland* (Farrar Straus Giroux, New York, 1993).
Sappho, trans. M.L. West, *Greek Lyric Poetry* (Worlds Classics, Oxford University Press, Oxford, 1993).
Sappho, eds Peter Jay and Caroline Lewis, *Sappho Through English Poetry* (Anvil Press, London, 1996).
Sappho, trans. Robert Chandler, *Sappho* (J.M. Dent, London, 1998).
Sappho, recueillies par Philippe Brunet, preface de Karen Haddad-Wotling, *L'égal des dieux, cent versions d'un poème de Sappho* (Allia, Paris, 1998).
Sartre, Jean Paul, *L'Idiot de la famille*, 2 vols (Gallimard, Paris, 1971).
Sedgwick, Eve Kosofsky, *Between Men: English Literature and Male Homosocial Desire* (Columbia University Press, New York, 1985).
Segal, Charles, 'Eros and Incantation: Sappho and Oral Poetry' in *Reading Sappho: Contemporary Approaches*, ed. Ellen Greene (University of California Press, Berkeley and Los Angeles, 1995), pp. 58–78.
Seltman, Charles, *Women in Antiquity* (St Martin's Press, New York, 1955).
Setzer, Sharon, 'Mary Robinson as Sylphid Self: The End of Feminine Self-Fashioning', *Philological Quarterly* 75:4 (Fall 1996), pp. 501–20.
Sewter, A.C., 'The Life, Work and Letters of William Artaud' (MA thesis, University of Manchester, 1951).
Schefold, Karl, *Die Bildnisse der Antiken Dichter* (Benno Schwabe, Basel, 1943).
Sheriff, Mary D., *The Exceptional Woman: Elisabeth Vigée-Lebrun and the Cultural Politics of Art* (University of Chicago Press, Chicago and London, 1996).
Showalter, Elaine, *Sexual Anarchy: Gender and Culture at the Fin de Siècle* (Bloomsbury, London, 1991).
Simpson, Mark, 'A Crying Shame: Transvestism and Misogyny in [Neil Jordan's film] "The Crying Game"' in *Male Impersonators: Men Performing Masculinity* (Cassell, London, 1994), pp. 164–76.
Sinfield, Alan, *Alfred Tennyson* (Basil Blackwell, Oxford, 1986).

Skinner, Marilyn B., 'Woman and Language in Archaic Greece, or, Why is Sappho a Woman?' in *Feminist Theory and the Classics*, eds Nancy Sorkin Rabinowitz and Amy Richlin (Routledge, London and New York, 1993), pp. 125–44.

Skovgaard, Bente, *Catalogue of Abildgaard's Drawings*, Kobberstiksamling-ens 110, 11, 113 billedhefter 4 (The Royal Museum of Fine Arts, Copenhagen, 1978).

Sligo, John, *The Faces of Sappho* (Penguin and the Literature Board of the Australia Council, Ringwood Victoria, 1990).

Smith, Alison, *The Victorian Nude: Sexuality, Morality and Art* (Manchester University Press, Manchester and New York, 1996).

Snyder, Jane McIntosh, *Lesbian Desire in the Lyrics of Sappho* (Columbia University Press, New York, 1997).

Stehle, Eva, *Performance and Gender in Ancient Greece: Non Dramatic Poetry in its Setting* (Princeton University Press, Princeton New Jersey, 1997).

Stein, Judith, 'The Iconography of Sappho 1775–1875' (unpublished PhD thesis, University of Pennsylvannia, 1981).

Stray, Christopher, *Classics Transformed: Schools, Universities, and Society in England, 1830–1960* (Clarendon Press, Oxford, 1998).

Stott, Rebecca, *The Fabrication of the Late Victorian Femme Fatale* (Macmillan, London, 1992).

Sturgis, Matthew, *Passionate Attitudes: The English Decadence of the Eighteen Nineties* (Macmillan, London, 1995).

Svenbro, Jesper, 'Death by Writing: Sappho, the Poem, and the Reader' in *Phrasikleia: An Anthropology of Reading in Ancient Greek*, trans. Janet Lloyd (Cornell University Press, Ithaca, New York, 1993), pp. 152–61.

Swinburne, Algernon Charles, *The Swinburne Letters*, ed. Cecil Y. Lang, 6 vols (Yale University Press and Oxford University Press, New Haven and London, 1962).

Tennyson, Alfred, *The Poems of Tennyson*, ed. Christopher Ricks (Longmans, London, 1969).

Tennyson, Alfred, *Poems, Chiefly Lyrical* (1830), facsimile reprint, with an introduction by Jonathan Wordsworth (Woodstock Books, Oxford and New York, 1991).

Tennyson, Alfred, *The Letters of Alfred Lord Tennyson*, eds Cecil Y. Lang and Edgar F. Shannon Jr. (Oxford University Press, Oxford, 1982).

Thurman, Judith, *Colette: A Biography* (Chatto and Windus, London, 2000).

Tomory, Peter, 'The Fortunes of Sappho, 1770–1850' in *Re-discovering Hellenism: The Hellenic Inheritance and the English Imagination*, ed. G.W. Clarke with J.C. Eade (Cambridge University Press, Cambridge, 1989), pp. 121–35.

Vanita, Ruth, *Sappho and the Virgin Mary: Same Sex Love and the English Literary Imagination* (Columbia University Press, New York, 1996).

Vickers, Nancy, 'The Body Re-Membered: Petrarchan Lyrics and the Strategies of Description' in *Mimesis: From Mirror to Method, Augustine to Descartes*, eds J.D. Lyons and S.G. Nichols (University Press of New England, Hanover New Hampshire, 1982).

Voigt, Eva-Maria, ed., *Sappho et Alcaeus: Fragmenta* (Amsterdam-Polak and Van Gennep, Amsterdam, 1971).

Warner, Michael, 'Homo-Narcissism, or, Heterosexuality' in *Engendering Men: The Question of Male Feminist Criticism*, eds Joseph A. Boone and Michael Cadden (Routledge, London and New York, 1990), pp. 190–206.

Weeks, Jeffrey, *Coming Out: Homosexual Politics in Britain from the Nineteenth Century to the Present* (Quartet Books, London and New York, 1977).

Weiskel, Thomas, *The Romantic Sublime: Studies in the Structure and Psychology of Transcendence* (Johns Hopkins University Press, Baltimore and London, 1976).

West, M.L., *Introduction to Greek Metre* (Clarendon Press, Oxford, 1987).

West, M.L., trans., *Greek Lyric Poetry* (Worlds Classics, Oxford University Press, Oxford, 1993).
Whigham, Peter, *Things Common, Properly* (Anvil Press Poetry Ltd, London, 1984).
White, Allon *The Uses of Obscurity* (Routledge, London and New York, 1981).
White, Chris, '"Poets and Lovers Evermore": Interpreting Female Love in the Poetry and Journals of Michael Field', *Textual Practice*, vol. 4 (1990), pp. 197–212.
White, Chris, 'The One Woman (in Virgin Haunts of Poesie): Michael Field's Sapphic Symbolism' in *Volcanoes and Pearl Divers: Essays in Lesbian Feminist Studies*, ed. Suzanne Raitt (Onlywomen Press, London, 1995).
White, Chris, 'The Tiresian Poet: Michael Field' in *Victorian Women Poets: A Critical Reader*, ed. Angela Leighton (Basil Blackwell, Oxford, 1996), pp. 148–61.
Wilde, Oscar, *The Picture of Dorian Gray* (1890), in *The Complete Works of Oscar Wilde* with an introduction by Vyvyan Holland (Collins, London, 1988).
Wilde, Oscar, *De Profundis* (1905), in *The Complete Works of Oscar Wilde* with an introduction by Vyvyan Holland (Collins, London, 1988).
Wildenstein, Georges, *The Paintings of Fragonard* (Phaidon, London, 1960).
Wilkes, Joanne, *Lord Byron and Madame De Stael: Born for Opposition* (Ashgate Publishing Ltd, Aldershot, 1999).
Williams, William Carlos, *Paterson*, Book V (New Directions Publishing Corporation, New York, 1958).
Williamson, Margaret, *Sappho's Immortal Daughters* (Harvard University Press, Cambridge Mass., 1995).
Williamson, Margaret, 'Sappho and the Other Woman' in *Reading Sappho: Contemporary Approaches*, ed. Ellen Greene (University of California Press, Berkeley and Los Angeles, 1995).
Wilson, Lyn Hatherly, *Sappho's Sweet Bitter Songs: Configurations of Female and Male in Ancient Greek Lyric* (Routledge, London and New York, 1996).
Winkler, John J., *The Constraints of Desire: The Anthropology of Sex and Gender in Ancient Greece* (Routledge, New York and London, 1990).
Winkler, Jack, 'Gardens of Nymphs: Public and Private in Sappho's Lyrics', in *Reading Sappho: Contemporary Approaches*, ed. Ellen Greene (University of California Press, Berkeley and Los Angeles, 1995).
Wolf, Naomi, *The Beauty Myth* (Chatto and Windus, London, 1990).
Woolf, Virginia, *The Diary of Virginia Woolf*, eds Anne Olivier Bell and Andrew McNeillie (The Hogarth Press, London, 1984).
Wroth, Warwick, *Catalogue of the Greek Coins of Troas, Aeolis and Lesbos* (British Museum, London, 1894).
Young, Douglas, *Auntran Ballads: An Outwale o'Verses* (William McLellan, Edinburgh, 1943).
Zeiger, Melissa, 'A Muse Funereal: The Critique of Elegy in Swinburne's "Ave Atque Vale"', *Victorian Poetry*, Vol. 24, part 2 (1986), pp. 173–88.
Zonana, Joyce, 'Swinburne's Sappho: The Muse as Sister-Goddess', *Victorian Poetry* 28 (1990), pp. 39–50.

Index

Compiled by Sue Carlton